Microsoft

Microsoft
Word 2016
Step by Step

Joan Lambert

PUBLISHED BY
Microsoft Press
A division of Microsoft Corporation
One Microsoft Way
Redmond, Washington 98052-6399

Library of Congress Control Number: 2015934878
ISBN: 978-0-7356-9777-5

Printed and bound in the United States of America.

First Printing

Microsoft Press books are available through booksellers and distributors worldwide. If you need support related to this book, email Microsoft Press Support at mspinput@microsoft.com. Please tell us what you think of this book at http://aka.ms/tellpress.

This book is provided "as-is" and expresses the author's views and opinions. The views, opinions, and information expressed in this book, including URL and other Internet website references, may change without notice.

Some examples depicted herein are provided for illustration only and are fictitious. No real association or connection is intended or should be inferred.

Microsoft and the trademarks listed at www.microsoft.com on the "Trademarks" webpage are trademarks of the Microsoft group of companies. All other marks are property of their respective owners.

Acquisitions and Developmental Editor: Rosemary Caperton
Editorial Production: Online Training Solutions, Inc. (OTSI)
Technical Reviewers: Kathy Krause, Steve Lambert, Jaime Odell (OTSI)
Copyeditors: Kathy Krause and Val Serdy (OTSI)
Indexers: Susie Carr, Angela Martin, and Ginny Munroe (OTSI)
Cover: Twist Creative • Seattle

Contents

Part 1: Get started with Word 2016

Give us feedback
Tell us what you think of this book and help Microsoft
improve our products for you. Thank you!
http://aka.ms/tellpress

Create and manage documents 29

Enter and edit text 69

Part 2: Create professional documents

Part 3: Enhance document content

Part 4: Review and finalize documents

Part 5: Use advanced Word functions

Give us feedback
Tell us what you think of this book and help Microsoft
improve our products for you. Thank you!
http://aka.ms/tellpress

Introduction

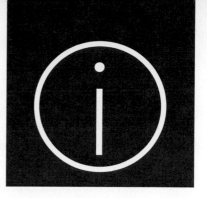

Welcome! This *Step by Step* book has been designed so you can read it from the beginning to learn about Microsoft Word 2016 and then build your skills as you learn to perform increasingly specialized procedures. Or, if you prefer, you can jump in wherever you need ready guidance for performing tasks. The how-to steps are delivered crisply and concisely—just the facts. You'll also find informative, full-color graphics that support the instructional content.

Who this book is for

Microsoft Word 2016 Step by Step is designed for use as a learning and reference resource by home and business users of Microsoft Office programs who want to use Word to create and edit documents. The content of the book is designed to be useful for people who have previously used earlier versions of Word and for people who are discovering Word for the first time.

The *Step by Step* approach

The book's coverage is divided into parts representing general Word skill sets. Each part is divided into chapters representing skill set areas, and each chapter is divided into topics that group related skills. Each topic includes expository information followed by generic procedures. At the end of the chapter, you'll find a series of practice tasks you can complete on your own by using the skills taught in the chapter. You can use the practice files that are available from this book's website to work through the practice tasks, or you can use your own files.

Download the practice files

Before you can complete the practice tasks in this book, you need to download the book's practice files to your computer from *http://aka.ms/word2016sbs/downloads*. Follow the instructions on the webpage.

> ⚠ **IMPORTANT** Word 2016 is not available from the book's website. You should install that app before working through the procedures and practice tasks in this book.

You can open the files that are supplied for the practice tasks and save the finished versions of each file. If you later want to repeat practice tasks, you can download the original practice files again.

> 🔍 **SEE ALSO** For information about opening and saving files, see "Open and move around in documents" in Chapter 2, "Create and manage documents."

The following table lists the practice files for this book.

Chapter	Folder	File
Part 1: Get started with Word 2016		
1: Word 2016 basics		None
2: Create and manage documents	Ch02	DisplayViews.docx
		EditProperties.docx
		NavigateFiles.docx
3: Enter and edit text	Ch03	EditText.docx
		FindText.docx
		ImportText.docx
		ResearchText.docx
Part 2: Create professional documents		
4: Modify the structure and appearance of text	Ch04	ApplyStyles.docx
		ChangeTheme.docx
		CreateLists.docx
		FormatCharacters.docx
		FormatParagraphs.docx
		StructureContent.docx

Chapter	Folder	File
5: Organize information in columns and tables	Ch05	AddColumns.docx
		CreateTabbedLists.docx
		CreateTables.docx
		FormatTables.docx
6: Add simple graphic elements	Ch06	AddWordArt.docx
		Bamboo1.jpg
		EditPictures.docx
		InsertClippings.docx
		InsertPictures.docx

Part 3: Enhance document content

Chapter	Folder	File
7: Insert and modify diagrams	Ch07	Chickens.jpg
		CreateDiagrams.docx
		CreatePictograms.docx
		Fish.jpg
		ModifyDiagrams.docx
		Penguins.jpg
		Tiger.jpg
8: Insert and modify charts	Ch08	CreateCharts.docx
		FormatCharts.docx
		ModifyCharts.docx
		Temperatures.xlsx
9: Add visual elements	Ch09	AddWatermarks.docx
		Clouds.jpg
		InsertBuildingBlocks.docx
		InsertHeadersFooters.docx
		OTSI-Logo.png
10: Organize and arrange content	Ch10	ArrangeObjects.docx
		Bamboo1.jpg
		Bamboo2.jpg
		ControlLayout.docx
		ReorganizeOutlines.docx

Chapter	Folder	File
Part 4: Review and finalize documents		
11: Collaborate on documents	Ch11	ControlChanges.docx
		MergeDocs1.docx
		MergeDocs2.docx
		ReviewComments.docx
		TrackChanges.docx
12: Finalize and distribute documents	Ch12	ControlLayout.docx
		CorrectErrors.docx
		PrepareDocument.docx
		PreviewPages.docx
		PrintDocument.docx
Part 5: Use advanced Word functions		
13: Reference content and content sources	Ch13	CompileBibliography.docx
		CreateIndexes.docx
		CreateTOC.docx
		DisplayFields.docx
		InsertBookmarks.docx
		InsertFootnotes.docx
14: Merge data with documents and labels	Ch14	CreateEnvelopes.docx
		CustomerList.xlsx
		InsertFields.docx
		PolicyholdersList.xlsx
		RefineData.docx
		StartMerge.docx
15: Create custom document elements	Ch15	ChangeTheme.docx
		CreateBuildingBlocks.docx
		CreateStyles.docx
		CreateTemplates.docx
		CreateThemes.docx
16: Customize options and the user interface	None	

Ebook edition

If you're reading the ebook edition of this book, you can do the following:

- Search the full text
- Print
- Copy and paste

You can purchase and download the ebook edition from the Microsoft Press Store at *http://aka.ms/word2016sbs/detail*.

Get support and give feedback

This topic provides information about getting help with this book and contacting us to provide feedback or report errors.

Errata and support

We've made every effort to ensure the accuracy of this book and its companion content. If you discover an error, please submit it to us at *http://aka.ms/word2016sbs /errata*.

If you need to contact the Microsoft Press Support team, please send an email message to *mspinput@microsoft.com*.

For help with Microsoft software and hardware, go to *http://support.microsoft.com*.

We want to hear from you

At Microsoft Press, your satisfaction is our top priority, and your feedback our most valuable asset. Please tell us what you think of this book at *http://aka.ms/tellpress*.

The survey is short, and we read every one of your comments and ideas. Thanks in advance for your input!

Stay in touch

Let's keep the conversation going! We're on Twitter at *http://twitter.com /MicrosoftPress*.

Part 1

Get started with Word 2016

Word 2016 basics

When you use a computer app to create, edit, and format text documents, you are performing a task known as *word processing*. Word 2016 is one of the most sophisticated word-processing apps available. You can use Word to efficiently create a wide range of business and personal documents, from the simplest letter to the most complex report. Word includes many desktop publishing features that you can use to enhance the appearance of documents so that they are visually appealing and easy to read.

The elements that control the appearance of Word and the way you interact with it while you create documents are collectively referred to as the *user interface*. Some user interface elements, such as the color scheme, are cosmetic. Others, such as toolbars, menus, and buttons, are functional. The default Word configuration and functionality is based on the way that most people work with the app. You can modify cosmetic and functional user interface elements to suit your preferences and working style.

This chapter guides you through procedures related to starting Word, working in the Word user interface, and managing Office and app settings.

In this chapter

- Start Word
- Work in the Word user interface
- Manage Office and app settings

Practice files

No practice files are necessary to complete the practice tasks in this chapter.

Start Word

The way that you start Word 2016 is dependent on the operating system you're running on your computer. For example:

- In Windows 10, you can start Word from the Start menu, the All Apps menu, the Start screen, or the taskbar search box.

- In Windows 8, you can start Word from the Apps screen or Start screen search results.

- In Windows 7, you can start Word from the Start menu, All Programs menu, or Start menu search results.

You might also have a shortcut to Word on your desktop or on the Windows taskbar.

When you start Word without opening a specific document, the Word Start screen appears. The Start screen is a hybrid of the Open and New pages of the Backstage view. It displays links to recent files in the left pane, and new file templates in the right pane.

> **TIP** You can turn off the appearance of the Start screen if you want to go directly to a new, blank document. For information, see "Change default Word options" in Chapter 16, "Customize options and the user interface."

To start Word by opening a document

1. Do either of the following:

   - In File Explorer, double-click the document.

     > **TIP** File Explorer is the current version of the browsing utility that was formerly known as Windows Explorer. If you're working on a Windows 7 computer, use Windows Explorer whenever this book refers to File Explorer.

   - In Microsoft Outlook, double-click a document that is attached to an email message.

     > **TIP** By default, Word opens documents from online sources in protected mode.

To start Word on a Windows 10 computer

1. Click the **Start** button, and then click **All apps**.

2. In the app list, click any index letter to display the alphabet index, and then click **W** to scroll the app list to the apps starting with that letter.

3. Scroll the list if necessary, and then click **Word 2016** to start the app.

To start Word on a Windows 8 computer

1. From the **Start** screen, display the **Apps** screen.

2. Sort the **Apps** screen by name, and then click any index letter to display the alphabet index.

3. In the alphabet index, click **W** to scroll the app list to the apps starting with that letter. Then click **Word 2016** to start the app.

Work in the Word user interface

The Word user interface provides intuitive access to all the tools you need to develop a sophisticated document tailored to the needs of your audience. You can use Word 2016 to do the following:

- Create professional-looking documents that incorporate impressive graphics.

- Give documents a consistent look by applying styles and themes that control the font, size, color, and effects of text and the page background.

- Store and reuse preformatted elements such as cover pages and sidebars.

- Create personalized mailings to multiple recipients without repetitive typing.

- Track reference information and compile tables of contents, indexes, and bibliographies.

- Coauthor documents with team members.

- Safeguard documents by controlling who can make changes and the types of changes that can be made, and by removing personal and confidential information.

When you're working with a document, it is displayed in an app window that contains all the tools you need to add and format content.

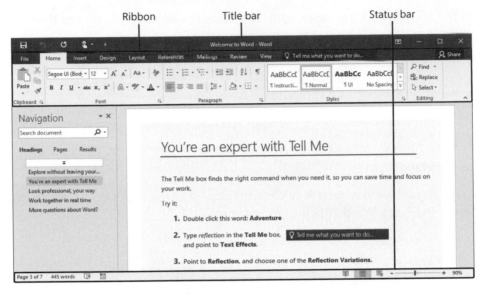

A document displayed in the app window

About Office

Word 2016 is part of the Microsoft Office 2016 suite of apps, which also includes Microsoft Access, Excel, Outlook, and PowerPoint. The apps in the Office suite are designed to work together to provide highly efficient methods of getting things done. You can install one or more Office apps on your computer. Some apps have multiple versions designed for different platforms. For example, you can install different versions of Word on a computer, a smartphone, an iPad, and an Android device; you can also work in a version of Word that is hosted entirely online. Although the core purpose of an app remains the same regardless of the platform on which it runs, the available functionality and the way you interact with the app might be different.

The app that is described and depicted in images throughout this book is a standard desktop installation of Word 2016 on a Windows 10 computer.

It is available as part of the Office 2016 suite of apps, as a freestanding app, or as part of an Office 365 subscription. Until recently, the standard way of acquiring Office software was to purchase a disc, packaged in a box, and install the software from the disc. In the recent past, the standard distribution model has changed to an online installation, often as part of an Office 365 subscription licensing package.

Office 365, which was originally available only to businesses, now has many subscription options designed for individual home and business users, students, households, small businesses, midsize businesses, enterprises, government agencies, academic institutions, and nonprofits; in other words, whatever your needs may be, there is an Office 365 subscription option that will be a close fit. Many of the Office 365 subscription options include licensing for the desktop Office apps, and permit users to run Office on multiple devices, including Windows computers, Mac computers, Windows tablets, Android tablets, iPads, and smartphones.

If you have an Office 365 subscription and are working on a document that is stored on a Microsoft SharePoint site or in a Microsoft OneDrive folder, you'll also have access to Word Online. You can review and edit documents in Word Online, which runs directly in your browser instead of on your computer. Office Online apps are installed in the online environment in which you're working and are not part of the desktop version that you install directly on your computer.

SEE ALSO For information about connecting to OneDrive and SharePoint sites, see "Manage Office and app settings" later in this chapter.

Word Online displays the contents of a document very much like the desktop app does, and offers a limited subset of the commands and content formatting options that are available in the full desktop app. If you're working with a document in Word Online and find that you need more functionality than is available, and you have the full version of Word installed on your computer, you can click Open In Word to open the document in the full version.

Identify app window elements

The Word app window contains the elements described in this section. Commands for tasks you perform often are readily available, and even those you might use infrequently are easy to find.

Title bar

At the top of the app window, this bar displays the name of the active file, identifies the app, and provides tools for managing the app window, ribbon, and content.

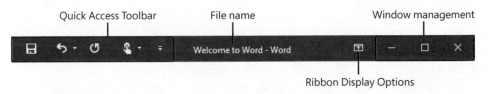

The title bar elements are always on the left end, in the center, and on the right end of the title bar

The Quick Access Toolbar at the left end of the title bar can be customized to include any commands that you want to have easily available. The default Quick Access Toolbar in the Word app window displays the Save, Undo, and Redo/Repeat buttons. On a touchscreen device, the default Quick Access Toolbar also includes the Touch/Mouse Mode button.

> **SEE ALSO** For information about Touch mode, see "Work with the ribbon and status bar" later in this topic.

You can change the location of the Quick Access Toolbar and customize it to include any command to which you want to have easy access.

> **TIP** You might find that you work more efficiently if you organize the commands you use frequently on the Quick Access Toolbar and then display it below the ribbon, directly above the workspace. For information, see "Customize the Quick Access Toolbar" in Chapter 16, "Customize options and the user interface.""

Four buttons at the right end of the title bar serve the same functions in all Office apps. You control the display of the ribbon by clicking commands on the Ribbon

Display Options menu, temporarily hide the app window by clicking the Minimize button, adjust the size of the window by clicking the Restore Down/Maximize button, and close the active document or exit the app by clicking the Close button.

> **SEE ALSO** For information about different methods of closing documents and exiting Word, see "Save and close documents" in Chapter 2, "Create and manage documents."

Ribbon

The ribbon is located below the title bar. The commands you'll use when working with a document are gathered together in this central location for efficiency.

Your ribbon might display additional tabs

> **TIP** The available ribbon tabs and the appearance of commands on the ribbon might differ from what is shown in this book, based on the apps that are installed on your computer, the Word settings and window size, and the screen settings. For more information, see the sidebar "Adapt procedure steps" later in this chapter.

Across the top of the ribbon is a set of tabs. Clicking a tab displays an associated set of commands arranged in groups.

Commands related to managing Word and documents (rather than document content) are gathered together in the Backstage view, which you display by clicking the File tab located at the left end of the ribbon. Commands available in the Backstage view are organized on named pages, which you display by clicking the page tabs in the colored left pane. You redisplay the document and the ribbon by clicking the Back arrow located above the page tabs.

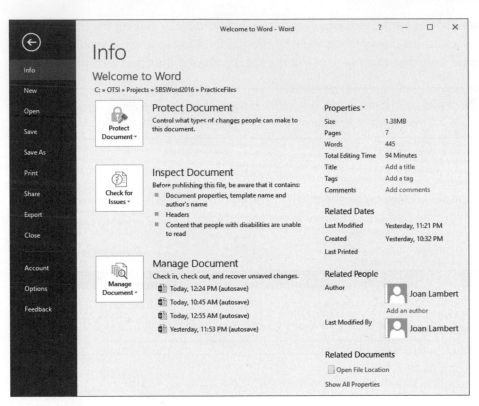

You manage files and app settings in the Backstage view

Commands related to working with document content are represented as buttons on the remaining tabs of the ribbon. The Home tab, which is active by default, contains the most frequently used commands.

When a graphic element such as a picture, table, or chart is selected on a page, one or more *tool tabs* might appear at the right end of the ribbon to make commands related to that specific object easily accessible. Tool tabs are available only when the relevant object is selected.

> **TIP** Some older commands no longer appear as buttons on the ribbon but are still available in the app. You can make these commands available by adding them to the Quick Access Toolbar or the ribbon. For more information, see "Customize the Quick Access Toolbar" and "Customize the ribbon" in Chapter 16, "Customize options and the user interface."

On each tab, buttons representing commands are organized into named groups. You can point to any button to display a ScreenTip that contains the command name, a description of its function, and its keyboard shortcut (if it has one).

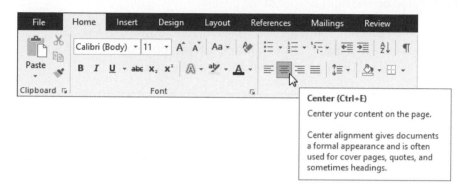

ScreenTips can include the command name, keyboard shortcut, and description

> **TIP** You can control the display of ScreenTips and of feature descriptions in ScreenTips. For more information, see "Change default Word options" in Chapter 16, "Customize options and the user interface."

Some buttons include an arrow, which might be integrated with or separate from the button. To determine whether a button and its arrow are integrated, point to the button to activate it. If both the button and its arrow are shaded, clicking the button displays options for refining the action of the button. If only the button or arrow is shaded when you point to it, clicking the button carries out its default action or applies the current default formatting. Clicking the arrow and then clicking an action carries out the action. Clicking the arrow and then clicking a formatting option applies the formatting and sets it as the default for the button.

Examples of buttons with separate and integrated arrows

When a formatting option has several choices available, they are often displayed in a gallery of images, called *thumbnails*, that provide a visual representation of each choice. When you point to a thumbnail in a gallery, the Live Preview feature shows you what the active content will look like if you click the thumbnail to apply the associated formatting. When a gallery contains more thumbnails than can be shown in the available ribbon space, you can display more content by clicking the scroll arrow or More button located on the right border of the gallery.

Related but less common commands are not represented as buttons in a group. Instead, they're available in a dialog box or pane, which you open by clicking the dialog box launcher located in the lower-right corner of the group.

> **TIP** To the right of the groups on the ribbon is the Collapse The Ribbon button, which is shaped like a chevron. For more information, see "Work with the ribbon and status bar," later in this topic.

Tell me what you want to do

Entering a term in the Tell Me What You Want To Do box located to the right of the ribbon tabs displays a list of related commands and links to additional resources online. Or you can press F1 to open the Help window for the current app.

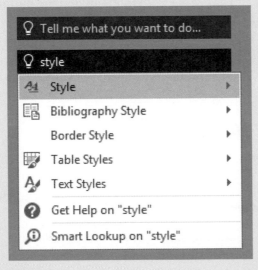

The easy path to help when working in Word

Status bar

Across the bottom of the app window, the status bar displays information about the current document and provides access to certain Word functions. You can choose which statistics and tools appear on the status bar. Some items, such as Document Updates Available, appear on the status bar only when that condition is true.

Customize Status Bar		
Formatted Page Number	1	
Section	1	
✓ Page Number		
Vertical Page Position		
Line Number		
Column		
✓ Word Count		✓ Signatures	Off
✓ Spelling and Grammar Check		Information Management Policy	Off
✓ Language		Permissions	Off

✓ Signatures	Off
Information Management Policy	Off
Permissions	Off
Track Changes	Off
Caps Lock	Off
Overtype	Insert
Selection Mode	
Macro Recording	Not Recording
✓ Upload Status	
✓ Document Updates Available	No
✓ View Shortcuts	
✓ Zoom Slider	
✓ Zoom	100%

Page 3 of 7   445 words

You can specify which items you want to display on the status bar

The View Shortcuts toolbar, Zoom Slider tool, and Zoom button are at the right end of the status bar. These tools provide you with convenient methods for changing the display of document content.

View Shortcuts   Zoom Slider   Zoom

— ———|——— +   100%

You can display different content views and change the magnification from the status bar

SEE ALSO For information about displaying updates when coauthoring a Word document, see Chapter 11, "Collaborate on documents." For information about changing the content view, see "Display different views of documents" in Chapter 2, "Create and manage documents."

Work with the ribbon and status bar

The goal of the ribbon is to make working with document content as intuitive as possible. The ribbon is dynamic, meaning that as its width changes, its buttons adapt to the available space. As a result, a button might be large or small, it might or might not have a label, or it might even change to an entry in a list.

For example, when sufficient horizontal space is available, the buttons on the References tab of the Word app window are spread out, and you can review the commands available in each group.

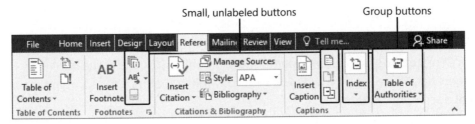

At 1024 pixels wide, most button labels are visible

If you decrease the horizontal space available to the ribbon, small button labels disappear and entire groups of buttons might hide under one button that represents the entire group. Clicking the group button displays a list of the commands available in that group.

When insufficient horizontal space is available, labels disappear and groups collapse under buttons

When the ribbon becomes too narrow to display all the groups, a scroll arrow appears at its right end. Clicking the scroll arrow displays the hidden groups.

1

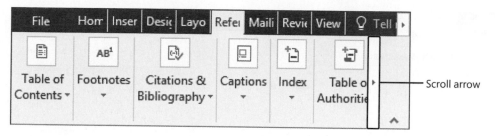

Scroll arrow

Scroll to display additional group buttons

The width of the ribbon depends on these three factors:

- **Window width** Maximizing the app window provides the most space for the ribbon.

- **Screen resolution** Screen resolution is the size of your screen display expressed as pixels wide × pixels high. The greater the screen resolution, the greater the amount of information that will fit on one screen. Your screen resolution options are dependent on the display adapter installed in your computer, and on your monitor. Common screen resolutions range from 800 × 600 to 2560 × 1440 (and some are larger). The greater the number of pixels wide (the first number), the greater the number of buttons that can be shown on the ribbon.

- **The magnification of your screen display** If you change the screen magnification setting in Windows, text and user interface elements are larger and therefore more legible, but fewer elements fit on the screen.

You can hide the ribbon completely if you don't need access to any of its buttons, or hide it so that only its tabs are visible. (This is a good way to gain vertical space when working on a smaller screen.) Then you can temporarily redisplay the ribbon to click a button, or permanently redisplay it if you need to click several buttons.

If you're working on a touchscreen device, you can turn on Touch mode, which provides more space between buttons on the ribbon and status bar. (It doesn't affect the layout of dialog boxes or panes.) The extra space is intended to lessen the possibility of accidentally tapping the wrong button with your finger.

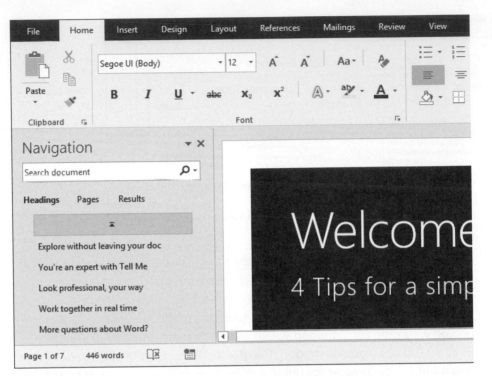

Touch mode has a greater amount of space in the ribbon, status bar, and Navigation pane

The same commands are available in Touch mode, but they're often hidden under group buttons.

> 🔍 **SEE ALSO** For information about working with a modified ribbon, see the sidebar "Adapt procedure steps" later in this topic.

You can switch between Touch mode and Mouse mode (the standard desktop app user interface) from the Quick Access Toolbar. Switching any one of the primary Office apps (Access, Excel, Outlook, PowerPoint, and Word) to Touch mode turns it on in all of them.

To maximize the app window

1. Do any of the following:

   - Click the **Maximize** button.

   - Double-click the title bar.

   - Drag the borders of a non-maximized window.

   - Drag the window to the top of the screen. (When the pointer touches the top of the screen, the dragged window maximizes.)

To change the screen resolution

1. Do any of the following:

   - Right-click the Windows 10 desktop, and then click **Display settings**. At the bottom of the **Display** pane of the **Settings** window, click the **Advanced display settings** link.

   - Right-click the Windows 8 or Windows 7 desktop, and then click **Screen resolution**.

   - Enter screen resolution in Windows Search, and then click **Change the screen resolution** in the search results.

   - Open the **Display** Control Panel item, and then click **Adjust resolution**.

2. Click or drag to select the screen resolution you want, and then click **Apply** or **OK**. Windows displays a preview of the selected screen resolution.

3. If you like the change, click **Keep changes** in the message box that appears. If you don't, the screen resolution reverts to the previous setting.

To completely hide the ribbon

1. Near the right end of the title bar, click the **Ribbon Display Options** button.

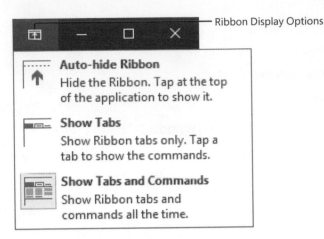

The Ribbon Display Options button is on the title bar so that it is available when the ribbon is hidden

2. On the **Ribbon Display Options** menu, click **Auto-hide Ribbon**.

> ✓ **TIP** To redisplay the ribbon, click the Ribbon Display Options button and then click Show Tabs or Show Tabs And Commands.

To display only the ribbon tabs

1. Do any of the following:

   - Double-click any active tab name.

   - Near the upper-right corner of the app window, click the **Ribbon Display Options** button, and then click **Show Tabs**.

   - In the lower-right corner of the ribbon, click the **Collapse the Ribbon** button.

   - Press **Ctrl+F1**.

To permanently redisplay the ribbon

1. Do any of the following:

   - Double-click any tab name.

   - Near the upper-right corner of the app window, click the **Ribbon Display Options** button, and then click **Show Tabs and Commands**.

   - Press **Ctrl+F1**.

To temporarily redisplay the ribbon

1. Click any tab name to display the tab until you click a command or click away from the ribbon.

To optimize the ribbon for touch interaction

1. On the Quick Access Toolbar, click or tap the **Touch/Mouse Mode** button, and then click **Touch**.

To specify the items that appear on the status bar

1. Right-click the status bar to display the Customize Status Bar menu. A check mark indicates each item that is currently enabled.

2. Click to enable or disable a status bar indicator or tool. The change is effected immediately. The menu remains open to permit multiple selections.

3. When you finish, click away from the menu to close it.

Adapt procedure steps

This book contains many images of user interface elements (such as the ribbons and the app windows) that you'll work with while performing tasks in Word on a Windows computer. Depending on your screen resolution or app window width, the Word ribbon on your screen might look different from that shown in this book. (If you turn on Touch mode, the ribbon displays significantly fewer commands than in Mouse mode.) As a result, procedural instructions that involve the ribbon might require a little adaptation.

Simple procedural instructions use this format:

1. On the **Insert** tab, in the **Illustrations** group, click the **Chart** button.

If the command is in a list, our instructions use this format:

1. On the **Home** tab, in the **Editing** group, click the **Find** arrow and then, in the **Find** list, click **Go To**.

If differences between your display settings and ours cause a button to appear differently on your screen than it does in this book, you can easily adapt the steps to locate the command. First click the specified tab, and then locate the specified group. If a group has been collapsed into a group list or under a group button, click the list or button to display the group's commands. If you can't immediately identify the button you want, point to likely candidates to display their names in ScreenTips.

Multistep procedural instructions use this format:

1. To select the paragraph that you want to format in columns, triple-click the paragraph.

2. On the **Layout** tab, in the **Page Setup** group, click the **Columns** button to display a menu of column layout options.

3. On the **Columns** menu, click **Three**.

1

On subsequent instances of instructions that require you to follow the same process, the instructions might be simplified in this format because the working location has already been established:

1. Select the paragraph that you want to format in columns.

2. On the **Columns** menu, click **Three**.

The instructions in this book assume that you're interacting with on-screen elements on your computer by clicking (with a mouse, touchpad, or other hardware device). If you're using a different method—for example, if your computer has a touchscreen interface and you're tapping the screen (with your finger or a stylus)—substitute the applicable tapping action when you interact with a user interface element.

Instructions in this book refer to user interface elements that you click or tap on the screen as *buttons*, and to physical buttons that you press on a keyboard as *keys*, to conform to the standard terminology used in documentation for these products.

Manage Office and app settings

You access app settings from the Backstage view; specifically, from the Account page and the Word Options dialog box.

The Account page of the Backstage view in Word displays information about your installation of Word (and other apps in the Office suite) and the resources you connect to. This information includes:

- Your Microsoft account and links to manage it.
- The current app window background and theme.
- Storage locations and services (such as Facebook and LinkedIn) that you've connected Office to.
- Your subscription information and links to manage the subscription, if you have Office through an Office 365 subscription.
- The app version number and update options.

Account information in Word

Microsoft account options

If you use Office 365, Skype, OneDrive, Xbox Live, Outlook.com, or a Windows Phone, you already have a Microsoft account. (Microsoft account credentials are also used by many non-Microsoft products and websites.) If you don't already have a Microsoft account, you can register any existing account as a Microsoft account, sign up for a free Outlook.com or Hotmail.com account and register that as a Microsoft account, or create an alias for an Outlook.com account and register the alias.

TIP Many apps and websites authenticate transactions by using Microsoft account credentials. For that reason, it's a good idea to register a personal account that you control, rather than a business account that your employer controls, as your Microsoft account. That way, you won't risk losing access if you leave the company.

Two ways you can personalize the appearance of your Word app window are by choosing an Office background and an Office theme. (These are specific to Office and aren't in any way associated with the Windows theme or desktop background.) The background is a subtle design that appears in the title bar of the app window. There are 14 backgrounds to choose from, or you can choose to not have a background.

Backgrounds depict a variety of subjects

At the time of this writing, there are three Office themes:

- **Colorful** Displays the title bar and ribbon tabs in the color specific to the app, and the ribbon commands, status bar, and Backstage view in light gray

- **Dark Gray** Displays the title bar and ribbon tabs in dark gray, and the ribbon commands, status bar, and Backstage view in light gray

- **White** Displays the title bar, ribbon tabs, and ribbon commands in white, and the status bar in the app-specific color

There are rumors that another theme will be released in the near future, but it hasn't yet made an appearance.

 TIP The images in this book depict the No Background option to avoid interfering with the display of any user interface elements, and the Colorful theme.

From the Connected Services area of the page, you can connect Office to Facebook, Flickr, and YouTube accounts to access pictures and videos; to SharePoint sites and OneDrive storage locations; and to LinkedIn and Twitter accounts to share documents. You must already have an account with one of these services to connect Office to it.

Until you connect to storage locations, they aren't available to you from within Word. For example, when inserting a picture onto a page, you will have the option to insert a locally stored picture or to search online for a picture. After you connect to your Facebook, SharePoint, or OneDrive accounts, you can also insert pictures stored in those locations.

The changes that you make on the Account page apply to all the Office apps installed on all the computers associated with your account. For example, changing the Office background in Word on one computer also changes it in Outlook on any other computer on which you've associated Office with the same account.

Some of the settings on the Account page are also available in the Word Options dialog box, which you open from the Backstage view. This dialog box also contains hundreds of options for controlling the way Word works. Chapter 16, "Customize options and the user interface," provides in-depth coverage of these options. It's a good idea to familiarize yourself with the dialog box content so you know what you can modify.

To display your Office account settings

1. With Word running, click the **File** tab to display the Backstage view.

2. In the left pane of the Backstage view, click **Account**.

To manage your Microsoft account settings

1. Display the **Account** page of the Backstage view.

2. In the **User Information** area, click any of the links to begin the selected process.

To change the app window background for all Office apps

1. Display the **Account** page of the Backstage view.

2. In the **Office Background** list, point to any background to display a live preview in the app window, and then click the background you want.

To change the app window color scheme for all Office apps

1. Display the **Account** page of the Backstage view.

2. In the **Office Theme** list, click **Colorful**, **Dark Gray**, or **White**.

To connect to a cloud storage location or social media service

1. Display the **Account** page of the Backstage view.

2. At the bottom of the **Connected Services** area, click **Add a service**, click the type of service you want to add, and then click the specific service.

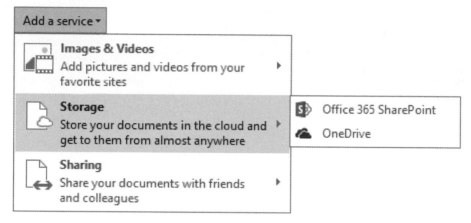

You can connect to OneDrive and OneDrive For Business sites by clicking the OneDrive link

To manage your Office 365 subscription

1. Display the **Account** page of the Backstage view.

2. In the **Product Information** area, click the **Manage Account** button to display the sign-in page for your Office 365 management interface.

3. Provide your account credentials and sign in to access your options.

To manage Office updates

1. Display the **Account** page of the Backstage view.

2. Click the **Update Options** button, and then click the action you want to take.

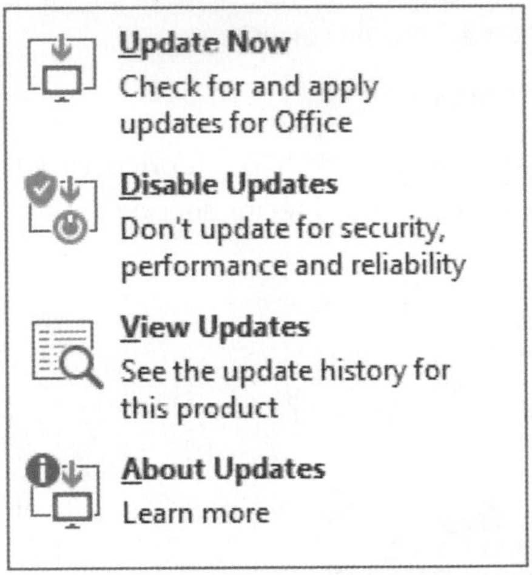

You can install available updates from the Backstage view before the automatic installation occurs

To open the Word Options dialog box

1. In the left pane of the Backstage view, click **Account**.

Skills review

In this chapter, you learned how to:

- Start Word

- Work in the Word user interface

- Manage Office and app settings

Practice tasks

No practice files are necessary to complete the practice tasks in this chapter.

Start Word

Perform the following tasks:

1. Using the technique that is appropriate for your operating system, start Word.

2. When the **Start** screen appears, press the **Esc** key to create a new blank document.

Work in the Word user interface

Start Word, create a new blank document, maximize the app window, and then perform the following tasks:

1. On each tab of the ribbon, do the following:

    • Review the available groups and commands.

    • Display the ScreenTip of any command you're not familiar with. Notice the different levels of detail in the ScreenTips.

    • If a group has a dialog box launcher in its lower-right corner, click the dialog box launcher to display the associated dialog box or pane.

2. Change the width of the app window and notice the effect it has on the ribbon. When the window is narrow, locate a group button and click it to display the commands.

3. Maximize the app window. Hide the ribbon entirely, and notice the change in the app window. Redisplay the ribbon tabs (but not the commands). Temporarily display the ribbon commands, and then click away from the ribbon to close it.

4. Use any of the procedures described in this chapter to permanently redisplay the ribbon tabs and commands.

5. Display the status bar shortcut menu, and identify the tools and statistics that are currently displayed on the status bar. Add any indicators to the status bar that will be useful to you.

6. Keep the document open in Word for use in the next set of practice tasks.

Manage Office and app settings

With a new blank document open in Word, perform the following tasks:

1. Display the **Account** page of the Backstage view and review the information that is available there.

2. Expand the **Office Background** list. Point to each theme to display a live preview of it. Then click the theme you want to apply.

3. Apply each of the Office themes, and consider its merits. Then apply the theme you like best.

> ✅ **TIP** If you apply a theme other than Colorful, your interface colors will be different from the interface shown in the screenshots in this book, but the functionality will be the same.

4. Review the services that Office is currently connected to. Expand the **Add a service** menu and point to each of the menu items to display the available services. Connect to any of these that you want to use.

5. Click the **Update Options** button and note whether updates are currently available to install.

> ✅ **TIP** The update process takes about 10 minutes and requires that you exit all the Office apps and Internet Explorer. If updates are available, apply them after you finish the practice tasks in this chapter.

6. On the **Update Options** menu, click **View Updates** to display the *What's New and Improved in Office 2016* webpage in your default browser. Review the information on this page to learn about any new features that interest you.

7. Return to Word, and open the **Word Options** dialog box.

8. Explore each page of the dialog box. Notice the sections and the settings in each section. Note the settings that apply only to the current file.

9. Review the settings on the **General** page, and modify them as necessary to fit the way you work. Then close the dialog box.

10. Close the document without saving changes.

Create and manage documents

You can use Word 2016 to create many different types of documents, for many different purposes. Word is widely used in schools, businesses, and organizations of many kinds to create letters, newsletters, reports, resumes, and other documents that contain text. Word provides a lot of flexibility in document design, so you can also create documents that contain images and content that doesn't fit a standard sheet of paper, such as trifold brochures, greeting cards, business cards, certificates, and signs.

You can open and work with documents from a variety of locations. Word 2016 introduces methods of quickly accessing documents from multiple computers that can save you time and conserve storage space. When working in a Word document, you can display different views of the content and the document structure, and use different methods to move around within the document. You can also display and modify the information that is stored with each file (its properties).

This chapter guides you through procedures related to creating documents, opening and moving around in documents, displaying different views of documents, displaying and editing file properties, and saving and closing documents.

In this chapter

- Create documents
- Open and move around in documents
- Display different views of documents
- Display and edit file properties
- Save and close documents

Practice files

For this chapter, use the practice files from the Word2016SBS\Ch02 folder. For practice file download instructions, see the introduction.

Create documents

When creating a document in Word, you can create a blank document of the default file type or create a document based on one of the templates provided with Word. Each template incorporates specific design elements such as fonts and colors. Many templates also include typical information that you can modify or build on to create a useful document.

When you start Word, the app displays a Start screen that gives you options for opening an existing file or creating a new one.

The Start screen appears by default but can be disabled

If you create custom templates and save them in your Personal Templates folder, Featured and Personal links appear below the search box. You can click these links to switch between viewing app-supplied templates and your own.

> **SEE ALSO** For information about creating custom templates, see "Create and attach templates" in Chapter 15, "Create custom document elements."

> **TIP** The document templates that are available in Word include standard templates that have been available for many years, and featured templates that change occasionally. The templates on the New page of the Backstage view in your installation of Word might be different from those shown in images in this book.

If you're already working in Word, you can create a new document from the New page of the Backstage view. The same templates and search options are available from both pages.

Word provides document templates for a wide variety of purposes

You can start from a blank document that contains one page. You can then add content, apply structure and design elements, and make any necessary configuration changes.

New blank documents are based on the built-in Normal template. You can save time by basing your document on a content template, and then customizing the content provided in the template to meet your needs.

Many templates are available when you're working in Word 2016. Most are for specific types of documents, and many are pre-populated with text, tables, images, and other content that you can modify to fit your needs. A few of the templates are installed on your computer with Word. Many more templates are maintained on the Microsoft Office website, but you can locate and use them directly from within Word (provided you have an Internet connection).

The available templates vary depending on whether you're working online or offline:

- When you're working online (that is, when your computer has an active Internet connection, whether or not you're using it to do anything else), the New page displays thumbnails of featured templates. These vary based on the season; for example, they might include holiday-specific or season-specific templates for creating announcements, invitations, and newsletters. The search box at the top of the page is active; you can enter a search term to display related online templates, or click a category below the search box to display online templates in that category.

- When you're working offline, the New page displays only templates that are stored on your computer. These include any templates that you have already used, and a selection of letter, newsletter, report, and resume templates. The search box is unavailable (you can only search the offline templates by scrolling through the thumbnails on the New page).

Word document templates contain elements such as the following:

- **Formatting** Most templates contain formatting information, which in addition to styles can include page layout settings, backgrounds, themes, and other types of formatting. A template that contains only formatting defines the look of the document; you add your own content.

- **Text** Templates can also contain text that you customize for your own purposes. For example, if you base a new document on an agenda template from

Office.com, the text of the agenda is already in place, and all you have to do is customize it. Sometimes, a document based on a template displays formatted text placeholders surrounded by square brackets—for example, [Company Name]—instead of actual text. You replace a placeholder with your own text by clicking it and then typing the replacement. If you don't need a placeholder, you can simply delete it.

- **Graphics, tables, charts, and diagrams** Templates can contain ready-made graphic elements, either for use as is or as placeholders for elements tailored to the specific document.

- **Building blocks** Some templates make custom building blocks, such as headers and footers or a cover page, available for use with a particular type of document. They might also include AutoText, such as contact information or standard copyright or privacy paragraphs.

> **SEE ALSO** For information about working with building blocks, see "Insert preformatted document parts" in Chapter 9, "Add visual elements," and "Create custom building blocks" in Chapter 15, "Create custom document elements."

- **Custom tabs, commands, and macros** Sophisticated templates might include custom ribbon tabs or toolbars with commands and macros that are specific to the purposes of the template. A macro is a recorded series of commands that permits a user to perform a process with the click of a button. The topic of macros is beyond the scope of this book; for information, refer to Word Help.

> **TIP** Word 2016 template files have one of two file name extensions, depending on their content. Those that contain macros have the .dotm file name extension; those that don't contain macros have the .dotx extension.

When you base a new document on a template, that template is said to be *attached* to the document. The styles defined in the attached template appear in the Styles pane so that you can easily apply them to any content you add to the document. You can change the document template by attaching a different one.

> **SEE ALSO** For information about attaching templates to existing documents, see Chapter 15, "Create custom document elements."

To create a new blank document

1. Start Word.

2. When the **Start** screen appears, press the **Esc** key.

Or

1. If Word is already running, click the **File** tab to display the Backstage view.

2. In the left pane of the Backstage view, click **New** to display the New page.

3. On the **New** page of the Backstage view, click the **Blank document** thumbnail.

To preview design templates

1. Display the **New** page of the Backstage view.

2. On the **New** page, scroll the pane to view the design templates that were installed with Word.

3. Click any thumbnail to open a preview window that displays a sample document page.

4. Do any of the following:

    *   To create a document based on the template that is active in the preview window, click the **Create** button.

    *   To view the next template, click the arrow to the right of the preview window; to view the previous template, click the arrow to the left.

    *   To close the preview window without creating a document, click the **Close** button in the upper-right corner of the preview window.

To create a document based on an installed template

1. Display the **New** page of the Backstage view.

2. Scroll the pane to locate the design you want to use.

3. Double-click the thumbnail to create the document.

To create a document based on an online template

1. Display the **New** page of the Backstage view.

2. Do either of the following to display templates related to a specific topic:

   - In the search box at the top of the page, enter a term related to the template content or design you're looking for, and then click the **Search** button.

   - Below the search box, click one of the suggested searches.

3. In the **Category** list, click any category or categories to further filter the templates. Active category filters are indicated by colored bars at the top of the Category list.

Clicking multiple categories applies multiple filters

4. Scroll the pane to locate a design that fits your needs.

5. Double-click any thumbnail to create a file based on the template.

To remove a template search filter

1. Do either of the following:

    - In the **Category** list, point to the applied filter, and then click the **X** that appears to the right of the category name.

    - Double-click the category name.

To clear a template search

1. To the left of the search box, click the **Home** button.

Open and move around in documents

The Start screen that appears by default when you start Word displays a list of documents you worked on recently, and a link to open other existing documents.

Open existing documents

If the document you want to open appears on the Start screen, you can open it directly from there. Otherwise, you can open documents that are stored locally on your computer, or in a remote storage location such as a Microsoft OneDrive folder or a Microsoft SharePoint document library, either from within Word or from the document storage location.

> **TIP** If you receive a document as an attachment to an email message, you can open the attached document and start Word, if it isn't already running, from within Outlook 2016, or you can preview the document content directly in the Outlook Reading pane without starting Word.

2

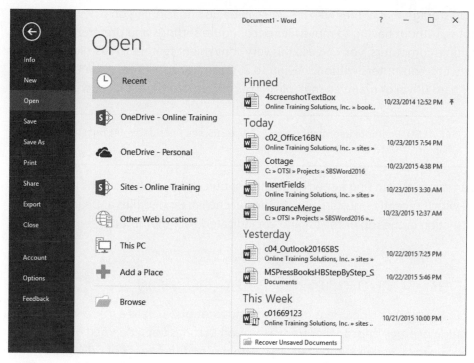

The Open page includes all the locations you've linked to from Office apps

The Open page displays only documents that are saved in the Word-specific file formats (.docx and .doc), and templates created for those standards. For more information about file formats, see "Save and close documents" later in this chapter.

The Recent list in the right pane of the Open page provides quick access to the documents you've worked with recently. The Recent list includes locally stored documents and documents that you've worked with while signed in with your current account on any computer, tablet, or other device, if the documents are stored in a shared location. This is one of the tremendous benefits of the Office 365 subscription model and the cloud storage that comes with it—you can be up and running on a new computer in minutes, without having to move files or configure settings and preferences. If you use multiple computers, you can use this very convenient feature to seamlessly transition between computers without having to actually transport files (on a USB flash drive or hard drive) or maintain multiple copies of files in different locations.

> **SEE ALSO** For more information about Office 365, see the sidebar "About Office" in Chapter 1, "Word 2016 basics."

To ensure that you can find a specific document quickly regardless of whether you've worked with it recently, you can pin it to the Recent list. Pinned files appear in the Pinned section at the top of the list and are indicated by a thumbtack.

Open documents in Protected view

When you open a document from an online location (such as a cloud storage location or email message) or from a location that has been deemed unsafe, Word opens the file in Protected view, with most editing functions disabled. The purpose of this is to prevent any malicious code from gaining access to your computer. If you're uncertain about the origin of a file that you're opening, you can choose to open the file in Protected view.

In Protected view, the title bar displays *Read-Only* in brackets to the right of the file name, and a yellow banner at the top of the content pane provides information about why the file has been opened in Protected view. If you know that the document is from a safe location or sender, and you want to edit the file content, you can choose to enable editing. If you don't intend to modify the file content, you can hide the banner by clicking the Close button (the X) at its right end.

If you want to open documents from a specific online storage folder without going into Protected view, you can add that folder (and its subfolders, if you want) to your Trusted Locations list. For information about trusted locations and other Trust Center settings, see "Manage add-ins and security options" in Chapter 16, "Customize options and the user interface."

To open a recent document

1. Start Word.

2. On the **Start** screen, in the **Recent** list, click the file name of the file you want to open.

Or

1. With Word running, click the **File** tab to display the Backstage view.

2. In the left pane of the Backstage view, click **Open** to display the Open page.

3. With **Recent** selected at the top of the left pane of the Open page, scroll the file list in the right pane if necessary to locate the document you want to open. Then click the file name to open it.

To pin a document to the Recent file list

1. Display the **Recent** list on the **Open** page of the Backstage view.

2. If necessary, scroll through the list to locate the file you want to pin.

3. Point to the file name, and then click the **Pin** button that appears to the right of the file name to add the file to the **Pinned** area at the top of the **Recent** list.

To open any existing document

1. Start Word.

2. Do either of the following to display the **Open** page of the Backstage view:

    • On the **Start** screen, at the bottom of the left pane, click **Open Other Documents**.

    • With Word running, display the Backstage view, and then click **Open**.

3. In the **Places** list, click the local or network storage location where the file is stored.

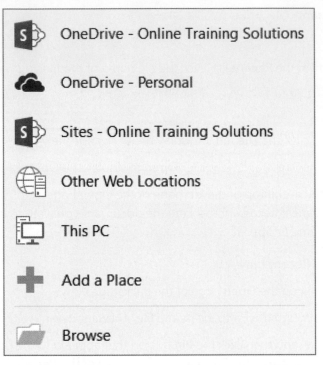

The Places list includes all the locations you've connected Office to

4. Navigate to the file storage folder by using one of the following methods:

   - In the right pane, click a recent folder. Then click any subfolders until you reach the folder you want.

   - In the left pane, click **Browse** to open the Open dialog box. Then click folders in the **Navigation** pane, double-click folders in the file pane, or enter the folder location in the **Address** bar.

5. Double-click the document you want to open.

> **TIP** In the Open dialog box, clicking a file name and then clicking the Open arrow displays a list of alternative ways to open the selected document. To look through a document without making any inadvertent changes, you can open the document as read-only, open an independent copy of the document, or open it in Protected view. You can also open the document in a web browser. In the event of a computer crash or other similar incident, you can tell the app to open the document and try to repair any damage.

To open a file directly from a OneDrive storage site

1. In your browser, navigate to the OneDrive folder.

2. Browse to and click the file you want to open.

3. If prompted to do so, enter the Microsoft account credentials associated with your OneDrive, and then click **Sign in**.

Or

1. In File Explorer, navigate to the OneDrive folder.

2. Browse to and double-click the file you want to open.

3. If prompted to do so, enter the Microsoft account credentials associated with your OneDrive, and then click **Sign in**.

Edit PDF files in Word

A useful feature of Word 2016 is the ability to open PDF files and edit them by using all the standard Word proofing tools. When you finish, you can save the file as a document or as a PDF.

To open a PDF file in Word, do either of the following:

- In File Explorer, right-click the file, click Open, and then click **Word (Desktop)**.

- In Word, display the **Open** page of the Backstage view, navigate to the file location, click the file, and then click **Open**. (In the Open dialog box, PDF files now fall into the category of Word Documents.)

Word converts the file to an editable Word document. If the file contains complicated formatting and layout, the Word version of the document might not be a perfect replica of the PDF, but most simple files convert quite cleanly.

Move around in documents

If you open a document that is too long or too wide to fit in the content pane, you can bring off-screen content into view without changing the location of the cursor by using the vertical and horizontal scroll bars. The scroll bars appear only when the document is longer or wider than the content pane. The scroll bars and pointer fade from sight when you're not using the mouse, to remove distractions. You can make them reappear by moving the mouse.

You can also move around in a document by moving the cursor. You can place the cursor in a specific location by clicking there, or you can move the cursor different distances and in different directions and by pressing keyboard keys.

The location of the cursor is displayed on the status bar. By default, the status bar displays the page the cursor is on, but you can also display the cursor's location by section, line number, and column, and in inches from the top of the page.

> **SEE ALSO** For information about displaying information on the status bar, see "Work with the ribbon and status bar" in Chapter 1, "Word 2016 basics."

In a long document, you might want to move quickly among elements of a certain type; for example, from heading to heading, from page to page, or from graphic to graphic. You can do this from the Navigation pane.

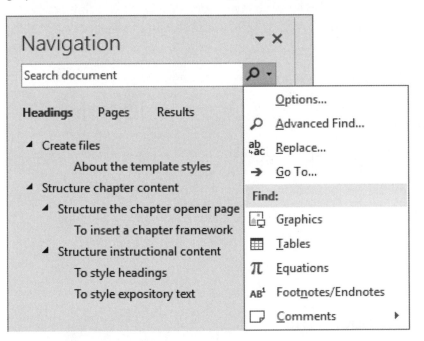

Move to the next object of a specific type

> **SEE ALSO** For information about working in the Navigation pane, see "Display different views of documents," later in this chapter.

2

A greater variety of browsing options is available from the Go To tab of the Find And Replace dialog box. From this tab, you can locate pages, sections, lines, bookmarks, comments, footnotes, endnotes, fields, tables, graphics, equations, objects, or headings. You can jump directly to a specific object if you know its position within the sequence of that type of object in the document (for example, if it is the fifth equation), move forward or backward a specific number of objects, or browse from one to the next.

Find and Replace	? ✕

Find   Replace   **Go To**

Go to what:

Page
Section
Line
Bookmark
Comment
Footnote

Enter line number:

Enter + and – to move relative to the current location. Example: +4 will move forward four items.

Previous   Next   Close

Move to a specific object

🔍 **SEE ALSO** For information about using the Navigation pane to search for specific content in a document, see "Find and replace text" in Chapter 3, "Enter and edit text."

To change the area of a document that is displayed in the content pane

1. On the vertical scroll bar, do any of the following:

   - Click the scroll arrows to move up or down by one line.

   - Click above or below the scroll box to move up or down by the height of one screen.

   - Drag the scroll box on the scroll bar to display the part of the document corresponding to the location of the scroll box. For example, dragging the scroll box to the middle of the scroll bar displays the middle of the document.

Or

1. On the horizontal scroll bar, do any of the following to move side to side:

   - Click the scroll arrows.

   - Click to the left or right of the scroll box.

   - Drag the scroll box on the scroll bar to display the part of the document corresponding to the location of the scroll box.

To move the cursor by using the keyboard keys

1. Move the cursor by pressing the key or key combination described in the following table.

To move the cursor	Press
Left one character	Left Arrow
Right one character	Right Arrow
Up one line	Up Arrow
Down one line	Down Arrow
Left one word	Ctrl+Left Arrow
Right one word	Ctrl+Right Arrow
Up one paragraph	Ctrl+Up Arrow
Down one paragraph	Ctrl+Down Arrow
To the beginning of the current line	Home
To the end of the current line	End
To the beginning of the document	Ctrl+Home
To the end of the document	Ctrl+End
To the beginning of the previous page	Ctrl+Page Up
To the beginning of the next page	Ctrl+Page Down
Up one screen	Page Up
Down one screen	Page Down

To show or hide the Navigation pane in a document

1. On the **View** tab, in the **Show** group, select the **Navigation Pane** check box.

2

To browse by object from the Navigation pane

1. Open the **Navigation** pane, and then do any of the following:

   - At the top of the **Navigation** pane, click **Headings**. Then click any heading to move directly to that location in the document.

   - At the top of the **Navigation** pane, click **Pages**. Then click any thumbnail to move directly to that page of the document.

   - At the right end of the search box, click the arrow. In the **Find** list, click the type of object you want to browse by. Then click the **Next** and **Previous** arrows to move among those objects.

To display the Go To tab of the Find And Replace dialog box

1. Do any of the following:

   - On the **Home** tab, in the **Editing** group, click the **Find** arrow, and then click **Go To**.

   - In the **Navigation** pane, click the **Search** arrow, and then in the **Search for more things** list, click **Go To**.

   - Press **Ctrl+G**.

To browse by object from the Go To What list

1. Display the **Go To** tab of the **Find and Replace** dialog box.

2. In the **Go to what** list, click the type of object you want to search for.

3. Do any of the following:

   - Click the **Next** button to move to the next object of that type.

   - Click the **Previous** button to move to the previous object of that type.

   - In the adjacent box, enter either of the following, and then click the **Go To** button:

     - Enter a number identifying the position of the object within the total objects of that type in the document. (For example, to move to the fourth field in the document, you would enter **4**.)

     - Enter + (plus sign) or – (minus sign) and then a number to move forward or backward by that many objects of the selected type.

Display different views of documents

You can display a document in different views that provide different types of information and make it easier to interact with specific document elements. If you want to take a closer look at the document content, you can increase the magnification of the content pane. If you want a high-level view of the content—for example, to quickly review all the pages of a document for length—you can decrease the magnification and view multiple pages at the same time.

Word 2016 has five views in which you can create, organize, and preview documents. Each view is suited to a specific purpose. The views are:

- **Print Layout view** This view displays a document on the screen the way it will look when printed. You can review elements such as margins, page breaks, headers and footers, and watermarks. This is the default view and the view you'll use most frequently (or perhaps the only view you'll use) when developing content.

- **Read Mode view** This view displays as much document content as will fit on the screen at a size that is comfortable for reading. In this view, the ribbon is replaced by one toolbar at the top of the screen with buttons for searching and navigating in the document. You can display comments, but you can't edit the document in this view.

- **Web Layout view** This view displays the document the way it will look when viewed in a web browser, so that you can review the way that text wraps to fit the window and the positioning of graphics. Web Layout view also displays page backgrounds and effects.

- **Outline view** This view displays the structure of a document as nested levels of headings and body text, and provides tools for viewing and changing the hierarchy.

> **SEE ALSO** For information about displaying and modifying a document in Outline view, see "Reorganize document outlines" in Chapter 10, "Organize and arrange content."

- **Draft view** This view displays the content of a document with a simplified layout so that you can quickly enter and edit text. Draft view doesn't display images or layout elements such as headers and footers.

You manage the display of views and of window elements from the View tab of the ribbon. Three of the views are also available from the View Shortcuts toolbar near the right end of the status bar.

The active view is shaded

When you are developing a document in Print Layout view, the primary content pane displays the content of the document that you're working in. Each page is represented at the size specified in the document layout settings, with margins and other white space represented as they will appear when the document is printed. As you scroll a multipage document, spaces appear between the pages. If you want to fit more content on the screen, you can hide the white space on and between pages.

The junction of two pages with and without white space

When working in Outline or Draft view, you can display the paragraph style of each paragraph in the left margin, in an area called the style area pane. (It's not a pane, though, it's just a marginal area of the page.) By default, the style area pane width is set to zero inches wide, so it is effectively closed. If you want to display it, you can increase the width.

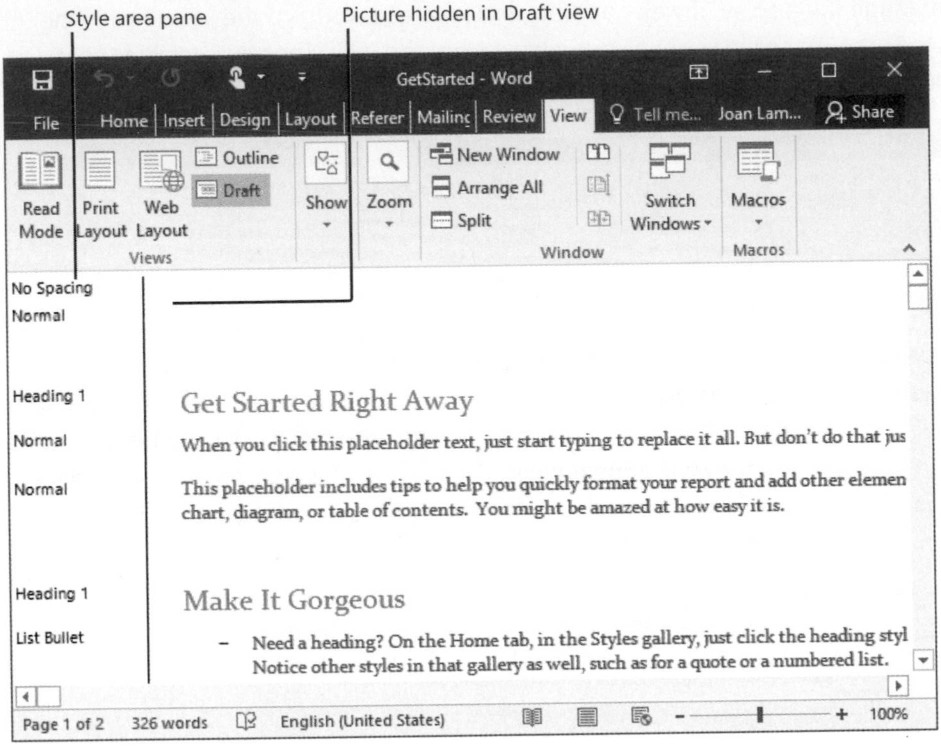

Style area pane   Picture hidden in Draft view

The style area pane is available only in Draft view and Outline view

If your document uses styles to control the appearance and hierarchy of the content, you can display the headings in the Navigation pane and styles in the Style pane so that you can more quickly access and work with styles and styled content. You can also use the Navigation pane to display and move among page thumbnails or search results, as described in the previous topic.

Word has many other task-specific panes in which you can, for example, display Clipboard content, research terminology, review spelling, and format graphics. These panes usually appear to the right or left of the content pane and span the full height of the content pane. Some of them can float within or outside of the Word window or be docked to other sides of the window. I discuss these panes in the context of their functionality in other chapters. Regardless of the purpose of the pane, however, you use the same methods to resize or move it.

You can change the space available for document content and app window elements by resizing the window, adjusting the relative sizes of the panes, or collapsing or hiding the ribbon. A new feature introduced with Word 2016 permits you to entirely hide not only the ribbon content, but also the ribbon tabs and the app window title bar.

> **SEE ALSO** For information about hiding, collapsing, and displaying the ribbon, see "Work with the ribbon and status bar" in Chapter 1, "Word 2016 basics."

When you want to focus on the layout of a document, you can display rulers and grid-lines to help you position and align elements. You can also adjust the magnification of the content area by using the tools available in the Zoom group on the View tab and at the right end of the status bar.

Clicking the Zoom button opens the Zoom dialog box

> **SEE ALSO** For information about controlling paragraph formatting from the ruler, see "Apply paragraph formatting" in Chapter 4, "Modify the structure and appearance of text."

If you want to work with different parts of a document, you can open the same instance of the document in a second window and display both, or you can split a window into two panes and scroll through each pane independently.

You're not limited to working with one document at a time. You can easily switch among multiple open documents. If you want to compare or work with the content of multiple documents, you can simplify the process by displaying the documents next to each other.

A feature that can be invaluable when you are fine-tuning the layout of a document in Word is the display of nonprinting characters (such as tabs, paragraph marks, and section breaks) that control the layout of your document. You can control the display of these characters for each window.

To switch among views of a document

1. Do either of the following:

    - On the **View** tab, in the **Views** group, click the view you want.

    - On the **View Shortcuts** toolbar, click the view button you want.

To hide or display white space in Print Layout view

1. Point to the space between two pages.

2. When the pointer changes to display a representation of that space, double-click.

To show or hide the Navigation pane

1. On the **View** tab, in the **Show** group, select the **Navigation Pane** check box.

To adjust the size of the Navigation pane

1. Point to the right border of the **Navigation** pane. When the pointer changes to a double-headed arrow, drag to the right or left.

TIP The Navigation pane is available in all views other than Read Mode. When you adjust the width of the Navigation pane, the pane content changes accordingly. For example, the Navigation pane displays more page thumbnails in a narrow pane and fewer page thumbnails in a wide pane.

To display the style area pane in Draft view or Outline view

1. In the Backstage view, click the **Options** page tab to open the Word Options dialog box.

2. In the **Word Options** dialog box, click the **Advanced** page tab.

3. On the **Advanced** page, scroll to the **Display** area (about halfway down the page) and change the **Style area pane width in Draft and Outline views** setting to any number greater than 0. Then click **OK**.

To resize the style area pane in Draft view or Outline view

1. Point to the right border of the style area pane.

2. When the pointer changes to a double-headed arrow, drag the border to the left or right.

To change the magnification of document content

1. Do either of the following to open the **Zoom** dialog box:

   • On the **View** tab, in the **Zoom** group, click the **Zoom** button.

   • At the right end of the status bar, click the **Zoom** button.

2. In the **Zoom** dialog box, select a **Zoom to** option or enter a specific percentage in the **Percent** box, and then click **OK**.

Or

1. In the zoom controls at the right end of the status bar, do any of the following:

   • Drag the slider to the left to decrease the magnification or to the right to increase the magnification.

   • At the left end of the slider, click the **Zoom Out** button to decrease the magnification in 10-percent increments.

   • At the right end of the slider, click the **Zoom In** button to increase the magnification in 10-percent increments.

To display or hide rulers or gridlines in a document

1. On the **View** tab, in the **Show** group, do either of the following:

   - Select or clear the **Ruler** check box.

   - Select or clear the **Gridlines** check box.

 SEE ALSO For information about controlling document gridlines, see "Arrange objects on a page" in Chapter 10, "Organize and arrange content."

To display or hide nonprinting characters and formatting marks in a document

1. Do either of the following:

   - On the **Home** tab, in the **Paragraph** group, click the **Show/Hide ¶** button.

   - Press **Ctrl+***.

   > **TIP** You need to hold down the Shift key to activate the * key. So, in effect, you are pressing Ctrl+Shift+8.

To split a window into two panes

1. On the **View** tab, in the **Window** group, click the **Split** button.

To display a different open document

1. Do either of the following:

   - On the **View** tab, in the **Window** group, click the **Switch Windows** button, and then click the file you want to view.

   - Point to the **Word** button on the Windows taskbar, and then click the thumbnail of the document you want to display.

To display multiple open documents at the same time

1. On the **View** tab, in the **Window** group, click the **Arrange All** button.

Display and edit file properties

Properties are file attributes or settings, such as the file name, size, created date, author, and read-only status. Some properties exist to provide information to computer operating systems and apps. You can display properties within the content of a document (for example, you can display the page number on the document pages). Word automatically tracks some of the file properties for you, and you can set others.

You can examine the properties that are attached to a file from the Info page of the Backstage view.

Properties ▾

Size	0.98MB
Pages	43
Words	8532
Total Editing Time	652 Minutes
Title	Finalize and distribute ...
Tags	Add a tag
Comments	Add comments

Related Dates

Last Modified	10/22/2015 6:48 PM
Created	8/8/2015 9:26 PM
Last Printed	

Related People

Author
Joan Lambert

Last Modified By
Kathy Krause

Related Documents

Open File Location

Show All Properties

Some of the properties stored with a typical Word document

You can change or remove basic properties in the default Properties pane or expand the Properties pane to make more available, or you can display the Properties dialog box to access even more properties.

To display file properties

1. Display the **Info** page of the Backstage view. The Properties area in the right pane displays the standard properties associated with the document.

2. At the bottom of the **Properties** pane, click **Show All Properties** to expand the pane.

3. At the top of the **Properties** pane, click **Properties**, and then click **Advanced Properties** to display the Properties dialog box.

To edit file properties

1. In the **Properties** pane, click the value for the property you want to edit to activate the content box.

2. Enter or replace the property value, and then press **Enter**.

Or

1. In the **Properties** dialog box, do either of the following:

    • On the **Summary** page, click the box to the right of the property you want to modify, and then enter or replace the property value.

    • On the **Custom** page, select the property you want to modify in the **Name** list, and then enter or replace the property value in the **Value** box.

Save and close documents

When you save a document in Word, it is saved in the default .docx file format, but you can also choose a different format from many other choices. For example, if you plan to distribute the document electronically to people who use a different word-processing program, you can choose a compatible format, or if you want to protect the document content, you can save it as a PDF file.

Manually save documents

You save a document the first time by clicking the Save button on the Quick Access Toolbar or by displaying the Backstage view and then clicking Save As. Both actions open the Save As page, where you can select a storage location.

2

	GetStarted - Word	? — ☐ ✕

← Save As

Info
New
Open
Save
Save As
Print
Share
Export
Close

Account
Options
Feedback

S OneDrive - Online Training Solu...

☁ OneDrive - Personal

S Sites - Online Training Solutions,...

⊕ Other Web Locations

🖥 This PC

➕ Add a Place

📁 Browse

Current Folder
PracticeFiles
C: » OTSI » Projects » SBSWord2016 » Practice...

Today
PracticeFiles
C: » OTSI » Projects » SBSWord2016 » Pra...
OTSI
C: » OTSI

This Week
Documents

SBSWord2016
C: » OTSI » Projects » SBSWord2016

Last Week
Templates
C: » OTSI » Templates

Older
Desktop

Projects
E: » Projects

Save your document in an online location to access it from anywhere

You can save the document in a folder on your computer or, if you have an Internet connection, in a folder on your OneDrive. If your company is running SharePoint, you can add a SharePoint site so that it is available from the Places pane of the Save As page, just like any other folder.

 SEE ALSO For information about OneDrive, see the sidebar "Save files to OneDrive" later in this chapter.

Clicking Browse at the bottom of the left pane displays the Save As dialog box, in which you assign a name to the document.

The dialog box shows other files of the same type that are saved in the current folder

> **TIP** If you want to create a new folder in which to store the document, click the New Folder button on the dialog box's toolbar.

After you save a document for the first time, you can save changes simply by clicking the Save button on the Quick Access Toolbar. The new version of the document then overwrites the previous version.

To save a document for the first time

1. Click the **File** tab to display the Backstage view.

2. In the left pane of the Backstage view, click **Save As**.

3. On the **Save As** page of the Backstage view, click a storage location, and then click a recently accessed folder in the right pane, or click **Browse**.

4. In the **Save As** dialog box, browse to the folder you want to save the document in.

5. In the **File name** box, enter a name for the document.

6. If you want to save a document in a format other than the one shown in the Save As Type box, click the **Save as type** arrow and then, in the **Save as type** list, click the file format you want.

7. In the **Save As** dialog box, click **Save**.

2

To add a cloud storage location

1. On the **Save As** page of the Backstage view, click **Add a Place**.

2. In the **Add a Place** list, click **Office 365 SharePoint** or **OneDrive**.

3. In the **Add a service** dialog box, enter the email address you use to sign in to the cloud storage service, and then click **Next**.

4. In the **Sign in** dialog box, enter the password associated with the account, and then click **Sign In** to add the cloud storage location associated with that account to the Places list.

To save a copy of a document

1. Display the **Save As** page of the Backstage view.

2. Save the document with a different name in the same location or with any name in a different location. (You can't store two documents with the same name in the same folder.)

To save a document without changing its name or location

1. Do any of the following:

   - On the Quick Access Toolbar, click the **Save** button.

   - In the left pane of the Backstage view, click **Save**.

   - Press **Ctrl+S**.

Save files to OneDrive

When you save a document to OneDrive, you and other people with whom you share the document can work on it by using a local installation of Word or by using Word Online, which is available in the OneDrive environments.

If you're new to the world of OneDrive, here's a quick tutorial to help you get started.

OneDrive is a cloud-based storage solution. The purpose of OneDrive is to provide a single place for you to store and access all your files. Although this might seem like a simple concept, it provides major value for people who use Word or other Office products on multiple devices, including Windows computers, Mac computers, iPads and other tablets, and Windows, iPhone, and Android smartphones.

For example, you can create a document on your desktop computer at work, edit it on your laptop at home, and review it on your smartphone while you're waiting for your lunch to be served at a restaurant. If you use the full suite of Office products within your organization, you can even present the document in a Skype for Business meeting from your tablet PC, all while the document is stored in the same central location.

There are currently two types of OneDrive—one for personal use and one for business use:

- **OneDrive** A *personal* OneDrive storage site is provided free with every Microsoft account. Each OneDrive is linked to a specific account.

- **OneDrive for Business** An *organizational* OneDrive storage site is provided with every business-level Office 365 subscription license. These storage locations are part of an organization's Office 365 online infrastructure.

You might have both types of OneDrive available to you; if you do, you can connect to both from within Word (or any Office app).

In this book, the personal and organizational versions are referred to generically as *OneDrive* sites.

2

To make OneDrive a realistic one-stop storage solution, Microsoft has chosen to support the storage of very large files (up to 10 gigabytes [GB] each) and to provide a significant amount of free storage—from a minimum of 15 GB for every Microsoft account, to unlimited storage for Office 365 subscribers!

By default, documents that you store on your OneDrive site are password-protected and available only to you. You can share specific files or folders with other people by sending a personalized invitation or a generic link that allows recipients to view or edit files. You can access documents stored on your OneDrive in several ways:

- From within Word when opening or saving a file.

- Through File Explorer, when you synchronize your OneDrive site contents with the computer.

- Through a web browser. Personal OneDrive sites are available at *https://onedrive.live.com*; organizational OneDrive sites have addresses linked to your Office 365 account, such as *https://contoso-my.sharepoint.com/personal/joan_contoso_com/*.

Because OneDrive and OneDrive for Business file storage locations are easy to add to any version of Word 2016, OneDrive is a simple and useful cloud storage option. And best of all, it's completely free!

Automatically save documents

By default, Word automatically saves the document you're working on and tracks saved versions so that you can gracefully recover documents without losing data, or you can revert to an earlier version.

When the AutoSave function is turned on:

- If you're working in a new, unnamed file, the app saves a temporary copy of the file to your default storage location.

- If you're working in a previously saved file, the app saves a copy of the file to the location in which you opened or last saved it.

You can turn off the automatic file-saving function if you prefer to save changes manually (but I'd advise against it), and you can change the time interval between saves.

To adjust the time interval between saves

1. Display the Backstage view, and then click **Options** to open the Word Options dialog box.

2. In the left pane, click **Save**.

3. On the **Save** page, in the **Save AutoRecover information every** box, specify the frequency (in minutes) at which you'd like Word to save the document.

> **SEE ALSO** For information about working with document versions, see "Compare and merge documents" in Chapter 11, "Collaborate on documents." For information about configuring other Word options, see "Change default Word options" in Chapter 16, "Customize options and the user interface."

Save documents in other formats

Word 2016 uses file formats based on a programming language called *Extensible Markup Language*, or more commonly, *XML*. These file formats, called the *Microsoft Office Open XML Formats*, were introduced with Microsoft Office 2007.

Word 2016 offers a selection of file formats intended to provide specific benefits. Each file format has a file name extension that identifies the file type to the system. The file formats and file name extensions for Word 2016 files include the following:

- Word Document (.docx)
- Word Macro-Enabled Document (.docm)
- Word Template (.dotx)
- Word Macro-Enabled Template (.dotm)
- Word XML Document (.xml)

Other file types that are not specific to Word, such as text files, webpages, PDF files, and XPS files, are available from the Save As dialog box.

2

File name:	GetStarted	∨
Save as type:	Word Document	∨
Authors:	**Word Document**	

Word Macro-Enabled Document
Word 97-2003 Document
Word Template
Word Macro-Enabled Template
Word 97-2003 Template
⌃ Hide Folders PDF
XPS Document
Single File Web Page
Web Page
Web Page, Filtered
Rich Text Format
Plain Text
Word XML Document
Word 2003 XML Document
Strict Open XML Document
OpenDocument Text

You can save a document in any of these file formats

The default file format for files created in Word 2016 is the .docx format, which provides the following benefits over the .doc file format that was the previous standard:

- **Decreased file size** Files are compressed when saved, decreasing the amount of disk space and bandwidth needed to store and transmit files.

- **Simpler retrieval and editing of content** XML files can be opened in text-editing apps such as Notepad.

- **Increased security** Personal data can be located and removed from the document, and files can't store macros. (The .docm file format is designed for documents that contain macros.)

If you want to save a Word document in a format that can be opened by the widest variety of programs (including text editors that are installed with most operating systems), use one of these two formats:

- **Rich Text Format (*.rtf)** This format preserves the document's formatting.

- **Plain Text (*.txt)** This format preserves only the document's text.

If you want people to be able to view a document exactly as it appears on your screen, use one of these two formats:

- **PDF (.pdf)** This format is preferred by commercial printing facilities. Recipients can display the file in the free Microsoft Reader or Adobe Reader apps, and can display and edit the file in Word 2016 or Adobe Acrobat.

- **XPS (.xps)** This format precisely renders all fonts, images, and colors. Recipients can display the file in Microsoft Reader or the free XPS Viewer app.

> **TIP** Another way to create a PDF file or XPS file is by selecting that option when sending the document by email. For more information, see "Print and send documents" in Chapter 12, "Finalize and distribute documents."

The PDF and XPS formats are designed to deliver documents as electronic representations of the way they appear when printed. Both types of files can easily be sent by email to many recipients and can be made available on a webpage for downloading by anyone who wants them. However, the files are no longer Word documents. A PDF file can be converted to the editable Word format. An XPS file cannot be opened, viewed, or edited in Word.

You can create a PDF file from all or part of a document

When you save a Word document in PDF or XPS format, you can optimize the file size of the document for your intended distribution method—the larger Standard file size is better for printing, whereas the Minimum file size is suitable for online publishing.

2

Maintain compatibility with earlier versions of Word

Word 2003 and earlier versions of Word used the .doc file format. You can open .doc files in Word 2016, but some Word 2016 features will be unavailable.

When you open a file created in Word 2010 or an earlier version of Word, the title bar displays *[Compatibility Mode]* to the right of the document name. You can work in Compatibility mode, or you can convert the document to Word 2016 format by clicking the Convert button on the Info page of the Backstage view, or by saving a copy of the document with Word Document as the file type.

If you work with people who are using a version of Word earlier than Word 2007, you can save your documents in a format that they will be able to use by choosing the *Word 97-2003* file format in the Save As Type list, or they can install the free Microsoft Office Compatibility Pack for Word, Excel, and PowerPoint File Formats from the Microsoft Download Center (located at *download.microsoft.com*). The Compatibility Pack doesn't provide additional functionality in the older versions of the apps, but it does enable users to open current documents, workbooks, and presentations.

To save part or all of a document in PDF format

1. Open the **Save As** dialog box. In the **File type** list, click **PDF**. The dialog box content changes to provide additional options.

2. If you want to create a PDF file that has a smaller file size (but lower quality), click **Minimum size (publishing online)**.

3. To modify any of the default settings, click the **Options** button, do any of the following, and then click **OK**:

   - Specify the pages to include in the file.

   - Include or exclude comments and tracked changes.

   - Include or exclude nonprinting elements such as bookmarks and properties.

   - Select compliance, font embedding, and encryption options.

4. If you don't want to automatically open the new PDF file in your default PDF viewer, clear the **Open file after publishing** check box.

5. In the **Save As** dialog box, click **Save**.

Close documents

Every time you open a document, a new instance of Word starts. When you close the file, you can exit that instance of Word. If you have only one document open, you can close the file and exit Word, or you can close the file but leave Word running.

To close a document

1. Do any of the following:

   - At the right end of the title bar, click the **Close** button to close the document and the Word window.

   - Display the Backstage view, and then click **Close** to close the document without exiting Word.

   - On the Windows taskbar, point to the Word button to display thumbnails of all open documents. Point to the thumbnail of the document you want to close, and then click the **Close** button that appears in its upper-right corner.

Skills review

In this chapter, you learned how to:

- Create documents

- Open and move around in documents

- Display different views of documents

- Display and edit file properties

- Save and close documents

Practice tasks

The practice files for these tasks are located in the Word2016SBS\Ch02 folder. You can save the results of the tasks in the same folder.

Create documents

Perform the following tasks:

1. Start Word and create a new, blank document.

2. Display the available templates for new documents. Scroll through the list of featured templates and note the types of documents you can create from them.

3. Search for a template that is related to something you're interested in. (For example, you could use a search term such as **food**, **school**, **children**, or **customers**.)

4. Review the categories in the right pane of the search results. Filter the results by two categories and notice the effect. Then remove one of the category filters. Preview a template from the search results. If the template preview includes multiple images, preview each of those by clicking the arrows below the image.

5. Without closing the preview window, preview the next or previous template by clicking the arrows to the sides of the preview window.

6. From the preview window, create a document based on the currently displayed template. Notice that the unsaved blank document remains open.

7. Close the blank document without saving it. Leave the template-based document open for use in a later set of practice tasks.

Open and move around in documents

In Word, perform the following tasks:

1. Display the **Open** page of the **Backstage** view.

2. If there are files in the **Recent** list, notice the groups they're divided into, their file storage locations, and whether any are pinned to the list.

3. From the **Open** page, browse to the practice files folder, and open the **NavigateFiles** document.

4. In the second line of the document title, click at the right end of the paragraph to position the cursor.

5. Use a keyboard method to move the cursor to the beginning of the line.

6. Use a keyboard method to move the cursor to the beginning of the word *Regulations*.

7. Use a keyboard method to move the cursor to the end of the document.

8. Use the scroll bar to move to the middle of the document.

9. Use the scrollbar to change the view of the document by one screen.

10. Open the **Navigation** pane.

11. In the **Navigation** pane, click the *Landscaping* heading to move the cursor directly to the selected heading.

12. At the top of the **Navigation** pane, click **Pages**. On the **Pages** page, scroll through the thumbnails to review the amount of visible detail, and then click the thumbnail for page **5** to move the cursor directly to the top of the selected page.

13. At the right end of the **Navigation** pane title bar, click the **Close** button (the X) to close the pane.

14. On the **Open** page of the Backstage view, pin the **NavigateFiles** document to the **Recent** list.

15. Close the document without saving it.

Display different views of documents

Open the DisplayViews document in Word, and then perform the following tasks:

1. If the document is not already in Print Layout view, display it in that view.

2. Switch to Web Layout view and scroll through the document to the end. Notice that the lines break differently and that there are no longer any page breaks.

3. Move the cursor back to the beginning of the document, and switch to Read Mode view.

4. On the Read Mode toolbar, click **Tools** to review the commands on the menu, and then click **View** to review the commands on that menu. Then, on the **View** menu, click **Edit Document** to return to Print Layout view.

5. In Print Layout view, hide the white space between pages. Scroll through the document and notice the change in the page lengths when the white space is hidden.

6. Open the **Navigation** pane and display the document headings. Adjust the pane width to the minimum necessary to display the headings.

7. Close the **Navigation** pane.

8. In the **Word Options** dialog box, set the width of the style area pane to 2". Then click **OK** to return to the document.

9. Display the document in Draft view. Notice that the style area is visible along the left side of the document, but it is wider than necessary.

10. Drag the style area pane's right border to the left until it takes up about half the original amount of space.

11. Display the document in Print Layout view, and use any method described in this chapter to change the magnification to **75%**.

12. Split the window into two panes, position the cursor in the top pane, and then change the magnification to **100%**. Notice that only the active pane changes. Then remove the split.

13. Use commands on the **View** tab to arrange the **DisplayViews** document and the document you created in the first set of practice tasks side by side on the screen.

14. In the **DisplayViews** document, display the gridlines. Notice that they appear in both open documents.

15. Switch to the document you created in the first set of practice tasks. Display the rulers. Notice the effect of this action in the other open document.

16. Save and close both documents.

Display and edit file properties

Open the EditProperties document in Word, and then perform the following tasks:

1. On the **Info** page of the Backstage view, do the following:

    - Review the information in the **Properties** list. Notice the types of information that have been saved with the document.

    - Point to each of the property values, and notice the values that you can edit.

    - Set the **Title** property to Welcome to Word.

2. Expand the **Properties** list to display all properties, and then do the following:

    - Notice the additional properties that were not previously visible. (If necessary, click **Show Fewer Properties** to switch back to the original list for comparison purposes.)

    - Point to the **Manager** and **Author** property values, and notice that Check Names and Address Books buttons appear. Experiment with adding a Manager property from your address book.

3. Click the **Properties** header, and then display the advanced properties. In the **EditProperties Properties** dialog box, do the following:

    - Compare the properties on the **Summary** tab with those in the **Properties** list. Notice the properties that you added in steps 1 and 2.

    - In the **Author** box, enter your name.

    - In the **Keywords** box, enter Word 2016 new features.

    - Review the information on the **General**, **Statistics**, **Contents**, and **Custom** tabs. Notice the information that is available only in the Properties dialog box.

    - Click **OK**.

4. Verify that the information you entered in the **Properties** dialog box appears in the **Properties** list. If it doesn't, save, close, and reopen the document to update the properties.

Save and close documents

In Word, perform the following tasks:

1. Save a copy of the EditProperties document in the practice file folder as MyDocument. Close the document and this instance of Word.

2. Close the document you created in the first task without exiting Word.

3. Close the remaining open documents, and exit Word.

Enter and edit text

Word is a word-processing app designed to be used primarily for working with text. This can be text that you enter yourself or text that you import from another file.

After you have entered or imported text into a document, you can select and edit it as needed. For example, you can select a word, a sentence, a line, or a paragraph. You can select one of these elements at a time, or you can select several at the same time. These words, sentences, lines, or paragraphs can be adjacent (that is, next to each other in your document) or non-adjacent (that is, in different areas of the document). You can also select all the content in a document at the same time.

Word also makes it easy to find and replace text—for example, if you realize you made a mistake and want to locate and fix each instance of the error. Word also includes a wide array of reference and research tools.

This chapter guides you through procedures related to entering or importing text; moving, copying, and deleting text; finding and replacing text; and using reference and research tools.

In this chapter

- Enter and import text
- Move, copy, and delete text
- Find and replace text
- Use reference and research tools

Practice files

For this chapter, use the practice files from the Word2016SBS\Ch03 folder. For practice file download instructions, see the introduction.

Enter and import text

Entering new text in a document is easy. A blinking cursor shows where the next character you enter will appear. When you begin entering text, any existing text to the right of the cursor moves to make room for the new text. When the cursor reaches the right margin, the word you are entering moves to the next line.

Parks Appreciation Day

Help beautify our city by participating in the annual cleanup of Log Drift Park, Swamp Creek Park, and Tall Tree Park. Volunteers will receive a free T-shirt and barbecue lunch. Bring your own gardening tools and gloves, and be ready to have fun!

|

Entering new text in a document is easy

> **TIP** If a wavy line appears under a word or phrase, Word is flagging a possible error. For information about proofing errors, see "Locate and correct text errors" in Chapter 12, "Finalize and distribute documents."

Another way to add text to a document is to import it from another document.

To enter text

1. Click to position the cursor where you want to add your text, and begin typing.

To start a new paragraph

1. Press the **Enter** key.

To import text

1. In the target document, position the cursor where you want to insert text from another document.

> **TIP** It isn't necessary to open the source document to complete this operation.

2. On the **Insert** tab, in the **Text** group, click the **Object** arrow (not the button). Then click **Text from File** to open the Insert File dialog box.

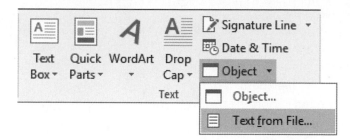

Import entire documents

3. Browse to the file that contains the text you want to insert, click the file, and then click the **Insert** button to import the text into your document.

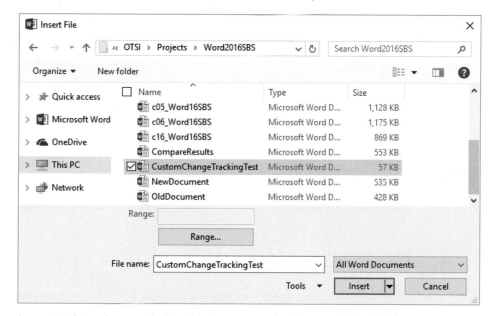

Import text into a document by inserting the contents of one document into another

Import text from multiple documents

Sometimes you'll want to insert the contents of more than one existing document into another document. For example, you might want to compile 12 monthly reports into an annual report. It would be tedious to select and copy the text of each report and then paste it into the annual report document. Instead, you can have Word import the text from those documents in one easy operation. Here's how:

1. In the target document, position the cursor where you want to insert the existing documents.

2. On the **Insert** tab, in the **Text** group, click the **Object** arrow (not the button) and then, in the list, click **Text from File**.

3. In the **Insert File** dialog box, open the folder that contains the source files you want to insert.

4. If the files containing the text you want to import are listed together, click the first file. Then, while pressing the **Shift** key, press the last file. All the files will be selected. If the files are not listed together, click the first file. Then, while pressing the **Ctrl** key, click each additional file.

5. Click the **Insert** button. The content of each file you selected will be added to the target document.

Move, copy, and delete text

You'll rarely write a perfect document that requires no editing. You'll almost always want to add or remove a word or two, change a phrase, or move text from one place to another. Or you might want to edit a document that you created for one purpose so that you can use it for a different purpose. You can edit a document as you create it, or you can write it first and then revise it.

It's easy to modify a few characters, but if you want to edit more than that efficiently, you need to know how to select text. Selected text appears highlighted on the screen.

> ✓ **TIP** Many instructional materials incorrectly refer to selecting text as *highlighting text*, which is misleading. To highlight text is to apply the Highlight character format.

You can select content by using the mouse, using the keyboard, tapping, or combining multiple tools. Some methods of selecting use an area of the document's left margin called the *selection area*. When the mouse pointer is in the selection area, it changes to an arrow that points toward the upper-right corner of the page.

3

> Parks Appreciation Day
>
> Help beautify our city by participating in the annual cleanup of Log Drift Park, Swamp Creek Park, and Tall Tree Park. Volunteers will receive a free T-shirt and barbecue lunch. Bring your own gardening tools and gloves, and be ready to have fun!
>
> The Park Service Committee is coordinating group participation in this event. If you are interested in spending time outdoors with family and friends while improving the quality of our parks, contact Nancy Anderson by email at nancy@adventure-works.com.

You can select an entire line of text with just one click

> ✓ **TIP** When you select content, Word displays the Mini Toolbar, from which you can quickly format the selection or perform other actions, depending on the type of content you select. For information about applying formatting from the Mini Toolbar, see Chapter 4, "Modify the structure and appearance of text." For information about turning off the display of the Mini Toolbar, see "Change default Word options" in Chapter 16, "Customize options and the user interface."

You can move or copy selected text within a document or between documents by using these methods:

- You can drag a selection from one location to another. This method is easiest to use when you can display the original location and destination on the screen at the same time. (You can create a copy by holding down a key while dragging.)

- You can cut or copy the text from the original location to the Clipboard and then paste it from the Clipboard into the new location. There are multiple methods for cutting, copying, and pasting text. No matter which method you use, when you cut text, Word removes it from its original location. When you copy text, Word leaves the original text intact.

The Clipboard is a temporary storage area that is shared by the Office apps. You can display items that have been cut or copied to the Clipboard in the Clipboard pane.

The Clipboard stores items that have been cut or copied from any Microsoft Office app

You can cut and copy content to the Clipboard and paste the most recent item from the Clipboard without displaying the Clipboard pane. If you want to work with items other than the most recent, you can display the Clipboard pane and then do so.

If you make a change to a document and then realize that you made a mistake, you can easily reverse, or undo, one or more recent changes. You can redo changes that you've undone, or repeat your most recent action elsewhere in the document.

In addition to moving and copying text, you can also simply delete it. The easiest way to do this is by using the Delete key or the Backspace key. However, when you delete text by using one of these keys, the text is not saved to the Clipboard and you can't paste it elsewhere.

To select text

1. Do any of the following:

   - To select adjacent words, lines, or paragraphs, drag through the text.

   - Position the cursor at the beginning of the text you want to select, and then do any of the following:

     - To select one character at a time, hold down the **Shift** key and then press the **Left Arrow** or **Right Arrow** key.

     - To select one word at a time, hold down the **Shift** and **Ctrl** keys and then press the **Left Arrow** or **Right Arrow** key.

     - To select one line at a time, hold down the **Shift** key and then press the **Up Arrow** or **Down Arrow** key.

     - To select any amount of adjacent content, hold down the **Shift** key and then click at the end of the content that you want to select.

   - To select a word, double-click anywhere in the word. Word selects the word and the space immediately after the word, but not any punctuation after the word.

   - To select a sentence, hold down the **Ctrl** key and click anywhere in the sentence. Word selects all the characters in the sentence, from the first character through the space following the ending punctuation mark.

   > ⚠ **IMPORTANT** You cannot select a sentence by using this technique if other text is already selected. This activates the non-adjacent multi-selection functionality described in a later procedure.

- To select a line, click in the selection area to the left of the line.

- To select a paragraph, do either of the following:

  - Triple-click anywhere in the paragraph.

  - Double-click in the selection area to the left of the paragraph.

  Word selects the text of the paragraph and the paragraph mark.

  > ✓ **TIP** Paragraph marks are nonprinting characters that are usually hidden. For information about displaying nonprinting characters, see "Display different views of documents" in Chapter 2, "Create and manage documents."

- To select non-adjacent words, lines, or paragraphs, select the first text segment and then hold down the **Ctrl** key while selecting the next text segment.

- To select all the content in a document or text container, do either of the following:

  - Triple-click in the selection area.

  - Press **Ctrl+A**.

To release a selection

1. Click anywhere in the window other than the selection area.

To cut text to the Clipboard

1. Select the text, and then do any of the following:

   - On the **Home** tab, in the **Clipboard** group, click the **Cut** button.

   - Right-click the selection, and then click **Cut**.

   - Press **Ctrl+X**.

To copy text to the Clipboard

1. Select the text, and then do any of the following:

   - On the **Home** tab, in the **Clipboard** group, click the **Copy** button.

   - Right-click the selection, and then click **Copy**.

   - Press **Ctrl+C**.

To paste the most recent item from the Clipboard

1. Position the cursor where you want to insert the text, and then do any of the following:

   - On the **Home** tab, in the **Clipboard** group, click the **Paste** button.

   - Press **Ctrl+V**.

Or

1. Right-click where you want to insert the text, and then in the **Paste Options** section of the menu, click a paste option.

To move text

1. Do either of the following:

    -   Cut the text from the original location, and then paste it into the new location.

    -   Drag the text from the original location to the new location.

3

To copy text from one location to another

1. Do either of the following:

    -   Copy the text from the original location, and then paste it into the new location.

    -   Hold down the **Ctrl** key and drag the text from the original location to the new location.

> ✅ **TIP** To drag selected text, point to it, hold down the mouse button and move the pointer to the insertion location (indicated by a thick vertical line), and then release the mouse button.

To display the Clipboard pane

1. On the **Home** tab, click the **Clipboard** dialog box launcher.

To manage cut and copied items in the Clipboard pane

1. Do any of the following:

    -   To paste an individual item at the cursor, click the item, or point to the item, click the arrow that appears, and then click **Paste**.

    -   To paste all the items stored on the Clipboard at the same location, click the **Paste All** button at the top of the Clipboard pane.

    -   To remove an item from the Clipboard, point to the item in the Clipboard pane, click the arrow that appears, and then click **Delete**.

    -   To remove all items from the Clipboard, click the **Clear All** button at the top of the Clipboard pane.

Paste options

Clicking the Paste arrow on the Home tab displays the Paste menu of options for controlling the way Word inserts content that you paste into a document. The available options vary depending on the type of content that you have cut or copied to the Clipboard. For example, when pasting text, the Paste menu includes buttons for keeping source formatting, merging formatting, or pasting only the text.

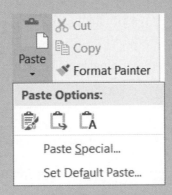

Word offers several different methods of pasting content

Pointing to a button displays a preview of how the source content will look if you use that option to paste it at the current location. In addition to these buttons, the Paste menu includes Paste Special and Set Default Paste options. Clicking Paste Special opens a dialog box in which you can choose from additional options.

Clicking Paste Special opens a dialog box in which you can choose from additional options.

Paste Special		?	✕
Source:	Microsoft Word Document		
	C:\Users\Documents\Step By Step Books\c03_Word16SBS.docx		

As:

⦿ Paste:	Microsoft Word Document Object		☐ Display as icon
◯ Paste link:	**Formatted Text (RTF)**		
	Unformatted Text		
	Picture (Enhanced Metafile)		
	HTML Format		
	Unformatted Unicode Text		

Result

Inserts the contents of the Clipboard as text with font and table formatting.

	OK	Cancel

The Paste Special dialog box offers several options for pasting text

Clicking Set Default Paste on the Paste Options menu displays the Advanced page of the Word Options dialog box. In the Cut, Copy, And Paste section of this page, you can set default paste options. For more information, see Chapter 16, "Customize options and the user interface."

To control the behavior of the Clipboard pane

1. At the bottom of the pane, click **Options**, and then click the display option you want.

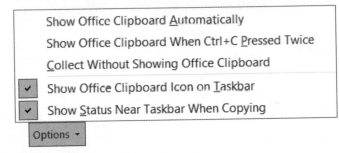

Clipboard pane display options

To undo your last editing action

1. Do either of the following:

   - On the **Quick Access Toolbar**, click the **Undo** button.

   - Press **Ctrl+Z**.

To undo two or more actions

1. On the **Quick Access Toolbar**, in the **Undo** list, click the first action you want to undo. Word reverts that action and all those that follow.

To delete only one or a few characters

1. Position the cursor immediately to the left of the text you want to delete.

2. Press the **Delete** key once for each character you want to delete.

Or

1. Position the cursor immediately to the right of the text you want to delete.

2. Press the **Backspace** key once for each character you want to delete.

To delete any amount of text

1. Select the text you want to delete.

2. Press the **Delete** key or the **Backspace** key.

Find and replace text

One way to ensure that the text in your documents is consistent and accurate is to use the Find feature to search for and review every occurrence of a particular word or phrase. For example, if you are responsible for advertising a trademarked product, you can search your marketing materials to check that every occurrence of the product's name is correctly identified as a trademark.

You can use the search box at the top of the Navigation pane to locate all instances of a specific word, phrase, or formatting mark in the current document. When you enter characters in the search box at the top of the pane, Word highlights all occurrences of those characters in the document and displays them on the Results page of the Navigation pane. When you point to a search result on the Results page, a ScreenTip displays the number of the page on which that result appears and the name of the heading preceding the search result. You can click a search result to move directly to that location in the document, or you can click the Next and Previous arrows to move between results.

> $\bigodot$ **SEE ALSO** For more information about working with the Navigation pane, see Chapter 2, "Create and manage documents."

Navigation ▾ ✕

employees ✕ ▾

21 results ▲ ▼

Headings   Pages   **Results**

Familiarize **employees** with the concept of service.

Forge a sense of teamwork among all **employees** across departments.

What kinds of things are your **employees** interested in?

What is the skill level of these **employees**?

do you see as being successful for these **employees** (collection, activity, fundraising; see

leader, a Committee member, and other interested **employees** for one hour to decide the following:

When will the project be introduced to the **employees**?

tasks? (As much as possible, leave room for **employees** to participate in planning and carrying out

The Results page of the Navigation pane displays each instance of the search term in context

> **TIP** The Results page of the Navigation pane allows you to continue editing your document as you normally would while still having access to all the search results.

If you want to be more specific about the text you are looking for—for example, if you want to look for occurrences that match the exact capitalization of your search term—you can do so from the Find tab of the Find And Replace dialog box.

You can make a search more specific by using the criteria in the Search Options area of the Find tab

If you want to substitute a specific word or phrase for another, you can use the Replace function. As on the Find tab, the Replace tab contains options you can use to carry out more complicated replacement operations. Note that the settings in the Search Options area apply to the search term and not to its replacement.

| Find and Replace | ? | × |

Find | **Replace** | **Go To**

Find what: `Committee`

Options: Search Down

Replace with: `Team`

<< Less | Replace | Replace All | Find Next | Cancel

Search Options

Search: Down

☐ Match case
☐ Find whole words only
☐ Use wildcards
☐ Sounds like (English)
☐ Find all word forms (English)

☐ Match prefix
☐ Match suffix

☐ Ignore punctuation characters
☐ Ignore white-space characters

Replace

Format ▾ | Special ▾ | No Formatting

Correcting errors and inconsistencies is easy when you use the Replace feature

You can evaluate and decide whether to replace individual instances of the search term, or you can replace all occurrences of the search term in the document at the same time.

To display the Results page of the Navigation pane

1. Do any of the following:

   - On the **Home** tab, in the **Editing** group, click the **Find** button.

   - On the **View** tab, in the **Show** group, select the **Navigation Pane** check box and then, at the top of the **Navigation** pane, click **Results**.

   - Press **Ctrl+F.**

To search for text

1. On the **Results** page of the **Navigation** pane, enter the text you want to find in the search box.

To find a search result in the document

1. On the **Results** page of the **Navigation** pane, point to a search result to display a ScreenTip with the number of the page on which that result appears and the name of the heading that precedes that search result.

2. Click the search result to move directly to that location in the document.

To display the Find tab of the Find And Replace dialog box

1. Do either of the following:

    *   In the **Navigation** pane, click the **Search for more things** arrow at the right end of the search box, and then click **Advanced Find**.

    *   On the **Home** tab, in the **Editing** group, in the **Find** list, click **Advanced Find**.

To conduct a more specific search

1. Display the **Find** page of the **Find and Replace** dialog box.

2. Click **More** in the lower-left corner of the dialog box to display additional search options.

3. In the **Find what** box, enter the text you want to search for, or click the **Special** button and then click the symbol or formatting symbol you want to locate.

4. Modify your search by selecting any of the following options in the expanded dialog box:

    *   Guide the direction of the search by selecting **Down**, **Up**, or **All** from the **Search** list.

    *   Locate only text that matches the capitalization of the search term by selecting the **Match case** check box.

    *   Exclude occurrences of the search term that appear within other words by selecting the **Find whole words only** check box.

    *   Find two similar words, such as *effect* and *affect*, by selecting the **Use wildcards** check box and then including one or more wildcard characters in the search term.

> **TIP** The two most common wildcard characters are ?, which represents any single character in this location in the Find What text, and *, which represents any number of characters in this location in the Find What text. For a list of the available wildcards, select the Use Wildcards check box and then click the Special button.

3

- Find occurrences of the search text that sound the same but are spelled differently, such as *there* and *their,* by selecting the **Sounds like** check box.

- Find occurrences of a particular word in any form, such as *try, tries,* and *tried,* by selecting the **Find all word forms** check box.

- Locate formatting, such as bold, or special characters, such as tabs, by selecting them from the **Format** or **Special** list.

- Locate words with the same beginning or end as the search term by selecting the **Match prefix** or **Match suffix** check box.

- Locate words with different hyphenation or spacing by selecting the **Ignore punctuation characters** or **Ignore white-space characters** check box.

5. Click the **Find Next** button to find the next instance of the text in the document.

> **TIP** You can conduct a more specific search directly from the Navigation pane by clicking the Search For More Things arrow at the right end of the search box and then clicking Options. The Find Options dialog box opens, where you can select many of these same settings while continuing to use the Results page of the Navigation pane to conduct your search.

To display the Replace tab of the Find And Replace dialog box

1. Do any of the following:

- If the **Find and Replace** dialog box is already open, click the **Replace** tab.

- If the **Navigation** pane is open, click the **Search for more things** arrow at the right end of the search box, and then click **Replace**.

- On the **Home** tab, in the **Editing** group, click the **Replace** button.

- Press **Ctrl+H**.

To replace text

1. Display the **Replace** tab of the **Find and Replace** dialog box.

2. In the **Find what** box, enter the text you want to replace.

3. In the **Replace with** box, enter the replacement text.

> **TIP** Click the More button in the lower-left corner to expand the dialog box to display the Search Options area, which contains additional search options.

4. Do one of the following:

   - Click **Replace** to find the next occurrence of the text in the **Find what** box, replace it with the text in the **Replace with** box, and move to the next occurrence.

   - Click **Replace All** to replace all occurrences of the text in the **Find what** box with the text in the **Replace with** box.

> **TIP** Before clicking Replace All, ensure that the replacement is clearly defined. For example, if you want to change *trip* to *journey*, be sure to tell Word to find only the whole word *trip*; otherwise, *triple* could become *journeyle*.

   - Click **Find Next** to find the first occurrence of the text in the **Find What** box or to leave the selected occurrence as it is and locate the next one.

Use reference and research tools

Language is often contextual. That is, you use different words and phrases in a marketing brochure than you would in a letter requesting immediate payment of an invoice or in an informal memo about a social gathering after work. To help ensure that you're using the words that best convey your meaning in any given context, you can look up definitions, synonyms, and antonyms of words from within a document by using the built-in proofing tools. You can also use the selected word as a jumping-off point for further research.

You can display definitions of words on the Define page of the Smart Lookup pane. By default, this pane displays dictionary definitions from online sources.

3

Smart Lookup ▾ ×

Explore | **Define**

Professional
pro·fes·sion·al [prə'feSH(ə)n(ə)l] ◄)

adjective

adjective: professional

1. of, relating to, or connected with a profession:

"young professional people"

synonyms: white-collar, nonmanual

antonyms: blue-collar

2. (of a person) engaged in a specified activity as one's main paid occupation rather than as a pastime:

"a professional boxer"

synonyms: paid, salaried

antonyms: amateur

noun

noun: professional, plural noun: professionals

The Smart Lookup pane displays information about the selected word

You can also install free dictionaries from the Microsoft Office Store. After you install a dictionary, you can display definitions in the Thesaurus pane when you're online or offline.

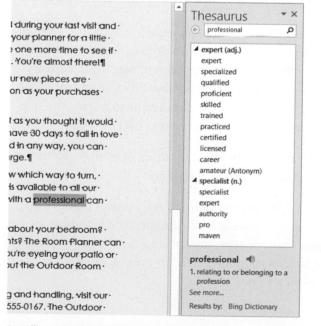

Installing a dictionary makes definitions available at any time

Install Office tools

A dictionary isn't the only tool, or *app*, that you can install. There are many other useful apps available for Word and other Office apps, including fax services, maps, newsfeeds, and social connectors.

To locate apps that are available for Word, follow these steps:

1. On the **Insert** tab, in the **Add-ins** group, click the **Store** button to display the Store tab of the Office Add-ins dialog box.

2. Browse the available apps or use the search box to search for a specific app.

To display and manage your installed add-ins, do the following:

1. On the **Insert** tab, in the **Add-ins** group, click the **My Add-ins** button to display a list of the apps you've installed.

2. To remove an app, right-click it on the **My Add-ins** page of the **Office Add-ins** dialog box, click **Remove**, and then click **Remove** again to confirm the removal.

Sometimes it's difficult to think of the best word to use in a specific situation. You can display a list of synonyms (words that have the same meaning) and usually an antonym (a word that has the opposite meaning) from the shortcut menu that appears when you click a word. You can display a more comprehensive list of synonyms in the Thesaurus pane. You can click any synonym in the Thesaurus pane to display the synonyms and definition of that word, until you find the word that best suits your needs.

You can use built-in and online tools to translate words, phrases, or even entire documents into other languages. These tools include the following:

- **Mini Translator** When the Mini Translator is turned on, you can point to a word or selected phrase to display a translation in the specified language. In the Bilingual Dictionary pane that appears, you can choose to display more information and options, copy the translated word or phrase, or hear the original word or phrase spoken for you.

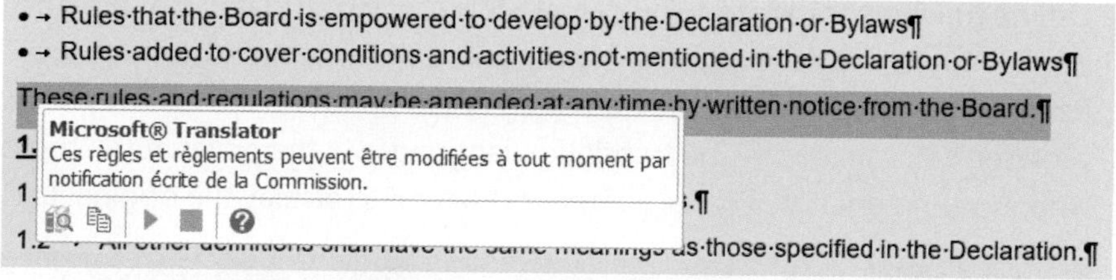

• → Rules·that·the·Board·is·empowered·to·develop·by·the·Declaration·or·Bylaws¶
• → Rules·added·to·cover·conditions·and·activities·not·mentioned·in·the·Declaration·or·Bylaws¶

These·rules·and·regulations·may·be·amended·at·any·time·by·written·notice·from·the·Board.¶

Microsoft® Translator
Ces règles et règlements peuvent être modifiées à tout moment par notification écrite de la Commission.

1.2 → All·other·definitions·shall·have·the·same·meanings·as·those·specified·in·the·Declaration.¶

Using the Mini Translator is the quickest way to obtain the translation of a selection

3

■ **Online bilingual dictionary** You can choose this option to display a translation of selected text in the Research pane. You can also use the Research pane to obtain a translation of a word or phrase that does not appear in the text of the document.

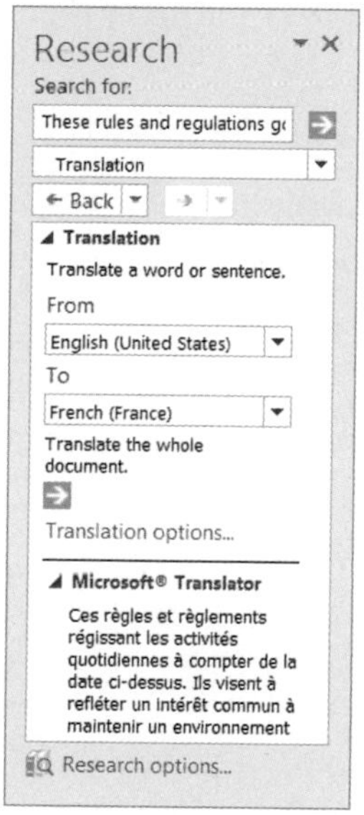

Research ▾ ✕
Search for:
These rules and regulations g(⮕
Translation ▾
← Back ▾ → ▾

◢ **Translation**
Translate a word or sentence.
From
English (United States) ▾
To
French (France) ▾
Translate the whole document.
⮕
Translation options...

◢ **Microsoft® Translator**
Ces règles et règlements régissant les activités quotidiennes à compter de la date ci-dessus. Ils visent à refléter un intérêt commun à maintenir un environnement

🔍 Research options...

The available translation options vary depending on the language selected

■ **Online machine translator** You can use this tool to translate an entire document. When you choose this option, Word sends the document to the Microsoft Translator service (which is free); the translated document then appears in your web browser. You can modify the translation languages in the boxes at the top of the webpage and point to any part of the translation to display the original text.

You can use the free Microsoft Translator service to translate a document into more than 40 languages

You can translate from and to many languages, including Arabic, Chinese, Greek, Hebrew, Italian, Japanese, Korean, Polish, Portuguese, Russian, Spanish, and Swedish. You set which languages you want to use in the Translation Language Options dialog box.

Set the language for each translator independently

Display document statistics

Word displays information about the size of a document at the left end of the status bar. To show the number of words in only part of the document, such as a few paragraphs, simply select that part. You can review more statistics and specify the content to include in the statistics in the Word Count dialog box. To open it, click the Word Count indicator on the status bar or the Word Count button in the Proofing group on the Review tab.

Word Count	?	✕

Statistics:

Pages	8
Words	3,517
Characters (no spaces)	17,681
Characters (with spaces)	21,108
Paragraphs	131
Lines	305

☐ Include textboxes, footnotes and endnotes

Close

In addition to counting pages and words, Word counts characters, paragraphs, and lines

To display the definition of a word while online

1. Click or select the word that you want the definition of.

2. Open the **Insights** pane by doing either of the following:

   • On the **Review** tab, in the **Insights** group, click **Smart Lookup**.

   • Right-click the word, and then click **Smart Lookup**.

3. Click the **Define** link in the **Insights** pane to display the Define page, which provides various definitions of the word.

To install a dictionary

1. On the **Insert** tab, in the **Add-ins** group, click the **Store** button to open the Office Add-ins dialog box.

2. In the search box in the dialog box, enter **dictionary**. A list of available dictionaries appears.

3. Click the dictionary you want to install. The Office Add-ins dialog box changes to display information about the dictionary.

4. Click the **Trust It** button to install the dictionary.

To display synonyms for a word

1. Right-click the word, and then click **Synonyms**.

To display synonyms, antonyms, and the definition of a word

1. Right-click the word, click **Synonyms**, and then on the submenu, click **Thesaurus**.

Or

1. Click or select the word.

2. Do either of the following:

    • On the **Review** tab, in the **Proofing** group, click the **Thesaurus** button.

    • Press **Shift+F7**.

To replace a word with a synonym

1. Do either of the following:

    • Display the list of synonyms, and then click the synonym you want to use.

    • Display the **Thesaurus**, point to the synonym you want to use, click the arrow that appears, and then click **Insert**.

To change the languages used by the translator tools

1. On the **Review** tab, in the **Language** group, click the **Translate** button, and then click **Choose Translation Language** to display the **Translation Language Options** dialog box.

2. In the **Choose document translation languages** section, do the following:

   - In the **Translate from** list, click the original language.

   - In the **Translate to** list, click the translation language.

3. In the **Choose Mini Translator language** section, in the **Translate to** list, click the translation language.

4. Click **OK**.

To translate text within Word

1. Select the word or phrase you want to translate.

2. On the **Review** tab, in the **Language** group, click the **Translate** button, and then click **Translate Selected Text**. If you're prompted to approve sending the text for translation, click **Yes**.

3. The Research pane opens and displays the selected text in the Search For box. The From and To boxes display the currently selected original and translation languages. If either language is different than the current selection, change the selection. Then click the **Search** button (the green arrow) to display the translated word or phrase in the Translation page.

4. If you translated a phrase, you can do either of the following:

   - To replace the selected text with the translation, click the **Insert** button.

   - To copy the translation, click the **Insert** arrow, and then click **Copy**.

To turn on the Mini Translator

1. On the **Review** tab, in the **Language** group, click the **Translate** button, and then click **Mini Translator**.

To translate text by using the Mini Translator

1. Turn on the Mini Translator, and then do either of the following:

   - To translate a single word, point to the word to display the **Online Bilingual Dictionary**, which contains a translation in the specified language.

   - To translate a phrase or other longer piece of text, select the text you want to translate, and then point to it to display the **Microsoft Translator** dialog box, which contains a translation in the specified language.

2. In the **Online Bilingual Dictionary** dialog box or the **Microsoft Translator** dialog box, do any of the following:

   - Click the **Expand** button to display more information and options in the **Research** pane.

   - Click the **Copy** button to copy the entire contents of the dialog box to the Clipboard.

   - Click the **Play** button to hear the word or phrase spoken for you.

To insert translated text from the Online Bilingual Dictionary into the document, replacing the text selection

1. In the **Research** pane, in the translation text below **Bilingual Dictionary**, select and copy the translated word you want to insert.

2. In the document, replace the original word with the copied word.

To change the translation languages in the Research pane

1. Do any of the following:

   - In the **From** list, click the original language.

   - In the **To** list, click the translation language.

To translate a word that does not appear in the text of a document

1. In the **Research** pane, on the **Translation** page, enter the word you want to translate in the search box.

2. In the **From** list, select the original language of the text you want to translate.

3. In the **To** list, select the language to which the text should be translated.

4. Click the **Start Searching** button.

To use the online machine translator to translate an entire document

1. Open the document you want to translate in Word.

2. On the **Review** tab, in the **Language** group, click the **Translate** button, and then click **Translate Document**.

3. Word displays a message that the document will be sent for translation by the Microsoft Translator service (which is free). Click **Send** to display the translated document in your web browser.

Skills review

In this chapter, you learned how to:

- Enter and import text

- Move, copy, and delete text

- Find and replace text

- Use reference and research tools

3

Practice tasks

The practice files for these tasks are located in the Word2016SBS\Ch03 folder. You can save the results of the tasks in the same folder.

Enter and import text

Start Word, and then perform the following tasks:

1. Create a new document based on the blank document template.

2. With the cursor at the beginning of the new document, enter **Parks Appreciation Day**, and then create a new paragraph.

3. Enter **Help beautify our city by participating in the annual cleanup of Log Drift Park, Swamp Creek Park, and Tall Tree Park. Volunteers will receive a free T-shirt and barbeque lunch. Bring your own gardening tools and gloves, and be ready to have fun!**

4. Create a new paragraph, and then enter **The Park Service Committee is coordinating group participation in this event. If you are interested in spending time outdoors with family and friends while improving the quality of our parks, contact Nancy Anderson by email at nancy@adventure-works.com.**

5. Create a new paragraph, and with the cursor in the first blank line, insert the text from the **ImportText** file from the practice file folder.

6. Save the document as **EnterText**, and close it.

Move, copy, and delete text

Open the EditText document in Print Layout view, display formatting marks, and then perform the following tasks:

> **TIP** Press Ctrl+* to turn on and off the display of formatting marks and hidden text.

1. In the second bullet point under **Project Goals**, delete the word **natural**.

2. In the third bullet point, use the arrow keys to select the words **and motivate** and the following space, and then delete the selection.

3. In the fourth bullet point, select the word **Forge**, and then replace it by entering **Build**. Notice that you don't have to enter a space after *Build*. Word inserts the space for you.

4. In the middle of page **1**, use the selection area to select the entire first bullet point after **Questions for Team Leaders**.

5. Copy the selection to the Clipboard.

6. At the bottom of page **1**, click to the left of **What** in the first bullet point after **Questions for Department Reps**. Then in the **Clipboard** group, expand the **Paste Options** menu. Notice that, because you're pasting a list item into a list, two of the three available buttons have list-related icons.

7. Point to each of the paste option buttons to review how the source text will look with that paste option implemented.

8. Click the **Merge List** button to paste the copied bullet point into the second list and retain its formatting.

9. On page **2**, in the **Set Up Team** section, select the entire paragraph that begins with **Explain the position's responsibilities**.

10. Cut the selection, and then paste it before the preceding paragraph to reverse the order of the two paragraphs.

11. In the **Undo** list, point to the third action (**Paste Merge List**). Notice that the text at the bottom of the list indicates that three actions will be undone if you click this list entry.

12. In the **Undo** list, click **Paste Merge List** to undo the previous cut-and-paste operation and the pasting of the copied text.

13. In the **Pre-Plan Project** section, select the **If some employee input** paragraph.

14. Drag the paragraph to the left of the word **If** at the beginning of the preceding bullet point to switch the order of the bullet points.

15. Release the selection and move the cursor to the end of the paragraph.

16. Delete the paragraph mark to merge the two bullet points. Add a space to separate the two sentences.

17. If you prefer to not show formatting symbols, turn them off.

18. Save and close the document.

Find and replace text

Open the FindText document in Print Layout view, and then perform the following tasks:

1. With the cursor at the beginning of the document, open the **Results** page of the **Navigation** pane.

2. Enter **Board** in the search box.

3. Click the **Next** button (the downward-pointing triangle under the search box) to move through the first few search results.

4. Scroll through the document to show other highlighted results. Notice that on page **2**, in section **4**, Word has highlighted the *board* portion of *skateboards*. You need to restrict the search to the whole word *Board*.

5. Open the **Find Options** dialog box.

6. Select the **Match case** and **Find whole words only** check boxes, and then click **OK**.

7. Enter **Board** in the search box again and scroll through the list of results. Notice that the word *skateboards* is no longer highlighted.

8. Move the cursor to the beginning of the document.

9. Open the **Find and Replace** dialog box with the **Replace** page active. Notice that the **Find What** box retains the entry from the previous search.

10. Display the **Search options** area. Notice that the **Match case** and **Find whole words only** options are still selected.

11. In the **Search Options** area, ensure that **Down** is selected in the **Search** list. Then click **Less** to hide the **Search Options** area.

12. Enter **Association Board** in the **Replace with** box and click **Find Next** to have Word highlight the first occurrence of *Board*.

13. Click **Replace** to have Word replace the selected occurrence of *Board* with *Association Board* and then find the next occurrence.

14. Click **Replace All**. Word tells you how many replacements it made from the starting point forward.

15. Close the **Find and Replace** dialog box.

16. Close the **Navigation** pane.

17. Save and close the document.

Use reference and research tools

> ⚠️ **IMPORTANT** You must have an active Internet connection to complete the following tasks.

Open the ResearchText document in Print Layout view, and perform the following tasks:

1. In the second line of the first paragraph, select the word *acclaimed*. Then do the following:

   a. Display a definition of the word *acclaimed* in the Insights pane.

   b. Display a list of synonyms for the word *acclaimed* in the Thesaurus pane.

   c. Scroll through the list of synonyms. Notice that an antonym appears at the bottom of the list.

   d. In the synonym list, click a synonym of *acclaimed* to replace the word in the search box at the top of the pane.

   e. From the synonym list, replace the word *acclaimed* in the document with one of its synonyms.

   f. Close the open panes.

2. Open the **Translation Language Options** dialog box, and set the Mini Translator language to translate text into French.

3. Turn on the **Mini Translator**.

4. In the first line of the first paragraph, point to the word *mistake*, and then move the pointer over the translucent box that appears above the word to display the **Mini Translator**, showing French translations for the word *mistake*.

5. Expand the **Mini Translator** box to display the Research pane.

6. In the **Research** pane, in the **mistake** translation below **Bilingual Dictionary**, select and copy the word *erreur*.

7. In the document, replace *mistake* with the copied word.

8. Close the **Research** pane, and turn off the **Mini Translator**.

9. Save and close the document.

Part 2

Create professional documents

Modify the structure and appearance of text

Documents contain text that conveys information to readers, but the appearance of the document content also conveys a message. You can provide structure and meaning by formatting the text in various ways. Word 2016 provides a variety of simple-to-use tools that you can use to apply sophisticated formatting and create a navigational structure.

In a short document or one that doesn't require a complex navigational structure, you can easily format words and paragraphs so that key points stand out and the structure of your document is clear. You can achieve dramatic flair by applying predefined WordArt text effects. To keep the appearance of documents and other Microsoft Office files consistent, you can format document elements by applying predefined sets of formatting called *styles*. In addition, you can change the fonts, colors, and effects throughout a document with one click by applying a theme.

This chapter guides you through procedures related to applying character and paragraph formatting, structuring content manually, creating and modifying lists, applying styles to text, and changing a document's theme.

In this chapter

- Apply paragraph formatting
- Structure content manually
- Apply character formatting
- Create and modify lists
- Apply built-in styles to text
- Change the document theme

Practice files

For this chapter, use the practice files from the Word2016SBS\Ch04 folder. For practice file download instructions, see the introduction.

Apply paragraph formatting

A paragraph is created by entering text and then pressing the Enter key. A paragraph can contain one word, one sentence, or multiple sentences. Every paragraph ends with a paragraph mark, which looks like a backward P (¶). Paragraph marks and other structural characters (such as spaces, line breaks, and tabs) are usually hidden, but you can display them. Sometimes displaying these hidden characters makes it easier to accomplish a task or understand a structural problem.

> **SEE ALSO** For information about working with hidden structural characters, see "Structure content manually" later in this chapter.

You can change the look of a paragraph by changing its indentation, alignment, and line spacing, in addition to the space before and after it. You can also put borders around it and shade its background. Collectively, the settings you use to vary the look of a paragraph are called *paragraph formatting*.

You can modify a paragraph's left and right edge alignment and vertical spacing by using tools on the Home tab of the ribbon, and its left and right indents from the Home tab or from the ruler. The ruler is usually hidden to provide more space for the document content.

The left indent can be changed from the Home tab or the ruler

If you modify a paragraph and aren't happy with the changes, you can restore the original paragraph and character settings by clearing the formatting to reset the paragraph to its base style.

> **SEE ALSO** For information about styles, see "Apply built-in styles to text" later in this chapter.

When you want to make several adjustments to the alignment, indentation, and spacing of selected paragraphs, it is sometimes quicker to make changes in the Paragraph dialog box than to click buttons and drag markers.

The Paragraph dialog box

Configure alignment

The alignment settings control the horizontal position of the paragraph text between the page margins. There are four alignment options:

- **Align Left** This is the default paragraph alignment. It sets the left end of each line of the paragraph at the left page margin or left indent. It results in a straight left edge and a ragged right edge.

- **Align Right** This sets the right end of each line of the paragraph at the right page margin or right indent. It results in a straight right edge and a ragged left edge.

- **Center** This centers each line of the paragraph between the left and right page margins or indents. It results in ragged left and right edges.

- **Justify** This alignment adjusts the spacing between words so that the left end of each line of the paragraph is at the left page margin or indent and the right end of each line of the paragraph (other than the last line) is at the right margin or indent. It results in straight left and right edges.

The icons on the alignment buttons on the ribbon depict the effect of each alignment option.

To open the Paragraph dialog box

1. Do either of the following:

   - On the **Home** tab or the **Layout** tab, in the **Paragraph** group, click the **Paragraph** dialog box launcher.

   - On the **Home** tab, in the **Paragraph** group, click the **Line and Paragraph Spacing** button, and then click **Line Spacing Options**.

To set paragraph alignment

1. Position the cursor anywhere in the paragraph, or select all the paragraphs you want to adjust.

2. Do either of the following:

   - On the **Home** tab, in the **Paragraph** group, click the **Align Left**, **Center**, **Align Right**, or **Justify** button.

   - Open the **Paragraph** dialog box. On the **Indents and Spacing** tab, in the **General** area, click **Left**, **Centered**, **Right**, or **Justified** in the **Alignment** list.

Configure vertical spacing

Paragraphs have two types of vertical spacing:

- **Paragraph spacing** The space between paragraphs, defined by setting the space before and after each paragraph. This space is usually measured in points.

- **Line spacing** The space between the lines of the paragraph, defined by setting the height of the lines either in relation to the height of the text (Single, Double, or a specific number of lines) or by specifying a minimum or exact point measurement.

The default line spacing for documents created in Word 2016 is 1.08 lines. Changing the line spacing changes the appearance and readability of the text in the paragraph and, of course, also changes the amount of space it occupies on the page.

> *The line spacing of this paragraph is set to the default, 1.08 lines.* A paragraph can contain one word, one sentence, or multiple sentences. You can change the look of a paragraph by changing its indentation, alignment, and line spacing, as well as the space before and after it. You can also put borders around it and shade its background. Collectively, the settings you use to vary the look of a paragraph are called *paragraph formatting*.
>
> *The line spacing of this paragraph is set to Double (2 lines).* A paragraph can contain one word, one sentence, or multiple sentences. You can change the look of a paragraph by changing its indentation, alignment, and line spacing, as well as the space before and after it. You can also put borders around it and shade its background. Collectively, the settings you use to vary the look of a paragraph are called *paragraph formatting*.

The effect of changing line spacing

You can set the paragraph and line spacing for individual paragraphs and for paragraph styles. You can quickly adjust the spacing of most content in a document by selecting an option from the Paragraph Spacing menu on the Design tab. (Although the menu is named Paragraph Spacing, the menu options control both paragraph spacing and line spacing.) These options, which are named by effect rather than by specific measurements, work by modifying the spacing of the Normal paragraph style and any other styles that depend on the Normal style for their spacing. (In standard templates, most other styles are based on the Normal style.) The Paragraph Spacing options modify the Normal style in only the current document, and do not affect other documents.

The following table describes the effect of each Paragraph Spacing option on the paragraph and line spacing settings.

Paragraph spacing option	Before paragraph	After paragraph	Line spacing
Default	Spacing options are controlled by the style set		
No Paragraph Space	0 points	0 points	1 line
Compact	0 points	4 points	1 line
Tight	0 points	6 points	1.15 lines
Open	0 points	10 points	1.15 lines
Relaxed	0 points	6 points	1.5 lines
Double	0 points	8 points	2 lines

To quickly adjust the vertical spacing before, after, and within all paragraphs in a document

1. On the **Design** tab, in the **Document Formatting** group, click the **Paragraph Spacing** button to display the Paragraph Spacing menu.

Each paragraph spacing option controls space around and within the paragraph

2. Click the option you want to apply to all of the paragraphs in the document.

To adjust the spacing between paragraphs

1. Select all the paragraphs you want to adjust.

2. On the **Layout** tab, in the **Paragraph** group, adjust the **Spacing Before** and **Spacing After** settings.

The settings in the Spacing boxes are measured in points

To adjust spacing between the lines of paragraphs

1. Position the cursor anywhere in the paragraph, or select all the paragraphs you want to adjust.

2. To make a quick adjustment to selected paragraphs, on the **Home** tab, in the **Paragraph** group, click **Line And Paragraph Spacing**, and then click any of the line spacing commands on the menu.

1.0
1.15
1.5
2.0
2.5
3.0
Line Spacing Options...
≛ Add Space <u>B</u>efore Paragraph
≛ Remove Space <u>A</u>fter Paragraph

You can choose from preset internal line spacing options or adjust paragraph spacing

> ✅ **TIP** You can also adjust the space before and after selected paragraphs from the Line And Paragraph Spacing menu. Clicking one of the last two options adds or removes a preset amount of space between the selected paragraphs.

Or

1. Position the cursor anywhere in the paragraph, or select all the paragraphs you want to adjust.

2. Open the **Paragraph** dialog box. On the **Indents and Spacing** tab, in the **Spacing** area, make the adjustments you want to the paragraph spacing, and then click **OK**.

Configure indents

In Word, you don't define the width of paragraphs and the length of pages by defining the area occupied by the text; instead, you define the size of the white space—the left, right, top, and bottom margins—around the text.

> 🔍 **SEE ALSO** For information about setting margins, see "Preview and adjust page layout" in Chapter 12, "Finalize and distribute documents." For information about sections, see "Control what appears on each page" in the same chapter.

Although the left and right margins are set for a whole document or for a section of a document, you can vary the position of the paragraphs between the margins by indenting the left or right edge of the paragraph.

A paragraph indent is the space from the page margin to the text. You can change the left indent by clicking buttons on the Home tab, or you can set the indents directly on the ruler. Three indent markers are always present on the ruler:

- **Left Indent** This defines the outermost left edge of each line of the paragraph.

- **Right Indent** This defines the outermost right edge of each line of the paragraph.

- **First Line Indent** This defines the starting point of the first line of the paragraph.

The ruler indicates the space between the left and right page margins in a lighter color than the space outside of the page margins.

First Line Indent   Left Indent   Right Indent

Periodically you might want to experiment with structural or content modifications, or you might simply find that a change you've made didn't work as intended, and want to undo your changes. The Office apps provide three levels of change reversion:

- You can undo one change at a time (and redo that change if you want to).
- You can undo all the changes in the current app session.
- You can roll back to a previous version of the document.

The indent markers on the ruler

The default setting for the Left Indent and First Line Indent markers is 0.0", which aligns with the left page margin. The default setting for the Right Indent marker is the distance from the left margin to the right margin. For example, if the page size is set to 8.5" wide and the left and right margins are set to 1.0", the default Right Indent marker setting is 6.5".

You can arrange the Left Indent and First Line Indent markers to create a hanging indent or a first line indent. Hanging indents are most commonly used for bulleted and numbered lists, in which the bullet or number is indented less than the main text (essentially, it is *out*dented). First line indents are frequently used to distinguish the beginning of each subsequent paragraph in documents that consist of many consecutive paragraphs of text. Both types of indents are set by using the First Line Indent marker on the ruler.

> **TIP** The First Line Indent marker is linked to the Left Indent marker. Moving the Left Indent marker also moves the First Line Indent marker, to maintain the first line indent distance. You can move the First Line Indent marker independently of the Left Indent marker to change the first line indent distance.

To display the ruler

1. On the **View** tab, in the **Show** group, select the **Ruler** check box.

> **TIP** In this book, we show measurements in inches. If you want to change the measurement units Word uses, open the Word Options dialog box. On the Advanced page, in the Display area, click the units you want in the Show Measurements In Units Of list. Then click OK.

To indent or outdent the left edge of a paragraph

1. Position the cursor anywhere in the paragraph, or select all the paragraphs you want to adjust.

2. Do any of the following:

   - On the **Home** tab, in the **Paragraph** group, click the **Increase Indent** or **Decrease Indent** button to move the left edge of the paragraph in 0.25" increments.

> **TIP** You cannot increase or decrease the indent beyond the margins by using the Increase Indent and Decrease Indent buttons. If you do need to extend an indent beyond the margins, you can do so by setting negative indentation measurements in the Paragraph dialog box.

- Open the **Paragraph** dialog box. On the **Indents and Spacing** tab, in the **Indentation** area, set the indent in the **Left** box, and then click **OK**.

- On the ruler, drag the **Left Indent** marker to the ruler measurement at which you want to position the left edge of the body of the paragraph.

To create a hanging indent or first line indent

1. Position the cursor anywhere in the paragraph, or select all the paragraphs you want to adjust.

2. Open the **Paragraph** dialog box. On the **Indents and Spacing** tab, in the **Indents** area, click **First line** or **Hanging** in the **Special** box.

3. In the **By** box, set the amount of the indent, and then click **OK**.

Or

1. Set the left indent of the paragraph body.

2. On the ruler, drag the **First Line Indent** marker to the ruler measurement at which you want to begin the first line of the paragraph.

To indent or outdent the right edge of a paragraph

1. Position the cursor anywhere in the paragraph, or select all the paragraphs you want to adjust.

2. Do either of the following:

   - On the ruler, drag the **Right Indent** marker to the ruler measurement at which you want to set the maximum right edge of the paragraph.

   - Open the **Paragraph** dialog box. On the **Indents and Spacing** tab, in the **Indentation** area, set the right indent in the **Right** box, and then click **OK**.

> **TIP** Unless the paragraph alignment is justified, the right edge of the paragraph will be ragged, but no line will extend beyond the right indent or outdent.

Configure paragraph borders and shading

To make a paragraph really stand out, you might want to put a border around it or shade its background. (For real drama, you can do both.) You can select a predefined border from the Borders menu, or design a custom border in the Borders And Shading dialog box.

You can customize many aspects of the border

After you select the style, color, width, and location of the border, you can click the Options button to specify its distance from the text.

Structure content manually

At times it's necessary to manually position text within a paragraph. You can do this by using two different hidden characters: line breaks and tabs. These characters are visible only when the option to show paragraph marks and formatting symbols is turned on.

The hidden characters have distinctive appearances:

- A line break character looks like a bent left arrow: ↵

- A tab character looks like a right-pointing arrow: →

You can use a line break, also known as a *soft return*, to wrap a line of a paragraph in a specific location without ending the paragraph. You might use this technique to display only specific text on a line, or to break a line before a word that would otherwise be hyphenated.

> ✓ **TIP** Inserting a line break does not start a new paragraph, so when you apply paragraph formatting to a line of text that ends with a line break, the formatting is applied to the entire paragraph, not only to that line.

> 🔍 **SEE ALSO** For information about page and section breaks, see "Control what appears on each page" in Chapter 12, "Finalize and distribute documents."

A tab character defines the space between two document elements. For example, you can separate numbers from list items, or columns of text, by using tabs. You can then set tab stops that define the location and alignment of the tabbed text.

You can align text in different ways by using tabs

You can align lines of text in different locations across the page by using tab stops. The easiest way to set tab stops is directly on the horizontal ruler. By default, Word sets left-aligned tab stops every half inch (1.27 centimeters). (The default tab stops aren't shown on the ruler.) To set a custom tab stop, start by clicking the Tab button (located at the intersection of the vertical and horizontal rulers) until the type of tab stop you want appears.

The tab settings

You have the following tab options:

- **Left Tab** Aligns the left end of the text with the tab stop

- **Center Tab** Aligns the center of the text with the tab stop

- **Right Tab** Aligns the right end of the text with the tab stop

- **Decimal Tab** Aligns the decimal point in the text (usually a numeric value) with the tab stop

- **Bar Tab** Draws a vertical line at the position of the tab stop

If you find it too difficult to position tab stops on the ruler, you can set, clear, align, and format tab stops from the Tabs dialog box.

You can specify the alignment and tab leader for each tab

You might also work from this dialog box if you want to use tab leaders—visible marks such as dots or dashes connecting the text before the tab with the text after it. For example, tab leaders are useful in a table of contents to carry the eye from the text to the page number.

When you insert tab characters, the text to the right of the tab character aligns on the tab stop according to its type. For example, if you set a center tab stop, pressing the Tab key moves the text so that its center is aligned with the tab stop.

To display or hide paragraph marks and other structural characters

1. Do either of the following:

   - On the **Home** tab, in the **Paragraph** group, click the **Show/Hide ¶** button.

   - Press **Ctrl+Shift+*** (asterisk).

To insert a line break

1. Position the cursor where you want to break the line.

2. Do either of the following:

   - On the **Layout** tab, in the **Page Setup** group, click **Breaks**, and then click **Text Wrapping**.

   - Press **Shift+Enter**.

To insert a tab character

1. Position the cursor where you want to add the tab character.

2. Press the **Tab** key.

To open the Tabs dialog box

1. Select any portion of one or more paragraphs that you want to manage tab stops for.

2. Open the **Paragraph** dialog box.

3. In the lower-left corner of the **Indents and Spacing** tab, click the **Tabs** button.

To align a tab and set a tab stop

1. Select any portion of one or more paragraphs that you want to set the tab stop for.

2. Click the **Tab** button at the left end of the ruler to cycle through the tab stop alignments, in this order: Left, Center, Right, Decimal, Bar.

3. When the **Tab** button shows the alignment you want, click the ruler at the point where you want to set the tab.

> **TIP** When you manually align a tab and set a tab stop, Word removes any default tab stops to the left of the one you set.

4

Or

1. Open the **Tabs** dialog box.

2. In the **Tab stop position** box, enter the position for the new tab stop.

3. In the **Alignment** and **Leader** areas, set the options you want for this tab stop.

4. Click **Set** to set the tab, and then click **OK**.

To change the position of an existing custom tab stop

1. Do either of the following:

   - Drag the tab marker on the ruler.

   - Open the **Tabs** dialog box. In the **Tab stop position** list, select the tab stop you want to change. Click the **Clear** button to clear the existing tab stop. Enter the replacement tab stop position in the **Tab stop position** box, click **Set**, and then click **OK**.

To remove a custom tab stop

1. Do either of the following:

   - Drag the tab marker away from the ruler.

   - In the **Tabs** dialog box, select the custom tab stop in the **Tab stop position** list, click **Clear**, and then click **OK**.

Apply character formatting

The appearance of your document helps to convey not only the document's message but also information about the document's creator—you. A neatly organized document that contains consistently formatted content and appropriate graphic elements, and that doesn't contain spelling or grammatical errors, invokes greater confidence in your ability to provide any product or service.

Earlier in this chapter, you learned about methods of applying formatting to paragraphs. This topic covers methods of formatting the text of a document. Formatting that you apply to text is referred to as *character formatting*. In Word documents, you can apply three types of character formatting:

- Individual character formats including font, font size, bold, italic, underline, strikethrough, subscript, superscript, font color, and highlight color
- Artistic text effects that incorporate character outline and fill colors
- Preformatted styles associated with the document template, many of which convey structural information (such as titles and headings)

When you enter text in a document, it is displayed in a specific font. By default, the font used for text in a new blank document is 11-point Calibri, but you can change the font of any element at any time. The available fonts vary from one computer to another, depending on the apps installed.

You can vary the look of a font by changing the following attributes:

- **Size** Almost every font has a range of sizes you can select from. (Sometimes you can set additional sizes beyond those listed.) The font size is measured in points, from the top of the ascenders to the bottom of the descenders. A point is approximately 1/72 of an inch (about 0.04 centimeters).
- **Style** Almost every font has a range of font styles. The most common are regular (or plain), italic, bold, and bold italic.
- **Effects** Fonts can be enhanced by applying effects, such as underlining, small capital letters (small caps), or shadows.
- **Character spacing** You can alter the spacing between characters by pushing them apart or squeezing them together.

Although some attributes might cancel each other out, they are usually cumulative. For example, you might use a bold font style in various sizes and various shades of green to make words stand out in a newsletter.

You apply character formatting from one of three locations:

- **Mini Toolbar** Several common formatting buttons are available on the Mini Toolbar that appears when you select text.

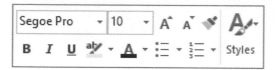

The Mini Toolbar appears temporarily when you select text, becomes transparent when you move the pointer away from the selected text, and then disappears entirely

- **Font group on the Home tab** This group includes buttons for changing the font and most of the font attributes you are likely to use.

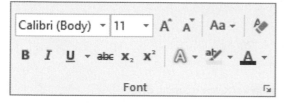

The most common font formatting commands are available on the Home tab

- **Font dialog box** Less-commonly applied attributes such as small caps and special underlining are available from the Font dialog box.

Font attributes that aren't available on the Home tab can be set here

In addition to applying character formatting to change the look of characters, you can apply predefined text effects (sometimes referred to as *WordArt*) to a selection to add more zing. The available effects match the current theme colors.

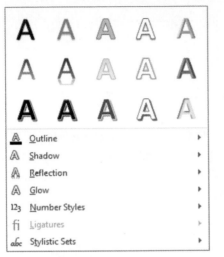

You can apply any predefined effect in the gallery or define a custom effect

These effects are somewhat dramatic, so you'll probably want to restrict their use to document titles and similar elements to which you want to draw particular attention.

To change the font of selected text

1. On the **Mini Toolbar** or in the **Font** group on the **Home** tab, in the **Font** list, click the font you want to apply.

To change the font size of selected text

1. Do any of the following on the **Mini Toolbar** or in the **Font** group on the **Home** tab:

   - In the **Font Size** list, click the font size you want to apply.

   - In the **Font Size** box, enter the font size you want to apply (even a size that doesn't appear in the list). Then press the **Enter** key.

   - To increase the font size in set increments, click the **Increase Font Size** button, or press **Ctrl+>**.

   - To decrease the font size in set increments, click the **Decrease Font Size** button, or press **Ctrl+<**.

To format selected text as bold, italic, or underlined

1. Do any of the following:

    *   On the **Mini Toolbar**, click the **Bold**, **Italic**, or **Underline** button.

    *   On the **Home** tab, in the **Font** group, click the **Bold**, **Italic**, or **Underline** button.

    *   Press **Ctrl+B** to format the text as bold.

    *   Press **Ctrl+I** to format the text as italic.

    *   Press **Ctrl+U** to underline the text.

> ✔ **TIP** To quickly apply a different underline style to selected text, click the arrow next to the Underline button on the Home tab, and then in the list, click the underline style you want to apply.

To cross out selected text by drawing a line through it

1. On the **Home** tab, in the **Font** group, click the **Strikethrough** button.

To display superscript or subscript characters

1. Select the characters you want to reposition.

2. On the **Home** tab, in the **Font** group, do either of the following:

    *   Click the **Subscript** button to shift the characters to the bottom of the line.

    *   Click the **Superscript** button to shift the characters to the top of the line.

To apply artistic effects to selected text

1. On the **Home** tab, in the **Font** group, click the **Text Effects and Typography** button, and then do either of the following:

    *   In the gallery, click the preformatted effect combination that you want to apply.

    *   On the menu, click **Outline**, **Shadow**, **Reflection**, **Glow**, **Number Styles**, **Ligatures**, or **Stylistic Sets**. Then make selections on the submenus to apply and modify those effects.

To change the font color of selected text

1. On the **Home** tab, in the **Font** group, click the **Font Color** arrow to display the **Font Color** menu.

2. In the **Theme Colors** or **Standard Colors** palette, select a color swatch to apply that color to the selected text.

> ✔ **TIP** To apply the Font Color button's current color, you can simply click the button (not its arrow). If you want to apply a color that is not shown in the Theme Colors or Standard Colors palette, click More Colors. In the Colors dialog box, click the color you want in the honeycomb on the Standard page, or click the color gradient or enter values for a color on the Custom page.

To change the case of selected text

1. Do either of the following:

    -   On the **Home** tab, in the **Font** group, click the **Change Case** button, and then click **Sentence case**, **lowercase**, **UPPERCASE**, **Capitalize Each Word**, or **tOGGLE cASE**.

    -   Press **Shift+F3** repeatedly to cycle through the standard case options (Sentence case, UPPERCASE, lowercase, and Capitalize Each Word).

> ⚠ **IMPORTANT** The case options vary based on the selected text. If the selection ends in a period, the Capitalize Each Word option is unavailable. If the selection does not end in a period, the Sentence Case option is unavailable.

To highlight text

1. Select the text you want to change, and then do either of the following in the **Mini Toolbar** or in the **Font** group on the **Home** tab:

    -   Click the **Text Highlight Color** button to apply the default highlight color.

    -   Click the **Text Highlight Color** arrow, and then click a color swatch to apply the selected highlight color and change the default highlight color.

Or

1. Without first selecting text, do either of the following:

   - Click the **Text Highlight Color** button to select the default highlight color.

   - Click the **Text Highlight Color** arrow, and then click a color swatch to select that highlight color.

2. When the pointer changes to a highlighter, drag it across one or more sections of text to apply the highlight.

3. Click the **Text Highlight Color** button or press the **Esc** key to deactivate the highlighter.

To copy formatting to other text

1. Click anywhere in the text that has the formatting you want to copy.

2. On the **Home** tab, in the **Clipboard** group, do either of the following:

   - If you want to apply the formatting to only one target, click the **Format Painter** button once.

   - If you want to apply the formatting to multiple targets, double-click the **Format Painter** button.

3. When the pointer changes to a paintbrush, click or drag across the text you want to apply the copied formatting to.

4. If you activated the Format Painter for multiple targets, repeat step 3 until you finish applying the formatting. Then click the **Format Painter** button once, or press the **Esc** key, to deactivate the tool.

To repeat the previous formatting command

1. Select the text to which you want to apply the repeated formatting.

2. Do either of the following to repeat the previous formatting command:

   - On the **Quick Access Toolbar**, click the **Repeat** button.

   - Press **Ctrl+Y**.

To open the Font dialog box

1. Do either of the following:

   - On the **Home** tab, in the **Font** group, click the **Font** dialog box launcher.

   - Press **Ctrl+Shift+F**.

To remove character formatting

1. Select the text you want to clear the formatting from.

2. Do any of the following:

   - Press **Ctrl+Spacebar** to remove only manually applied formatting (and not styles).

   - On the **Home** tab, in the **Font** group, click the **Clear All Formatting** button to remove all styles and formatting other than highlighting from selected text.

   > ⚠️ **IMPORTANT** If you select an entire paragraph, clicking Clear All Formatting will reset the paragraph to the default paragraph style.

   - On the **Home** tab, in the **Font** group, click the **Text Highlight Color** arrow and then, on the menu, click **No Color** to remove highlighting.

To change the character spacing

1. Select the text you want to change.

2. Open the **Font** dialog box, and then click the **Advanced** tab to display character spacing and typographic features.

3. In the **Spacing** list, click **Expanded** or **Condensed**.

4. In the adjacent **By** box, set the number of points you want to expand or condense the character spacing.

5. In the **Font** dialog box, click **OK**.

4

Character formatting and case considerations

The way you use character formatting in a document can influence its visual impact on your readers. Used judiciously, character formatting can make a plain document look attractive and professional, but excessive use can make it look amateurish and detract from the message. For example, using too many fonts in the same document is the mark of inexperience, so don't use more than two or three.

Bear in mind that lowercase letters tend to recede, so using all uppercase (capital) letters can be useful for titles and headings or for certain kinds of emphasis. However, large blocks of uppercase letters are tiring to the eye.

TIP Where do the terms *uppercase* and *lowercase* come from? Until the advent of computers, individual characters made of lead were assembled to form the words that would appear on a printed page. The characters were stored alphabetically in cases, with the capital letters in the upper case and the small letters in the lower case.

Create and modify lists

Lists are paragraphs that start with a character (usually a number or bullet) and are formatted with a hanging indent so that the characters stand out on the left end of each list item. Fortunately, Word takes care of the formatting of lists for you. You simply indicate the type of list you want to create. When the order of items is not important—for example, for a list of people or supplies—a bulleted list is the best choice. And when the order is important—for example, for the steps in a procedure—you will probably want to create a numbered list.

You can format an existing set of paragraphs as a list or create the list as you enter information into the document. After you create a list, you can modify, format, and customize the list as follows:

- You can move items around in a list, insert new items, or delete unwanted items. If the list is numbered, Word automatically updates the numbers.

- You can modify the indentation of the list. You can change both the overall indentation of the list and the relationship of the first line to the other lines.

- For a bulleted list, you can sort list items into ascending or descending order, change the bullet symbol, or define a custom bullet (even a picture bullet).

- For a numbered list, you can change the number style or define a custom style, and you can specify the starting number for a list.

To format a new bulleted or numbered list as you enter content

1. With the cursor at the position in the document where you want to start the list, do either of the following:

   - To start a new bulleted list, enter * (an asterisk) at the beginning of a paragraph, and then press the **Spacebar** or the **Tab** key before entering the list item text.

   - To start a new numbered list, enter 1. (the number 1 followed by a period) at the beginning of a paragraph, and then press the **Spacebar** or the **Tab** key before entering the list item text.

   When you start a list in this fashion, Word automatically formats it as a bulleted or numbered list. When you press Enter to start a new item, Word continues the formatting to the new paragraph. Typing items and pressing Enter adds subsequent bulleted or numbered items. To end the list, press Enter twice; or click the Bullets arrow or Numbering arrow in the Paragraph group on the Home tab, and then in the gallery, click None.

> **TIP** If you want to start a paragraph with an asterisk or number but don't want to format the paragraph as a bulleted or numbered list, click the AutoCorrect Options button that appears after Word changes the formatting, and then in the list, click the appropriate Undo option. You can also click the Undo button on the Quick Access Toolbar or press Ctrl+Z.

To convert paragraphs to bulleted or numbered list items

1. Select the paragraphs that you want to convert to list items.

2. On the **Home** tab, in the **Paragraph** group, do either of the following:

   - Click the **Bullets** button to convert the selection to a bulleted list.

   - Click the **Numbering** button to convert the selection to a numbered list.

To create a list that has multiple levels

1. Start creating a bulleted or numbered list.

2. When you want the next list item to be at a different level, do either of the following:

   - To create the next item one level lower (indented more), press the **Tab** key at the beginning of that paragraph, before you enter the lower-level list item text.

   - To create the next item one level higher (indented less), press **Shift+Tab** at the beginning of the paragraph, before you enter the higher-level list item text.

   In the case of a bulleted list, Word changes the bullet character for each item level. In the case of a numbered list, Word changes the type of numbering used, based on a predefined numbering scheme.

> **TIP** For a multilevel list, you can change the numbering pattern or bullets by clicking the Multilevel List button in the Paragraph group on the Home tab and then clicking the pattern you want, or you can define a custom pattern by clicking Define New Multilevel List.

To modify the indentation of a list

1. Select the list items whose indentation you want to change, and do any of the following:

   - On the **Home** tab, in the **Paragraph** group, click the **Increase Indent** button to move the list items to the right.

   - In the **Paragraph** group, click the **Decrease Indent** button to move the list items to the left.

   - Display the horizontal ruler, and drag the indent markers to the left or right.

> **TIP** You can adjust the space between the bullets and their text by dragging only the Hanging Indent marker.

> **SEE ALSO** For information about paragraph indentation, see "Apply paragraph formatting" earlier in this chapter.

To sort bulleted list items into ascending or descending order

1. Select the bulleted list items whose sort order you want to change.

2. On the **Home** tab, in the **Paragraph** group, click the **Sort** button to open the Sort Text dialog box.

3. In the **Sort by** area, click **Ascending** or **Descending**. Then click **OK**.

To change the bullet symbol

1. Select the bulleted list whose bullet symbol you want to change.

2. On the **Home** tab, in the **Paragraph** group, click the **Bullets** arrow.

3. In the **Bullets** gallery, click the new symbol you want to use to replace the bullet character that begins each item in the selected list.

To define a custom bullet

1. In the **Bullets** gallery, click **Define New Bullet**.

2. In the **Define New Bullet** dialog box, click the **Symbol**, **Picture**, or **Font** button, and make a selection from the wide range of options.

3. Click **OK** to apply the new bullet style to the list.

To change the number style

1. Select the numbered list whose number style you want to change.

2. On the **Home** tab, in the **Paragraph** group, click the **Numbering** arrow to display the Numbering gallery.

3. Make a new selection to change the style of the number that begins each item in the selected list.

To define a custom number style

1. In the **Numbering** gallery, click **Define New Number Format**.

2. In the **Define New Number Format** dialog box, do any of the following:

   - Change the selections in the **Number Style**, **Number Format**, or **Alignment** boxes.

   - Click the **Font** button, and make a selection from the wide range of options.

3. Click **OK** to apply the new numbering style to the list.

To start a list or part of a list at a predefined number

1. Place the cursor within an existing list, in the list paragraph whose number you want to set.

2. Display the **Numbering** gallery, and then click **Set Numbering Value** to open the Set Numbering Value dialog box.

3. Do either of the following to permit custom numbering:

   - Click **Start new list**.

   - Click **Continue from previous list**, and then select the **Advance value (skip numbers)** check box.

4. In the **Set value to** box, enter the number you want to assign to the list item. Then click **OK**.

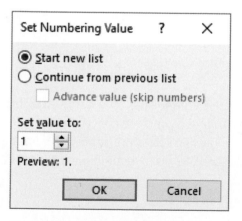

You can start or restart a numbered list at any number

4

Format text as you type

The Word list capabilities are only one example of the app's ability to intuit how you want to format an element based on what you type. You can learn more about these and other AutoFormatting options by exploring the Auto-Correct dialog box, which you can open from the Proofing page of the Word Options dialog box.

The AutoFormat As You Type page shows the options Word implements by default, including bulleted and numbered lists.

You can select and clear options to control automatic formatting behavior

One interesting option in this dialog box is Border Lines. When this check box is selected, typing three consecutive hyphens (-) or three consecutive under-scores (_) and pressing Enter draws a single line across the page. Typing three consecutive equal signs (=) draws a double line, and typing three consecutive tildes (~) draws a zigzag line.

Apply built-in styles to text

You don't have to know much about character and paragraph formatting to be able to format your documents in ways that will make them easier to read and more professional looking. With a couple of mouse clicks, you can easily change the look of words, phrases, and paragraphs by using styles. More importantly, you can build a document outline that is reflected in the Navigation pane and can be used to create a table of contents.

> **SEE ALSO** For information about tables of contents, see "Create and modify tables of contents" in Chapter 13, "Reference content and content sources."

4

Apply styles

Styles can include character formatting (such as font, size, and color), paragraph formatting (such as line spacing and outline level), or a combination of both. Styles are stored in the template that is attached to a document. By default, blank new documents are based on the Normal template. The Normal template includes a standard selection of styles that fit the basic needs of most documents. These styles include nine heading levels, various text styles including those for multiple levels of bulleted and numbered lists, index and table of contents entry styles, and many specialized styles such as those for hyperlinks, quotations, placeholders, captions, and other elements.

By default, most common predefined styles are available in the Styles gallery on the Home tab. You can add styles to the gallery or remove those that you don't often use.

AaBbCcDc	AaBbCcDc	AaBbCc	AaBbCcD	AaB	AaBbCcD
¶ Normal	¶ No Spac...	Heading 1	Heading 2	Title	Subtitle
AaBbCcD	***AaBbCcD***	*AaBbCcD*	**AaBbCcD**	*AaBbCcDd*	*AaBbCcDd*
Subtle Em...	Emphasis	Intense E...	Strong	Quote	Intense Q...
AABBCCDC	AABBCCDC	***AaBbCcD***	AaBbCcDc		
Subtle Ref...	Intense R...	Book Title	¶ List Para...		

* Create a Style
* Clear Formatting
* Apply Styles...

The Styles gallery in a new, blank document based on the Normal template

Initially, the Normal template displays only a limited number of styles in the Styles gallery, but in fact it contains styles for just about every element you can think of. Although they are available, these styles aren't actually used unless you apply the style or add the corresponding element to the document. For example, nine paragraph styles are available for an index, but none of them is used until you create and insert an index in the document.

You can display style names or previews in the Styles pane, and configure it to show all styles, styles that are in the template, styles that are used in the document, or recommended styles.

Styles ▾ ✕	Styles ▾ ✕
Clear All	Clear All
Default ¶	
Normal ¶	Default ¶
No Spacing ¶	**Normal** ¶
Heading 1 ¶a	No Spacing ¶
Heading 2 ¶a	Heading 1 ¶a
Heading 3 ¶a	Heading 2 ¶a
Heading 4 ¶a	Heading 3 ¶a
Title ¶a	Heading 4 ¶a
Subtitle ¶a	Title ¶a
Subtle Emphasis a	SUBTITLE ¶a
Emphasis a	Subtle Emphasis a
Intense Emphasis a	
Strong a	
Quote ¶a	
Intense Quote ¶a	
Subtle Reference a	
Intense Reference a	
☐ Show Preview	☑ Show Preview
☐ Disable Linked Styles	☐ Disable Linked Styles
Options...	Options...

The Styles pane can display style names or previews of the styles

If you don't have room to display the entire Styles pane, you can apply styles from the floating Apply Styles pane. The Style Name list in the Apply Styles pane displays the same set of styles that are in the Styles pane; that is, if the pane shows only the styles in use, so does the Style Name list.

Apply Styles ▾ ✕

Style Name:

Intense Reference ▾

Reapply | Modify... | 𝐀𝐚

☑ AutoComplete style names

The Style Name box displays the style applied to the active selection

There are three primary types of styles, identified in the Styles pane by icons:

- **Paragraph** These styles can include any formatting that can be applied to a paragraph. They can also include character formatting. Paragraph styles are applied to the entire paragraph containing the cursor. In the Styles pane, a paragraph style is identified by a paragraph mark to the right of its name.

- **Character** These styles can include any formatting that can be applied to selected text. They are applied on top of the character formatting defined for the paragraph style. Like direct character formatting, character styles are applied to selected text; to apply them to an entire paragraph, you must select the paragraph. In the Styles pane, a character style is identified by a lowercase letter *a*.

- **Linked** These styles are hybrids. If you click in a paragraph and then apply the style, the style is applied to the entire paragraph like a paragraph style. If you select text and then apply the style, the style is applied to the selection only. In the Styles pane, a linked style is identified by both a paragraph mark and a lowercase letter *a*.

> 🔍 **TIP** Two additional style types, Table and List, are reserved for styles for those document elements.

Styles stored in a template are usually based on the Normal style and use only the default body and heading fonts associated with the document's theme, so they all go together well. For this reason, formatting document content by using styles produces a harmonious effect. After you apply named styles, you can easily change the look of an entire document by switching to a different style set that contains styles with the same names but different formatting.

> 🔍 **SEE ALSO** For information about document theme elements, see "Change the document theme," later in this chapter.

Style sets are available from the Document Formatting gallery on the Design tab.

Pointing to a style set in the gallery displays a live preview of the effects of applying that style set to the entire document

> ✓ **TIP** Style sets provide a quick and easy way to change the look of an existing document. You can also modify style definitions by changing the template on which the document is based. For more information about styles and templates, see Chapter 15, "Create custom document elements."

To open the Styles pane

1. Do either of the following:

   - On the **Home** tab, click the **Styles** dialog box launcher.

   - Press **Alt+Ctrl+Shift+S**.

> ✓ **TIP** If the Styles pane floats above the page, you can drag it by its title bar to the right or left edge of the app window to dock it. If it's docked, you can drag it away from the edge of the window to float it.

To change which styles are displayed in the Styles pane

1. At the bottom of the **Styles** pane, click the **Options** link to open the Style Pane Options dialog box.

To make it easier to find specific styles, sort the list alphabetically

2. In the **Style Pane Options** dialog box, do any of the following, and then click **OK**:

   - In the **Select styles to show** list, click one of the following:

     - **Recommended** Displays styles that are tagged in the template as recommended for use

     - **In use** Displays styles that are applied to content in the current document

     - **In current document** Displays styles that are in the template that is attached to the current document

     - **All styles** Displays built-in styles, styles that are in the attached template, and styles that were brought into the document from other templates

- In the **Select how list is sorted** list, click **Alphabetical**, **As Recommended**, **Font**, **Based on**, or **By type**

- In the **Select formatting to show as styles** area, select each check box for which you want to display variations from named styles

- In the **Select how built-in style names are shown** area, select the check box for each option you want to turn on

To display or hide style previews in the Styles pane

1. Open the **Styles** pane, and then select or clear the **Show Preview** check box.

 TIP Selecting the Show Preview check box displays style names in the formatting assigned to the style. Pointing to a style displays its formatting specifications.

To open the Apply Styles pane

1. On the **Home** tab, in the **Styles** group, click the **More** button (in the lower-right corner of the Styles gallery pane) to display the Styles gallery and menu.

2. On the **Styles** menu, click **Apply Styles**.

To apply a style from the Apply Styles pane

1. Do either of the following:

   - To apply the style that is shown in the Style Name list, click the **Reapply** button.

   - To apply a different style, click the **Style Name** list and then click the style you want to apply.

To apply a built-in style

1. Select the text or paragraph to which you want to apply the style.

 TIP If the style you want to apply is a paragraph style, you can position the cursor anywhere in the paragraph. If the style you want to apply is a character style, you must select the text.

2. In the **Styles** gallery on the **Home** tab, or in the **Styles** pane, click the style you want to apply.

To change the style set

1. On the **Design** tab, in the **Document Formatting** group, click the **More** button if necessary to display all the style sets.

2. Point to any style set to preview its effect on the document.

3. Click the style set you want to apply.

Manage outline levels

Styles can be used for multiple purposes: to affect the appearance of the content, to build a document outline, and to tag content so that you can easily locate it.

Heading styles define a document's outline

Each paragraph style has an associated Outline Level setting. Outline levels include Body Text and Level 1 through Level 9. (Most documents make use only of body text and the first three or four outline levels.)

Paragraph   ?   ✕

Indents and Spacing   **Line and Page Breaks**

General

Alignment: Left   ⌄

Outline level: Level 1   ⌄   ☐ Collaps*e*d by default

                Body Text ⌃
                Level 1
Indentation   Level 2
                Level 3
Left: Level 4   S*p*ecial: B*y*:
                Level 5
Right: Level 6   (none)   ⌄   ⬍
                Level 7
   ☐ *M*irror inde Level 8
                Level 9 ⌄

Most documents use only two to four of the outline levels

Paragraphs that have the Level 1 through Level 9 outline levels become part of the hierarchical structure of the document. They appear as headings in the Navigation pane and act as handles for the content that appears below them in the hierarchy. You can collapse and expand the content below each heading, and move entire sections of content by dragging the headings in the Navigation pane.

To display the document outline in the Navigation pane

1. In the **Navigation** pane, click **Headings** to display the document structure.

> ✓ **TIP** Only headings that are styled with the document heading styles appear in the Navigation pane.

To expand or collapse the outline in the Navigation pane

1. In the **Navigation** pane, do either of the following:

   - If there is a white triangle to the left of a heading, click it to expand that heading to show its subheadings.

   - If there is a downward-angled black triangle to the left of a heading, click it to collapse the subheadings under that heading.

> **TIP** If there is no triangle next to a heading, that heading does not have subheadings.

To expand or collapse sections in the document

1. In a document that contains styles, point to a heading to display a triangle to its left. Then do either of the following:

   - If the triangle is a downward-angled gray triangle, click the triangle to hide the content that follows the heading.

   - If the triangle is a white triangle, click the triangle to display the hidden document content.

4

Change the document theme

Every document you create is based on a template, and the look of the template is controlled by a theme. The theme is a combination of coordinated colors, fonts, and effects that visually convey a certain tone. To change the look of a document, you can apply a different theme from the Themes gallery.

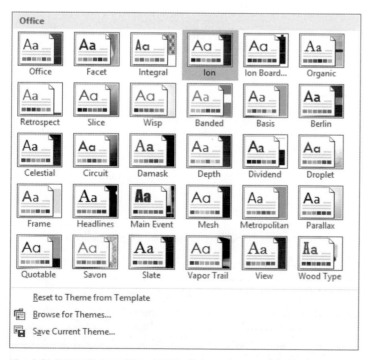

The default installation of Word 2016 offers 30 themes to choose from

Each theme has a built-in font set and color set, and an associated effect style.

- Each font set includes two fonts—the first is used for headings and the second for body text. In some font sets, the heading and body fonts are the same.

- Each color in a color set has a specific role in the formatting of styled elements. For example, the first color in each set is applied to the Title and Intense Reference styles, and different shades of the third color are applied to the Subtitle, Heading 1, and Heading 2 styles.

If you like the background elements of a theme but not the colors or fonts, you can mix and match theme elements.

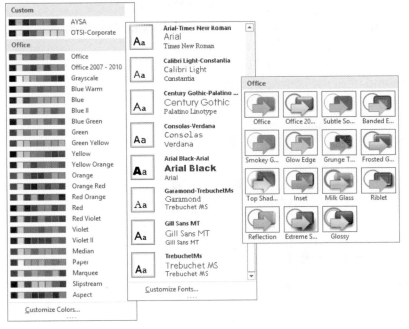

Word 2016 offers thousands of different combinations for creating a custom theme that meets your exact needs

SEE ALSO For information about creating custom themes, see "Create and manage custom themes" in Chapter 15, "Create custom document elements."

TIP In addition to colors and fonts, you can control the more subtle design elements, such as paragraph spacing and visual effects that are associated with a theme.

By default, Word applies the Office theme to all new, blank documents. In Word 2016, the Office theme uses a primarily blue palette, the Calibri font for body text, and Calibri Light for headings. If you plan to frequently use a theme other than the Office theme, you can make that the default theme.

To apply a built-in theme to a document

1. On the **Design** tab, in the **Document Formatting** group, click the **Themes** button, and then click the theme you want to apply.

> ✓ **TIP** If you have manually applied formatting to document content, the theme does not override the manual formatting. To ensure that all document elements are controlled by the theme, click Reset To The Default Style Set on the Document Formatting menu.

To change theme elements in a document

1. On the **Design** tab, in the **Document Formatting** group, do any of the following:

   - Click the **Colors** button (the ScreenTip says *Theme Colors*), and then click the color set you want to apply.

   - Click the **Fonts** button (the ScreenTip says *Theme Fonts*), and then click the font set you want to apply.

   - Click the **Effects** button (the ScreenTip says *Theme Effects*), and then click the effect style you want to apply.

To change the default theme

1. In the document, apply the theme you want to use as the default theme.

2. On the **Design** tab, in the **Document Formatting** group, click **Set as Default**.

Skills review

In this chapter, you learned how to:

- Apply paragraph formatting
- Structure content manually
- Apply character formatting
- Create and modify lists
- Apply built-in styles to text
- Change the document theme

Practice tasks

The practice files for these tasks are located in the Word2016SBS\Ch04 folder. You can save the results of the tasks in the same folder.

Apply paragraph formatting

Open the FormatParagraphs document, display formatting marks, and then complete the following tasks:

1. Display the rulers and adjust the zoom level to display most or all of the paragraphs in the document.

2. Select the first two paragraphs (*Welcome!* and the next paragraph) and center them between the margins.

3. Select the second paragraph, and apply a first line indent.

4. Select the third paragraph and then apply the following formatting:

   - Format the paragraph so that the edges of the paragraph are flush against both the left and right margins.

   - Indent the paragraph by a half inch on the left and on the right.

5. Indent the *Be careful* paragraph by 0.25 inches.

6. Simultaneously select the *Pillows*, *Blankets*, *Towels*, *Limousine winery tour*, and *In-home massage* paragraphs. Change the paragraph spacing to remove the space after the paragraphs.

7. At the top of the document, apply an outside border to the *Please take a few minutes* paragraph.

8. Save and close the document.

Structure content manually

Open the StructureContent document, display formatting marks, and then complete the following tasks:

1. Display the rulers and adjust the zoom level to display most or all of the paragraphs in the document.

2. In the second paragraph (*We would like...*), insert a line break immediately after the comma and space that follow the word *cottage*.

3. Select the *Pillows*, *Blankets*, *Towels*, and *Dish towels* paragraphs. Insert a left tab stop at the **2** inch mark and clear any tab stops prior to that location.

4. In the *Pillows* paragraph, replace the space before the word *There* with a tab marker. Repeat the process to insert tabs in each of the next three paragraphs. The part of each paragraph that follows the colon is now aligned at the 2-inch mark, producing more space than you need.

5. Select the four paragraphs containing tabs, and then do the following:

   - Change the left tab stop from the **2** inch mark to the **1.25** inch mark.

   - On the ruler, drag the **Hanging Indent** marker to the tab stop at the **1.25** inch mark (the Left Indent marker moves with it) to cause the second line of the paragraphs to start in the same location as the first line. Then press the **Home** key to release the selection so you can review the results.

6. At the bottom of the document, select the three paragraphs containing dollar amounts, and then do the following:

   - Set a **Decimal Tab** stop at the **3** inch mark.

   - Replace the space to the left of each dollar sign with a tab to align the prices on the decimal points.

7. Hide the formatting marks to better display the results of your work.

8. Save and close the document.

Apply character formatting

Open the FormatCharacters document, and then complete the following tasks:

1. In the second bullet point, underline the word *natural*. Then repeat the formatting command to underline the word *all*, in the fourth bullet point.

2. In the fourth bullet point, click anywhere in the word *across*. Apply a thick underline to the word in a way that also assigns the **Thick underline** format to the **Underline** button. Then apply the thick underline to the word *departments*.

3. Select the *Employee Orientation* heading, and apply bold formatting to the heading.

4. Copy the formatting, and then paint it onto the *Guidelines* subtitle, to make the subtitle a heading.

5. Select the *Guidelines* heading, and apply the following formatting:

   - Change the font to **Impact**.

   - Set the font size to **20** points.

   - Apply the **Small caps** font effect.

   - Expand the character spacing by **10** points.

6. Change the font color of the words *Employee Orientation* to **Green, Accent 6**.

7. Select the *Community Service Committee* heading, and apply the following formatting:

   - Outline the letters in the same color you applied to *Employee Orientation*.

   - Apply an **Offset Diagonal Bottom Left** outer shadow. Change the shadow color to **Green, Accent 6, Darker 50%**.

   - Fill the letters with the **Green, Accent 6** color, and then change the text outline to **Green, Accent 6, Darker 25%**.

You have now applied three text effects to the selected text by using three shades of the same green.

8. In the first bullet point, select the phrase *the concept of service* and apply a **Bright Green** highlight.

9. In the fifth bullet point, simultaneously select the words *brainstorming*, *planning*, and *leadership* and change the case of all the letters to uppercase.

10. Save and close the document.

Create and modify lists

Open the CreateLists document, display formatting marks and rulers, and then complete the following tasks:

1. Select the first four paragraphs below *The rules fall into four categories*. Format the selected paragraphs as a bulleted list. Then change the bullet character for the four list items to the one that is composed of four diamonds.

2. Select the two paragraphs below the *Definitions* heading. Format the selected paragraphs as a numbered list.

3. Select the first four paragraphs below the *General Rules* heading. Format the paragraphs as a second numbered list. Ensure that the new list starts with the number 1.

4. Format the next three paragraphs as a bulleted list. (Notice that Word uses the bullet symbol you specified earlier.) Indent the bulleted list so that it is a subset of the preceding numbered list item.

5. Format the remaining three paragraphs as a numbered list. Ensure that the list numbering continues from the previous numbered list.

6. Locate the *No large dogs* numbered list item. Create a new second-level numbered list item (**a**) from the text that begins with the word *Seeing*. Then create a second item (**b**) and enter **The Board reserves the right to make exceptions to this rule.**

7. Create a third list item (**c**). Promote the new list item to a first-level item, and enter **All pets must reside within their Owners' Apartments.** Notice that the *General Rules* list is now organized hierarchically.

8. Sort the three bulleted list items in ascending alphabetical order.

9. Save and close the document.

Apply built-in styles to text

Open the ApplyStyles document in Print Layout view, and then complete the following tasks:

1. Scroll through the document to gain an overview of its contents. Notice that the document begins with a centered title and subtitle, and there are several headings throughout.

2. Open the **Navigation** pane. Notice that the Headings page of the Navigation pane does not reflect the headings in the document, because the headings are formatted with local formatting instead of styles.

3. Open the **Styles** pane and dock it to the right edge of the app window.

4. Set the zoom level of the page to fit the page content between the Navigation pane and the Styles pane.

5. Apply the **Title** style to the document title, *All About Bamboo*.

6. Apply the **Subtitle** style to the *Information Sheet* paragraph.

7. Apply the **Heading 1** style to the first bold heading, *Moving to a New Home*. Notice that the heading appears in the Navigation pane.

8. Hide the content that follows the heading. Then redisplay it.

9. Apply the **Heading 1** style to *Staying Healthy*. Then repeat the formatting to apply the same style to *Keeping Bugs at Bay*.

10. Scroll the page so that both underlined headings are visible. Select the *Mites* and *Mealy Bugs* headings. Then simultaneously apply the **Heading 2** style to both selections.

11. Configure the **Styles** pane to display all styles, in alphabetical order.

12. In the **Navigation** pane, just above the headings, click the *Jump to the beginning* button to return to the document title.

13. In the first paragraph of the document, select the company name *Wide World Importers*, and apply the **Intense Reference** style.

14. In the second paragraph, near the end of the first sentence, select the word *clumping*, and apply the **Emphasis** style. Then, at the end of the sentence, apply the same style to the word *running*.

15. Close the **Navigation** pane and the **Styles** pane. Then configure the view setting to display both pages of the document in the window.

16. Apply the **Basic (Elegant)** style set to the document. Change the view to **Page Width** and notice the changes to the styled content.

17. Save and close the document.

Change the document theme

Open the ChangeTheme document, and then complete the following tasks:

1. Apply the **Facet** theme to the document.

2. Change the theme colors to the **Orange** color scheme.

3. Change the theme fonts to the **Georgia** theme set.

4. Set the **Facet** theme as the default theme for the document.

5. Save and close the document.

Organize information in columns and tables

In Word documents, text is most commonly presented in paragraph form. To make certain types of information more legible, you can arrange it in two or more columns or display it in a table. For example, flowing text in multiple columns is a common practice in newsletters, flyers, and brochures, whereas presenting information in tables is common in reports.

When you need to present facts and figures in a document, using columns or tables is often more efficient than describing the data in a paragraph, particularly when the data consists of numeric values. You can display small amounts of data in simple columns separated by tabs, which creates a *tabbed list*. Larger amounts of data and data that is more complex are better presented in table form—that is, in a structure of rows and columns, frequently with row and column headings. Tables make data easier to read and understand.

This chapter guides you through procedures related to presenting information in columns, creating tabbed lists, presenting information in tables, and formatting tables.

In this chapter

- Present information in columns
- Create tabbed lists
- Present information in tables
- Format tables

Practice files

For this chapter, use the practice files from the Word2016SBS\Ch05 folder. For practice file download instructions, see the introduction.

Present information in columns

By default, Word displays text in one column that spans the width of the page between the left and right margins. If you prefer, however, you can specify that text be displayed in two, three, or more columns to create layouts like those used in newspapers and magazines.

When you format text to flow in columns, the text fills the first column on each page and then moves to the top of the next column. When all the columns on one page are full, the text moves to the next page. You can manually indicate where you want the text within each column to end.

Simple·Room·Design¶

With·the·Room·Planner,·you'll·never·make·a·design·mistake·again.·Created·by·acclaimed·interior·designers·to·simplify·the·redecorating·process,·this·planning·tool·incorporates·elements·of·color,·dimension,·and·style·to·guide·your·project.·It·includes·a·furniture·location·guide;·room·grid;·drawing·tools;·and·miniature·furniture,·rugs,·accessories,·and·color·swatches·that·match·our·large·in-store·selection.·Here's·how·to·use·the·planner·to·create·the·room·of·your·dreams!¶

¶ ————————Section Break (Continuous)————————

Take·a·look·at·how·your·home·is·decorated·and·note·the·things·you·like·and·dislike.·Pay·special·attention·to·the·color·scheme·and·to·how·each·room·"feels"·to·you.·Is·it·inviting?·Does·it·feel·comfortable?·Does·it·relax·you·or·does·it·invigorate·you?¶

Focus·on·the·room(s)·you·would·most·like·to·change.·Brainstorm·all·the·things·you·would·change·in·that·room·if·you·could.·Don't·give·a·thought·to·any·financial·considerations;·just·let·your·imagination·go·wild!·It·might·be·helpful·to·write·down·all·the·negatives·and·positives.·

love,·and·the·rest·will·fall·into·place.¶

Take·your·Room·Planner·home·and·get·to·work!·Adjust·the·planner·so·that·it·models·the·room·dimensions.·Don't·forget·to·place·the·windows·and·doors.·Arrange·the·furniture·placeholders·to·mirror·how·your·room·is·currently·set·up.·Add·the·current·colors,·too.¶

This·is·where·the·fun·begins!·Start·changing·things·around·a·bit.·Move·the·furniture,·add·different·colors,·and·watch·the·room·come·together!·Here's·where·you·can·tell·if·that·rich·red·rug·

design·for·a·day·or·two.·Then·review·it·again.·Does·it·still·look·perfect,·or·is·something·not·quite·right?·You·might·need·to·"live"·with·the·new·plan·for·a·few·days,·especially·if·you've·made·big·changes.·When·everything·feels·just·right·to·you,·you're·ready·for·the·next·big·step!¶

Come·back·to·the·store.·Look·again·at·the·pieces·you·liked·during·your·last·visit·and·see·if·you·still·love·them.·If·you're·not·quite·sure,·go·back·to·your·planner·for·a·little·more·tweaking.·If·you·are·sure,·take·a·look·around·the·store·

You can format text to flow in columns

> **IMPORTANT** Assistive devices such as screen readers do not always correctly process text that is arranged in columns. Consider the limitations of these devices if you want your document to meet accessibility requirements.

The Columns gallery in the Page Setup group on the Layout tab displays several standard options for dividing text into columns. You can choose one, two, or three columns of equal width or two columns of unequal width.

The Columns gallery displays the predefined column options

If the standard options don't suit your needs, choose More Columns. This opens the Columns dialog box, where you can specify the number and width of columns. The number of columns is limited by the width and margins of the page. Each column must be at least a half inch (or 0.27 centimeter) wide.

For more options, you can open the Columns dialog box

You can format an entire document or a section of a document in columns. When you select a section of text and format it in columns, Word inserts *section breaks* at the beginning and end of the selected text to delineate the area in which the columnar formatting is applied. Within the columnar text, you can insert *column breaks* to specify where you want to end one column and start another. Section breaks and column breaks are visible when you display hidden formatting marks in the document.

> **SEE ALSO** For information about formatting marks, see "Display different views of documents" in Chapter 2, "Create and manage documents."

> **TIP** You can format the content within a specific section of a document independently of other sections. For example, you can place a wide table in its own section and change the page orientation of that section to landscape to accommodate the wider table. For more information about sections, see "Control what appears on each page" in Chapter 12, "Finalize and distribute documents."

You apply character and paragraph formatting to columnar text in the same way you do to any other text. Here are some formatting tips for columnar text:

- When presenting text in columns, justify the paragraphs to give the page a clean and organized appearance. When you justify text, Word adjusts the spacing between words to align all the paragraphs in the document with both the left and right margins.

Justify text in columns for a clean look

> **SEE ALSO** For information about justifying paragraphs, see "Apply paragraph formatting" in Chapter 4, "Modify the structure and appearance of text."

- You can change the column widths, minimizing the space between columns. That way, you can fit more text on the page. You can choose to change the column widths in the entire section, in the entire document, or from the current cursor location to the end of the document.

> ✓ **TIP** Selecting the Line Between check box in the Columns dialog box inserts a vertical line between columns. This can more clearly denote the separation of the columns, which is especially helpful if you have reduced the space between columns to fit more content on a page.

5

¶ ————————————————Section Break (Continuous)————————————————

Take a look at how your home is decorated and note the things you like and dislike. Pay special attention to the color scheme and to how each room "feels" to you. Is it inviting? Does it feel comfortable? Does it relax you or does it invigorate you?¶

Focus on the room(s) you would most like to change. Brainstorm all the things you would change in that room if you could. Don't give a thought to any financial considerations; just let your imagination go wild! It might be helpful to write down all the negatives and positives. You don't need to come up with solutions all at once. Just be clear on what you like and what you hate about that room.¶

Visit our showroom and purchase a Room Planner. While

to place the windows and doors. Arrange the furniture placeholders to mirror how your room is currently set up. Add the current colors, too.¶

This is where the fun begins! Start changing things around a bit. Move the furniture, add different colors, and watch the room come together! Here's where you can tell if that rich red rug you saw in the showroom enhances or overwhelms your room. What about that overstuffed chair that caught your eye? Place a furniture or accessory shape, and then color it. Does it look great or is it too jarring? Change the color... does that help? Don't forget about the walls. Try different colors to see the effect on the room overall.¶

Come back to the store. Look again at the pieces you liked during your last visit and see if you still love them. If you're not quite sure, go back to your planner for a little more tweaking. If you are sure, take a look around the store one more time to see if anything else catches your eye. Then make your purchases. You're almost there!¶

NOTE: If you decided to paint your room, do that before your new pieces are delivered. You'll want to start enjoying your new room as soon as your purchases arrive.¶

After a few weeks, ask yourself whether the room is as great as you thought it would be. Does it achieve the look and feel you were after? You have 30 days to

Wider columns display more content and generally look neater on the page

- To lessen the amount of white space within a line, you can set up Word to hyphenate the text and break longer words into syllables.

Hyphenation	?	X
☑ **A**utomatically hyphenate document		
☑ **H**yphenate words in **C**APS		
Hyphenation zone:	[ ] ▲▼	
Limit consecutive hyphens to:	1 ▲▼	
[**M**anual...]	[OK]	[Cancel]

When hyphenating a document, you can specify whether you want to allow stacked hyphens at the ends of consecutive lines of a paragraph

■ To emphasize certain portions of the text, you can indent it in the column.

> if· anything· else· catches· your·
> eye.·Then·make·your·purchases.·
> You're·almost·there!¶
>
> NOTE:· If· you· decided· to· paint·
> your· room,· do· that· before·
> your·new·pieces·are·delivered.·
> You'll· want· to· start· enjoying·
> your· new· room· as· soon· as·
> your·purchases·arrive.¶
>
> After· a· few· weeks,· ask· yourself·
> whether·the·room·is·as·great·as·
> you·thought·it·would·be.·Does·it·
> achieve· the· look· and· feel· you·
> were·after?·You·have·30·days·to·
> fall· in· love· with· our· furniture·
> and· accessories,· so· if· you· are·

You can change the indentation of individual paragraphs within a column

■ You can manually break columns. When you break a column, the text after the break moves to the top of the next column. You might manually break a column to even out the text along the bottom of the page or if you just want certain text to appear at the top of the next column.

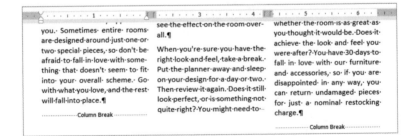

Manually break columns to even out the text at the end of a page

To lay out text in columns

> ✓ **TIP** To make columns easier to work with, display formatting marks and the ruler before you begin.

1. Do either of the following:

   - To format only a section of the document, select the paragraphs that you want to display in columns.

   - To format the entire document with the same number of columns, click anywhere in the document—you don't have to select the text.

2. On the **Layout** tab, in the **Page Setup** group, click the **Columns** button.

3. In the **Columns** gallery, do either of the following:

   - Select one of the thumbnails to flow the selected text into that column configuration.

   - At the bottom of the gallery, click **More Columns** to display the **Columns** dialog box. Make the adjustments you want, and then click **OK**.

To justify column text

1. Select the columns you want to align.

2. Do either of the following:

   - On the **Home** tab, in the **Paragraph** group, click the **Justify** button.

   - Press **Ctrl+J**.

> 🔍 **SEE ALSO** For more information about keyboard shortcuts, see "Keyboard shortcuts" at the end of this book.

To resize columns

1. Click anywhere in the columnar text.

2. On the **Layout tab**, at the bottom of the **Columns** gallery, click **More Columns** to open the Columns dialog box.

3. In the **Width** box for any of the columns, enter or select a new width. The Width measurements for the other columns change to match, and the width of all the columns changes. The columns in the Preview thumbnail reflect the new settings.

4. When the column width is changed to your satisfaction, click **OK**.

Or

1. Click anywhere in the columnar text.

 TIP If the rulers aren't turned on, select the Ruler check box in the Show group on the View tab.

2. On the horizontal ruler, drag the margins to expand or contract the columns to the width you want.

To hyphenate document content

1. In the **Page Setup** group of the **Layout** tab, click the **Hyphenation** button, and then click **Automatic** to hyphenate the text of the document.

To change the indentation of a paragraph in a column

1. Click anywhere in the paragraph you want to indent.

2. On the horizontal ruler, do any of the following:

   • Drag the column's **First Line Indent** marker to the right to indent only the first line of the paragraph.

   • Drag the column's **Hanging Indent** marker to the right to indent all but the first line of the paragraph.

   • Drag the column's **Left Indent** marker to the right to indent all lines of the paragraph.

To insert a column break

1. Click at the beginning of the line you want to flow to the next column.

2. In the **Page Setup** group of the **Layout** tab, click the **Breaks** button, and then click **Column** to insert a column break. The text that follows moves to the top of the next column.

Create tabbed lists

If you have a relatively small amount of data to present, you might choose to display it in a tabbed list. A tabbed list arranges text in simple columns separated by tabs. If some text items in the list are longer than others, the columns might not line up at first. You can align the text within the columns by using left, right, centered, or decimal tab stops.

Consultation·Fee·Schedule¶

Location	→	Discount·Applies	→	Hourly·Rate¶
In·home	→	No	→	$50.00¶
Phone	→	Yes	→	$35.00¶
In·store	→	Yes	→	$40.00¶

An easy way to present data is to create a tabbed list

> 🔍 **SEE ALSO** For more information about setting tab stops, see "Structure content manually" in Chapter 4, "Modify the structure and appearance of text."

When entering text in a tabbed list, many inexperienced Word users simply press the Tab key multiple times to align the columns of the list with the default tab stops. This approach offers no control over the column widths, however. In addition, if you change the text between two tabs, you might inadvertently misalign the next section of text. To be able to fine-tune the columns, you must set custom tab stops rather than relying on the default ones.

When setting up a tabbed list, you first enter the text, pressing Tab only once between the items that you want to appear in separate columns. Then you apply any necessary formatting, such as bold formatting, so you can accurately set the column width. You can also adjust the spacing of the list—for example, to make it single-spaced. To set the list apart from the rest of the document, you can indent it. Finally, you can set custom tab stops—left (the default), right, centered, or decimal—to align the text in each column. By setting the tabs in order from left to right, you can check the alignment of the text within each column as you go.

> ✓ **TIP** It's more efficient to make all character and paragraph formatting changes to the text before setting tab stops. Otherwise, you might have to adjust the tab stops after applying the formatting.

To create a tabbed list

1. Open a document to which you want to add a tabbed list, and display formatting marks and the rulers.

2. Click in the document where you want to create the tabbed list, enter the text that you want to appear in the top line of the left column, and press **Tab**.

3. Enter the text you want to appear in the top line of the second column, and press **Tab**.

4. Repeat this action for each additional column you want to create. After you enter the text for the top line in the final column, press **Enter**.

5. Add more lines to the list by entering your content and pressing the **Tab** key to move to the next column or the **Enter** key to move to the next row.

6. When you have finished creating the list, select the entire list.

7. Set the custom tab stops you want for the list.

To format column headings for a tabbed list

1. Select the first line of the tabbed list.

2. On the **Mini Toolbar** that appears, click the **Bold**, **Italic**, **Underline**, or **Font Color** button.

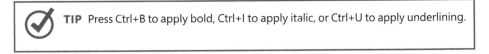

> **TIP** Press Ctrl+B to apply bold, Ctrl+I to apply italic, or Ctrl+U to apply underlining.

To indent a tabbed list

1. Select all the lines of the tabbed list, including the headings.

2. On the **Layout** tab, in the **Paragraph** group, in the **Indent** area, enter or select a value in the **Left** box.

To change the alignment of a column

1. Select all the lines of the tabbed list.

2. On the horizontal ruler, double-click any tab marker to open the **Tabs** dialog box.

3. In the **Tab stop position** box, select the tab stop you want to change and then, in the **Alignment** area, click the alignment you want.

4. In the **Tabs** dialog box, click **OK**.

Present information in tables

A *table* is a structure of vertical columns and horizontal rows. Each column and each row can be identified by a heading, although some tables have only column headings or only row headings. The box at the junction of each column and row is a *cell* in which you can store data (text or numeric information).

You can create tables in a Word document in the following ways:

- To create a blank table of up to 10 columns and eight rows, you can display the Insert Table gallery and menu. The gallery is a simple grid that represents columns and rows of cells. When you point to a cell in the grid, Word outlines the cells that would be included in a table created by clicking that cell and displays a live preview of the prospective table. Clicking a cell in the grid inserts an empty table the width of the text column. The table has the number of rows and columns you indicated in the grid, with each row one line high and all the columns of an equal width.

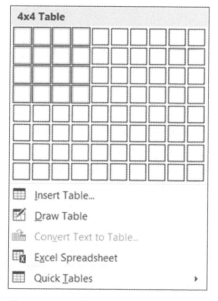

The intended table dimensions (expressed as columns x rows) are shown in the gallery header

- To create a more customized empty table, use the Insert Table dialog box. Here, you can specify the number of columns and rows and the width of the table and its columns.

You can create a custom table from the Insert Table dialog box

- To manually create an empty table, use the Draw Table feature, available from the Insert Table menu. This displays a pencil with which you can draw cells directly in the Word document to create a table. The cells you draw connect by snapping to a grid, but you have some control over the size and spacing of the rows and columns.

> **TIP** When drawing a table, you can display the rulers or gridlines to help guide you in placing the lines. For more information about rulers, see "Display different views of documents" in Chapter 2, "Create and manage documents." For information about controlling document gridlines, see "Arrange objects on a page" in Chapter 10, "Organize and arrange content."

> ⚠️ **IMPORTANT** Assistive devices such as screen readers can usually access content in tables that are created by using the Insert Table command but not in manually drawn tables. Consider the limitations of these devices if you want your document to meet accessibility requirements.

- To present data that already exists in the document (either as regular text or as a tabbed list) as a table, you can use the Convert Text To Table feature. When you do, Word prompts you to specify the number of columns; whether the column width should be fixed or if AutoFit settings should apply; and whether columns should correlate to paragraph marks, commas, tabs, or some other character.

You can cleanly convert content that is separated by paragraph marks, tabs, commas, or any single character that you specify

Insert an Excel spreadsheet

In addition to inserting a table, you can insert a Microsoft Excel spreadsheet in your document. To do so, click Excel Spreadsheet on the Insert Table menu. Then enter the data you want in the spreadsheet window that appears in the document. You can use Excel features such as functions and formulas to create or manipulate the data.

When you insert an Excel spreadsheet into your document and activate it, the Excel ribbon is made available

Inserting Excel spreadsheet content into your document does not create a Word table. Rather, it creates a snapshot of the Excel content. You cannot work with the content in Word or use any of the table tools discussed in this chapter. You can, however, format the data in the spreadsheet window by using various Excel tools and features. To access the spreadsheet for editing, double-click it.

A table appears in a document as a set of cells, usually delineated by borders or grid-lines. Each cell contains an end-of-cell marker, and each row ends with an end-of-row marker. You can easily move and position the cursor in the table by pressing the Tab key or the arrow keys or by clicking in a table cell.

> ✓ **TIP** In some Quick Tables, borders and gridlines are turned off. For more information about Quick Tables, see the sidebar "Quick Tables" in the next topic.

> ✓ **TIP** Two separate elements in Word 2016 are named *gridlines*, and both can be used in association with tables. From the Show group on the View tab, you can display the *document gridlines*, which you can use to position content on the page. From the Table group on the Layout tool tab, you can display the *table gridlines*, which define the cells of a table.

When you point to a table, a move handle appears in its upper-left corner and a size handle in its lower-right corner. When the cursor is in a table, two Table Tools tabs—Design and Layout—appear on the ribbon.

A table has its own controls and tool tabs

> ✓ **TIP** The end-of-cell markers and end-of-row markers are identical in appearance and are visible only when you display formatting marks in the document. The move handle and size handle appear only in Print Layout view and Web Layout view.

After you create a table in Word, you can enter data (such as text, numbers, or graphics) into the table cells. You can format the data in a table as you would any other text in Word, changing the font, aligning the text, and so on. You can also sort data in a table. For example, in a table that has the column headings Name, Address, Postal Code, and Phone Number, you can sort on any one of those columns to arrange the information in alphabetical or numerical order.

When you want to perform calculations on numbers in a Word table, you can create a formula by using the tools in the Formula dialog box.

You can easily create a formula to calculate a value in a table

To use a function other than SUM in the Formula dialog box, you click the function you want in the Paste Function list. You can use built-in functions to perform a number of calculations, including averaging (AVERAGE) a set of values, counting (COUNT) the number of values in a column or row, or finding the maximum (MAX) or minimum (MIN) value in a series of cells.

Although formulas commonly refer to the cells above or to the left of the active cell, you can also use the contents of specified cells in formulas by entering the cell address in the parentheses following the function name. The *cell address* is a combination of the column letter and the row number. For example, A1 is the cell at the intersection of the first column and the first row. A series of cells in a row can be addressed as a range consisting of the first cell and the last cell separated by a colon, such as A1:D1. For example, the formula =SUM(A1:D1) totals the values in row 1 of columns A through D. A series of cells in a column can be addressed in the same way. For example, the formula =SUM(A1:A4) totals the values in column A of rows 1 through 4. You can also use constants in formulas.

You can modify a table's structure in any number of ways. These include the following:

- **Insert rows or columns** With Word 2016, you can insert a row or column with just one click. Adding multiple rows and columns is also very easy.

Item	Repair Type	Quantity	Cost in $
Elastomeric Decks	Resurface	400 sq. ft.	1,600
Wood Decks	Replace	1,200 sq. ft.	6,500
Building Exterior	Repaint	9,000 sq. ft.	9,000
Roof	Reseal	5,000 sq. ft.	2,700
Entry Doors	Repaint	4	600
Carpet	Replace	150 sq. yds.	4,500
Intercom	Replace	1	2,500
Garage Door Opener	Replace	1	2,000
Steel Doors	Repaint	10	750
Exterior Trim	Repaint	800 ft.	4,500
Elevator Hydraulics	Replace	1	55,000
Fire Alarm System	Replace	1	3,000
TOTAL			92,650

Inserting a row or column now takes only one click

- **Insert cells** You can insert cells in a Word table. When you do, you must specify the direction in which adjacent cells should move to accommodate the new cells.

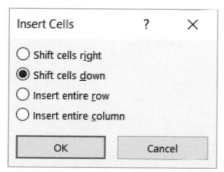

When inserting less than a full row or column, you must specify the movement of the surrounding cells

- **Resize an entire table** You can easily make a table larger or smaller, maintaining its original aspect ratio if you want.

- **Resize a single column or row** You can drag to resize a single column or row. For finer control, you can use the commands in the Cell Size group on the Layout tool tab.

■ **Merge and split cells** You can merge cells so they span multiple columns or rows. For example, if you wanted to enter a title for a table in the table's first row, you could merge the cells in that row to create one merged cell that spans the table's width. You could then enter the title in the merged cell. (For added flair, you could even center the title.) In addition to merging multiple cells to create a single cell, you can split a single cell to create multiple cells. When you do, you must specify the number of columns and rows into which you want to split the cell.

When you split a cell, you must specify the number of columns and rows into which you want to split the cell

■ **Delete table elements** You can delete table elements, including cells, columns, rows, and the entire table, from the Mini Toolbar or the Layout tool tab.

You can delete table elements from the Mini Toolbar

> ✓ **TIP** You can move a table by using the same techniques you would use to move text or pictures in Word. For more information, see "Move, copy, and delete text" in Chapter 3, "Enter and edit text."

To create a table from a preset grid

1. Position the cursor where you want to insert the table.

2. On the **Insert** tab, in the **Tables** group, click the **Table** button.

3. In the **Insert Table** gallery, point to (don't click) a cell in the gallery to preview the effect of creating the table in the document.

4. Select a cell to create a blank table consisting of the selected number of columns and rows.

To create a custom table

1. Position the cursor where you want to insert the table.

2. In the **Insert Table** gallery, click **Insert Table** to open the Insert Table dialog box.

3. In the **AutoFit behavior** area, do any of the following, and then click **OK**:

   • Click **Fixed column width**, and then specify a standard width for the table columns.

   • Click **AutoFit to contents** to size the table columns to fit their contents. The width of the resulting table can be less than the width of the page.

   • Click **AutoFit to window** to create a table that fits within the page margins and is divided into columns of equal size.

To draw a table

1. In the **Insert Table** gallery, click **Draw Table**. The cursor changes to a pencil.

2. In the document, point to the location where you want the upper-left corner of the table to be, and then click to start the table.

3. Move the cursor to the location where you want the lower-right corner of the table to be, and click to complete the table footprint. If there is text within the footprint of the table, it moves to accommodate the table.

4. Click along the table borders to create columns and rows.

5. When you have finished adding columns and rows, click the **Esc** key to turn off the table-drawing function.

5

Other table layout options

You can control many aspects of a table in the Table Properties dialog box, which you display by clicking the Properties button in the Table group on the Layout tool tab.

You can control many aspects of a table

The Table Properties dialog box contains the following tabs:

- **Table** On the Table tab, you can specify the width of the table and the way it interacts with the surrounding text. You can also access border and shading options, including those for the internal margins of table cells.

- **Row** On the Row tab, you can specify the height of the selected rows, whether rows can break across pages (when the table is wider than the page), and whether the header row is repeated at the top of each page when a table is longer than one page. Note that the Repeat As Header Row option applies to the entire table rather than the selected row. This option is available only when the cursor is in the top row of the table. Selecting this option helps readers of a document to more easily interpret data in multi-page tables. It also allows assistive devices such as screen readers to correctly interpret the table contents.

- **Column** On the Column tab, you can set the width of each column.

- **Cell** On the Cell tab, you can set the width of selected cells and the vertical alignment of text within them. Click the Options button on this page to set the internal margins and text wrapping of individual cells.

- **Alt Text** On the Alt Text tab, you can enter text that describes the table. Alt text might appear when a table can't be displayed on the page or when the document is read aloud by an assistive device. Including alt text or a table caption improves the accessibility of the table.

You can also control cell width, alignment, and margins by using the settings in the Cell Size and Alignment groups on the Layout tool tab.

5

To enter data in a table

1. Position the cursor in the cell in which you want to enter data.

2. Enter the data.

3. Continue entering data in cells, pressing the **Tab** key and the arrow keys to move from cell to cell.

To navigate within a table

1. With the cursor in a table cell, do either of the following:

   - Press the **Tab** key to move the cursor to the next cell in the row, or from the last cell of a row to the first cell of the next row.

   - Press **Shift+Tab** to move the cursor to the previous cell.

To convert a tabbed list to a table

1. Select the tabbed list.

2. On the **Insert** tab, in the **Tables** group, click the **Table** button, and then click **Convert Text to Table**.

3. In the **Convert Text to Table** dialog box, verify that the **Number of columns** box displays the number of columns you want, and then click **OK**.

> **TIP** Conversely, you can convert a table to regular text by selecting the table and clicking Convert To Text in the Data group on the Layout tool tab.

To add calculations to a table cell

1. Position the cursor in the cell to which you want to add a calculation.

2. On the **Layout** tool tab, in the **Data** group, click the **Formula** button to open the Formula dialog box.

3. If the rows above the selected cell contain numeric data, the **Formula** box contains a simple formula for adding the amounts in the rows above the cell. To apply a different formula, delete the existing formula and choose a different formula from the **Paste function** list.

4. Verify that the parentheses following the function name include the correct cells, and then click **OK**.

To update a calculation in a table

1. In the cell that contains a calculation you want to update, right-click the formula results, and click **Update Field**.

To align text in a table cell

1. Click in or select the cell or cells that you want to align.

2. On the **Layout** tool tab, in the **Alignment** group, select an alignment button to align the text in the cell.

To sort data in a table

1. Click anywhere in the table.

2. On the **Layout** tool tab, in the **Data** group, click the **Sort** button.

3. In the **Sort** dialog box, do the following, and then click **OK**:

   a. In the **Sort by** area, select the primary column by which you want to sort the content, the content type (**Text**, **Number**, or **Date**) if necessary to set the correct numeric sorting order, and **Ascending** or **Descending**.

   b. In the **Then by** area, select and configure up to two additional nested sorting criteria.

To select table cells

1. Do either of the following:

   - To select a single cell, double-click in the cell.

   - To select multiple cells, click the first cell you want to select, and then do either of the following:

     - To select adjacent cells, hold down the **Shift** key, and click the last cell you want to select. The first cell, the last cell, and all the cells in between will be selected.

     - To select non-adjacent cells, hold down the **Ctrl** key, and click each additional cell you want to select. All the cells you clicked will be selected.

5

To select table columns

1. Do either of the following:

   - To select a single column, point to the top of the column. When the cursor changes to a downward-pointing arrow, click to select the column.

   - To select multiple columns, when the cursor changes to a downward-pointing arrow, click to select the first column. Then do either of the following:

     - To select adjacent columns, hold down the **Shift** key, and then click to select the last column.

     - To select non-adjacent columns, hold down the **Ctrl** key, and then click to select each additional column.

To select table rows

1. Do either of the following:

   - To select a single row, point to the left edge of the row. When the cursor changes to an upward-pointing arrow, click to select the row.

   - To select multiple rows, when the cursor changes to an upward-pointing arrow, click to select the first row. Then do either of the following:

     - To select adjacent rows, hold down the **Shift** key, and then click to select the last row.

     - To select non-adjacent rows, hold down the **Ctrl** key, and then click to select each additional row.

To select a table

1. Point to the table to display the move handle, and then click the move handle.

To resize a table column

1. Do any of the following:

   - Point to the right border of the column you want to resize. When the cursor changes to a vertical line with arrows on each side, click and drag the border to the left or right to make the column narrower or wider.

   - Double-click the right border of a column to adjust the width so that it is as narrow as possible while accommodating the contents of the column.

   - Click in the column you want to resize. Then, on the **Layout** tool tab, in the **Cell Size** group, change the **Width** setting.

To resize a table row

1. Do either of the following:

    -   Point to the bottom border of the row you want to resize. When the cursor changes to a horizontal line with arrows on each side, click and drag the border up or down to make the row shorter or taller.

    -   Click in the row you want to resize. Then, on the **Layout** tool tab, in the **Cell Size** group, change the **Height** setting.

To resize a table

1. Point to the table.

2. Click the size handle that appears in the lower-right corner of the table and drag it inward to make the table smaller or outward to make it larger.

> **TIP** To maintain the table's original aspect ratio, hold down the Shift key as you drag.

To insert a table column

1. Point to the top of the table where you want to insert a column. A gray insertion indicator with a plus sign appears.

2. Point to the plus sign. Then, when it turns blue, click it to insert a column where indicated.

> **TIP** To insert multiple columns, select the same number of columns you want to insert in the table. Then, on the Mini Toolbar that appears, click Insert and choose Insert Left or Insert Right. The number of columns you selected will be inserted.

To insert one table row

1. To insert a row at the end of a table, click in the last cell of the last row, and then press **Tab** to create a new row with the same formatting as the previous row.

Or

1. Point to the left of the table where you want to insert a row. A gray insertion indicator with a plus sign appears.

2. Point to the plus sign. When it turns blue, click it to insert a row where indicated.

To insert multiple table rows

1. Select the number of rows that you want to insert in the table, adjacent to the location you want to insert them.

2. Do either of the following:

   - On the **Mini Toolbar** that appears, click **Insert**, and then click **Insert Above** or **Insert Below**.

   - On the **Layout** tool tab, in the **Rows & Columns** group, click **Insert Above** or **Insert Below**.

To insert table cells

1. Select the number of cells you want to insert adjacent to the location where you want to insert them.

2. Click the **Rows & Columns** dialog box launcher on the **Layout** tool tab to open the Insert Cells dialog box.

3. Specify the direction to move adjacent cells to accommodate the new cells.

4. Click **OK**.

To merge table cells

1. Select the cells you want to merge.

2. On the **Layout** tool tab, in the **Merge** group, click the **Merge Cells** button to combine the selected cells into one cell.

To delete table elements

1. Select one or more cells, columns, or rows that you want to delete.

2. Do either of the following:

   - On the **Mini Toolbar** that appears, click **Delete**, and then click **Delete Cells**, **Delete Columns**, or **Delete Rows**.

   - On the **Layout** tool tab, in the **Rows & Columns** group, click the **Delete** button and choose from the same set of options.

To delete a table

1. Click anywhere in the table.

2. On the **Mini Toolbar** or on the **Layout** tool tab, in the **Rows & Columns** group, click the **Delete** button.

Format tables

Manually formatting a table to best convey its data can be a process of trial and error. With Word 2016, you can quickly get started by applying one of the table styles available in the Table Styles gallery on the Design tool tab. The table styles include a variety of borders, colors, and other attributes that give the table a very professional appearance.

In Word 2016, the Table Styles gallery is divided into sections for plain tables, grid tables, and list tables

The Table Styles gallery includes three categories of styles:

- **Plain Tables** These have very little formatting.
- **Grid Tables** These include vertical separators between columns.

Item	Repair Type	Quantity	Cost in $
Elastomeric Decks	Resurface	400 sq. ft.	1,600
Wood Decks	Replace	1,200 sq. ft.	6,500
Building Exterior	Repaint	9,000 sq. ft.	9,000
Roof	Reseal	5,000 sq. ft.	2,700
Entry Doors	Repaint	4	600
Carpet	Replace	150 sq. yds.	4,500
Intercom	Replace	1	2,500
Garage Door Opener	Replace	1	2,000
Steel Doors	Repaint	10	750
Exterior Trim	Repaint	800 ft.	4,500
Elevator Hydraulics	Replace	1	55,000
Fire Alarm System	Replace	1	3,000
TOTAL			92,650

An example of a simple grid table

- **List Tables** These do not include vertical column separators.

If you want to control the appearance of a table more precisely, you can use the commands on the Design and Layout tool tabs for tables to format the table elements. For example, you can do the following:

- Apply formatting to emphasize the header row and total row.

Item	Repair Type	Quantity	Cost in $
Elastomeric Decks	Resurface	400 sq. ft.	1,600
Wood Decks	Replace	1,200 sq. ft.	6,500
Building Exterior	Repaint	9,000 sq. ft.	9,000
Roof	Reseal	5,000 sq. ft.	2,700
Entry Doors	Repaint	4	600
Carpet	Replace	150 sq. yds.	4,500
Intercom	Replace	1	2,500
Garage Door Opener	Replace	1	2,000
Steel Doors	Repaint	10	750
Exterior Trim	Repaint	800 ft.	4,500
Elevator Hydraulics	Replace	1	55,000
Fire Alarm System	Replace	1	3,000
TOTAL			92,650

You can apply special formatting to emphasize the header and total rows

- Apply formatting to emphasize the first and last columns.

Item	Repair Type	Quantity	Cost in $
Elastomeric Decks	Resurface	400 sq. ft.	1,600
Wood Decks	Replace	1,200 sq. ft.	6,500
Building Exterior	Repaint	9,000 sq. ft.	9,000
Roof	Reseal	5,000 sq. ft.	2,700
Entry Doors	Repaint	4	600
Carpet	Replace	150 sq. yds.	4,500
Intercom	Replace	1	2,500
Garage Door Opener	Replace	1	2,000
Steel Doors	Repaint	10	750
Exterior Trim	Repaint	800 ft.	4,500
Elevator Hydraulics	Replace	1	55,000
Fire Alarm System	Replace	1	3,000
TOTAL			92,650

You can also apply special formatting to emphasize the first and last columns in the table

- Apply formatting to the rows or columns so the rows or columns appear banded.

Item	Repair Type	Quantity	Cost in $
Elastomeric Decks	Resurface	400 sq. ft.	1,600
Wood Decks	Replace	1,200 sq. ft.	6,500
Building Exterior	Repaint	9,000 sq. ft.	9,000
Roof	Reseal	5,000 sq. ft.	2,700
Entry Doors	Repaint	4	600
Carpet	Replace	150 sq. yds.	4,500
Intercom	Replace	1	2,500
Garage Door Opener	Replace	1	2,000
Steel Doors	Repaint	10	750
Exterior Trim	Repaint	800 ft.	4,500
Elevator Hydraulics	Replace	1	55,000
Fire Alarm System	Replace	1	3,000
TOTAL			92,650

Applying banding can help to differentiate the text in each row or column

■ Apply a border to a cell, row, column, or table.

Item	Repair Type	Quantity	Cost in $
Elastomeric Decks	Resurface	400 sq. ft.	1,600
Wood Decks	Replace	1,200 sq. ft.	6,500
Building Exterior	Repaint	9,000 sq. ft.	9,000
Roof	Reseal	5,000 sq. ft.	2,700
Entry Doors	Repaint	4	600
Carpet	Replace	150 sq. yds.	4,500
Intercom	Replace	1	2,500
Garage Door Opener	Replace	1	2,000
Steel Doors	Repaint	10	750
Exterior Trim	Repaint	800 ft.	4,500
Elevator Hydraulics	Replace	1	55,000
Fire Alarm System	Replace	1	3,000
TOTAL			92,650

A heavy border applied to a row

■ Change the shading of a cell, row, or column.

Item	Repair Type	Quantity	Cost in $
Elastomeric Decks	Resurface	400 sq. ft.	1,600
Wood Decks	Replace	1,200 sq. ft.	6,500
Building Exterior	Repaint	9,000 sq. ft.	9,000
Roof	Reseal	5,000 sq. ft.	2,700
Entry Doors	Repaint	4	600
Carpet	Replace	150 sq. yds.	4,500
Intercom	Replace	1	2,500
Garage Door Opener	Replace	1	2,000
Steel Doors	Repaint	10	750
Exterior Trim	Repaint	800 ft.	4,500
Elevator Hydraulics	Replace	1	55,000
Fire Alarm System	Replace	1	3,000
TOTAL			92,650

Set off specific content by using unique shading

You can apply character formatting—for example, making text bold or changing the font color—to the text in tables just as you would to regular text: by clicking buttons on the Mini Toolbar and in the Font, Paragraph, and Styles groups on the Home tab.

> **TIP** If the first row of your table has several long headings that make it difficult to fit the table on one page, you can turn the headings sideways. Simply select the heading row and click the Text Direction button in the Alignment group on the Layout tool tab.

To apply a table style to a table

1. Click anywhere in the table.

2. On the **Design** tool tab, in the **Table Styles** group, click the **More** button to expand the gallery of available table styles.

3. Scroll through the gallery and preview styles that you like.

4. Select a thumbnail to format the table to match the thumbnail. The selected thumbnail moves to the visible row of the Table Style gallery on the ribbon.

To apply special formatting to the header or total row

1. Click anywhere in the table.

2. In the **Table Style Options** group, select the **Header Row** or **Total Row** check box.

 TIP When you choose options in the Table Style Options group, the thumbnails in the Table Styles gallery are updated to reflect your selections.

To apply special formatting to the first or last column

1. Click anywhere in the table.

2. In the **Table Style Options** group, select the **First Column** or **Last Column** check box.

To apply banding to table rows or columns

1. Click anywhere in the table.

2. In the **Table Style Options** group, select the **Banded Rows** or **Banded Columns** check box.

To add a border to a table element

1. Select the cell, row, or column to which you want to add a border, or select the whole table.

2. On the **Design** tool tab, in the **Borders** group, in the **Line Weight** list, click a border thickness.

3. In the **Borders** group, in the **Borders** list, click the border option you want.

To change the background color of a table element

1. In the table, select the cell, row, or column to which you want to add a background color.

2. In the **Table Styles** group, in the **Shading** list, click a color swatch.

Quick Tables

In addition to inserting empty tables, you can insert any of the available Quick Tables, which are predefined tables of formatted data that you can replace with your own information. Built-in Quick Tables include a variety of calendars and simple tables.

Double Table

The Greek alphabet

Letter name	Uppercase	Lowercase	Letter name	Uppercase	Lowercase
Alpha	A	α	Nu	N	ν
Beta	B	β	Xi	Ξ	ξ
Gamma	Γ	γ	Omicron	O	o
Delta	Δ	δ	Pi	Π	π
Epsilon	E	ε	Rho	P	ρ
Zeta	Z	ζ	Sigma	Σ	σ
Eta	H	η	Tau	T	τ

Matrix

City or Town	Point A	Point B	Point C	Point D	Point E
Point A	—				
Point B	87	—			
Point C	64	56	—		
Point D	37	32	91	—	
Point E	93	35	54	43	—

Tabular List

ITEM	NEEDED
Books	1
Magazines	3
Notebooks	1
Paper pads	1
Pens	3
Pencils	2
Highlighter	2 colors
Scissors	1 pair

With Subheads 1

Enrollment in local colleges, 2005

College	New students	Graduating students	Change
	Undergraduate		
Cedar University	110	103	+7
Elm College	223	214	+9
Maple Academy	197	120	+77

With Subheads 2

Save Selection to Quick Tables Gallery...

The predefined Quick Tables can be a convenient starting point

To insert a Quick Table:

1. On the **Insert** tab, in the **Tables** group, click the **Table** button. Then click **Quick Tables** to expand the Quick Tables gallery.

2. Scroll through the gallery, noticing the types of tables that are available, and then click the one you want.

3. Modify content and apply formatting to tailor the Quick Table to your needs.

You can also save a modified Quick Table, or any customized table, to the Quick Tables gallery. Saving a table saves both the table structure and the table content to the gallery. You can then easily insert an identical table into any document.

To save a table to the Quick Tables gallery:

1. Select the table.

2. On the **Insert** tab, in the **Tables** group, click the **Table** button, click **Quick Tables**, and then click **Save Selection to Quick Tables Gallery**.

3. In the **Create New Building Block** dialog box, assign a name to the table, and then click **OK**.

4. When you exit Word, you will be prompted to save the Building Blocks template. Click the **Save** button to ensure that the table will be available in the Quick Tables gallery for future use.

SEE ALSO For information about building blocks, see "Insert preformatted document parts" in Chapter 9, "Add visual elements."

5

Skills review

In this chapter, you learned how to:

- Present information in columns
- Create tabbed lists
- Present information in tables
- Format tables

Practice tasks

The practice files for these tasks are located in the Word2016SBS\Ch05 folder. You can save the results of the tasks in the same folder.

Present information in columns

Open the AddColumns document in Print Layout view, display formatting marks and rulers, and then perform the following tasks:

1. Select all the paragraphs except the heading and the first paragraph.

2. Lay out the selected text in three columns. Notice that a section break precedes the columns.

3. Justify all the text in the document except for the title.

4. With the cursor in the first column on the first page, use the commands in the **Columns** dialog box to change the spacing to **0.2"**, applying the change to this section only.

5. Turn on automatic hyphenation for the document.

6. In the third column, change the hanging indent of the *NOTE* paragraph so that the text after the first line indents at the first mark (0.125 in.).

7. At the bottom of page **1**, insert a column break at the beginning of the *Take your Room Planner home* paragraph in the first column.

8. At the bottom of the third column on page **1**, insert another column break at the beginning of the *If you're not sure* paragraph.

9. Save and close the document.

Create tabbed lists

Open the CreateTabbedLists document in Print Layout view, display formatting marks and rulers, and then perform the following tasks:

1. On the blank line at the end of the document, enter Location, press **Tab**, enter Discount Applies, press **Tab**, enter Hourly Rate, and then press **Enter**.

2. Add three more lines to the list by typing the following text, pressing the **Tab** key between each row entry, and the **Enter** key at the end of each row.

In home	No	$50.00
Phone	Yes	$35.00
In store	Yes	$40.00

3. Apply bold formatting to the first line of the tabbed list.

4. Select all four lines of the tabbed list, including the headings.

5. Change the left indent of the list to **0.5"** and the spacing after each line to **0 pt**.

6. With the entire list still selected, set a centered tab at the **2.5** inch mark and a right tab at the **4.5** inch mark.

7. Save and close the document.

Present information in tables

Open the CreateTables document in Print Layout view, display formatting marks and rulers, and then perform the following tasks:

1. On the second blank line below *Please complete this form*, insert a table that contains five rows and five columns.

2. Merge the five cells in the first row into a single cell and center-align the cell content. Then enter **Consultation Estimate** in the cell as a table title.

3. Insert the following text in the cells of the second row, and then format the text as bold:

Type	Location	Consultant	Hourly Rate	Total

4. Insert the following text in the cells of the third row:

Window treatments	In home	Patrick Hines	$50.00	$50.00

5. Add two rows to the end of the table.

6. Merge the first four cells of the last row of the table into a single cell. Enter **Subtotal** in the cell, and align the word with the right edge of the cell.

7. Create two new rows with the same formatting as the **Subtotal** row. Enter **Add trip charge** in the first cell of the first new row, and **Total** in the first cell of the second new row.

8. In the cells to the right of *Subtotal* and *Total* enter the SUM formula in the cell and display the formula results.

9. In the cell to the right of *Add trip charge*, enter **$10.00**. Then update the results in the *Total* cell.

10. At the end of the document, under the *In-Home Trip Charge* heading, convert the tabbed list to a table.

11. Resize the columns to fit their longest entries.

12. In the last row of the table, replace the existing text in the first cell with **50+ miles**, and replace the existing text in the second cell with **Email for an estimate**.

13. Add a third cell to the last row, and enter **info@wideworldimporters.com** in that cell.

14. Save and close the document.

Format tables

Open the FormatTables document in Print Layout view, and perform the following tasks:

1. Select the table, and display the **Table Styles** gallery.

2. Apply the **Grid Table 4 – Accent 1** table style (the second thumbnail in the fourth row of the **Grid Tables** section) to the table.

3. Apply the table style options to the header row, total row, first column, and last column.

4. Apply banded formatting to the table rows.

5. Add an outside border to the last row in the table. The border should have the line style that features a thick line on top and a thin line below it, with a line weight of 3 points.

6. Apply orange shading to the last row of the table.

7. Save and close the document.

Add simple graphic elements

Many documents that you create in Word 2016 contain only text. Others might benefit from the addition of graphic elements to reinforce their concepts, to grab the reader's attention, or to make them more visually appealing.

The term *graphics* generally refers to several kinds of visual objects, including photos, "clip art" images, diagrams, charts, and shapes. You can insert all these types of graphics as objects in a document and then size, move, and copy them.

This chapter guides you through procedures related to inserting, moving, and resizing pictures; editing and formatting pictures; inserting screen clippings; drawing and modifying shapes; and adding WordArt text.

> **SEE ALSO** For information about diagrams, see Chapter 7, "Insert and modify diagrams." For information about charts, see Chapter 8, "Insert and modify charts."

In this chapter

- Insert, move, and resize pictures
- Edit and format pictures
- Insert screen clippings
- Draw and modify shapes
- Add WordArt text

Practice files

For this chapter, use the practice files from the Word2016SBS\Ch06 folder. For practice file download instructions, see the introduction.

Insert, move, and resize pictures

You can place digital photographs and images created and saved in other programs into Word documents. Collectively, these types of images are referred to as *pictures*. You can use pictures to make documents more visually interesting or to convey information in a way that words cannot.

You can insert a picture into a document either from your computer or from an online source, such as the Internet or your cloud storage drive.

Choose an online storage location or search for an image

> **TIP** Pictures you acquire from the web are often copyrighted, meaning that you cannot use them without the permission of the image's owner. Sometimes owners will grant permission if you give them credit. Professional photographers usually charge a fee to use their work. Always assume that pictures are copyrighted unless the source clearly indicates that they are license free.

After you insert a picture, you can make it larger or smaller and position it anywhere you want on the page. Inserting or selecting a picture activates its sizing handles and the Format tool tab in the Picture Tools tab group.

This tab contains commands for formatting the appearance of a picture and control-ling its position relative to text, images, and other page elements.

When you select a picture, the tools for managing it become active

By default, Word inserts pictures in line with the text, which means that it increases the line spacing to accommodate the picture. If you enter text adjacent to the picture, the bottom of the picture will align with the bottom of the text on the same line.

> **TIP** You can move or copy a picture just as you would anything else in Word: by clicking it to select it and then either dragging it where you want it to go (to move it) or holding down the Ctrl key as you drag (to copy it).

To insert a picture from your computer

1. On the **Insert** tab, in the **Illustrations** group, click the **Pictures** button to open the Insert Picture dialog box.

2. In the **Insert Picture** dialog box, browse to and select the picture (or pictures) you want to insert. Then click the **Insert** button.

> ✅ **TIP** If a picture might change, you can ensure that the document is always up to date by clicking the Insert arrow and then clicking Link To File to insert a link to the picture, or by clicking Insert And Link to both insert the picture and link it to its graphic file.

The inserted picture is surrounded by a frame to indicate that it is selected. You can use the handles around the frame to size and rotate the picture.

To insert a picture from an online source

1. On the **Insert tab**, in the **Illustrations** group, click the **Online Pictures** button to open the Insert Pictures window.

2. In the **Insert Pictures** window, click the source you want to use, or enter a search term in the search box.

3. Browse to and select the picture you want to insert. Then click the **Insert** button.

To select a picture for editing

1. Click the picture once.

To move a picture

1. Point to the image. When the cursor changes to a four-headed arrow, drag the picture to its new location.

To resize a picture

1. Select the picture, and then do any of the following:

   - To change only the width of the picture, drag the left or right size handle.

   - To change only the height of the picture, drag the top or bottom size handle.

   - To change both the height and the width of the picture without changing its aspect ratio, drag a corner size handle or set the **Height** or **Width** measurement in the **Size** group on the **Format** tool tab. (Depending on the technique you use to set the measurements, the dimensions might not change until you press Enter or Tab, or click away from the measurement entry box.)

Graphic formats

Many common graphic formats store graphics as a series of dots, or *pixels*. Each pixel is made up of bits. The number of bits per pixel (bpp) determines the number of distinct colors that can be represented by a pixel.

The mapping of bits to colors isn't 1:1; it's 2^bpp. In other words:

- 1 bpp = 2 colors
- 2 bpp = 4 colors
- 4 bpp = 16 colors
- 8 bpp = 256 colors
- 16 bpp = 65,536 colors
- 32 bpp = 4,294,967,296 colors
- 64 bpp = 18,446,744,073,709,551,616 colors

Image files that you will use in a Word document are usually in one of the following file formats:

- **BMP (bitmap)** There are different qualities of BMPs.

- **GIF (Graphics Interchange Format)** This format is common for images that appear on webpages, because the images can be compressed with no loss of information and groups of them can be animated. GIFs store at most 8 bits per pixel, so they are limited to 256 colors.

- **JPEG (Joint Photographic Experts Group)** This compressed format works well for complex graphics such as scanned photographs. Some information is lost in the compression process, but often the loss is imperceptible to the human eye. Color JPEGs store 24 bits per pixel. Grayscale JPEGs store 8 bits per pixel.

- **PNG (Portable Network Graphic)** This format has the advantages of the GIF format but can store colors with 24, 32, 48, or 64 bits per pixel and grayscales with 1, 2, 4, 8, or 16 bits per pixel. A PNG file can also specify whether each pixel blends with its background color and can contain color correction information so that images look accurate on a broad range of display devices. Graphics saved in this format are smaller, so they display faster.

Of the commonly available file formats, PNG images are usually the best choice because they provide high quality images with a small file size, and support transparency.

6

Edit and format pictures

After you insert any picture into a document, you can modify it by using the commands on the Format tool tab. For example, you can do the following:

- Remove the background by designating either the areas you want to keep or those you want to remove.

- Sharpen or soften the picture, or change its brightness or contrast.

- Enhance the picture's color.

- Make one of the picture's colors transparent.

- Choose an effect, such as Pencil Sketch or Paint Strokes.

- Apply effects such as shadows, reflections, and borders; or apply combinations of these effects.

- Add a border consisting of one or more solid or dashed lines of whatever width and color you choose.

- Rotate the picture to any angle, either by dragging the rotating handle or by choosing a rotating or flipping option.

- Crop away the parts of the picture that you don't want to show on the page. (The picture itself is not altered—parts of it are simply covered up.)

All these changes are made to the representation of the picture that is on the page and do not affect the original picture.

The Format tool tab contains the following groups:

- **Adjust** The Adjust group contains commands that you can use to remove the picture's background, change the picture's brightness and contrast, recolor it, apply artistic effects to it, and compress it to reduce the size of the document containing it.

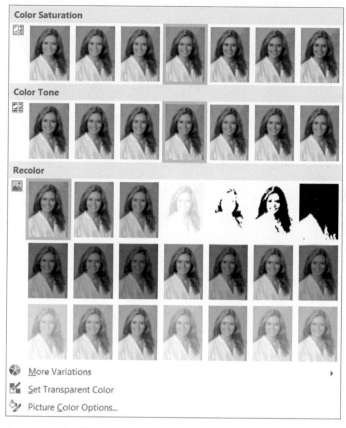

You can recolor the picture

- **Picture Styles** The Picture Styles group offers a wide range of picture styles that you can apply to a picture to change its shape and orientation and to add borders and picture effects.

- **Arrange** The Arrange group contains commands for specifying the relationship of the picture to the page and to other elements on the page.

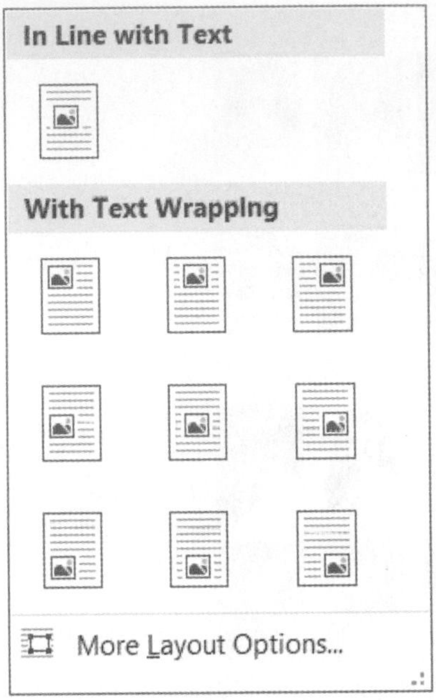

In Line with Text

With Text Wrapping

More Layout Options...

You can control the position of the picture in relation to the surrounding text

> **SEE ALSO** For more information about positioning objects and wrapping text around them, see "Add WordArt text" later in this chapter and "Arrange objects on a page" in Chapter 10, "Organize and arrange content."

- **Size** You can use the commands in the Size group to crop and resize pictures.

If you like the changes you've made to a picture, you can copy its formatting and apply it to another picture. If you don't like the changes you've applied to a picture, you can undo them.

To crop a picture

1. Select the picture. On the **Format** tool tab, in the **Size** group, click the **Crop** button to display thick black handles on the sides and in the corners of the picture.

2. Drag the handles to define the area you want to crop to. The areas that will be excluded from the cropped picture are shaded.

Cropping a photo

> ✓ **TIP** When you select a crop handle, be careful to not drag the picture sizing handles instead—they're very close to each other.

3. When you finish defining the area, click away from the picture, or click the **Crop** button again to apply the crop effect.

> ✓ **TIP** To redisplay the uncropped picture at any time, select it and click the Crop button.

Or

1. Select the picture. On the **Format** tool tab, in the **Size** group, click the **Crop** arrow, and then do one of the following:

   • Click **Crop to Shape**, and then click a shape.

   • Click **Aspect Ratio**, and then click an aspect ratio.

   Word crops the picture to meet your specifications.

You can crop photos to shapes

To frame a picture

1. Select the picture. On the **Format** tool tab, in the **Picture Styles** group, click the **More** button to display the Picture Styles gallery.

You can apply frames, shadows, glows, and three-dimensional effects from the Picture Styles gallery

2. Point to each picture style in turn to display a live preview of the frame applied to your picture. Click the picture style you want to apply.

To remove a background from a picture

1. Select the picture. On the **Format** tool tab, in the **Adjust** group, click the **Remove Background** button to display the Background Removal tool tab and apply purple shading to the areas of the picture that the tool thinks you want to remove.

The accuracy of the estimate depends on the intricacy of the background

2. Drag the white handles to define the area that you want to keep. The Background Removal tool updates its shading as you do.

3. On the **Background Removal** tool tab, click **Mark Areas to Keep**, and then click any areas of the photo that are shaded, that you'd like to expose and keep.

4. On the **Background Removal** tool tab, click **Mark Areas to Remove**, and then click any areas of the photo that aren't shaded, that you'd like to remove. Depending on the simplicity of the picture, you might need to make a lot of adjustments or only a few.

5. When you finish, click the **Keep Changes** button to display the results. You can return to the Background Removal tool tab at any time to make adjustments.

The background has been cleanly removed to leave only the cake

To adjust the color of a picture

1. Select the picture whose color you want to adjust.

2. On the **Format** tool tab, in the **Adjust** group, click the **Color** button to expand the gallery of color choices.

3. In the **Color** gallery, point to a thumbnail to preview its effect on the picture.

4. Click a thumbnail to apply the corresponding picture color to the picture.

To apply an artistic effect to a picture

1. Select the picture. On the **Format** tool tab, in the **Adjust** group, click the **Artistic Effects** button to display the Artistic Effects gallery.

2. Point to each effect to display a live preview of the effect on the selected photo.

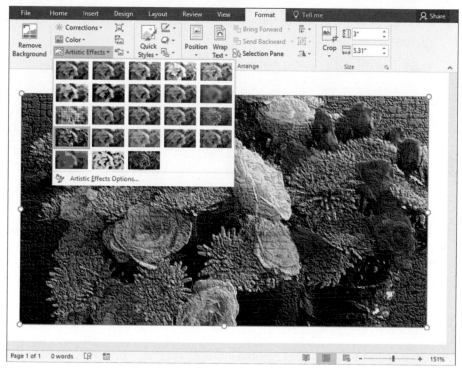

Try out all the effects

3. Click the effect that you want to apply.

To change the brightness, contrast, or sharpness of a picture

1. In the document, select the picture you want to correct.

2. On the **Format** tool tab, in the **Adjust** group, click the **Corrections** button to display the picture correction gallery.

3. In the gallery, point to a thumbnail to preview its effect on the picture.

4. Click a thumbnail to apply the corresponding correction to the picture.

> **TIP** The following procedures apply to most images and objects, including pictures, shapes, and WordArt objects.

To position a picture on the page

1. Select the picture.

2. On the **Format** tool tab, in the **Arrange** group, click the **Position** button to display the available text wrapping options.

3. Point to each thumbnail in turn to preview where that option will place the picture.

4. Select a thumbnail to move the picture to that location on the page.

To change how text wraps around a picture

1. Select the picture.

2. In the **Arrange** group, click the **Wrap Text** button to display the **Wrap Text** menu.

3. Do either of the following:

   • Point to each option in turn to preview its effects, and then click an option.

   • Click **More Layout Options** to display the **Text Wrapping** page of the **Layout** dialog box, click the option you want, and then click **OK**.

To copy the formatting of one picture to another picture

1. Select a picture that has color adjustments, color corrections, or a picture style applied to it.

2. On the **Home** tab, in the **Clipboard** group, click the **Format Painter** button.

3. Click another picture to apply to it the color adjustments, color corrections, or picture style from the first picture.

To discard the changes made to a picture

1. Select the picture whose changes you want to discard.

2. On the **Format** tool tab, in the **Adjust** group, click the **Reset Picture** arrow.

3. Do either of the following:

   • Choose **Reset Picture** to discard formatting changes only.

   • Choose **Reset Picture & Size** to discard all formatting and size changes.

Add video content to documents

Sometimes the best way to ensure that your audience understands your message is to show a video. It would be more common to embed a video in a Microsoft PowerPoint presentation than in a Word document, but it is possible to do both. You can embed a video recording directly onto a page, and then play the video when displaying the document electronically.

You can insert a video onto a page from your computer or a connected local storage device, from your Facebook account, from YouTube, or from a website that provides an "embed code" (basically, an address that you can link to).

6

Insert Video

Bing Video Search
Search the web

YouTube
The largest worldwide video-sharing community!

Search YouTube

From a Video Embed Code
Paste the embed code to insert a video from a web site

Paste embed code here

You can insert video clips from a variety of sources

TIP If a publicly posted video clip has an "embed code" available, you can link to the online video rather than embedding it in the document. Word uses the embed code to locate and play the video. As long as the video remains available in its original location (and you have an active Internet connection), you will be able to access and play the video from the document at any time.

After you insert the video, you can format its representation on the page in all the ways that you can with other imagery. You can move and resize it, display it in a frame of your choice, and even adjust the brightness or color contrast.

Insert screen clippings

Many people rely on the web as a source of information. At times, there might be information that you want to include in a Word document. For example, you might display an image of a page of a client's website in a sales proposal. Word 2016 includes a screen clipping tool that you can use to capture an image of anything that is visible on your computer screen and insert the image, called a *screen clipping* or *screenshot*, into your document. After you insert a screen clipping into your document, you can format it as you would any other picture.

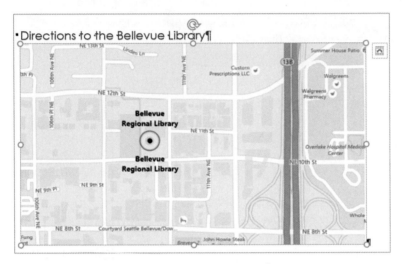

Word 2016 makes it easy to insert screen clippings into your documents

To insert an image of an on-screen window

1. Display the window that you want to capture and size it to display its contents as you want to show them.

2. Switch to Word and position the cursor where you want to insert the screen content.

3. On the **Insert** tab, in the **Illustrations** group, click **Screenshot**. The Screenshot menu displays thumbnails of all the windows on your screen that are currently available to insert.

Some open windows aren't available from this menu and must be captured as clippings

> ⚠️ **IMPORTANT** At the time of this writing, the Screenshot menu displays only desktop app windows; it doesn't display Store app windows.

4. On the **Screenshot** menu, click the window you want to insert an image of.

5. Resize the inserted image to suit your needs.

To capture a screen clipping from Word

1. Display the content that you want to capture.

2. Switch to Word and position the cursor where you want to insert the screen content.

3. On the **Insert** tab, in the **Illustrations** group, click **Screenshot**.

4. On the **Screenshot** menu, click **Screen Clipping**. The Word menu minimizes to the taskbar, and a translucent white layer covers the entire display.

> ✓ **TIP** If you change your mind about capturing the screen clipping, press the Esc key to remove the white layer.

5. When the cursor changes to a plus sign, point to the upper-left corner of the area you want to capture, and then drag down and to the right to define the screen clipping borders.

The screen clears from the area you select

When you release the mouse button, Word captures the clipping, restores the window, and inserts the clipping.

Draw and modify shapes

An extensive library of shapes is available in Word. Shapes can be simple, such as lines, circles, or squares; or more complex, such as stars, hearts, and arrows. Some shapes are three-dimensional (although most are two-dimensional). Some of the shapes have innate meanings or intentions, and others are simply shapes.

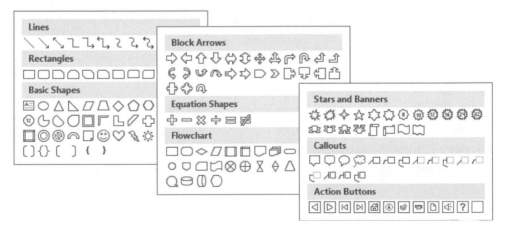

Simple representations of the shapes you can insert on a page

Pointing to any shape in the gallery displays a ScreenTip that contains the shape name.

Draw and add text to shapes

After you select a shape that you want to add to your document, you drag to draw it on the page. Shapes are also text boxes, and you can enter text directly into them. You can format the text in shapes just as you would regular text.

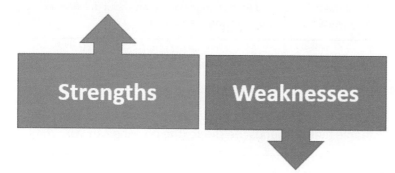

Shapes can help to visually reinforce a concept

With a little imagination, you'll soon discover ways to create images by combining shapes.

6

Use the drawing canvas to draw shapes

If your picture consists of more than a few shapes, you might want to draw the shapes on a drawing canvas instead of directly on the page. The drawing canvas keeps the parts of the picture together, helps you position the picture, and provides a frame-like boundary between your picture and the text on the page. To open a drawing canvas, you click New Drawing Canvas at the bottom of the Shapes menu. You can then draw shapes on the canvas in the usual ways. You can resize and move the drawing canvas and the shapes on it as one unit.

If you prefer to always use the drawing canvas when creating pictures with shapes, do the following:

1. Display the Backstage view, click **Options**, and in the **Word Options** dialog box, click **Advanced**.

2. On the **Advanced** page, in the **Editing Options** area, select the **Automatically create drawing canvas when inserting AutoShapes** check box, and click **OK**.

To create a shape on a page

1. On the **Insert** tab, in the **Illustrations** group, click the **Shapes** button and then, on the **Shapes** menu, click the shape you want to insert.

 TIP If you click a shape button and then change your mind about drawing the shape, you can release the shape by pressing the Esc key.

2. When the cursor changes to a plus sign, do either of the following:

   - Click on the page to create a shape of the default size.

   - Drag diagonally on the page to specify the upper-left and lower-right corners of the rectangle that surrounds the shape (the drawing canvas).

 TIP To draw a shape that has the same height and width (such as a circle or square), hold down the Shift key while you drag.

To add text to a shape

1. Select the shape, and then enter the text you want to display on the shape. There is no cursor to indicate the location of the text; simply start typing and it appears on the shape.

Locate additional formatting commands

You control the area of the shape that is available for text by formatting the Text Box margins of the shape. This setting is gathered with many others in the Format Shape pane, which you can display by clicking the dialog box launcher (the small diagonal arrow) in the lower-right corner of the Shape Styles or WordArt Styles group on the Format tool tab. You can display different pages of settings by clicking the text and icons at the top of the pane.

In Word 2016, the most frequently used formatting commands are located on the ribbon. If additional commands are available, the ribbon group includes a dialog box launcher. Clicking the dialog box launcher displays either a dialog box or a control pane.

Move and modify shapes

You can change the size, angles, outline and fill colors, and effects applied to the shape. You can apply different colors to the outline and inside (fill) of a shape.

When you first draw a shape and any time you select it thereafter, it has a set of handles.

You can easily modify the shape, size, and angle of an image

You can use the handles to manipulate the shape in the following ways:

- Drag the side or corner handles (hollow circles) to change the size or aspect ratio of the shape.

- Drag the angle handles (yellow circles) to change the angles or curves of the shape. Not all shapes have angle handles.

- Drag the rotate handle (circling arrow) to rotate the shape.

Nine shapes arranged to create a recognizable image

6

To select a shape for editing

1. Click the shape once.

To select multiple shapes

1. Do either of the following:

   - Click a shape, hold down the **Shift** or **Ctrl** key, and click each other shape.

   - Select one or more paragraphs to select all the shapes that are anchored to those paragraphs. This method doesn't activate the Format tool tab, but you can copy, cut, or delete the anchor paragraphs and associated shapes.

To resize a shape

2. Select the shape, and then do any of the following:

   - To change only the width of the shape, drag the left or right size handle.

   - To change only the height of the shape, drag the top or bottom size handle.

   - To change both the height and the width of the shape, drag a corner size handle.

   - To resize a shape without changing its aspect ratio, hold down the **Shift** key and drag a corner size handle or press an arrow key.

To rotate or flip a shape

1. Select the shape.

2. On the **Format** tool tab, in the **Arrange** group, click the **Rotate Objects** button.

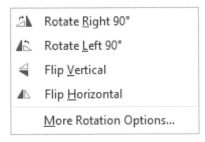

The menu illustrates the rotate and flip options

3. On the **Rotate Objects** menu, click the Rotate or Flip option you want.

> **TIP** You can rotate or flip any type of image. Rotating turns a shape 90 degrees to the right or left; flipping turns a shape 180 degrees horizontally or vertically.

Or

1. Select the shape.

2. Drag the **Rotate** handle in a clockwise or counterclockwise direction until the shape is at the angle of rotation you want.

To change a shape to another shape

1. Select the shape you want to change.

2. On the **Format** tool tab, in the **Insert Shapes** group, click the **Edit Shape** button, click **Change Shape**, and then click the new shape.

    Changing the shape doesn't affect the shape formatting or text.

Format shapes

When a shape is selected, the Format tool tab in the Drawing Tools tab group appears on the ribbon. You can use the commands on the Format tool tab to do the following:

- Replace the shape with another without changing the formatting.

- Change the fill and outline colors of the shape, and the effects applied to the shape.

- Separately, change the fill and outline colors and effects of any text that you add to the shape.

- Arrange, layer, and group multiple shapes.

Having made changes to one shape, you can easily apply the same attributes to another shape, or you can to apply the attributes to all future shapes you draw.

A happy fan cheering her team to victory!

When you have multiple shapes on a page, you can group them so that you can copy, move, and format them as a unit. You can change the attributes of an individual shape—for example, its color, size, or location—without ungrouping the shapes.

To format a shape

1. Select the shape that you want to format.

2. On the **Format** tool tab, in the **Shape Styles** group, click the **More** button to display the Shape Styles gallery.

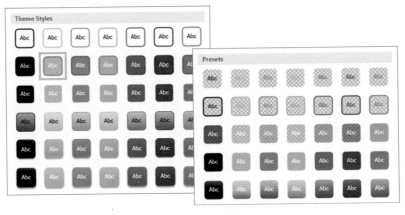

The shape style color options reflect the current color scheme

3. Point to thumbnails to display live previews of their effects, and then select a style thumbnail to apply the selected style.

To format text on a shape

1. Select the shape.

2. On the **Format** tool tab, in the **WordArt Styles** group, modify the style, text fill, text outline, or text effects.

Or

1. Select the text on the shape.

2. Do either of the following:

    - On the **Format** tool tab, in the **WordArt Styles** group, modify the style, text fill, text outline, or text effects.

    - On the **Home** tab, in the **Font** and **Paragraph** groups, use the standard text formatting commands.

To copy formatting from one shape to another

1. Select the formatting source shape.

2. On the **Home** tab, in the **Clipboard** group, click the **Format Painter** button.

3. Click the shape you want to copy the formatting to.

To set formatting as the default for the active document

1. Right-click the formatting source shape, and then click **Set as Default Shape**.

> **TIP** The Set As Default Shape command doesn't actually set a default shape; it sets only the default shape formatting.

To group shapes together as one object

1. Select all the shapes that you want grouped together.

2. On the **Format** tool tab, in the **Arrange** group, click the **Group** button (when you point to this button, the ScreenTip that appears says Group Objects) and then, in the list, click **Group**.

Grouped objects have a common set of handles

To move an entire group

1. Point to any shape in the group.

2. When the pointer changes to a four-headed arrow, drag the group to the new location.

To ungroup shapes

1. Select the group.

2. On the **Format** tool tab, in the **Arrange** group, click the **Group** button, and then click **Ungroup**.

Insert symbols

Some documents require characters not found on a standard keyboard. These characters might include the copyright (©) or registered trademark (®) symbols, currency symbols (such as € or £), Greek letters, or letters with accent marks. Or you might want to add arrows (such as ↗ or ↖) or graphic icons (such as ☎ or ✈). Like graphics or shapes, symbols can add visual information or eye appeal to a document. However, they are different from graphics in that they are characters associated with a particular font.

Word gives you easy access to a huge array of symbols that you can easily insert into any document. To insert a recently used symbol:

1. On the **Insert** tab, in the **Symbols** group, click the **Symbol** button to display a list of recently used symbols.

2. Click a symbol in the list to insert it in your document.

3. If the symbol you need does not appear in the list, click **More Symbols** to open the **Symbol** dialog box.

The Symbol dialog box offers easy access to hundreds of symbols

4. Click the symbol to select it, and then click the **Insert** button.

5. Click the **Close** button to close the Symbol dialog box.

You can also insert some common symbols by typing a key combination. For example, if you enter two consecutive dashes followed by a word and a space, Word automatically changes the two dashes to a professional-looking em-dash—like this one. (This symbol gets its name from the fact that it was originally the width of the character *m*.) These key combinations are controlled by the AutoCorrect feature. For information about displaying and modifying AutoCorrect options, see Chapter 16, "Customize options and the user interface."

You can review many of the available shortcuts on the Special Characters page of the Symbol dialog box.

6

Add WordArt text

You can use WordArt to apply a series of effects to text with one click. The 15 default WordArt styles included with Word 2016 combine outlines, fills, shadows, reflections, glow effects, beveled edges, and three-dimensional rotation to create text that really gets your attention. You can apply a default WordArt style, modify the effects of that style, or build a combination of effects from scratch.

WordArt differs from simple formatting in that text formatted as WordArt becomes an object that you can position anywhere on a page. Although the WordArt object is attached to the paragraph that contained the cursor when you created it, you can move it independently of the text, even positioning it in front of the text if you want.

With the Room Planner, you'll never make a design mistake again. Created b
ers to simplify the redecorating process, this planning tool incorporates ele
and style to guide your project. It includes a furniture location guide; roo
miniature furniture, rugs, accessories, and color swatches that match our lar
how to use the planner to create the room of your dreams!
Take a look at how your home is decorated and note the things you like and

You can position WordArt anywhere on the page—even in front of existing text

When it comes to creating WordArt, you have two options:

- You can convert existing text into WordArt.

- You can insert a new WordArt object and enter the text you want.

When a WordArt object is selected, the Format tool tab appears on the ribbon. You can use the commands on this tab to further format the WordArt object in the same ways that you can shapes. For example, you can:

- Add effects such as shadows and depth to create a three-dimensional appearance.

- Change the fill and outline colors.

- Change the text direction and alignment.

- Position the WordArt object in any of several predefined locations on the page.

- Specify how other text should wrap around the object.

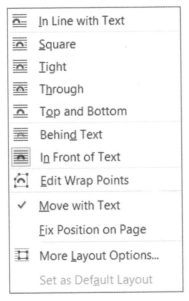

You can control how text wraps around the WordArt object

To convert existing text into WordArt

1. Select the text you want to convert to WordArt.

2. On the **Insert** tab, in the **Text** group, click the **WordArt** button.

3. Choose a text style in the **WordArt** gallery. The selected text is converted to WordArt.

> **TIP** The WordArt text styles are the same as the text effects available in the Text Effects gallery in the Font group on the Home tab.

To insert a WordArt object

1. Click in the document in the spot where you want to insert a new WordArt object.

2. On the **Insert** tab, in the **Text** group, click the **WordArt** button.

3. Choose a text style in the WordArt gallery. A placeholder WordArt object with the selected text effect is inserted at the cursor.

4. Select **Your text here**, and then enter your own text.

> **TIP** WordArt objects can accommodate multiple lines. Simply press Enter if you want to start a new line.

5. Click outside the WordArt object to view it.

Skills review

In this chapter, you learned how to:

- Insert, move, and resize pictures

- Edit and format pictures

- Insert screen clippings

- Draw and modify shapes

- Add WordArt text

Format the first letter of a paragraph as a drop cap

Many books, magazines, and reports begin the first paragraph of a section or chapter by using an enlarged, decorative capital letter. Called a dropped capital, or simply a *drop cap*, this effect can be an easy way to give a document a finished, professional look. When you format a paragraph to start with a drop cap, Word inserts the first letter of the paragraph in a text box and formats its height and font in accordance with the Drop Cap options.

W ith the Room Planner, you'll never make a design mistake again. Created by acclaimed interior designers to simplify the redecorating process, this planning tool incorporates elements of color, dimension, and style to guide your project. It includes a furniture location guide; room grid; drawing tools; and miniature furniture, rugs, accessories, and color swatches that match our large in-store selection. Here's how to use the planner to create the room of your dreams!
Take a look at how your home is decorated and note the things you like and dislike. Pay special attention to the color scheme and to how each room "feels" to you. Is it inviting? Does it feel comfortable? Does it relax you or does it invigorate you?

By default, a drop cap letter is the same font face as the rest of the paragraph and the height of three lines of text

Word 2016 has two basic drop-cap styles:

- **Dropped** The letter is embedded in the original paragraph.
- **In margin** The letter occupies its own column, and the remaining paragraph text is moved to the right.

To format the first letter of a paragraph as a drop cap:

1. Click anywhere in the paragraph.
2. On the **Insert** tab, in the **Text** group, click the **Add a Drop Cap** button and then click the drop cap style you want to apply.

To change the font, height, or distance between the drop cap and the paragraph text, click Drop Cap Options on the Drop Cap menu, and then format the options in the Drop Cap dialog box.

If you want to apply the drop cap format to more than the first letter of the paragraph, add the drop cap to the paragraph, click to the right of the letter in the text box, and enter the rest of the word or text that you want to make stand out. If you do this, don't forget to delete the word from the beginning of the paragraph!

Practice tasks

The practice files for these tasks are located in the Word2016SBS\Ch06 folder. You can save the results of the tasks in the same folder.

Insert, move, and resize pictures

Open the InsertPictures document in Print Layout view, and then perform the following tasks:

1. Position the cursor in the first paragraph after the *Beautiful Bamboo* heading, before the word *Bamboo*.

2. Insert the **Bamboo1** picture from the practice file folder into the document, and move the text that follows to the next line.

3. Move the picture to the beginning of the second paragraph, before the word *There*, and move the text that follows to the next line.

4. Resize the picture to a height of **2** inches.

5. Save and close the document.

Edit and format pictures

Open the EditPictures document in Print Layout view, and then perform the following tasks:

1. Do the following to the first picture in the document:

   - Crop the picture to a square shape.

   - Increase the contrast of the picture by 40 percent without changing the Brightness.

   - Change the picture's color setting to **Temperature: 8800K**.

   - Add a **Film Grain** artistic effect.

   - Apply the **Rotated, White** picture style to the picture.

   - Position the picture in the upper-right corner of the page.

   - Change the text wrapping to **Tight**.

2. Do the following to the second picture in the document:

   - Remove the background from the picture.

   - Change the text wrapping to **Tight**.

3. Copy the formatting of the first picture to the second picture.

4. Reset the first picture to discard all formatting changes.

5. Save and close the document.

Insert screen clippings

Open the InsertClippings document in Print Layout view, and then perform the following tasks:

1. Position the cursor on page **2** of the document, under the heading *Directions to the Bellevue Library*. Then minimize Word.

2. In your web browser, use the Bing Maps site (*www.bing.com/maps*) to display a map showing the location of the Bellevue Regional Library in Bellevue, Washington.

3. Insert a screen clipping of a portion of the map into the **InsertClippings** document.

4. Save and close the document.

Draw and modify shapes

Open a new blank document in Print Layout view, and then perform the following tasks:

1. In the upper-left corner of the page, insert a **Curved Right Arrow** shape.

2. Change the shape's **Height** setting to **3** inches and its **Width** setting to **2** inches.

3. Create a copy of the shape and move the copy to the upper-right corner of the page.

4. Flip the copy of the shape horizontally so it is a mirror image of the first shape.

5. Insert a **Rectangle** shape and move it so that its lower corners align with the points of each arrow. (You might have to adjust the size and position of the rectangle and the position of the arrows.)

6. In the rectangle, enter **What goes around comes around**.

7. Change the font of the text to **Century Gothic**, the size to **18** points, and the color to **Dark Blue**.

8. Group all the shapes as one object.

9. Apply the **Subtle Effect – Gold, Accent 4** to the grouped object.

10. Ungroup the shapes.

11. Save the document in the practice file folder as **MyShapes**, and then close it.

Add WordArt text

Open the AddWordArt document in Print Layout view, and then perform the following tasks:

1. Apply the **Gradient Fill – Purple, Accent 4, Outline - Accent 4** WordArt style to the first sentence in the document.

2. Position the cursor at the beginning of the third paragraph, and then create a new WordArt object that has the same WordArt style and the text **Room Planner rules!**

3. Position the second WordArt object in line with the text, and change the text wrapping to **Tight**.

4. Apply the **Subtle Effect – Aqua, Accent 5** shape style to the second WordArt object.

5. Save and close the document.

Part 3

Enhance document content

Insert and modify diagrams

Diagrams are graphics that convey information. Business documents often include diagrams to clarify concepts, describe processes, and show hierarchical relationships. Word 2016 includes a powerful diagramming feature called SmartArt that you can use to create diagrams directly in your documents. By using these dynamic diagram templates, you can produce eye-catching and interesting visual representations of information.

SmartArt graphics can illustrate many different types of concepts. Although they consist of collections of shapes, SmartArt graphics are merely visual containers for information stored as bulleted lists. You can also incorporate pictures and other images to create truly spectacular, yet divinely professional, diagrams.

This chapter guides you through procedures related to creating diagrams, modifying diagrams, and creating picture diagrams.

In this chapter

- Create diagrams
- Modify diagrams
- Create picture diagrams

Practice files

For this chapter, use the practice files from the Word2016SBS\Ch07 folder. For practice file download instructions, see the introduction.

Create diagrams

Sometimes the concepts you want to convey to an audience are best presented in diagrams. You can easily create a dynamic, appealing diagram by using SmartArt graphics, which visually express information in predefined sets of shapes. You can use SmartArt graphics to easily create sophisticated diagrams that illustrate the following concepts:

- **List** These diagrams visually represent lists of related or independent information—for example, a list of items needed to complete a task, including pictures of the items.

- **Process** These diagrams visually describe the ordered set of steps that are required to complete a task—for example, the steps for getting a project approved.

- **Cycle** These diagrams represent a circular sequence of steps, tasks, or events, or the relationship of a set of steps, tasks, or events to a central, core element— for example, the looping process for continually improving a product based on customer feedback.

- **Hierarchy** These diagrams illustrate the structure of an organization or entity—for example, the top-level management structure of a company.

- **Relationship** These diagrams show convergent, divergent, overlapping, merging, or containment elements—for example, how using similar methods to organize your email, calendar, and contacts can improve your productivity.

- **Matrix** These diagrams show the relationship of components to a whole— for example, the product teams in a department.

- **Pyramid** These diagrams illustrate proportional or interconnected relationships—for example, the amount of time that should ideally be spent on different phases of a project.

The layout of content in a SmartArt diagram is controlled by a behind-the-scenes bulleted list. When creating a SmartArt diagram in Word, you choose a layout first, and then populate the associated list in a window called the Text pane.

The dialog box from which you choose the SmartArt graphic layout displays mono-chromatic representations of the layouts—this is only so that the colors don't confuse the process of choosing a layout. The actual colors of the SmartArt diagram are based on the color scheme of the document, and you can choose from several different color patterns. The categories in the left pane of the dialog box are not mutually exclusive, so some diagrams appear in more than one category.

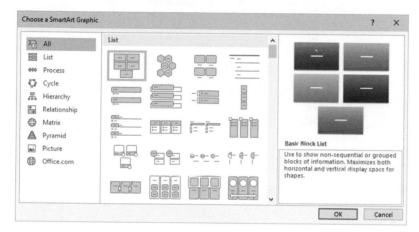

Word 2016 includes about 200 SmartArt templates

> **TIP** After you create a SmartArt diagram, you can change its content, layout, and colors. For information about changing the diagram colors, see "Modify diagrams" later in this chapter.

Clicking a layout in the Choose A SmartArt Graphic dialog box displays a color mockup of the diagram and information about any restrictions on the number of entries or list levels that the layout supports.

> **TIP** You can find the layout information in the Text pane after you create the diagram. Sometimes the Text pane displays the layout name and description at the bottom; other times only the layout name is displayed. When this is the case, simply point to the layout name to display the layout description in a ScreenTip.

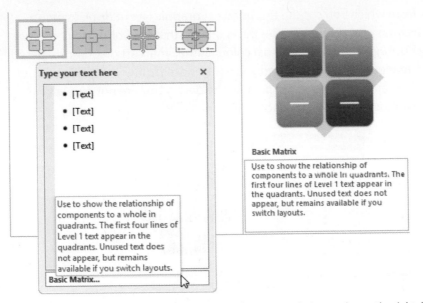

The detailed description of the selected SmartArt diagram can help you choose the right diagram for your needs

After you choose a layout, Word inserts the basic diagram into the document and displays the Text pane containing placeholder information. You can enter more or less information than is required by the original diagram.

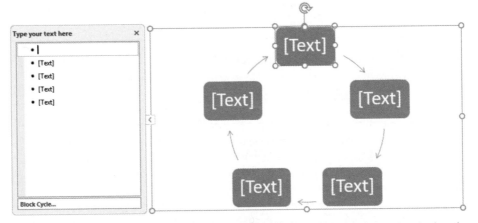

When you enter text in either the Text pane or the selected shape, that text also appears in the other location

You can insert and modify text either directly in the diagram shapes or in the associated Text pane. (You can hide the Text pane when you're not using it, and redisplay it if you need it.) The Text pane might display only a single-level bulleted list, or a multiple-level list if the diagram layout supports multiple levels. You can expand the diagram either by adding more list items or by adding more shapes. Some diagram layouts support a specific number of entries and others can be expanded significantly.

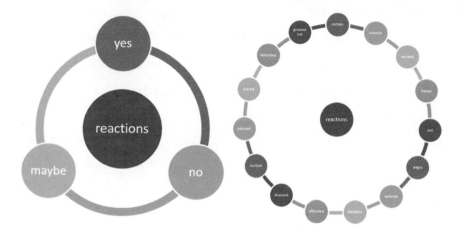

The number of items displayed by a diagram can be expanded or reduced to convey the precise meaning you want to convey

In layouts that support additional entries, the diagram shapes change to accommodate the content. Within a diagram, the shape size and font size always stay consistent. If a text entry is too long to fit a shape, the text size changes in all the shapes.

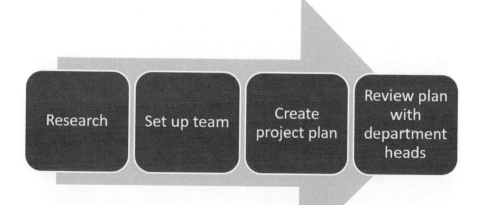

Word keeps your SmartArt diagrams looking professional by automatically adjusting text size as needed

> **TIP** You can move, resize, and wrap text around SmartArt graphics just as you can other types of images. For information about configuring image layout options, see "Arrange objects on a page" in Chapter 10, "Organize and arrange content."

To create a diagram in a document

1. Position the cursor in the document where you want to insert the diagram.

2. Do either of the following to open the Choose a SmartArt Graphic dialog box:

   - On the **Insert** tab, in the **Illustrations** group, click the **SmartArt** button.

   - Press **Alt+N+M**.

3. In the left pane, select a type of diagram. Then in the center pane, select a diagram layout thumbnail to view an example, along with a description of what the diagram best conveys, in the right pane.

4. Click **OK** to insert the selected diagram at the cursor.

To enter text into diagram shapes

1. If the **Text** pane isn't open, select the diagram, and then do either of the following:

   - Click the chevron on the left side of the diagram frame to open the Text pane.

   - On the **Design** tool tab for SmartArt (not the regular document Design tab), in the **Create Graphic** group, click the **Text Pane** button.

2. In the **Text** pane, select the first placeholder, and enter the text you want to display in the corresponding shape. Notice that the content you enter in the bulleted list appears immediately in the corresponding diagram shape. Then do any of the following:

   - Press the **Down Arrow** key to move to the next placeholder.

   - At the beginning of a list item, press **Tab** to increase the indent level of the current list item.

- At the end of a list item, press **Enter** to add an item to the bulleted list and add a shape to the diagram.

- Press **Delete** to remove an unused list item.

3. Repeat step 2 until you've entered all the diagram content.

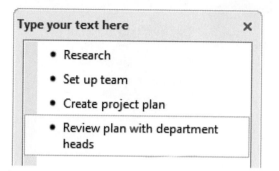

You can use the Text pane both to easily enter text and to quickly review your text for errors

> ✓ **TIP** For a clean look, don't use ending punctuation for the text that appears in the SmartArt graphic shapes.

4. In the **Text** pane, click the **Close** button (the **X**).

Modify diagrams

After you create a diagram and add the text you want to display in it, you can move and size it to fit the space, and format it to achieve professional-looking results.

If the diagram layout you originally selected doesn't precisely meet your needs, you can easily change to a different layout. Some layouts preserve information that doesn't fit, and others don't; a message at the bottom of the Text pane provides information so you can make an informed decision.

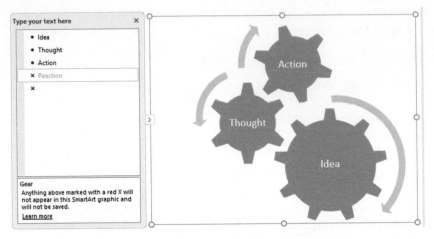

Some diagrams can support only a limited number of text entries

When a SmartArt graphic is active, the SmartArt Tools tab group on the ribbon includes two tabs: Design and Format.

The Design tool tab for SmartArt graphics

You can make many changes directly on the diagram canvas, but if you prefer, you can also make changes from the ribbon. From the Design tool tab, you can make changes such as the following:

- Add, move, and change the hierarchy of shapes.

- Change to a different layout.

- Change the color scheme of the diagram.

- Change the effects applied to the diagram shapes.

- Reset the diagram to its default settings.

The Format tool tab for SmartArt graphics

From the Format tool tab, you can make changes such as the following:

- Change the shape of an individual diagram shape—for example, change a square to a star to make it stand out.

- Change the size of an individual diagram shape.

- Apply a built-in shape style.

- Apply colors and effects to specific shapes.

- Apply WordArt text effects to the text in a shape.

- Position and resize the SmartArt graphic.

To add a shape to a SmartArt graphic

1. Select the diagram, and do either of the following:

   - Open the **Text** pane. At the end of a list item, press **Enter** to add an item to the bulleted list and a shape to the diagram.

   - On the **Design** tool tab, in the **Create Graphic** group, click the **Add Shape** button.

To remove a shape from a SmartArt graphic

1. Do either of the following:

   - In the diagram, select the shape.

   - In the **Text** pane, select the list item.

2. Press the **Delete** key.

To move a shape in a SmartArt graphic

1. Do either of the following:

   - In the diagram, drag the shape to a different position.

   - In the **Text** pane, drag the list item to a different position.

7

To change the hierarchy of shapes in a SmartArt graphic

> ⚠️ **IMPORTANT** You can promote and demote shapes only in SmartArt layouts that support multiple levels of content.

1. In the diagram, select a shape.
2. On the **Design** tool tab, in the **Create Graphic** group, do either of the following:
   - Click the **Promote** button to increase the level of the selected shape or list item.
   - Click the **Demote** button to decrease the level of the selected shape or list item.

Or

1. In the **Text** pane, click at the beginning of a list item.
2. Do either of the following:
   - Press **Tab** to demote the list item (and the shape).
   - Press **Shift+Tab** to promote the list item (and shape).

To change a SmartArt graphic to a different layout

1. Select the diagram.
2. On the **Design** tool tab, in the **Layouts** group, click the **More** button to expand the **Layouts** gallery. This view of the gallery displays only the available diagram layouts for the currently selected diagram layout category.
3. In the **Layouts** gallery, do either of the following:
   - Click a thumbnail to change the diagram to the new layout in the same category.
   - At the bottom of the gallery, click **More Layouts** to display the Choose A SmartArt Graphic dialog box. Locate and select the layout you want to apply, and then click **OK**.

To change the color scheme of a SmartArt graphic

1. On the **Design** tool tab, in the **SmartArt Styles** group, click the **Change Colors** button to display the SmartArt coloring options in the current color scheme.

The options are based on the document color scheme

2. Point to any color set to display a live preview of that option. Click the color set that you like to apply it to the diagram.

To change the effects applied to the shapes in a SmartArt graphic

1. Select the diagram. On the **Format** tool tab, in the **Shape Styles** group, click the **Shape Effects** button.

2. On the **Shape Effects** menu, click an effect category. Then on the **Variations** menu, point to any thumbnail to display a live preview of the effect.

3. Click a thumbnail to apply that effect to the diagram.

To reset a SmartArt graphic to its default formatting

1. Select the diagram, and on the **Design** tool tab, in the **Reset** group, click the **Reset Graphic** button.

To change the shape of an individual diagram shape

1. Right-click the diagram shape you want to change, and then click **Change Shape**.

2. In the **Shape** gallery, click any shape to change the diagram shape.

To change the size of an individual diagram shape

1. Select the shape, and then do either of the following:

   - Drag the sizing handle to the size you want.

   - On the **Format** tool tab, in the **Size** group, set the **Height** and **Width**.

To apply colors and effects to specific shapes

1. Select a shape. On the **Format** tool tab, in the **Shape Styles** group, do any of the following:

   - From the **Shape Styles** gallery, apply a preformatted set of styles.

   - From the **Shape Fill, Shape Outline, or Shape Effects** menu, apply individual style formats.

To apply WordArt text effects to the text in a shape

1. Do either of the following:

   - Select the diagram to apply WordArt text effects to all the text in a diagram.

   - Select a shape to apply WordArt text effects to only the selected shape.

2. On the **Format** tool tab, in the **WordArt Styles** group, click the **More** button to display the WordArt Styles gallery.

3. In the **WordArt Styles** gallery, point to any thumbnail to display a live preview of the effect.

4. Click a thumbnail to apply the effect to the selected shape or shapes.

> ✓ **TIP** For a custom WordArt effect, you can select the text fill color, the text outline color, and the text effect individually from the corresponding menus in the WordArt Styles group.

Create picture diagrams

Most SmartArt graphics present text information in shapes, but some can display pictures instead of, or in addition to, text. Most SmartArt graphic categories include some picture options, but picture diagrams are also available in their own category to help you locate them if you specifically want to create a diagram that includes pictures.

Diagrams that include spaces for pictures have "Picture" in the layout name

You can insert pictures into a SmartArt graphic from the same sources that you can insert them into a document: your computer or a connected storage location, a SharePoint library, a Facebook photo album, a OneDrive or OneDrive for Business storage folder, or the Internet. As always, take care when reusing pictures that you find on the Internet to ensure that you don't violate someone's copyright.

When you insert or select a picture in a SmartArt graphic, the SmartArt Tools tab group and the Picture Tools tab group are active. You can edit pictures that you insert in diagrams the same way you edit those you insert directly into documents.

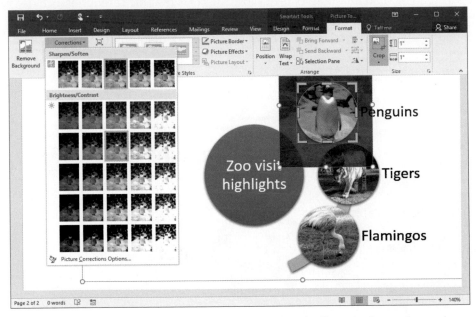

You can magnify the picture within the diagram space, remove the picture background, or apply an artistic effect

To insert a picture diagram in a document

1. Position the cursor in the document where you want to insert a picture diagram.

2. On the **Insert** tab, in the **Illustrations** group, click the **SmartArt** button to open the Choose a SmartArt Graphic dialog box.

3. In the left pane, click **Picture** to display the picture diagram options. Then in the middle pane, click any thumbnail to display information about the diagram and the number of pictures you can use in it.

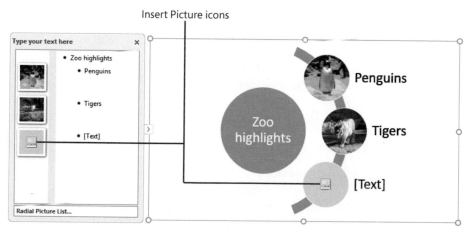

Picture diagram descriptions include information to help you decide how to best display your pictures

4. In the **Choose a SmartArt Graphic** dialog box, click **OK** to insert the selected picture diagram template.

To replace a picture placeholder in a diagram

1. In the **Text** pane or in a diagram shape, click the **Insert Picture** icon to open the Insert Pictures window.

Insert Picture icons

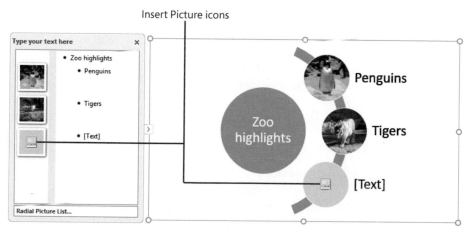

Word makes it easy to insert pictures in a picture diagram

2. In the **Insert Pictures** window, which displays the locations from which you can insert pictures into the diagram, click the source you want to use, or enter a term in the search box and then click the **Search** button.

The Insert Pictures window provides access to local and online resources

3. Browse to and select the picture you want to use. Then click the **Insert** button to replace the picture placeholder.

Skills review

In this chapter, you learned how to:

- Create diagrams
- Modify diagrams
- Create picture diagrams

Practice tasks

The practice files for these tasks are located in the Word2016SBS\Ch07 folder. You can save the results of the tasks in the same folder.

Create diagrams

Open the CreateDiagrams document, and then perform the following tasks:

1. Position the cursor below the existing page title.

2. Open the **Choose a SmartArt Graphic** dialog box, and review the available layouts. Click any layout that interests you to display information about it in the right pane.

3. Display the **Cycle** category of layouts. Click the **Hexagon Radial** layout, and then click **OK** to create the diagram in the document.

4. If the **Text** pane for the SmartArt graphic isn't already open, open it. Notice that the Text pane displays two levels of bullets. The first-level bullet populates the center hexagon and the second-level bullets populate the six surrounding hexagons.

5. In the **Text** pane, select the first bullet and then enter **My Health**. The words appear in the center hexagon.

6. In the **Text** pane, select the second bullet, enter **Physical**, and then press the **Down Arrow** key to move to the third bullet. The word appears in one of the outer hexagons.

7. Repeat step 6 to enter **Mental** and **Emotional** in the next two hexagons.

8. In the diagram, click one of the empty outer hexagon shapes to select it, and then click it again to activate the text insertion point. In the hexagon, enter **Financial**.

9. Repeat step 8 to enter **Social** and **Spiritual** in the final two outer hexagons.

10. Save and close the document.

Modify diagrams

Open the ModifyDiagrams document, and then perform the following tasks:

1. The Balance diagram on the page displays balance scales with up to four shapes stacked on each side. Select the **Balance** diagram. If the **Text** pane doesn't automatically open, open it.

2. In the **Text** pane, click at the end of the word *Family*, and then press **Enter** to create a new second-level bullet and add a corresponding shape to the diagram. Notice that with three shapes on each side, the scale moves to show that the two sides are balanced.

3. In the new shape, enter **Sports**.

4. In the diagram, click the **Job** shape to select it.

5. From the **Design** tool tab, add a shape to the **Work** side of the diagram. In the new shape, enter **Household management**. Notice that the scale tips to show that there are more shapes on the **Work** side.

6. In the diagram, select the word *Life*. From the **Format** tool tab, apply a WordArt style of your choice. Then apply a WordArt style to the word *Work*.

7. Select the entire diagram. On the **Design** tool tab, display the **Change Colors** gallery, and click the thumbnail of the color and pattern you want to use.

8. Display the **SmartArt Styles** gallery. Point to each of the thumbnails to display a live preview of the style. Then apply the style you like best.

9. Open the **Text** pane, and move the **Troop leader** and **Coach** shapes from the **Work** side of the diagram to the **Life** side. Notice that when there is more content than the shape supports, the unused content is dimmed and preceded by an X.

10. Select the diagram and expand the **Layouts** gallery. Point to each of the other layouts to find one that you can use to illustrate this same information. Click the layout you like best.

11. Experiment with any other modifications you'd like to make to the diagram.

12. Save and close the document.

Create picture diagrams

Open the CreatePictograms document, and then perform the following tasks:

1. Position the cursor below the existing page title.

2. Open the **Choose a SmartArt Graphic** dialog box, and click the **Picture** category.

3. Click any picture diagram layout that interests you to display information about it in the right pane.

4. Click the **Bending Picture Blocks** layout, and then click **OK** to insert the diagram in the document.

5. Populate the diagram by inserting the **Chickens**, **Penguins**, and **Tiger** pictures from the practice file folder into the picture placeholders.

6. Enter the corresponding animal names next to the pictures.

7. Add a shape to the diagram. Insert the **Fish** picture and corresponding name in the new shape.

8. Select the four shapes that contain animal names. From the **Format** tool tab for SmartArt, apply a different shape style.

9. Close the **Text** pane, and then click the **Tiger** picture. From the **Format** tool tab for pictures, crop the picture so that the animal fills the width of the picture shape.

10. Make any other improvements to the graphics that you want.

11. From the **Design** tool tab, apply a color set and effects of your choice.

12. Save and close the document.

Insert and modify charts

You'll often find it helpful to reinforce the argument you are making in a document by providing facts and figures. When it's more important for your audience to understand trends than identify precise values, you can use a chart to present numerical information in visual ways.

You can create a chart directly in a document or import a completed chart from another app. The chart takes on the design elements of the document template and blends in with the rest of the document content. You can modify the chart layout and the included elements to provide the visual imagery that you want.

This chapter guides you through procedures related to creating, modifying, and formatting charts.

In this chapter

- Create charts
- Modify charts
- Format charts

Practice files

For this chapter, use the practice files from the Word2016SBS\Ch08 folder. For practice file download instructions, see the introduction.

Create charts

You can easily add a chart to a document to help identify trends that might not be obvious from looking at numbers. Word 2016 has 15 chart categories. Some categories include two-dimensional and three-dimensional variations. The Treemap, Sunburst, Histogram, Box & Whisker, and Waterfall categories are new to the Microsoft Office apps in Office 2016.

In the Insert Chart dialog box, you can choose from many types of charts

The most frequently used chart categories include:

- **Column** These charts show how values change over time.

- **Line** These charts show erratic changes in values over time.

- **Pie** These charts show how parts relate to the whole.

> ⊘ **SEE ALSO** For information about creating pie charts, see the sidebar "Pie charts" later in this chapter.

- **Bar** These charts show the values of several items at one point in time.

You can display multiple types of data by creating a combo chart. Combo charts display multiple data series independently on a common axis.

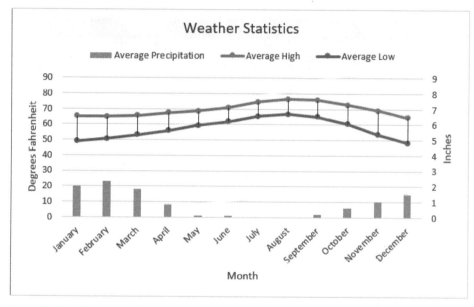

A combo chart that merges line and column charts

When you create a chart in Word, you specify the chart type and then Word opens a linked Microsoft Excel worksheet that contains sample data that is appropriate to the selected chart type. You replace the sample data in the worksheet with your own data, and the chart in the adjacent document window adapts to display your data.

> ⚠ **IMPORTANT** The procedures in this chapter assume that you have Excel 2016 installed on your computer. If you don't have this version of Excel, the procedures won't work as described.

8

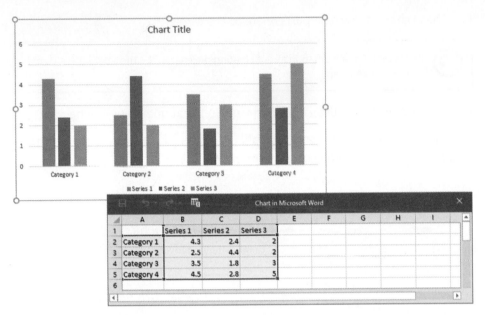

The worksheet title bar identifies it as specific to the chart

You can enter the data directly into the linked worksheet, or you can copy and paste it from an existing Microsoft Access table, Word table, or Excel worksheet.

After you plot the data in the chart, you can move and size the chart to fit the space available on the page, change the flow of text around the chart, and add and remove chart elements to most clearly define the chart content for the audience. You can edit the data in the worksheet at any time—both the values and the column and row headings. Word replots the chart to reflect your changes.

When a chart is active, you can work with the chart and its components by using commands from the Design and Format tool tabs that are available on the ribbon, and the Chart Elements, Chart Styles, and Chart Filters panes that open when you click the buttons to the right of the chart. The Layout Options button is also available.

> **TIP** The Chart Filters button appears only if it is appropriate for this type of chart.

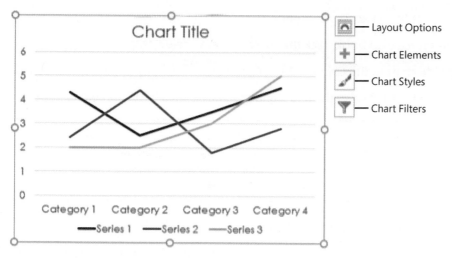

Manage a chart from the ribbon or from option panes

If you decide that the type of chart you initially selected doesn't adequately depict your data, you can change the type at any time.

To create a chart on a page

1. On the **Insert** tab, in the **Illustrations** group, click the **Chart** button.

2. In the left pane of the **Insert Chart** dialog box, click a chart category to display the chart variations in the right pane.

3. In the right pane, click the chart type that you want to create, and then click **OK** to insert a sample chart and open its associated Excel worksheet containing the plotted data.

4. In the linked Excel worksheet, enter the values to be plotted, following the pattern of the sample data.

> **TIP** If the data you want to plot on the chart already exists in another file, you can save time by reusing it. Set up the chart structure in the linked worksheet first, and then paste the existing data into the linked worksheet.

5. If the chart data range defined by the colored outlines doesn't automatically expand to include new data, drag the blue handle in the lower-right corner of the range to expand it.

6. Close the Excel window.

To insert a chart from Excel onto a page

1. In the source workbook, click the chart border to select it.

2. Copy the chart to the Clipboard.

3. Switch to Word, display the page, and then paste the chart from the Clipboard.

> ✓ **TIP** You can import data into your chart from a text file, webpage, or other external source, such as Microsoft SQL Server. To import data, first display the associated Excel worksheet. Then on the Excel Data tab, in the Get External Data group, click the button for your data source, and navigate to the source. For more information, refer to Excel Help.

To change the type of a selected chart

1. On the **Design** tool tab, in the **Type** group, click the **Change Chart Type** button.

2. In the **Change Chart Type** dialog box, click a category on the left, click a chart type at the top, and then click **OK**.

> ✓ **TIP** When you click a chart type in the top row, the dialog box displays a preview of that chart type as applied to the current data. You can point to the preview to display a larger version.

Modify charts

You can modify a chart by changing the data or elements that it displays.

Manage chart data

The Excel worksheet is composed of rows and columns of cells that contain values, which in charting terminology are called *data points*. Collectively, a set of data points is called a *data series*. Each worksheet cell is identified by an address consisting of its column letter and row number—for example, A2. A range of cells is identified by the address of the cell in the upper-left corner and the address of the cell in the lower-right corner, separated by a colon—for example, A2:D5.

By default, a chart is plotted based on the series of data points in the columns of the attached worksheet, and these series are identified in the legend. You can easily switch the chart to base it on the series in the rows instead, or you can select specific cells of the worksheet data to include in the chart.

You can edit the chart data at any time, either in the linked worksheet window or in Excel. The ribbon is available only when you open the worksheet in Excel.

To select a chart for editing

1. Point to a blank area of the chart, outside of the plot area.

2. When the *Chart Area* ScreenTip appears, click once.

To open the linked chart data worksheet in Word

1. Do either of the following:

    *   Right-click the chart, and then click **Edit Data**.

    *   Select the chart. Then on the **Design** tool tab, in the **Data** group, click the **Edit Data** button.

> ✓ **TIP** The chart must be active (surrounded by a frame) when you make changes to the data in the worksheet; otherwise, the chart won't automatically update.

To open the linked chart data worksheet in Excel

1. Select the chart.

2. On the **Design** tool tab, in the **Data** group, click the **Edit Data** arrow, and then click **Edit Data in Excel**.

> ✓ **TIP** If you open the worksheet in the linked window and then need access to commands on the ribbon, you can open the worksheet in Excel by clicking the Edit Data In Microsoft Excel button on the Quick Access Toolbar of the linked window.

To switch the data across the category and series axes

1. Open the linked chart data worksheet.

2. In Word, on the **Design** tool tab, in the **Data** group, click the **Switch Row/ Column** button.

8

TIP The Switch Row/Column button is active only when the linked worksheet is open.

To select worksheet data for editing

1. Do any of the following:

   - To select a cell, click it.

   - To select a column, click the column header (the letter at the top of the column).

   - To select a row, click the row header (the number at the left end of the row).

   - To select multiple cells, columns, or rows, do either of the following:

     - Select the first element, and then hold down the **Shift** key as you select subsequent elements.

     - Drag through adjacent cells, columns, or rows.

   - To select an entire worksheet, click the **Select All** button (the triangle in the upper-left corner of the worksheet, at the intersection of the row and column headers).

To change the area of a worksheet that is included in the chart

1. Drag the blue handle in the lower-right corner of the range to expand or contract it.

Sizing handle

	A	B	C	D	E	F	G	H
		January	February	March	April	May	June	July
1								
2	Average High	65.1	65	65.6	67.5	68.5	70.8	74.
3	Average Low	49	50.7	53.2	55.9	59.4	62	65.
4	Average Precipitation	2	2.3	1.8	0.8	0.1	0.1	
5								
6								

Chart in Microsoft Word

Different colors identify the series, categories, and values

To filter the chart to display only specific data

1. Select the chart, and then click the **Chart Filters** button to display the Chart Filters pane. The Chart Filters pane lists all the series and categories in the data set.

> **TIP** The Chart Filters button appears only if it is appropriate for this type of chart.

2. Point to any series or category to emphasize it.

3. Clear the check boxes of the series or categories you do not want to plot on the chart.

> **TIP** To clear all the check boxes in a group at once, clear the Select All check box.

4. At the bottom of the **Chart Filters** pane, click **Apply** to replot the data.

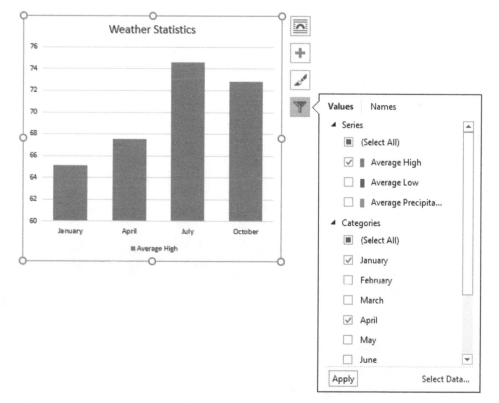

Filtering a chart to display only specific series and categories

5. Click the **Chart Filters** button to close the **Chart Filters** pane.

 SEE ALSO For information about working with the other two buttons to the right of the chart, see "Format charts" later in this chapter.

Modify the display of chart elements

Each data point in a data series is represented graphically in the chart by a data marker. The data is plotted against an x-axis—which is referred to as the *horizontal axis* or *category axis*—and a y-axis—which is referred to as the *vertical axis* or *value axis*. (Three-dimensional charts also have a z-axis—which is referred to as the *depth axis* or *series axis*.)

The primary components of a chart on a page are the following:

- **Chart area** This is the entire area within the chart frame.

- **Plot area** This is the rectangular area bordered by the axes.

- **Data markers** These are the graphical representations of the values, or data points, of each data series in the linked worksheet.

You can add chart elements to the chart components to help explain the data.

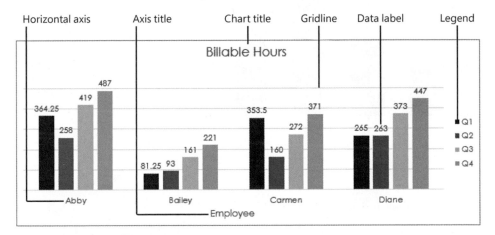

Some default and optional chart elements

The available chart elements include the following:

- **Axes** These elements control the display of the category and value axis labels, not the display of the data.

- **Axis titles** These identify the categories, values, or series along each axis.

- **Chart title** A title by which you identify the chart. The chart title can appear above the chart or overlaid across the center of the chart.

- **Data labels** These identify the exact values represented by the data markers on the chart. They can be displayed inside or outside of the data markers.

- **Data table** This table provides details of the plotted data points in table format, essentially mimicking the worksheet. A data table can incorporate a legend.

- **Error bars** These indicators mark a fixed amount or percentage of deviation from the plotted value for one or more series.

- **Gridlines** Major and minor horizontal and vertical gridlines identify measurement points along each axis and help to visually quantify the data points.

- **Legend** This listing correlates the data marker color and name of each data series. The legend can be displayed on any side of the plot area.

- **Lines** On charts that plot data that doesn't touch the category axis (such as an area chart or line chart), these lines drop from the plotted points to the corresponding value on the category axis.

- **Trendline** This line marks a value that is calculated on all the series values in a category. It most commonly marks the average of the values but can also be based on other equations.

- **Up/down bars** These bars indicate the difference between the high and low values for a category of data in a series.

All of the chart elements are optional. Some chart types don't support all of the elements. For example, a pie chart doesn't display axes or gridlines.

Each chart type has a set of Quick Layouts that you can use to display or position specific sets of chart elements.

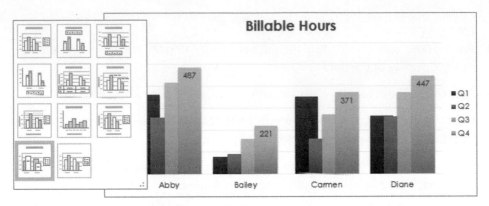

Apply a Quick Layout to quickly change multiple chart elements

The Quick Layouts are preset combinations of the available chart elements. When the preset layouts don't produce the chart you want, you can create a custom layout by mixing and matching different chart elements. You can control the display of chart elements from the Add Chart Element menu on the Design tool tab, and from the Chart Elements pane that opens when you click the button to the right of the chart.

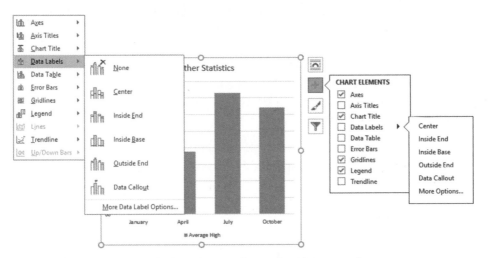

The menu and pane include only chart elements that apply to the current chart type

You can apply the same chart elements from both locations. The Add Chart Element menu provides a bit more visual guidance than the Chart Elements pane but is further from the chart.

You can adjust a chart layout by adding, deleting, moving, and sizing chart elements.

To perform any of those tasks, you must first select the element. The following table describes some of the options available for common chart elements.

Chart element	Options
Axes	Primary Horizontal, Primary Vertical, or both
Axis Titles	Primary Horizontal, Primary Vertical, or both
Chart Title	Above Chart or Centered Overlay
Data Labels	Center, Inside End, Inside Base, Outside End, or Data Callout
Data Table	With Legend Keys or No Legend Keys
Error Bars	Standard Error, Percentage, or Deviation
Gridlines	Primary Major Horizontal, Primary Major Vertical, Primary Minor Horizontal, Primary Minor Vertical, or any combination of the four options
Legend	Right, Top, Left, or Bottom
Lines	Drop Lines or High-Low Lines
Trendline	Linear, Exponential, Linear Forecast, or Moving Average
Up/Down Bars	(on or off)

> **TIP** You can use standard techniques to add pictures, shapes, and independent text boxes to pages to enhance charts.

To apply a preset layout to a chart

1. Select the chart. On the **Design** tool tab, in the **Chart Layouts** gallery, click the **Quick Layout** button, and then click the layout you want.

To display the Add Chart Element menu

1. Select the chart. On the **Design** tool tab, in the **Chart Layouts** group, click the **Add Chart Element** button.

To display the Chart Elements pane

1. Select the chart, and then click the **Chart Elements** button that appears to the right of the chart.

To specify which chart elements to display on the chart

1. Select the chart, and then open the **Add Chart Element** menu.

2. On the **Add Chart Element** menu, click the chart element, and then click one or more options to select or clear them.

Or

1. Select the chart, and then open the **Chart Elements** pane.

2. In the **Chart Elements** pane, do either of the following:

    - Clear the check box for the chart elements you want to remove from the chart.

    - Select the check box for the chart elements you want to open on the chart. Click the arrow that appears to the right of the element to display the display options menu for that element, and then click the option you want.

To change the size of a selected chart or chart element

1. Point to any sizing handle (the hollow dots around the chart frame), and when the pointer changes to a double-headed arrow, drag in the direction you want the chart to grow or shrink.

> **TIP** If an element cannot be resized, it doesn't have sizing handles when selected.

To change the position of a selected chart element

1. Point to the border around the element, away from any handles, and when the four-headed arrow appears, drag the chart to the new location.

> **TIP** Some elements cannot be moved, even if the four-headed arrow appears.

To rotate a three-dimensional chart layout

1. Right-click the chart, and then click **3-D Rotation**.

2. In the **3-D Rotation** area of the **Effects** page of the **Format Chart Area** pane, set the angle of rotation for each axis.

Pie charts

Unlike column, bar, and line charts, which plot at least two series of data points, pie charts plot only one series, with each data point, or *slice*, reflecting a fraction of the whole series. If you plot a multiseries chart and then change the chart type to a pie chart, Word hides all but the first series, retaining the hidden information in case you change back to a chart type capable of showing more than one series. You can switch to a different series by clicking the Chart Filters button to the right of the chart, selecting the series you want in the Series area of the Chart Filters pane, and clicking Apply.

When you plot a pie chart, you can use an effective formatting option that is not available with multiseries chart types. To draw attention to individual data points, you can "explode" the pie by dragging individual slices away from the center. Or you can double-click a slice to select it and open the Format Data Point pane, where you can set a precise Angle Of First Slice and Point Explosion percentage.

8

Format charts

You can quickly format a chart and its individual parts by applying fills, outlines, and effects to the following components:

- **Chart area** You can specify the background fill, the border color and style, effects such as shadows and edges, the 3-D format and rotation, and the size and position. You can also attach text to be displayed when someone points to the chart.

- **Plot area** You can specify the background fill, the border color and style, effects such as shadows and edges, and the 3-D format and rotation.

- **Data markers** You can specify the background fill, the border color and style, effects such as shadows and edges, and the 3-D format. You can also precisely determine the gap between data points.

- **Legend** You can specify the background fill, the border color and style, and effects such as shadows and edges. You can also specify the legend's position and whether it can overlap the chart.

- **Axes** You can specify the background fill, the line color and style, effects such as shadows and edges, and the 3-D format and rotation. For the category axis, you can also specify the scale, add or remove tick marks, adjust the label position, and determine the starting and maximum values. You can set the number format (such as currency or percentage), and set the axis label alignment.

- **Gridlines** You can set the line color, line style, and effects such as shadows and edges.

- **Data table** You can specify the background fill, the border color and style, effects such as shadows and edges, and the 3-D format. You can also set table borders.

- **Titles** You can specify the background fill, the border color and style, effects such as shadows and edges, and the 3-D format. You can also set the title's alignment, direction, and angle of rotation.

If you don't want to spend a lot of time formatting individual chart elements, you can apply a predefined chart style to create a sophisticated appearance with a minimum of effort. Chart styles affect only the formatting of the chart components and elements; they don't change the presence of the chart elements.

The Chart Styles pane has two pages: Style and Color. From the Style page, you can preview and apply the chart styles. From the Color page, you can change the colors that are used in the chart without affecting other document elements.

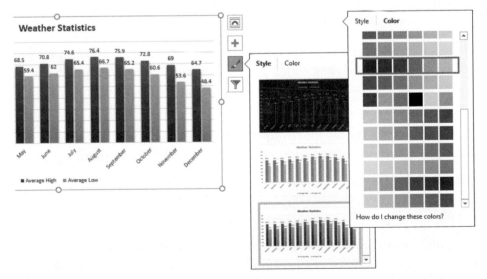

Change the chart colors without changing the template

You can apply these same styles and colors from the Chart Styles group on the Design tool tab. From the Format tool tab, you can apply shape styles and WordArt styles to chart elements.

You can fine-tune the formatting of a selected chart element in its Format pane. Each type of element has a specific Format pane. Most Format panes have settings that are divided into multiple pages, such as Fill & Line, Effects, Size & Position, and an Options page that is specific to the selected chart element. You can display different options by clicking the elements in the pane header.

Commands for formatting different elements are on separate pages of the pane

To apply a chart style to a chart

1. Select the chart, and then do either of the following:

    -   On the **Design** tool tab, in the **Chart Styles** gallery, click the style you want.

    -   Click the **Chart Styles** button, and then on the **Style** page of the **Chart Styles** pane, click the style you want.

To change the colors of chart elements without changing the template colors

1. Select the chart, and then do either of the following:

   - On the **Design** tool tab, in the **Chart Styles** gallery, click the **Change Colors** button, and then click the color set you want.

   - Click the **Chart Styles** button, and then on the **Color** page of the **Chart Styles** pane, click the style you want.

To select a chart component for formatting

1. Do either of the following:

   - On the chart, click the element once.

   - If the element is difficult to identify or click, on the **Format** tool tab, in the **Current Selection** group, display the **Chart Elements** list, and then click the component you want to select.

> **TIP** If you want to activate the chart (that is, select the chart area), be sure to click a blank area inside the chart frame. Clicking any of the chart's elements will activate that element, not the chart as a whole.

To apply a preset style to a selected chart component

1. On the **Format** tool tab, in the **Shape Styles** gallery, click the style you want.

To apply a fill color, outline color, or effect to a selected chart component

1. On the **Format** tool tab, in the **Shape Styles** group, click the **Shape Fill**, **Shape Outline**, or **Shape Effects** button, and then click the option you want.

To apply a WordArt style to the text in a selected chart

1. On the **Format** tool tab, in the **WordArt Styles** gallery, click the style you want.

To apply WordArt style components to a selected chart component

1. In the **WordArt Styles** group, click the **Text Fill**, **Text Outline**, or **Text Effects** button, and then click the option you want.

To open the Format pane for a chart element

1. Do any of the following:

    *   Double-click the chart element.

    *   Right-click the element, and then click **Format** *Element*.

    *   At the top of an open **Format** pane, click the downward-pointing triangle to the right of the **Options** label, and then click an element to open that Format pane.

Or

1. If you have trouble double-clicking a smaller chart element, on the **Format** tool tab, in the **Current Selection** group, display the **Chart Elements** list, and then click the element you want to select.

> ✓ **TIP** To open the Format Major Gridlines pane, right-click any gridline, and then click Format Gridlines. To open the Format Data Table pane, right-click the selected data table, and then click Format Data Table.

Skills review

In this chapter, you learned how to:

*   Create charts
*   Modify charts
*   Format charts

Custom chart templates

If you make extensive modifications to the design of a chart, you might want to save it as a template. Then when you want to plot similar data in the future, you can avoid having to repeat all the changes by applying the template as a custom chart type.

To save a customized chart as a template, follow these steps:

1. Select the chart (not a chart element).

2. Right-click the chart, and then click **Save as Template** to open the **Save Chart Template** dialog box displaying the contents of your **Charts** folder.

   TIP The default Charts folder is the *AppData\Roaming\Microsoft \Templates\Charts* subfolder of your user profile folder.

3. Enter a name for the chart template in the **File name** box, and then click **Save**.

You can work with custom chart templates in the following ways:

- To locate a custom chart type, open the Chart Type or Change Chart Type dialog box, and then click Templates.

- To delete a custom chart type, display the Templates folder in the Chart Type or Change Chart Type dialog box. In the lower-left corner, click Manage Templates. Then in the File Explorer window that opens, right-click the template and click Delete.

Practice tasks

The practice files for these tasks are located in the Word2016SBS\Ch08 folder. You can save the results of the tasks in the same folder.

Create charts

Open the CreateCharts document, and then perform the following tasks:

1. Position the cursor in the blank paragraph below the *Regional Averages* heading.

2. Insert a chart, using the **3-D Clustered Column** chart type (fourth from the left in the **Column** category).

3. In the linked chart data worksheet, select and delete all the sample data, leaving only the colors that identify the series, categories, and values.

4. In cell **B1**, enter March. Then press the **Tab** key to enter the heading on the chart and move to the next cell of the worksheet.

5. In cells **C1** through **E1**, enter June, September, and December.

> ✓ **TIP** If you were entering a sequential list of months, you could enter *January* and then drag the fill handle in the lower-right corner of the cell to the right to fill subsequent cells in the same row with the names of the months.

When you enter *December*, notice that it is outside of the colored guides and does not appear on the chart in the document. You will fix this in the next set of practice tasks.

6. In cells **A2** through **A4**, enter Minimum, Average, and Maximum, pressing the **Enter** key between entries.

> ✓ **TIP** Press Enter to move down in the column (or to the beginning of a data entry series) or Shift+Enter to move up. Press Tab to move to the right in the same row or Shift+Tab to move to the left.

7. In cell **B2**, enter 37, and press **Tab**. Notice that a corresponding column appears in the chart.

8. In cells **C2** through **E2**, enter **54, 53,** and **29**, pressing **Tab** to move from cell to cell. After you enter the last number, press **Enter** to move to cell **B3**.

9. Enter the following data into the chart worksheet, noticing as you enter data that the chart columns and scale change to reflect the data.

	B	C	D	E
3	47	67	66	35
4	56	80	70	41

10. Close the **Chart in Microsoft Word** window.

    Notice that the temperatures on the chart are grouped by category rather than by month, and the December temperatures are missing. You will fix these issues in the next set of practice tasks.

11. Open the **Temperatures** workbook from the practice file folder. Select the chart that is on the worksheet, and copy it to the Clipboard.

12. Return to the **CreateCharts** document. Position the cursor in the blank paragraph after the *Local Averages* heading, and then paste the chart from the Clipboard into the document. Notice that the chart takes on the color scheme of the document.

    The chart type used for this data, Stacked Column, sums the minimum, average, and maximum temperatures for each month.

13. Change the chart type of the new chart to **Line with Markers** (the fourth chart from the left in the **Line** category) to display the three temperature series individually.

14. Save and close the document. Then close the workbook.

Modify charts

Open the ModifyCharts document, and then perform the following tasks:

1. Select the chart, and open the linked chart data worksheet in Word.

2. In the worksheet, drag the blue handle so that the colored cells include only those that contain content (A1:E4). Notice that the December data appears in the chart.

3. In the document, select the chart. Then switch the data across the category and series axes to display the temperatures in groups by month.

4. In the worksheet, change the text in cells **B1:E1** to Spring, Summer, Fall, and Winter. Then close the linked chart data worksheet.

5. Open the **Chart Filters** pane, and then do the following:

    - Point to each item in the **Series** and **Category** areas of the pane to highlight those values on the chart.

    - Clear all the check boxes in the **Series** area, and then select only the **Average** check box.

    - Click **Apply** to modify the chart.

6. Repeat step 5 to display only the **Minimum** and **Maximum** series values.

7. From the **Quick Layout** gallery on the **Design** tool tab, apply **Layout 9** to the chart. Notice that this adds a chart title, axis titles, and a legend to the chart area.

8. Add the following elements to the chart:

    - Primary Minor Horizontal gridlines

    - Data labels

    > ✓ **TIP** You can add data labels to the chart only from the Chart Elements pane, not from the Add Chart Elements menu.

9. Remove the horizontal **Axis Title** placeholder from the chart.

10. Replace the vertical **Axis Title** placeholder with Degrees Fahrenheit.

11. Replace the **Chart Title** placeholder with Regional Averages.

12. Select the legend. Drag its top border to align with the top horizontal gridline, and its bottom border to align with the bottom horizontal gridline. Notice that the legend entries move to fill the space.

13. Drag the chart title to the right so that it right-aligns with the legend. Then click outside the chart to view the results.

14. Experiment with any other chart modification procedures that interest you. Then save and close the document.

Format charts

Open the FormatCharts document, and then perform the following tasks:

1. Select the chart. From the **Chart Styles** gallery on the **Design** tool tab, apply **Style 8** to the chart. Notice that the legend changes location.

2. Change the colors of the chart elements to the **Color 17** color set without affecting the document theme.

3. Select the legend. From the **Shape Styles** gallery on the **Format** tool tab, apply a **Moderate Effect** of your choice.

4. Select the chart title. From the **WordArt Styles** gallery, apply a WordArt style of your choice. Then change the fill and outline colors, and add a shadow effect if the WordArt style doesn't already have one.

5. Select the vertical axis title, and change the font size to **12** points.

6. Select the plot area (not the chart area), and double-click it to open its Format pane. In the **Format Plot Area** pane, explore the various options that are available for formatting this component.

7. At the top of the pane, click the downward-pointing arrow next to **Plot Area Options**, and select another chart component or element to display its Format pane.

8. Experiment with any other chart formatting procedures that interest you. Then save and close the document.

Add visual elements

You have already explored some of the more common graphic elements you can add to a document, such as pictures, diagrams, and charts. These elements reinforce concepts or help to make a document more visually appealing. You can also add other types of visual elements, such as document page backgrounds, which can be colors, textures, patterns, or pictures; and watermarks, which display text or an image behind the text on each page.

You can draw attention to specific information and add graphic appeal by incorporating preformatted document parts, also called *building blocks* and *Quick Parts*, into a document. These are combinations of drawing objects (and sometimes pictures) in a variety of formatting styles that you can select to insert elements such as cover pages, quotations pulled from the text (called *pull quotes*), and sidebars. Many of the built-in building blocks have graphic elements that coordinate with Office themes to add an extra visual impact to your document. You can use themed header, footer, and page number building blocks to provide useful information to readers, or you can create these page elements from scratch.

This chapter guides you through procedures related to formatting the page background; inserting a background watermark; inserting headers, footers, and page numbers; inserting preformatted document parts; and building equations.

In this chapter

- Format the page background
- Insert a background watermark
- Insert headers, footers, and page numbers
- Insert preformatted document parts
- Build equations

Practice files

For this chapter, use the practice files from the Word2016SBS\Ch09 folder. For practice file download instructions, see the introduction.

Format the page background

Whether you're creating a document that will be printed, viewed on a computer, or published on the Internet and viewed in a web browser, you can make the document pages stand out by changing the page background. You can configure a solid color background or apply any of the following effects:

- **Gradient** You can select a premade gradient, or choose two colors and the direction of the gradient—for example, horizontal, diagonal down, or from the center—to have Word blend them for you.

You can configure fill effects with multiple colors and in a variety of directions

- **Texture** Word offers 24 predefined textures, including textures designed to resemble papyrus, denim, woven mat, water droplets, granite, cork, and wood. In addition to these, you can apply textures saved as image files on your own computer, and even locate additional textures online.

A page with the Woven Mat texture applied to the background

- **Pattern** Word offers a variety of predefined patterns, such as polka dots, stripes, and checkerboards—and even plaid. In addition to choosing a pattern, you select a foreground and background color.

9

Word provides a preview of the selected effect in the Sample box

TIP When you use a texture or pattern background, Word configures it to repeat seamlessly across the page.

- **Picture** You can use a picture from your computer or any connected online storage locations as the document background.

Gradient	Texture	Pattern	Picture

Picture:

Clouds

Select Picture...

☐ Lock picture aspect ratio

Sample:

☐ Rotate fill effect with shape

A page with a picture of clouds applied to the background

You can insert a background picture from the Texture tab or Picture tab of the Fill Effects dialog box, though with slightly different results. Inserting an image from the Texture tab adds it to the Texture gallery.

Another way to change the background of your document is to apply a border. This is a good way to provide some definition to your document. Word offers several border styles from which to choose, including Box, Shadow, 3-D, and more. You can also change the style, color, and thickness of the border. For a bit more pizzazz, you can apply an Art border. Options include borders made of stars, suns, flowers, and more.

A blank page with a border applied

When it comes to backgrounds, the trick is to not overdo it. The effects should be subtle enough that they do not interfere with the text or other elements on the page or make the document difficult to read.

> **TIP** To make it easier to see the effect of your background changes on your document, display the whole page in the app window by clicking the One Page button on the View tab.

To apply a solid background color

1. On the **Design** tab, in the **Page Background** group, click the **Page Color** button.

2. On the **Page Color** menu, do one of the following:

   - In the **Theme Colors** or **Standard Colors** palette, click a color swatch.

   - Click **More Colors**, use the commands in the **Colors** dialog box to select a custom color, and then click **OK**.

To configure a preset gradient page background

1. On the **Page Color** menu, click **Fill Effects** to display the Gradient tab of the Fill Effects dialog box.

2. In the **Colors** area, click **Preset**.

3. Under **Preset colors**, select a background. The Variants and Sample areas change to show variations of the background.

4. In the **Shading styles** area, click the options to observe their effects in the Variants and Sample areas, and then click the shading style you want.

5. Click **OK**.

To configure a gradient color page background

1. Display the **Gradient** tab of the **Fill Effects** dialog box.

2. In the **Colors** area, click **One color** or **Two colors**.

3. In the color palette or palettes, click the colors you want to use. The Variants and Sample areas change to show variations of the background.

4. If you selected a one-color gradient, drag the **Darkness** slider until the colors in the Sample area look the way you want.

5. In the **Shading styles** area, click the options to observe their effects in the Variants and Sample areas, and then select a shading style.

6. Click **OK**.

To configure a textured page background

1. Display the **Texture** tab of the **Fill Effects** dialog box.

2. In the texture gallery, click the options to observe their effects in the Sample area, and then select a texture swatch.

3. Click **OK**.

To configure a patterned page background

1. Display the **Pattern** tab of the **Fill Effects** dialog box.

2. In the **Foreground** and **Background** color charts, click the colors you want to use for the pattern.

3. In the pattern gallery, click the options to observe their effects in the Sample area, and then click a pattern tile.

4. Click **OK**.

To configure a picture page background

1. Display the **Picture** tab of the **Fill Effects** dialog box.

2. Click the **Select Picture** button to open the Insert Pictures dialog box.

3. Do one of the following:

   - In the **From a file** area, click **Browse**. Then locate and select the picture you want to use and click **Insert**.

   - In the **Bing Image Search** area, enter a search word or phrase in the search box and press **Enter**. A dialog box containing pictures that match the word or phrase you entered appears; select the picture you want to use and click **Insert**.

   - In the **OneDrive** area, click **Browse**. Then locate and select the picture you want to use and click **Insert**.

4. Click **OK**.

> ⚠ **IMPORTANT** Word fills the page with as much of the picture as will fit. If one copy of the picture does not completely fill the page, Word inserts another copy, effectively "tiling" the image. If the picture is particularly large, only a portion of it will be visible. If you want to display the entire picture, resize it in a graphics app and then reselect it as the page background.

To remove the page background

1. On the **Design** tab, in the **Page Background** group, click the **Page Color** button.

2. On the **Page Color** menu, click **No Color**.

To apply a simple border

1. In the **Page Background** group, click the **Page Borders** button to display the Page Border page of the Borders And Shading dialog box.

2. In the **Setting** area of the **Borders and Shading** dialog box, click the type of border you want.

3. In the **Style**, **Color**, **Width**, and **Art** boxes, select the options you want.

4. When the border in the **Preview** box looks the way you want, click **OK**.

Insert a background watermark

A *watermark* is a faint text or graphic image that appears on the page behind the main content of a document. A common use of a text watermark is to indicate a status such as *DRAFT* or *CONFIDENTIAL*.

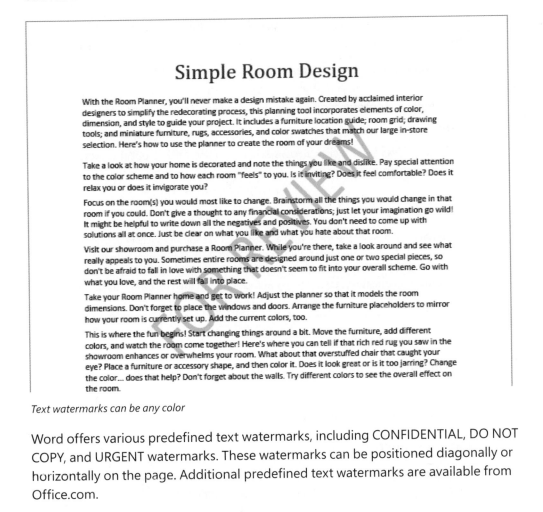

Text watermarks can be any color

Word offers various predefined text watermarks, including CONFIDENTIAL, DO NOT COPY, and URGENT watermarks. These watermarks can be positioned diagonally or horizontally on the page. Additional predefined text watermarks are available from Office.com.

In addition, you can create a custom text watermark that features whatever text you like. For example, you might create a text watermark that includes the name of your organization. When you create a custom text watermark, you can select the font, size, and color of the text, whether it appears diagonally or horizontally, and whether it is solid or semitransparent.

If you want to dress up the pages of your document without taking attention from the main text, you might consider displaying a graphic watermark, such as a company logo or an image that subtly reinforces your message. Watermarks are visible in printed and online documents, but because they are faint, they don't interfere with the readers' ability to view a document's main text.

Simple Room Design

With the Room Planner, you'll never make a design mistake again. Created by acclaimed interior designers to simplify the redecorating process, this planning tool incorporates elements of color, dimension, and style to guide your project. It includes a furniture location guide; room grid; drawing tools; and miniature furniture, rugs, accessories, and color swatches that match our large in-store selection. Here's how to use the planner to create the room of your dreams!

Take a look at how your home is decorated and note the things you like and dislike. Pay special attention to the color scheme and to how each room "feels" to you. Is it inviting? Does it feel comfortable? Does it relax you or does it invigorate you?

Focus on the room(s) you would most like to change. Brainstorm all the things you would change in that room if you could. Don't give a thought to any financial considerations; just let your imagination go wild! It might be helpful to write down all the negatives and positives. You don't need to come up with solutions all at once. Just be clear on what you like and what you hate about that room.

Visit our showroom and purchase a Room Planner. While you're there, take a look around and see what really appeals to you. Sometimes entire rooms are designed around just one or two special pieces, so don't be afraid to fall in love with something that doesn't seem to fit into your overall scheme. Go with what you love, and the rest will fall into place.

Take your Room Planner home and get to work! Adjust the planner so that it models the room dimensions. Don't forget to place the windows and doors. Arrange the furniture placeholders to mirror how your room is currently set up. Add the current colors, too.

This is where the fun begins! Start changing things around a bit. Move the furniture, add different colors, and watch the room come together! Here's where you can tell if that rich red rug you saw in the showroom enhances or overwhelms your room. What about that overstuffed chair that caught your eye? Place a furniture or accessory shape, and then color it. Does it look great or is it too jarring? Change the color... does that help? Don't forget about the walls. Try different colors to see the overall effect on the room.

You can use a picture, such as a company logo, as a watermark.

To add a predefined watermark to a document

1. Open the document to which you want to add a watermark.

2. On the **Design** tab, in the **Page Background** group, click the **Watermark** button to display the Watermark gallery and menu.

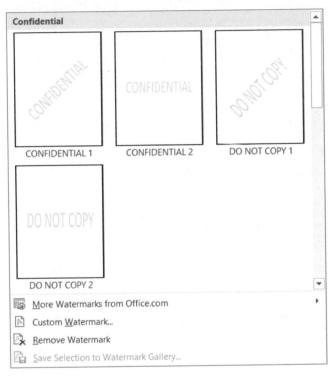

Scroll the gallery to display the Disclaimer and Urgent categories

3. In the gallery, click a watermark to insert it in light gray on every page of the document.

> ⚠️ **IMPORTANT** At the time of this writing, the More Watermarks From Office.com menu item doesn't provide any additional watermarks.

To add a custom text watermark

1. On the **Watermark** menu, click **Custom Watermark** to open the Printed Watermark dialog box.

Configure a custom picture or text watermark

2. Click **Text watermark**.

3. If necessary, in the **Language** list, click the language you want.

4. In the **Text** box, enter the text you want to appear in your watermark.

5. In the **Font**, **Size**, and **Color** boxes, choose the options you want.

6. If you want to reduce the opacity of the watermark color, select the **Semitransparent** check box.

7. In the **Layout** area, click either **Diagonal** or **Horizontal**.

8. Do either of the following:

   - Click **Apply** to apply the watermark to the document but leave the dialog box open, so that you can review the effect and make adjustments if you want.

   - Click **OK** to apply the watermark and close the dialog box.

To add a picture watermark to a document

1. Open the **Printed Watermark** dialog box, and click **Picture watermark**.

2. Click **Select Picture** to open the Insert Pictures dialog box.

3. Do one of the following:

   - In the **From a file** area, click **Browse**. Then locate and select the picture you want to use and click **Insert**.

   - In the **Bing Image Search** area, enter a search word or phrase in the search box and press **Enter**. A dialog box containing pictures that match the word or phrase you entered appears; select the picture you want to use and click **Insert**.

   - In the **OneDrive** area, click **Browse**. Then locate and select the picture you want to use and click **Insert**.

4. In the **Printed Watermark** dialog box, in the **Scale** list, click the scale you want to use.

    TIP If you're not sure what scale to choose, select Auto. Word will scale the picture automatically.

5. If you want the picture to appear washed out, select the **Washout** check box.

6. Do either of the following:

   - Click **Apply** to apply the watermark to the document but leave the dialog box open, so that you can review the effect and make adjustments if you want.

   - Click **OK** to apply the watermark and close the dialog box.

To remove a watermark

1. Display the **Watermark** menu, and click **Remove Watermark**.

Insert headers, footers, and page numbers

You can display information on every page of a document in regions at the top and bottom of a page by selecting a style from the Header or Footer gallery. Word displays dotted borders to indicate the header and footer areas, and displays a Design tool tab on the ribbon. You can enter and format information in the header and footer by using the same techniques you do in the document body and also by using commands on the Design tool tab.

Headers and footers are highly customizable. You can have a different header and footer on the first page of a document and different headers and footers on odd and even pages. You can manually insert text or graphic elements in a header or footer, select common elements (such as page number, date and time, or a document property) from a menu, or insert a preformatted building block. (For more information about building blocks, see "Insert preformatted document parts" later in this chapter.) You can also mix different headers, footers, and document themes to create a document that has the look and feel you want.

Headers and footers can include any information you want to display

9

> **TIP** If your document contains section breaks, each successive section inherits the headers and footers of the preceding section unless you break the link between the two sections. You can then create a different header and footer for the current section. For information about sections, see "Control what appears on each page" in Chapter 12, "Finalize and distribute documents."

It is quite common to insert page numbers in a document that will be printed. You can insert stylized page numbers in the header, footer, left margin, or right margin, or at the current cursor position on each page. You can manually insert a page number element in a header or footer, or you can use the separate Page Number feature to insert stylized page numbers. You can also quickly add headers and footers that include only page numbers and require no customization. There are several styles available in the Page Number galleries.

To insert custom header or footer content

1. Activate the header or footer by using one of these methods:

    - Position the cursor anywhere in the document. On the **Insert** tab, in the **Header & Footer** group, click the **Header** button or the **Footer** button, and then click the corresponding **Edit** command on the menu.

    - In Print Layout view, double-click in the top margin of a page to activate the header or in the bottom margin to activate the footer.

2. In the header or footer area, do any of the following:

    - Insert and format content by using the standard commands.

    - From the **Insert** group on the **Design** tool tab, insert the date, time, an image, document information, or any Quick Parts you want to include.

    - Use the preset tabs to align content at the left margin, in the center, and at the right margin, or modify the tabs to meet your needs.

3. In the **Close** group, click the **Close Header and Footer** button.

> **IMPORTANT** If your document includes a cover page, the header or footer first appears on the second page of the file and displays page number 1. Cover pages are counted separately from document pages.

To insert a preformatted header or footer

1. On the **Insert** tab, in the **Header & Footer** group, click the **Header** button or the **Footer** button.

2. In the **Header** gallery or the **Footer** gallery, click the design you want.

3. Replace any text placeholders and enter any other information you want to appear.

4. In the **Close** group, click the **Close Header and Footer** button.

To insert the current date or time in a header or footer

1. In the header or footer, position the cursor where you want the date or time to appear.

2. On the **Design** tool tab, in the **Insert** group, click the **Insert Date and Time** button.

3. In the **Date and Time** dialog box, do the following, and then click **OK**:

   - Click the format in which you want the date or time to appear in the header or footer.

   - If you want Word to update the date or time in the header each time you save the document, select the **Update automatically** check box.

To navigate among headers and footers

1. Click in the header or footer area, and then on the **Design** tool tab, in the **Navigation** group, do any of the following:

   - Click the **Go to Header** button to move the cursor to the header area at the top of the page.

   - Click the **Go to Footer** button to move the cursor to the footer area at the bottom of the page.

   - Click the **Next** button to move to the header or footer area of the next section.

   - Click the **Previous** button to move to the header or footer area of the previous section.

9

To modify standard header or footer settings

1. On the **Design** tool tab, in the **Options** group, do any of the following:

   - Select the **Different First Page** check box if you want to use a different header or footer on the first page of the document. You might want to do this if, for example, the first page of the document is a cover page.

   - Select the **Different Odd & Even Pages** check box if you want to use different headers or footers for odd pages and for even pages. Select this option if the content of the header or footer is not centered and the document content will be viewed on facing pages.

   - Clear the **Show Document Text** check box if you find that you're distracted by the main document text when you're working in the header or footer.

2. In the **Position** group, set the **Header from Top** or **Footer from Bottom** distance.

3. In the **Close** group, click the **Close Header and Footer** button.

To change the format of page numbers

1. On the **Insert** tab or **Design** tool tab (when the header or footer is active), in the **Header & Footer** group, click the **Page Number** button, and then click **Format Page Numbers**.

2. In the **Page Number Format** dialog box, in the **Number format** list, click the format you want.

3. Select any other options you want, and then click **OK**.

To insert a page number building block independently of a header or footer

1. On the **Insert** tab, in the **Header & Footer** group, click the **Page Number** button.

2. On the **Page Number** menu, click one of the following to display building blocks with page numbers in those locations:

   - Top of Page
   - Bottom of Page
   - Page Margins
   - Current Position

3. Scroll the submenu to review the available page number building blocks, and then click the one you want to insert.

To delete a header or footer

1. Do either of the following:

   - Activate the header or footer. Press **Ctrl+A** to select all the content of the header or footer, and then press the **Delete** key.

   - On the **Insert** tab, in the **Header & Footer** group, click **Header** or **Footer**, and then click the corresponding **Remove** command.

9

Insert preformatted document parts

To simplify the creation of professional-looking text elements, Word 2016 comes with ready-made visual representations of text, known as *building blocks*, which are available from various groups on the Insert tab. Headers and footers, which were covered in the previous topic, are one type of building block.

In addition to inserting headers and footers, you can insert the following types of building blocks:

- **Cover page** You can quickly add a formatted cover page to a document such as a report by selecting a style from the Cover Page gallery. The cover page includes text placeholders for elements such as a title so that you can customize the page to reflect the content of the document.

You can add document-specific information to the basic cover page

- **Text box** To reinforce key concepts and also alleviate the monotony of page after page of plain text, you can insert text boxes such as sidebars and quote boxes by selecting a style from the Text Box gallery. The formatted text box includes placeholder text that you replace with your own.

Focus on the room(s) you would most like to change. Brainstorm all the things you would change in that room if you could. Don't give a thought to any financial considerations; just let your imagination go wild! It might be helpful to write down all the negatives and positives. You don't need to come up with solutions all at once. Just be clear on what you like and what you dislike about that room.

Visit our showroom and purchase a Room Planner. While you're there, take a look around and see what really appeals to you. Sometimes entire rooms are designed around just one or two special pieces, so don't be afraid to fall in love with something that doesn't seem to fit into your overall scheme. Go with what you love, and the rest will fall into place.

[Grab your reader's attention with a great quote from the document or use this space to emphasize a key point. To place this text box anywhere on the page, just drag it.]

[Cite your source here.]

Take your Room Planner home and get to work! Adjust the planner so that it models the room dimensions. Don't forget to place the windows and doors. Arrange the furniture placeholders to mirror how your room is currently set up. Add the current colors, too.

Placeholder text in the quote box tells how to enter text and move the quote box on the page

Most building blocks include text fields that contain placeholders for information. For example, a cover page building block might contain placeholders for the date, title, subtitle, author name, company name, or company address. You can replace this text by selecting it and then typing over it with text of your own. For example, you can select the Document Title placeholder text in a cover page and replace it with the actual title of your document.

> **TIP** If any of the required information—such as Author—is already saved with the properties of the document into which you're inserting the cover page, Word inserts the saved information instead of the placeholders. For information about document properties, see "Prepare documents for electronic distribution" in Chapter 12, "Finalize and distribute documents."

Of course, you are not restricted to the default contents of the building block. You can change the building block in any way that you want to—altering the text and various visual elements. For example, if you insert a text box building block, you can change the box's size and other characteristics by using the Format tool tab that appears when the box is selected. Think of the building box as a convenient starting point.

You can display all available building blocks in the Building Blocks Organizer dialog box. The left pane of this dialog box displays a complete list of all the building blocks available on your computer. Clicking a building block in the left pane displays a preview in the right pane, along with its description and behavior.

9

Building Blocks Organizer   ?   ✕

Building blocks: Click a building block to see its preview

Name	Gallery	Categ...	Template	Beha
Bibliography	Bibliograp...	Built-In	Built-In...	Inser
References	Bibliograp...	Built-In	Built-In...	Inser
Works Cited	Bibliograp...	Built-In	Built-In.,..	Inser
Ion (Light)	Cover Pages	Built-in	Built-In...	Inser
Motion	Cover Pages	Built-in	Built-In...	Inser
ViewMaster	Cover Pages	Built-in	Built-In...	Inser
Ion (Dark)	Cover Pages	Built-in	Built-In...	Inser
Integral	Cover Pages	Built-in	Built-In...	Inser
Grid	Cover Pages	Built-in	Built-In...	Inser
Filigree	Cover Pages	Built-in	Built-In...	Inser
Slice (Light)	Cover Pages	Built-in	Built-In...	Inser
Austin	Cover Pages	Built-in	Built-In...	Inser
Slice (Dark)	Cover Pages	Built-in	Built-In...	Inser
Whisp	Cover Pages	Built-in	Built-In...	Inser
Banded	Cover Pages	Built-in	Built-In...	Inser
Retrospect	Cover Pages	Built-in	Built-In...	Inser
Facet	Cover Pages	Built-in	Built-In...	Inser
Semaphore	Cover Pages	Built-in	Built-In...	Inser
Sideline	Cover Pages	Built-in	Built-In...	Inser
Taylor Expa...	Equations	Built-In	Built-In...	Inser
Quadratic F...	Equations	Built-In	Built-In...	Inser

ABSTRACT

[DOCUMENT TITLE]

Integral
Large photo with title block beside abstract and contact info

Edit Properties...   Delete   Insert   Close

The Building Blocks Organizer includes all available building blocks

Initially, the building blocks are organized by type, as reflected in the Gallery column. If you want to insert building blocks of the same design in a document—for example, a cover page, footer, header, quote box, and sidebar all in the Whisp design—you might want to click the Name column heading to sort the list alphabetically by design name. Some elements, such as bibliographies, equations, tables of contents, tables, and watermarks, are not part of a design family and have their own unique names.

You can display a dialog box containing all the information about a selected building block in a more readable format. To do so, select the building block you want to learn more about, and then click the Edit Properties button in the lower-left corner of the

Building Blocks Organizer dialog box. Although you can use this dialog box to change the properties associated with any building block, be cautious when doing so. If you change the properties assigned to a building block that came with Word, you might accidentally render it unusable.

The Modify Building Block dialog box

If you frequently use a specific element in your documents, such as a formatted title-subtitle-author arrangement at the beginning of reports, you can define it as a custom building block. It will then then become available from the Quick Parts gallery.

> **SEE ALSO** For information about saving frequently used text as a building block, see "Create custom building blocks" in Chapter 15, "Create custom document elements."

To display all available building blocks

1. On the **Insert** tab, in the **Text** group, click the **Quick Parts** button, and then click **Building Blocks Organizer** to open the Building Blocks Organizer dialog box.

To insert and modify a cover page

1. On the **Insert** tab, in the **Pages** group, click the **Cover Page** button to display the gallery of available cover pages.

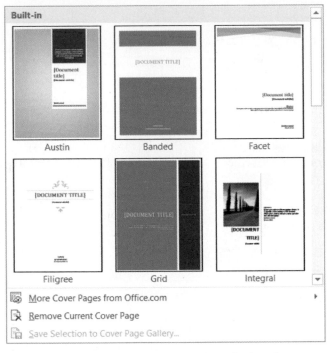

Thumbnails display cover page designs and standard text layout

2. Scroll through the **Cover Page** gallery to display the available options, and then select a thumbnail to insert the cover page at the beginning of the document.

3. Click a placeholder, click the arrow that appears, and then do any of the following:

   • Enter the text you want to use for the selected placeholder. As you enter the text, its appearance on the page reflects the character formatting applied to the placeholder.

   • If a control appears, such as for the date, use the control to enter the information required.

> **TIP** If you begin entering your name in a name placeholder, Word should recognize it from the user name information stored with the app and display a ScreenTip containing your completed name. Press Enter when the ScreenTip appears to have Word insert your name for you.

To insert a text box building block

1. On the **Insert** tab, in the **Text** group, click the **Text Box** button to display the available text box building blocks.

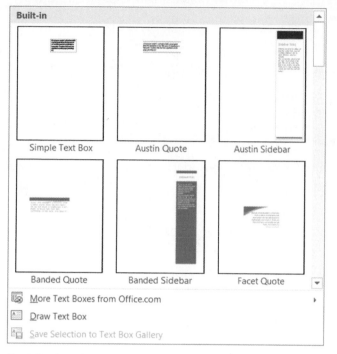

Predefined text boxes share graphic elements with themes

2. Scroll the gallery to review the available text boxes, and then click the one you want to insert.

Insert and link custom text boxes

If you prefer to start from scratch rather than using one of the preformatted text box building blocks, you can draw and format your own text box. Here's how:

1. On the **Insert** tab, click **Text Box**, and then click **Draw Text Box**.

2. Click and drag to draw a box of the approximate size you want anywhere on the page.

3. Enter the text and format it the way you would any other text.

4. Optionally, click the text box frame and format the text box shape, outline, fill, and other properties by using the commands on the **Format** tool tab.

When a text box has a solid border, you can reposition it by dragging it to another location or by pressing the arrow keys. You can rotate it by dragging the rotate handle, and change its size by dragging the size handles around its frame.

You can link text boxes so that text flows from one to the next. To do so:

1. Ensure that the second text box is empty.

2. Click the first text box.

3. On the **Format** tool tab, in the **Text** group, click **Create Link**. The pointer shape changes to a pitcher.

4. Point to the second text box. When the pointer changes to a pouring pitcher, click once.

Text boxes are not accessible to adaptive technologies, so if you want to ensure that a text-reading program can access the content of your document, do not use a text box.

Build equations

You can insert mathematical symbols, such as π (pi) or ∑ (sigma, or summation), the same way you would insert any other symbol. But you can also create entire mathematical equations in a document. You can insert some predefined equations, including the Quadratic Formula, the Binomial Theorem, and the Pythagorean Theorem, into a document with a few clicks. If you need something other than these standard equations, you can build your own equations by using a library of mathematical symbols.

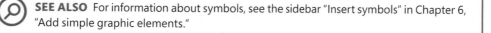 **SEE ALSO** For information about symbols, see the sidebar "Insert symbols" in Chapter 6, "Add simple graphic elements."

Equations are different from graphics in that they are accurately rendered mathematical formulas that appear in the document as fields. However, they are similar to graphics in that they can be displayed in line with the surrounding text or in their own space with text above and below them.

You can insert an equation in one of two ways:

- **Inserting a predefined equation** The Insert New Equation gallery contains several commonly used equations, including the following:

  - Area of a Circle

  - Binomial Theorem

  - Expansion of a Sum

  - Fourier Series

  - Pythagorean Theorem

  - Quadratic Formula

  - Taylor Expansion

  - Trig Identity 1

  - Trig Identity 2

  You can insert an equation from the gallery, or you can search the Office.com site for other predefined equations.

- **Building an equation from scratch** Clicking the Equation button instead of its arrow inserts a field in which you can build an equation.

9

When you opt to build an equation from scratch, Word displays the Design tool tab for equations. This tab provides access to mathematical symbols and structures such as fractions, scripts, radicals, integrals, and more.

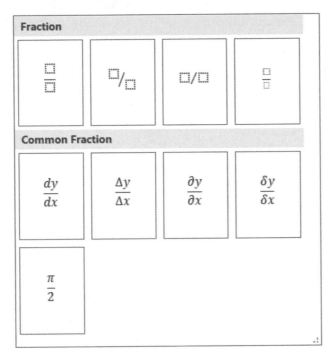

The Design tool tab for equations offers easy access to mathematical symbols and structures

Clicking a button on the Design tool tab—for example, the Fraction button—displays a gallery of related structures.

Fraction

Common Fraction

The Fraction gallery provides structures for forming fractions

By default, equations appear in professional, or two-dimensional, form. If you prefer linear form—equations in linear form are easier to edit—you can easily change the equation accordingly. You can also specify how the equation should be aligned on the page—left, right, or center.

The Equation Options dialog box

For even finer control over the equations you build, you can open the Equation Options dialog box by clicking the Tools dialog box launcher on the Design tool tab. Here, you can set many options that govern the appearance of equation expressions in a document, such as the following:

- The size of nested fractions

- The placement of integral limits

- The placement of n-ary limits

- The alignment of the equation

- The treatment of wrapped lines in the equation

You can fine-tune the appearance of equation expressions in a document

If you build an equation that you know you will want to reuse later, you can save it. When you save an equation, Word stores it as a building block. You can give the equation whatever name you like. You can then access the equation from the Equation gallery, with other predefined equations.

> **SEE ALSO** For information about building blocks, see "Insert preformatted document parts" earlier in this chapter.

To insert a predefined equation

1. On the **Insert** tab, in the **Symbols** group, click the **Equation** arrow.

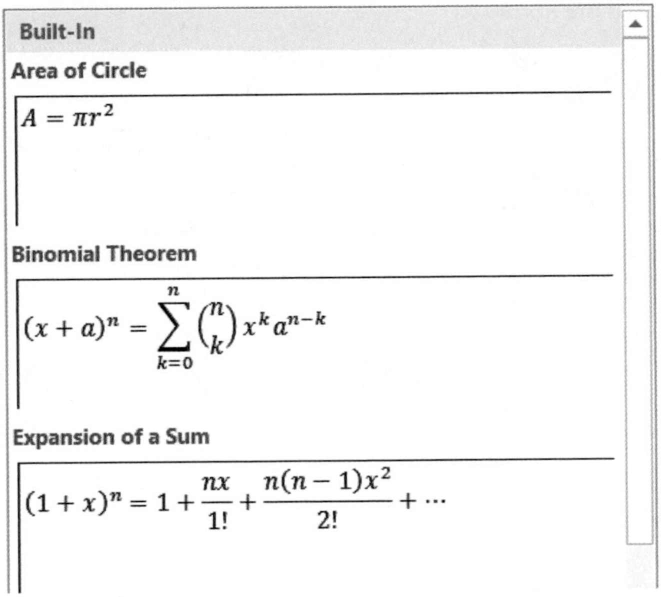

Built-In

Area of Circle

$$A = \pi r^2$$

Binomial Theorem

$$(x + a)^n = \sum_{k=0}^{n} \binom{n}{k} x^k a^{n-k}$$

Expansion of a Sum

$$(1 + x)^n = 1 + \frac{nx}{1!} + \frac{n(n-1)x^2}{2!} + \cdots$$

Clicking a predefined equation inserts it into the document at the cursor

2. In the **Insert an Equation** gallery, click the equation you want to insert.

To build an equation

1. On the **Insert** tab, in the **Symbols** group, click the **Equation** button to insert an equation field into the document.

    | Type equation here. |

    Word inserts a field in which you can build an equation

2. Enter an equation in the equation field.

To format an equation

1. Click the equation to select it.

2. Do any of the following:

    *   To change the equation to linear form, on the **Design** tool tab, in the **Tools** group, click the **Linear** button.

    *   To change the relationship of the equation with the text, do one of the following:

        *   To display the equation in line with the text rather than on its own line (the default), in the **Equation Options** list, click **Change to Inline**.

        *   If the equation is already displayed in line with the text and you want to set it apart on its own line, in the **Equation Options** list, click **Change to Display**.

    *   To change the alignment of the equation, in the **Equation Options** list, click **Justification**, and then click the alignment option you want (**Left**, **Right**, **Centered**, or **Centered as Group**).

    > ✓ **TIP** You can change the font, size, and other attributes of the equation as you would any other type of text element. Simply select the equation, right-click the selection, and choose Font from the menu that appears. The Font menu opens; change the settings as you want.

9

To save an equation

1. Click the equation to select it.

2. In the **Equation Options** list, click **Save as New Equation** to open the Create New Building Block dialog box.

3. In the **Name** box, replace the equation with a name you'll remember, and then click **OK**.

Skills review

In this chapter, you learned how to:

- Format the page background
- Insert a background watermark
- Insert headers, footers, and page numbers
- Insert preformatted document parts
- Build equations

Set mathematical AutoCorrect options

If you frequently create documents that contain mathematical formulas, you don't have to insert mathematical symbols by using the ribbon buttons. Instead, you can enter a predefined combination of characters and have Word automatically replace it with a corresponding math symbol. For example, if you enter \infty in an equation field, Word replaces the characters with the infinity symbol (∞).

This replacement is performed by the Math AutoCorrect feature. You can view all the predefined mathematical symbol descriptions by clicking the Math AutoCorrect button in the Equation Options dialog box, or by clicking Auto-Correct Options on the Proofing page of the Word Options dialog box, and then clicking the Math AutoCorrect tab.

The Math AutoCorrect feature simplifies the process of inserting mathematical symbols

You can create custom Math AutoCorrect entries in the same way you create text AutoCorrect entries. For information, see Chapter 16, "Customize options and the user interface."

Practice tasks

The practice files for these tasks are located in the Word2016SBS\Ch09 folder. You can save the results of the tasks in the same folder.

Format the page background

Create a new document in Word, and then perform the following tasks.

1. Apply a solid page background color of your choice.
2. Configure the page background to display a gradient, using any two colors of your choice and the **From Center** shading.
3. Configure the page background to display the **Woven Mat** texture.
4. Configure the page background to display the **Light Horizontal** pattern, using any two colors of your choice.
5. Configure the page background to display the **Clouds** picture from the practice file folder.
6. Remove the page background.
7. Apply a dark blue, double-line **Shadow** page border that is ½ point wide.
8. Save and close the document.

Insert a background watermark

Open the AddWatermarks document in Print Layout view, and then perform the following tasks:

1. Apply the **ASAP 2** watermark, and then remove it.
2. Create a text watermark with the text **First Draft**.
3. Style the watermark with the **Century Gothic** font and make it red, semitransparent, and horizontal.
4. Remove the watermark.
5. Begin creating a picture watermark.
6. Use the commands in the **Insert Pictures** dialog box to locate and insert the **OTSI-Logo** picture from the practice file folder.

7. Select a scale of **500%**, select the **Washout** check box, and click **OK**.

8. Save and close the document.

Insert headers, footers, and page numbers

Open the InsertHeadersFooters document in Print Layout view, and then perform the following tasks:

1. Move the cursor to the top of the first page after the cover page.

2. Insert a **Banded** header from the built-in headers menu. Notice that the title of the document appears in the header automatically.

3. Add a built-in **Banded** footer. Notice that page numbers appear in the footer automatically, and that page numbering begins on the first page after the cover page.

4. Remove the footer, leaving the header in place.

5. Activate the footer and, at the left end of the footer, insert a date that will update automatically. Use the date format of your choice.

6. Press the **Tab** key twice to move the cursor to the right end of the footer, and add page numbers in the current position in the **Large Color** style. Notice that the color matches the theme color of the document.

7. In the **Close** group, click the **Close Header and Footer** button.

8. Save and close the document.

Insert preformatted document parts

Open the InsertBuildingBlocks document in Print Layout view, and then perform the following tasks:

1. Move the cursor to the top of the document.

2. Add a **Banded** cover page, click in the **Document Title** placeholder, and enter **Office Procedures**.

3. If your name has not been entered automatically in the author placeholder, click the placeholder and enter your name.

4. Click in the **Company Name** placeholder and enter **Consolidated Messenger**.

5. Click in the **Company Address** placeholder and enter **1234 Main Street, New York, NY, 90012.**

6. On page **2** of the document, to the left of the *Warehouse* heading, insert a **Banded Quote** text box.

7. Click in the placeholder text and type **Consolidated Messenger believes in opportunity for all! We are an equal-opportunity employer.** Then click anywhere outside the text box building block.

8. Save and close the document.

Build equations

Create a new document in Word, and then perform the following tasks:

1. With the cursor on the first line of the document, insert the Pythagorean Theorem predefined equation.

2. On the next line, insert a blank equation field.

3. In the equation field, enter **(p-3)***.

4. Display the **Fraction** gallery, and click the first thumbnail in the first row (**Stacked Fraction**) to insert structured placeholders for a simple fraction in the equation field.

5. Enter **b** in the top box of the fraction structure, and enter **3** in the bottom box.

6. Change the equation to linear form.

7. Save the equation as a building block named **Additional People Cost**.

8. Display the **Insert an Equation** gallery. The equation you saved appears near the bottom of the gallery.

9. Save and close the document.

Organize and arrange content

Word 2016 provides many tools for organizing and arranging the content of a document. For example, you can use outlining tools to display the hierarchy of content within a document, and you can rearrange content in the Navigation pane and in Outline view. Word also includes positioning and alignment tools you can use to precisely position objects and control their alignment and stacking order.

You can also use the table functionality in Word to control the positions of blocks of information on the page in nested tables. For example, a table with two columns and two rows can hold a set of four paragraphs, four bulleted lists, or four tables in a format in which you can easily compare their data.

This chapter guides you through procedures related to reorganizing document outlines, arranging objects on a page, and using tables to control page layout.

In this chapter

- Reorganize document outlines
- Arrange objects on a page
- Use tables to control page layout

Practice files

For this chapter, use the practice files from the Word2016SBS\Ch10 folder. For practice file download instructions, see the introduction.

Reorganize document outlines

When you create a document, you can divide the document into logical sections by using headings. Heading styles define not only formatting but also outline levels. These outline levels are visible in the Navigation pane and also in Outline view.

> **SEE ALSO** For information about formatting headings by using styles, see "Apply built-in styles to text" in Chapter 4, "Modify the structure and appearance of text." For general information about styles, see "Create and modify styles" in Chapter 15, "Create custom document elements."

Manage content in the Navigation pane

When working in Print Layout view, you can display a hierarchical structure of the document headings in the Navigation pane. By default, the Navigation pane displays document content that is styled as Heading 1, Heading 2, or Heading 3. You can display up to nine heading levels in the Navigation pane. (The display is controlled by the outline level rather than by the heading name.) If you use custom styles, you can set the outline levels of the styles to control the Navigation pane content.

You can reorganize document content by dragging headings in the Navigation pane. You can also promote, demote, or remove sections by using commands on the Navigation pane shortcut menu.

Navigation

Search document

Headings   Pages   Results

10
Organize and arrange content
▲ Reorganize document outlines
    ▲ Manage content in the Navigation pane
            To display document structure in the Navig.   ← Pro**mo**te
            To change the outline levels displayed in th.   → De**mo**te
            To move a section in the Navigation pane
    ▲ Manage content in Outline view   New Heading **B**efore
            To display a document in Outline view   New Heading **A**fter
            To display only headings above a particular   New S**u**bheading
            To collapse a single section of an outline   ✕ **D**elete
            To expand a single section of an outline   **S**elect Heading and Content
            To display all text (expand the entire outline)   **P**rint Heading and Content
            To promote a heading   **E**xpand All
            To demote a heading   **C**ollapse All
            To move a section   Show **H**eading Levels   ▶
            To close Outline view
▲ Arrange objects on a page
            To apply a predefined position to the object

You can work with a document in the Navigation pane in much the same way you can in Outline view

10

To display the Navigation pane

1. On the **View** tab, in the **Show** group, select the **Navigation Pane** check box.

To change the outline levels displayed in the Navigation pane

1. Right-click anywhere in the **Navigation** pane, click **Show Heading Levels**, and then click the lowest outline level that you want to display.

To move a document section in the Navigation pane

2. In the **Navigation** pane, drag the heading of the section you want to move to the new location. (A bold horizontal line indicates the drop location.)

Manage content in Outline view

When you format headings by using Word's built-in heading styles, it's easy to view and organize the document in Outline view. In this view, you can hide all the body text and display only the headings at and above a particular level. You can also rearrange the sections of a document by moving their headings. When you display a document in Outline view, Word displays the document with a hierarchical structure, and the Outlining tab appears on the ribbon between the File and Home tabs.

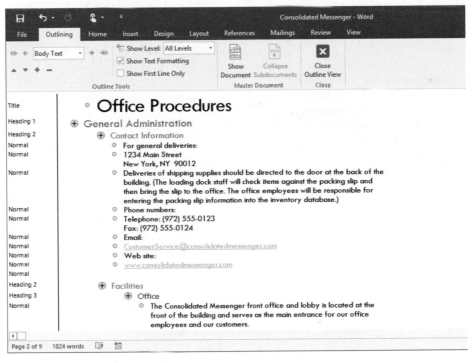

A document in Outline view

The indentations and symbols used in Outline view to indicate the level of a heading or paragraph in the document's structure don't appear in the document in other views or when you print it.

> **TIP** Word does not differentiate the Outlining tab by using a colored heading as it does for tool tabs, because Word always displays the Outlining tab in Outline view (not only when you select a specific type of content).

To easily reference paragraph styles while working in Outline view, you can display the style area pane to the left of the document. For information about displaying and resizing the style area pane, see "Display different views of documents" in Chapter 2, "Create and manage documents."

Double dotted lines indicate collapsed content

You can use commands in the Outline Tools group of the Outlining tab to do the following:

- Display only the headings at a specific level and above. Word displays a gray dotted line in the heading if the document contains text below it.

- Collapse or expand a specific heading.

- Expand the entire outline to display the document in its entirety.

- Promote or demote headings or body text by changing their level.

- Move headings and their text up or down in the document.

> **TIP** You can click the buttons in the Master Document group to create a master document with subdocuments that you can then display or hide. The topic of master documents and subdocuments is beyond the scope of this book. For information, use the Tell Me What You Want To Do text box.

10

To display a document in Outline view

1. On the **View** tab, in the **Views** group, click **Outline**.

To change the outline levels displayed in Outline view

1. Do either of the following:

    -   On the **Outlining** tab, in the **Outline Tools** group, in the **Outline Level** list, click **Level** *n*, where *n* is the lowest level of heading you want to display.

    -   Press **Alt+Shift+***n*, where *n* is the lowest level of head you want to display.

To collapse or expand a single document section in Outline view

1. Position the cursor in the heading of the section you want to collapse or expand.

2. Do either of the following:

    -   On the **Outlining** tab, in the **Outline Tools** group, click the **Collapse** or **Expand** button.

    -   Press **Alt+Shift+Minus Sign** to collapse the section or **Alt+Shift+Plus Sign** to expand the section.

To expand the entire document in Outline view

1. Do either of the following:

    -   On the **Outlining** tab, in the **Outline Tools** group, in the **Show Levels** list, click **All Levels**.

    -   Press **Alt+Shift+A**.

To promote or demote a heading in Outline view

1. Position the cursor in the heading you want to promote or demote.

2. Do either of the following:

    -   In the **Outline Tools** group, click the **Promote** or **Demote** button.

    -   Press **Alt+Shift+Left Arrow** to promote the heading or **Alt+Shift+Right Arrow** to demote the heading.

> ✓ **TIP** Promoting or demoting a heading also promotes or demotes subheadings within that section to maintain the content hierarchy.

To move a document section in Outline view

1. Click the plus sign to the left of the heading to select the section.

2. Do either of the following:

   - In the **Outline Tools** group, click the **Move Up** button or **Move Down** button as many times as necessary to move the section to the target location.

   - Press **Alt+Shift+Up Arrow** or **Alt+Shift+Down Arrow** as many times as necessary to move the section to the target location.

To close Outline view

1. On the **Outlining** tab, in the **Close** group, click the **Close Outline View** button to display the document in Print Layout view.

Arrange objects on a page

In previous chapters, you learned basic ways to position an object, such as a picture or shape, on a page. When you position an object on a page, text wraps around that object by default. You are not limited to the basic settings you've explored thus far, however. In fact, you can position objects and change text-wrap settings in several ways.

The Position gallery of layout options is available for most objects from the relevant Format tool tab. These options position the object in a specific location relative to the page margins.

10

The Position gallery offers several preconfigured position options

The Layout Options menu, which appears when you insert or select an object, provides text-wrapping options.

From the Layout Options menu, you can quickly set a text-wrapping option

The standard text-wrapping options include the following:

- **In Line with Text** As its name suggests, when you choose this option, the object is placed in line with the text. The text does not wrap around the object.

- **Square** When you choose Square, text wraps around the object in a square shape.

- **Tight** Choose this option if you want text to wrap more tightly around the object.

- **Through** The effects of this setting are most obvious when you insert an irregularly shaped object. When this option is selected, text appears to go through the object, filling in any blank spaces within it.

- **Top and Bottom** This option places the object on its own line, with no text on either side of it.

- **Behind Text** When you choose this option, the object is placed behind, or underneath, any existing text.

- **In Front of Text** This setting lays the object on top of existing text, thereby obscuring it.

You can display the Layout dialog box from either the Position menu or the Layout Options menu. The Text Wrapping tab of the Layout dialog box offers the same text-wrapping styles as the Layout Options menu. In addition, you can fine-tune text-wrapping settings—for example, indicating whether text should wrap on both sides of the object and how far the object should be from the text.

10

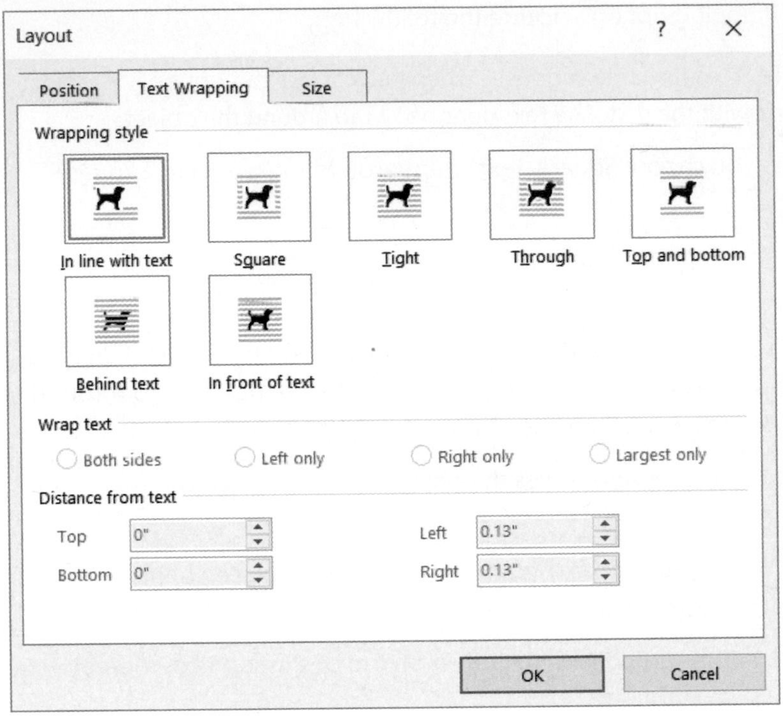

Layout   ?   ✕

Position | Text Wrapping | Size

Wrapping style

In line with text   Square   Tight   Through   Top and bottom

Behind text   In front of text

Wrap text
○ Both sides   ○ Left only   ○ Right only   ○ Largest only

Distance from text
Top   0"   Left   0.13"
Bottom 0"   Right 0.13"

OK   Cancel

For more exact text wrapping, configure the settings on this tab

For more position settings, including settings you can use to specify whether the position is absolute or relative (more on that in a moment), you can use the commands on the Position tab of the Layout dialog box. The available positions vary based on the selected text-wrapping option.

You can fine-tune position settings here

When you choose a text-wrapping option other than In Line With Text, you can specify that an object be positioned in a specific location on the page or relative to a page element, or you can anchor it to a paragraph so it moves with the content.

You can also use alignment commands to align objects with the margins and with each other. You can access these commands from the Align menu on the Format tool tab.

10

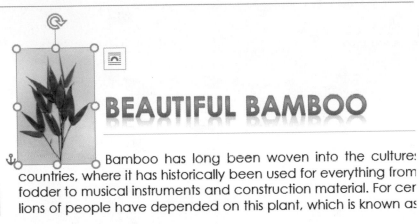

The picture is aligned with the top and left page margins

You can move an object manually by dragging it to another position on the page. To assist you in aligning objects, you can display a grid that divides the page content area into squares of specific dimensions.

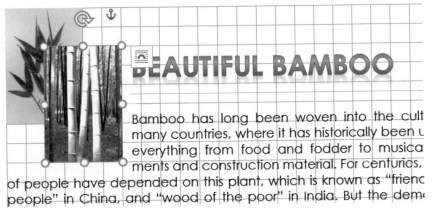

You can display a grid to help with aligning objects

You can change the grid settings in the Grid And Guides dialog box. You can choose whether to display alignment guides, such as margins, and whether items should be *snapped*, or automatically aligned, to the grid or to other objects. You can also change the size of the grid.

If you insert several objects and then position them so that they overlap, they are said to be *stacked*. The stacking order (which object appears on top of which) is initially determined by the order in which you inserted the objects, but it can also be determined by other factors, such as the type of text wrapping assigned to each object. If all the objects have the same kind of text wrapping, you can change their order. You do so by using buttons in the Arrange group on the Format tool tab, or from the Selection pane, which displays a list of all the objects on the page.

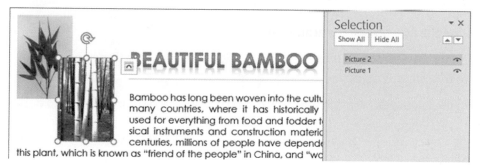

You can manage objects from the Selection pane

To display the Selection pane

1. Do either of the following:

   - On the **Home** tab, in the **Editing** group, click **Select**, and then in the list, click **Selection Pane**.

   - Select the object. Then on the **Format** tool tab, in the **Arrange** group, click the **Selection Pane** button.

To select an object

1. Do either of the following:

   - On the page, click the object.

   - In the **Selection** pane, click the object's name.

To position an object on a page

1. Select the object.

2. On the **Format** tool tab, in the **Arrange** group, click the **Position** button to display the Position gallery and menu.

10

3. In the **Position** gallery, point to a thumbnail to display a live preview of that option's effect on the position of the object. When you find the position you like, click the corresponding thumbnail.

Or

On the **Position** menu, click **More Layout Options** to display the **Position** tab of the **Layout** dialog box. In the **Horizontal** and **Vertical** areas, specify the absolute or relative position you want. Then click **OK**.

To change the way text wraps around an object

1. Select the object, and then click the **Layout Options** button that appears next to the selected object.

2. In the **Layout Options** gallery, click the text-wrapping option you want to apply.

Or

1. Select the object.

2. On the **Format** tool tab, in the **Arrange** group, click the **Wrap Text** button and then click **More Layout Options** to open the Layout dialog box with the Text Wrapping tab displayed.

3. In the **Wrapping Style** area, choose the text wrapping you want to apply.

4. In the **Wrap Text** area, indicate whether the text should wrap on both sides, on the left side only, on the right side only, or on the largest side only.

5. In the **Distance from Text** area, specify the minimum distance between each side of the object and the text.

6. Click **OK**.

To anchor an object to a paragraph or page

1. Position the object next to or within the paragraph you want to anchor it to, or in the position that you want to anchor it.

2. Select the object.

3. On the **Format** tool tab, in the **Arrange** group, click the **Wrap Text** button, and then do either of the following:

   - To anchor the object to the paragraph, click **Move with Text**.

   - To anchor the object to the page location, click **Fix Position on Page**.

To align an object on the page

1. Select the object.

2. On the **Format** tool tab, in the **Arrange** group, click the **Align Objects** button to display the Align menu.

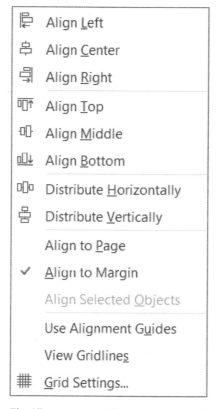

The Align menu provides easy access to all the alignment options

3. Click one of the six **Align** options at the top of the menu.

> ✅ **TIP** When objects have a text-wrapping setting other than In Line With Text, you can use the options on the Align menu to align multiple objects horizontally or vertically. You can also distribute selected objects equally between the first and last objects in the selection.

To display or hide gridlines in the content area

1. On the **Format** tool tab, in the **Arrange** group, click the **Align Objects** button, and then click **View Gridlines**.

To change grid settings

1. On the **Format** tool tab, in the **Arrange** group, click the **Align Objects** button, and then click **Grid Settings** to open the Grid And Guides dialog box.

You can specify the location and functionality of the on-screen alignment guides and grid

2. Make any changes you want, and then click **OK**.

To manually move an object

1. Select the object.

2. Drag the selected object to the target location.

> **TIP** If the grid is displayed and has been configured to allow snapping, the object will snap to the nearest gridline when it is dropped. To move an object without snapping it to the grid, hold down the Ctrl key while pressing an arrow key. The object will move in tiny increments.

To change the stacking order of objects

1. Select the object that you want to move.

2. On the **Format** tool tab, in the **Arrange** group, do one of the following:

    - Click the **Bring Forward** button to move the selected object one position closer to the top of the stack.

    - In the **Bring Forward** list, click **Bring to Front** to move the object to the top of the stack.

    - Click the **Send Backward** button to move the selected object one position closer to the bottom of the stack.

    - In the **Send Backward** list, click **Send to Back** to move the object to the bottom of the stack.

To hide objects on the page

1. Open the **Selection** pane. The eye icon to the right of each object indicates that it is currently visible on the page.

2. In the **Selection** pane, do either of the following:

    - To hide one object, click the eye icon to the right of the object name.

    - To hide all the objects in the document, click the **Hide All** button.

    The eye icon changes to a small horizontal bar to indicate that an object is hidden.

To display hidden objects

1. In the **Selection** pane, do either of the following:

    - To display one object, click the bar icon to the right of the object's name.

    - To display all the objects in the document, click the **Show All** button.

10

Use tables to control page layout

Most people are accustomed to thinking of a table as a means of displaying data in a quick, easy-to-grasp format. But tables can also serve to organize content in creative ways. For example, suppose you want to display two tables next to each other. The simplest way to do this is to first create a page-width table that has only one row and two columns, and then insert one of the tables you want to display in the first cell and the other table in the second cell. When the outer table borders are hidden, these nested tables appear side by side.

Consultation Fee		Trip Charges	
Location	Hourly Rate	Distance	Fee
In home	$50.00	0-10 miles	No charge
Phone	$35.00	11-20 miles	$10.00
In store	$40.00	Over 20 miles	$20.00

These tables are nested within the cells of a one-row, two-column table

As with regular tables, you can create a nested table in one of three ways:

- From scratch
- By formatting existing information
- By inserting Microsoft Excel data

And just like with other tables, you can format a nested table either manually or by using one of the ready-made table styles.

> **TIP** You can use tables to organize a mixture of elements such as text, tables, charts, and diagrams. For more information about creating tables, see Chapter 5, "Organize information in columns and tables."

If you are designing your document with accessibility in mind, be aware that screen readers and other assistive devices access content linearly—from left to right, row by row—whereas you might expect a person looking at the table to read its content from top to bottom, column by column. Some screen readers have a table reading mode that can help to ameliorate this problem, so if you're arranging content by using a simple table layout, this won't present as much of an issue (although the content meaning might still be less clear than when presented in normal text or in a list). If you create a fancy table layout that includes cells of varying heights and widths, with some merged cells and some split cells, it's likely that the screen reader will access and deliver the content out of order. Keep this in mind if you intend to deliver your content in an electronic format, and certainly if your organization is required to adhere to accessibility standards.

To create a nested table

1. In a document, position the cursor where you want to insert the nested table.

2. On the **Insert** tab, in the **Tables** group, click the **Table** button.

3. In the **Insert Table** gallery, click the box corresponding to the size of table you want for the container table.

> **IMPORTANT** It's inadvisable to create a container table of more than two columns. The procedures in this topic assume a two-column container table.

4. Create or locate the first table you want to nest within the container table, and click anywhere within it.

5. On the **Layout** tool tab, in the **Table** group, click **Select**, and then click **Select Table**.

6. On the **Home** tab, in the **Clipboard** group, click the **Cut** or **Copy** button to move or copy the selected table to the Clipboard.

> **TIP** Press Ctrl+C to copy the selected content to the Clipboard.

7. In the container table, right-click the left table cell, and then under **Paste Options**, click the **Nest Table** button to insert the table you copied into the cell and adjust the height of the container table to fit the nested table.

8. Create or locate the second table you want to nest within the container table, and then cut or copy the table to the Clipboard.

9. In the container table, click the right table cell, and then on the **Home** tab, in the **Clipboard** group, click the **Paste** button to insert the second table as a nested table.

> **TIP** Press Ctrl+V to paste the most recently copied content from the Clipboard.

10

To format a nested table

1. Point to the container table, and then click the table selector that appears just outside of its upper-left corner to select the table. (Be sure you select the container table and not the nested table.)

2. On the **Design** tool tab, in the **Borders** group, in the **Borders** list, click **No Border** to remove the borders from the container cells.

Skills review

In this chapter, you learned how to:

- Reorganize document outlines

- Arrange objects on a page

- Use tables to control page layout

Practice tasks

The practice files for these tasks are located in the Word2016SBS\Ch10 folder. You can save the results of the tasks in the same folder.

Reorganize document outlines

Open the ReorganizeOutlines document in Print Layout view, and then perform the following tasks:

1. Display the document in Outline view.

2. In the **Word Options** dialog box, set the style area pane width to 1", and then return to the document.

3. Use the commands on the **Outlining** tab to display only level 1 headings.

4. Expand the **General Administration** section, and then collapse it again.

5. Show all levels of the outline.

6. Promote the **Contact Information** heading to level 1, and then demote it back to level 2.

7. Move the **Warehouse** section up so that the heading and the text within it appear above the Office heading.

8. Close the outline to display the document in Print Layout view.

9. Open the **Navigation** pane.

10. In the **Navigation** pane, drag the Warehouse heading back to its original location, below the Office section.

11. Close the document, saving your changes if you want.

Arrange objects on a page

Open the ArrangeObjects document in Print Layout view, display formatting marks, and then perform the following tasks:

1. With the cursor next to the first word in the second paragraph, *There*, insert the **Bamboo1** picture from the practice file folder.

2. Use the buttons in the **Position** gallery to position the picture in the top center of the page, with square text wrapping.

3. Use the picture's **Layout Options** menu to set the text wrapping to **Tight**.

4. Use the commands on the **Text Wrapping** tab of the **Layout** dialog box to set the text wrapping to **Right only**, with the distance from text **0.5** on all sides.

5. Use the commands on the **Position** tab of the **Layout** dialog box to set the picture at a horizontal absolute position that is 2 inches to the right of the left margin, and a vertical absolute position that is 2 inches below the top margin.

6. With the cursor again next to the first word in the second paragraph, insert the **Bamboo2** picture from the practice file folder.

7. Use the buttons in the **Position** gallery to position the picture in the middle of the page, with square text wrapping.

8. Anchor the picture so that it moves with the text.

9. Select the paragraph containing the **Bamboo2** picture and move it to the end of the document. Notice that the picture moves with the paragraph.

10. Undo the move.

11. Anchor the picture so that it is in a fixed position on the page.

12. Select the paragraph containing the **Bamboo2** picture and move it to the end of the document. Notice that this time, the picture stays where it was on the page.

13. Undo the move.

14. Use the commands on the **Align Objects** menu to align the **Bamboo2** picture on the left side of the page.

15. Display the gridlines.

16. Drag the **Bamboo2** picture to the upper-left corner of the document, on top of the **Bamboo1** picture, using gridlines to align it.

17. Hide the gridlines.

18. Bring the **Bamboo1** picture to the front of the stack.

19. Open the **Selection** pane, and use it to hide either picture. Notice that the eye icon changes to a small horizontal bar to indicate that the object is hidden.

20. Redisplay the object.

21. Close the document, saving your changes if you want.

Use tables to control page layout

Open the ControlLayout document in Print Layout view, display formatting marks, and then perform the following tasks:

1. With the cursor on the line above the *Consultation Fee* table, insert a table that contains two columns and one row.

2. Cut the *Consultation Fee* table, and right-click in the left cell of the table you just created.

3. Use the options on the shortcut menu to nest the table into the container table.

4. Cut the *Trip Charges* table, and then click (don't right-click) in the right table cell of the container table.

5. Use any method described in this chapter to nest the *Trip Charges* table into the container table.

6. Remove the borders from the container table.

7. Close the document, saving your changes if you want.

Part 4

Review and finalize documents

Collaborate on documents

11

It's not unusual for several people to collaborate on the development of a document. Collaboration is simplest when contributors review electronic documents in files on a computer screen rather than paper printouts. On-screen review is very efficient; you can provide legible feedback, implement specific changes, and save trees at the same time.

One way to gather feedback from multiple reviewers is to send a file to each reviewer and then merge the reviewed versions into one file that displays all the changes for your review. If you save a file in a shared location, multiple people can review and edit the document at the same time. This highly efficient method of collaboration is called coauthoring.

Word 2016 has many tools that simplify document collaboration processes. You can make changes without deleting the original content, provide feedback in comments, and respond to comments and queries from other reviewers. To protect a document from unwanted changes, you can restrict the editing options so that Word tracks all changes, allows only certain types of changes, or doesn't allow changes at all.

This chapter guides you through procedures related to marking up and reviewing documents, comparing and merging document versions, restricting the changes that people can make to documents that you share with them, and coauthoring documents.

In this chapter

- Mark up documents
- Display and review document markup
- Compare and merge documents
- Control content changes
- Coauthor documents

Practice files

For this chapter, use the practice files from the Word2016SBS\Ch11 folder. For practice file download instructions, see the introduction.

Mark up documents

Comments and tracked changes are collectively referred to as *markup*.

Insert comments

A comment is a note that is attached to an anchor within the text. The anchor can be text or any type of object, or simply a location; wherever it is, Word displays the comment in the right margin of the document.

> You can configure a document to track all changes that people make, or you can specify the types of changes that are allowed. If you want other people to review a document but not change it, you can protect the document content with a password.
>
> This chapter guides you through procedures related to marking up and reviewing documents, comparing and merging document versions, restricting the changes that people can make to documents you share with them, and coauthoring documents.

> **Joan Lambert** 6 minutes ago
> CE: I paraphrased this a bit because the chapter opener page content is a bit longer than we can probably support.

Word automatically adds your name and a time stamp to the comment

Each comment is inside a container that is visible only when the comment is active (when you point to or click it). Comment containers are referred to as *balloons*. Balloons can be used for the display of various types of markup.

When comments are hidden, the hidden comments are indicated by conversation bubble icons.

> This chapter guides you through procedures related to marking up and reviewing documents, comparing and merging document versions, restricting the changes that people can make to documents you share with them, and coauthoring documents.

The conversation bubble indicates a hidden comment

You can insert comments for many reasons, such as to ask questions, make suggestions, provide reference information, or explain edits. You insert and work with comments by using the commands in the Comments group on the Review tab.

The commands in the Comments group make it easy to navigate through and remove comments

Multiple people can insert comments in a document. Word assigns a color to each person's comments and uses that color for the markup associated with comments, insertions, deletions, and formatting changes. (The color is assigned by user name, so if two people have the same user name their markup will be the same color.)

If you prefer to select specific colors and effects for comments and various types of markup, you can do so.

Advanced Track Changes Options		?	X
Insertions: Underline	**Color:** By author		
Deletions: Strikethrough	**Color:** By author		
Changed lines: Outside border			
Comments: By author			
☑ **Track moves**			
Moved from: Double strikethrough	**Color:** Green		
Moved to: Double underline	**Color:** Green		
Inserted cells: Light Blue	**Merged cells:** Light Yellow		
Deleted cells: Pink	**Split cells:** Light Orange		
☑ **Track formatting**			
Formatting: (none)	**Color:** By author		
Preferred width: 3.7"	**Measure in:** Inches		
Margin: Right			
☑ **Show lines connecting to text**			
Paper orientation in printing: Preserve			
OK	Cancel		

You can modify the types of changes that are tracked and the markup colors

Word uses standard colors to mark moved content and changes to table cells but doesn't track the editor, time, or date of the change. It is possible to customize these markup colors, but there really isn't any point to doing so because the custom colors won't travel with the document.

 TIP Display documents in Print Layout view so that all the collaboration commands are available.

11

To insert a comment

1. Select the text or object you want to anchor the comment to.

2. On the **Review** tab, in the **Comments** group, click the **New Comment** button.

3. In the comment balloon that appears in the right margin or in the **Revisions** pane, enter or paste your comment.

> **TIP** Comments are usually simple text but can include other elements and formatting such as images and active hyperlinks.

To specify the color of comments that you insert in any document

1. On the **Review** tab, click the **Tracking** dialog box launcher to open the **Track Changes Options** dialog box.

2. Click the **Advanced Options** button to open the **Advanced Track Changes Options** dialog box.

3. Click the arrow to the right of the **Comments** list to display a list of colors.

The named colors in the list are independent of the document color scheme and will not change between documents

4. In the **Comments** list, click the color you want to use for all the comments you insert in Word documents on the current computer.

5. Click **OK** in each open dialog box to close them and save your change.

Track changes

When two or more people collaborate on a document, one person usually creates and "owns" the document and the others review it, adding or revising content to make it more accurate, logical, or readable. When reviewing a document in Word, you can track your changes so they are available for review and retain the original text for comparison or reversion. You manage change tracking from the Tracking group on the Review tab.

A shaded button indicates that change tracking is active

> **TIP** Turning on the change tracking feature tracks changes in only the active document, not in any other open documents.

Word tracks insertions, deletions, movement, and formatting of content. When you display a document in All Markup view, tracked changes are indicated by different font colors and formatting. The default formatting is as follows:

- Insertions are underlined and in the color assigned to the reviewer.

- Deletions are crossed out and in the color assigned to the reviewer.

- Formatting changes appear in balloons in the markup area.

- Moves are double-underlined and green.

- All changes are marked in the left margin by a vertical line.

Moved text is green, and a double underline indicates its new location

As with comments, multiple people can track changes in a document. Word assigns a color to each person's changes and uses that color to format inserted and deleted text. If you prefer to select a color for your own changes, you can do so. You can also modify the formatting that indicates each type of change—for example, you could have Word indicate inserted text by formatting it as bold, italic, or with a double underline, but that change would be valid only for your profile on the computer you make the change on and would not affect the change formatting on other computers.

If you want to ensure that other reviewers track their changes to a document, you can turn on and lock the change-tracking feature and (optionally) require that reviewers enter a password to turn off change tracking.

 SEE ALSO For information about forcing change tracking by restricting editing, see "Control content changes" later in this chapter.

To turn change tracking on or off

1. Do either of the following:

   - On the **Review** tab, in the **Tracking** group, click the **Track Changes** button (not its arrow).

   - Press **Ctrl+Shift+E**.

    SEE ALSO For information about locking the change-tracking feature, see "Control content changes" later in this chapter. For information about keyboard shortcuts, see the "Keyboard shortcuts" section at the end of this book.

To track changes without displaying them on the screen

1. On the **Review** tab, in the **Tracking** group, click the **Display for Review** arrow.

2. In the **Display for Review** list, click **Simple Markup** or **No Markup**.

    SEE ALSO For more information about the markup views, see "Display and review document markup" later in this chapter.

To specify the color of the changes you track in any document

1. On the **Review** tab, click the **Tracking** dialog box launcher to open the **Track Changes Options** dialog box.

2. Click the **Advanced Options** button to open the **Advanced Track Changes Options** dialog box.

3. In the **Color** lists adjacent to **Insertions**, **Deletions**, and **Formatting**, click the color you want to use for that type of change in Word documents on the current computer.

4. Click **OK** in each open dialog box to close them and save your changes.

To prevent reviewers from turning off change tracking

1. On the **Review** tab, in the **Tracking** group, click the **Track Changes** arrow, and then click **Lock Tracking**.

2. In the **Lock Tracking** dialog box, enter and reenter a password to prevent other people from turning off this feature.

Lock Tracking	?	✕

Prevent other authors from turning off Track Changes.

Enter password (optional): `****`

Reenter to confirm: `****`

(This is not a security feature.)

OK Cancel

Use a password that you will remember, or make a note of it in a secure location so you can find it later

3. In the **Lock Tracking** dialog box, click **OK**.

To unlock change tracking

1. On the **Review** tab, in the **Tracking** group, click the **Track Changes** arrow, and then click **Lock Tracking**.

2. In the **Unlock Tracking** dialog box, enter the password you assigned when you enabled this feature, and then click **OK**.

Unlock Tracking	?	X
Password: ****		
OK	Cancel	

Unlocking tracking doesn't turn off change tracking; you must do that separately

Display and review document markup

After reviewers provide feedback by making changes and entering comments, you can review and process the tracked changes and comments.

Display markup

Usually you would display and review all the markup at one time, but you can also choose to display only certain types of markup, or only markup from specific reviewers.

Word 2016 has four basic Display For Review options that govern the display of tracked changes in a document. The settings are:

- **Simple Markup** This default markup view displays a red vertical line in the left margin adjacent to each tracked change. Markup is hidden.

- **All Markup** This view displays a gray vertical line in the left margin adjacent to each tracked change, and formats inserted, deleted, and moved content as configured in the Advanced Track Changes Options dialog box.

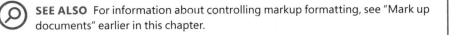

> **SEE ALSO** For information about controlling markup formatting, see "Mark up documents" earlier in this chapter.

- **No Markup** This view hides comments and displays the current document content as though all changes have been accepted. Changes that you make in this view are tracked (if change tracking is turned on) and visible when markup is shown.

- **Original** This view displays the original document content without any markup.

Depending on your view settings, comments are shown in the following ways:

- In balloons in the right margin

- Hidden and indicated by a comment icon in the right margin

- Hidden and indicated by highlighting in the text

You can click the comment icon or point to the highlight to display the comment text.

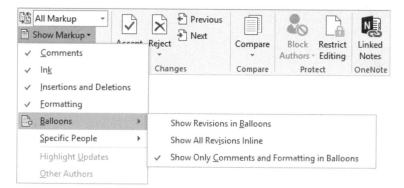

The individual markup display options

After you select a Display For Review option, you can additionally filter the display of markup in these ways:

- You can individually control the display of comments, insertions and deletions, and formatting.

- You can show all markup inline or in balloons, or keep comments in balloons and insertions, deletions, and moves inline.

- You can display or hide markup by reviewer.

If you prefer to display all the comments and tracked changes in a document at one time, you can do so in the Revisions pane. By default, this pane opens to the left of the document text (and to the right of the Navigation pane, if that is open) at the same height as the document content area. If you want to, you can dock it to the right side of the window instead.

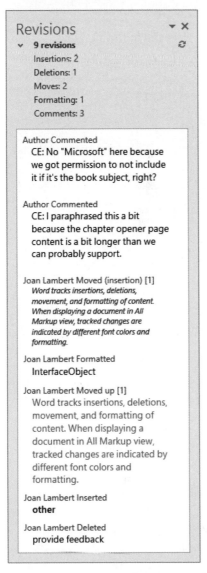

Information about the number and type of revisions is available at the top of the pane

From the ribbon, you can also display the Revisions pane horizontally. By default, the horizontal pane stretches across the bottom of the Word app window. If you want to, you can drag it to the top of the window.

You can display the pane vertically or horizontally

When the Revisions pane is docked, the document content display area becomes narrower or shorter to make space for the pane. You can undock the pane so that it floats independently of the app window and doesn't decrease the content pane size. The floating pane has a vertical format, but you can change its height and width to fit wherever it's convenient.

The best display location depends on the amount of space you have available on your device screen.

To change the display of markup in a document

1. On the **Review** tab, in the **Tracking** group, click the **Display for Review** arrow.

2. In the **Display for Review** list, click **Simple Markup**, **All Markup**, **No Markup**, or **Original**.

Or

1. To switch between Simple Markup view and All Markup view, click the red or gray vertical line in the margin to the left of any tracked change.

To display specific types of markup in balloons

1. In the **Display for Review** list, click **All Markup**.

2. In the **Show Markup** list, click **Balloons**, and then click **Show Revisions in Balloons**, **Show All Revisions Inline**, or **Show Only Comments and Formatting in Balloons**.

11

To hide or display all markup of a specific type

1. On the **Review** tab, in the **Tracking** group, click the **Show Markup** button, and then click **Comments, Ink, Insertions and Deletions**, or **Formatting**.

> **TIP** A check mark to the left of a markup type indicates that elements of that type are visible in views of the document that display those elements.

To display only markup by a specific person

1. On the **Review** tab, in the **Tracking** group, click the **Show Markup** button.

2. In the **Show Markup** list, click **Specific People**, and then click the name of any reviewer whose comments you don't want to display.

To display individual comments in Simple Markup view

1. Do any of the following:

   - Click a comment icon to display the comments on that line in comment balloons.

   - Point to a comment icon to highlight the comments on that line in the colors associated with the comments' authors.

   > **TIP** The reviewer name is taken from the user information stored with the user account. If you're signed in to Word with a Microsoft account, Word tracks revisions by the name associated with your Microsoft account. If the instance of Word you're working in is not linked to a Microsoft account, you can change the stored user information on the General page of the Word Options dialog box. Changing your user information affects revision tracking only when you aren't signed in with a Microsoft account.

   - Right-click highlighted, commented text, and then click **Edit Comment** to display only that comment in a comment balloon.

To display the Revisions pane

1. On the **Review** tab, in the **Tracking** group, click the **Reviewing Pane** button.

> ✓ **TIP** Clicking the button opens the Revisions pane in its most recent location. The default location in each new Word session is to the left of the page.

Or

1. In the **Tracking** group, click the **Reviewing Pane** arrow.

2. In the **Reviewing Pane** list, do either of the following:

   - Click **Reviewing Pane Vertical** to display the pane to the left or right of the document.

   - Click **Reviewing Pane Horizontal** to display the pane below the ribbon or above the status bar.

To change the location of the Revisions pane

1. Drag the pane by its header to any of the following locations:

   - Dock the pane vertically to the left or right side of the app window or against any other vertical pane,

   - Dock the pane horizontally below the ribbon or above the status bar.

   - Drag the pane inside or outside the app window to float it independently.

To change the width or height of the Revisions pane

1. Point to the right or top border of the pane.

2. When the pointer changes to a double-headed arrow, drag the border.

To display a breakdown of revision types

1. In the **Revisions** pane, to the left of the total number of revisions, click the **Expand** button (the caret symbol).

11

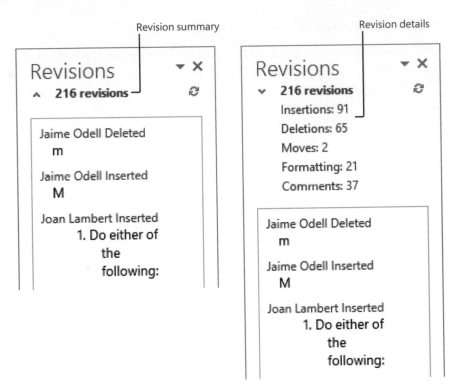

You can display a detailed list of revisions by type

To close the Revisions pane

1. Do either of the following:

    - In the upper-right corner of the pane, click the **Close** button.

    - On the **Review** tab, in the **Tracking** group, click the **Reviewing Pane** button.

Review and respond to comments

All the comments that are in a document are available for review, regardless of who created them. You can scroll through a document and review the comments as you come to them, or you can jump from comment to comment by clicking buttons on the ribbon.

> ✓ **TIP** If a document contains both comments and tracked changes, clicking the Next or Previous button in the Changes group on the Review tab moves sequentially among these elements, whereas clicking the Next or Previous button in the Comments group moves only among comments.

When reviewing comments, you can take the following actions:

- Respond to individual comments to provide further information or request clarification.

- Mark individual comments as Done to indicate that you've processed them, and retain them for later reference.

- Delete individual comments that you no longer require.

- Filter the comments by author and then delete all visible comments at the same time.

- Delete all comments in the document at the same time.

The purpose of each of these options is fairly clear. The ability to mark comments as Done was introduced in Word 2013 and is a useful feature, particularly if everyone on your review team is running Word 2013 or Word 2016. Marking a comment as Done leaves the comment intact but minimizes and recolors the comment elements so that it doesn't distract from the document content in the way that an active comment would.

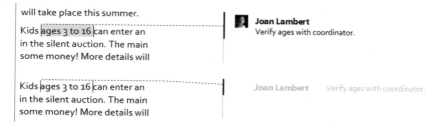

An example of a tracked comment before and after being marked as Done

To move among only comments

1. Do any of the following:

   - On the **Review** tab, in the **Comments** group, click the **Next** or **Previous** button to jump from balloon to balloon.

   - In the **Revisions** pane, click any comment to move to that comment in the document.

   - Scroll through the document to visually locate comment balloons.

11

To activate a comment for editing

1. Click the comment balloon.

2. Right-click the commented text, and then click **Edit Comment**.

To respond to a comment

1. In the upper-right corner of the comment balloon, click the **Reply to Comment** icon to create an indented response marked with your name and the time and date.

   Or

   Right-click the comment, and then click **Reply to Comment**.

2. Enter your additional comments, and then click away from the comment balloon to finish.

> **TIP** Word 2010 and earlier versions of Word will display your response in a separate comment balloon rather than in the original balloon.

To mark a comment as Done or reactivate a Done comment

1. Right-click the comment highlight (in the text) or balloon (in the margin), and then click **Mark Comment Done**.

To delete a comment

1. Do any of the following:

   - Click the comment balloon, and then click the **Delete** button in the **Comments** group.

   - Right-click the comment balloon, and then click **Delete Comment**.

   - Right-click the comment highlight (in the text), and then click **Delete Comment**.

Review and process tracked changes

As with comments, you can scroll through a document and review insertions, deletions, content moves, and formatting changes as you come to them, or you can jump from change to change by clicking buttons on the ribbon. You also have the option of accepting or rejecting multiple changes at the same time.

Here are the typical scenarios for reviewing and processing changes that you might consider:

- Display a document in Simple Markup view or No Markup view so you're viewing the final content. If you are happy with the document content in that view, accept all the changes at the same time.

- Display a document in All Markup view. Scan the individual changes visually. Individually reject any change that doesn't meet your requirements. As you complete the review of a section that meets your requirements, select the content of that section and approve all the changes within your selection.

- Display a document in All Markup view. Move to the first change. Accept or reject the change and move to the next. (You can perform both actions with one click.)

When reviewing tracked changes, you can take the following actions:

- Accept or reject individual changes.

- Select a section of content and accept or reject all changes therein at the same time.

- Filter the changes and then accept or reject all visible changes at the same time.

- Accept or reject all changes in the document at the same time.

To move among tracked changes and comments

1. Do either of the following:

   - On the **Review** tab, in the **Changes** group, click the **Next** or **Previous** button.

   - In the **Revisions** pane, click any comment to move to that comment in the document.

To display the time and author of a tracked change

1. Point to any revision in the text to display a ScreenTip identifying the name of the reviewer who made a specific change, and when the change was made.

To incorporate a selected change into the document and move to the next change

1. On the **Review** tab, in the **Changes** group, click the **Accept** button.

Or

11

1. On the **Review** tab, in the **Changes** group, click the **Accept** arrow.

2. In the **Accept** list, click **Accept and Move to Next**.

To incorporate a selected change into the document and remain in the same location

1. Do either of the following:

   - Right-click the change, and then click **Accept Deletion** or **Accept Insertion**.

   - On the **Review** tab, in the **Accept** list, click **Accept This Change**.

To remove the selected change, restore the original text, and move to the next change

1. Do either of the following:

   - On the **Review** tab, in the **Changes** group, click the **Reject** button.

   - On the **Review** tab, in the **Reject** list, click **Reject and Move to Next**.

To remove the selected change, restore the original text, and remain in the same location

1. On the **Review** tab, in the **Reject** list, click **Reject This Change**.

To accept or reject all the changes in a section of text

1. Select the text.

2. Do either of the following:

   - On the **Review** tab, in the **Changes** group, click the **Accept** button or the **Reject** button.

   - Right-click the selected text, and then click **Accept Deletion** or **Reject Deletion**.

To accept or reject all the changes in a document

1. Do either of the following:

   - On the **Review** tab, in the **Accept** list, click **Accept All Changes**.

   - On the **Review** tab, in the **Reject** list, click **Reject All Changes**.

To accept or reject all the changes of a certain type or from a certain reviewer

1. Configure the review display settings to display only the changes you want to accept or reject.

2. Do either of the following:

    - On the **Review** tab, in the **Accept** list, click **Accept All Changes Shown**.

    - On the **Review** tab, in the **Reject** list, click **Reject All Changes Shown**.

Remember to check for errors

It's a good idea to check for spelling issues in a document after you finish processing changes because it's easy to accidentally end up with a missing or extra space in the document. If the Check Spelling As You Type option is on (as it is by default), you can scroll through the document and visually scan for wavy red underlines that indicate suspected spelling errors or wavy blue underlines that indicate suspected grammar errors. Or to be entirely thorough, you can run the Spelling & Grammar tool and respond to each issue it identifies.

SEE ALSO For more information about checking spelling and grammar, see "Locate and correct text errors" in Chapter 12, "Finalize and distribute documents."

11

Compare and merge documents

Sometimes you might want to compare several versions of the same document. Word supports two types of document version comparison:

- Comparing a document to a separate copy of the document

- Comparing a document to a previous version of the same document

Compare and combine separate copies of a document

If you have sent a document out for soft-copy review by several colleagues, you might want to compare their edited versions with the original document. Or if you've made changes to a document and want to compare it to a previous version of the document, you can do so.

Instead of comparing multiple open documents visually, you can tell Word to compare the documents and merge the changes into one document. From within that one document, you can view all the changes from all the reviewers or view only those from a specific reviewer.

When you compare documents, Word generates a composite document in the center pane and displays the two original documents on the right. Differences between the documents, and changes that were tracked in either original document, are shown as tracked changes in the composite document and in the Revisions pane.

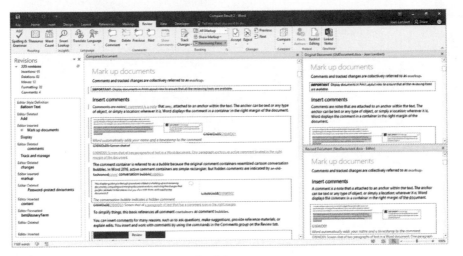

Scrolling any one of the documents scrolls all three

> **TIP** Word can't compare or combine documents that have Protection turned on.

You can compare any two documents. To compare multiple edited documents to one original, combine all the edited documents and then compare them with the original.

To compare or combine two documents and annotate changes

1. Start from a blank document or any existing document.

2. On the **Review** tab, in the **Compare** group, click **Compare** to track changes from only one document or **Combine** to track changes from both documents.

3. In the **Compare Documents** or **Combine Documents** dialog box, under **Original document**, click the arrow to expand the list. The list contains files you've recently worked with listed in alphabetical order.

4. If the document you want to designate as the first document appears in the list, click it. If not, click **Browse** (the first item in the list) to display the **Open** dialog box. In the dialog box, navigate to the document you want, click it, and then click **Open**.

5. Use the same technique in the **Revised document** area to select the document you want to designate as the second document.

6. In the **Label changes with** box or boxes, enter the name or names you want Word to assign as the reviewer when marking differences between the documents.

> **TIP** When comparing documents, you specify the reviewer for only the revised document; when combining documents, you specify reviewers for both documents.

11

Compare Documents	? ✕
Original document	**Revised document**
OldDocument.docx	NewDocument.docx
Label changes with	**Label changes with** Editor

⇄

| << **Less** | OK | Cancel |

Comparison settings
- ☑ Insertions and deletions
- ☑ Mo**v**es
- ☑ Comme**n**ts
- ☑ **F**ormatting
- ☑ Case chan**g**es
- ☑ White s**p**ace

- ☑ **T**ables
- ☑ **H**eaders and footers
- ☑ Footnotes and en**d**notes
- ☑ Te**x**tboxes
- ☑ Field**s**

Show changes

Show changes at:
- ○ **C**haracter level
- ◉ **W**ord level

Show changes in:
- ○ Original documen**t**
- ○ Re**v**ised document
- ◉ New do**c**ument

You can indicate what types of differences to identify and how to label them

7. If the dialog box doesn't include the **Comparison settings** and **Show changes** areas, click the **More** button to display them.

8. In the **Comparison settings** area of the dialog box, select the check boxes of the content differences you want to annotate.

> ✓ **TIP** By default, Word marks changes at the word level in a new document. You have the option to show changes at the character level and to show them in one of the two documents rather than in a third document. Until you're comfortable with the compare and combine operations, it's safest to retain the default settings in the Show Changes area.

9. In the **Compare Documents** or **Combine Documents** dialog box, click **OK** to create the combined document and display the combined and original documents.

> ✓ **TIP** If you compare documents that contain conflicting formatting, a message box will ask you to confirm which document's formatting should be used.

> ⚠ **IMPORTANT** If the Revisions pane does not open, click the Reviewing Pane button in the Tracking group on the Review tab. If the source documents are not displayed, click the Compare button, click Show Source Documents, and then click Show Both.

Compare separate versions of a document

Word automatically saves a temporary copy of your open documents every 10 minutes. Automatically saved versions of the document are displayed in the Manage Document area of the Info page of the Backstage view.

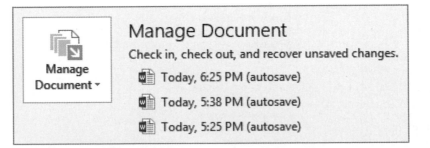

The ability to look back at an earlier version of a document you've heavily revised can come in handy

To display a previous version of a document

1. On the **Info** page of the Backstage view, in the **Manage Document** list, click the version you want to display.

To compare a document to a previous version

1. Display the previous version of the document.

2. On the information bar at the top of the previous version, click the **Compare** button.

To roll back to a previous version of a document

1. Display the previous version of the document.

2. On the information bar at the top of the previous version, click the **Revert** button.

To change how often Word automatically saves document recovery versions

1. Display the **Save** page of the **Word Options** dialog box.

2. In the **Save AutoRecover information every** box, enter the number of minutes Word should allow to pass before saving a recovery version of the document.

3. Click **OK** to close the dialog box.

Control content changes

Sometimes you'll want people to be able to display the contents of a document but not make changes to it. Other times you'll want to allow changes, but only of certain types, or only if they're tracked for your review. This section includes information about ways that you can protect the content of a document.

> **TIP** When considering content protection options, keep in mind that storing documents within a document management system that has version control can save you a lot of trouble. Word 2016 includes a built-in version tracking system that you can use to compare and restore previous versions of a document that are stored on your computer. Microsoft SharePoint document libraries provide access to previous versions of documents checked in by any team member. (At the time of this writing, SharePoint Online document libraries default to tracking 500 versions of each document.)

Restrict actions

To prevent people from introducing inconsistent formatting or unwanted changes into a document, you can restrict the types of changes that an individual document permits, in the following ways:

- **Restrict formatting** You can limit formatting changes to a specific list of styles that you select, or to the "recommended minimum" style set, which consists of all the styles needed by Word for features such as tables of contents. (The recommended minimum set doesn't necessarily include all the styles used in the document.) Restricting formatting prevents anyone from adding or applying styles that you don't want to have in your document.

> **SEE ALSO** For more information about styles, see "Apply character formatting" and "Apply built-in styles to text" in Chapter 4, "Modify the structure and appearance of text."

- **Restrict editing** You can limit changes to comments, tracked changes, or form field content, or you can permit no changes at all.

You can implement these types of restrictions from the Restrict Editing pane.

Restrict Editing ▾ ✕

1. Formatting restrictions

☑ Limit formatting to a selection of styles

Settings...

2. Editing restrictions

☑ Allow only this type of editing in the document:

Tracked changes ▾

3. Start enforcement

Are you ready to apply these settings? (You can turn them off later)

Yes, Start Enforcing Protection

You can restrict formatting so that other people don't make unapproved content or formatting changes

---

🔍 **SEE ALSO** For information about locking change tracking without restricting editing, see "Track changes" earlier in this chapter.

When restrictions are turned on, the Restrict Editing pane provides information about the actions you can perform in the document. Ribbon buttons that apply restricted formats are unavailable (grayed out).

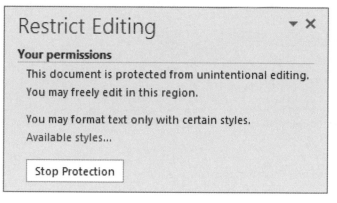

The pane reflects the specific formatting restrictions in place

To display the Restrict Editing pane

1. Do either of the following:

    - On the **Info** page of the Backstage view, click the **Protect Document** button, and then click **Restrict Editing**.

    - On the **Review** tab or **Developer** tab, in the **Protect** group, click the **Restrict Editing** button.

To restrict the styles permitted in a document

1. Display the **Restrict Editing** pane.

2. In the **Formatting restrictions** area of the **Restrict Editing** pane, select the **Limit formatting to a selection of styles** check box, and then click **Settings** to display the **Formatting Restrictions** dialog box.

Formatting Restrictions ? ✕

Styles

☑ Li_m_it formatting to a selection of styles

By restricting formatting to the styles you select, you prevent the ability to modify styles and the ability to apply direct formatting to the document. Select the styles you want to allow to be used in this document.

Checked styles are currently allowed:

☑ 1 / 1.1 / 1.1.1
☑ 1 / a / i
☑ AltProcedure
☑ AltText
☑ Article / Section
☑ Balloon Text (recommended)
☑ Bibliography (recommended)
☑ Block Text (recommended)
☑ bmAboutAuthorTitle

| A_ll | _R_ecommended Minimum | _N_one |

Formatting

☐ A_llow AutoFormat to override formatting restrictions
☐ Block Theme or Scheme s_w_itching
☐ Bloc_k_ Quick Style Set switching

| OK | Cancel |

The Allow AutoFormat option permits Word to apply automatic formatting, such as list formatting

3. Select the permitted styles by doing one of the following:

    -   To allow only the recommended minimum style set, click the **Recommended Minimum** button.

    -   To allow only specific styles, click the **None** button and then, in the **Checked styles are currently allowed** list box, select the check boxes of the styles you want to allow.

    -   To allow all styles and restrict only formatting, click the **All** button.

4. Select the permitted formatting by doing any of the following:

   • To permit Word to automatically format elements such as hyperlinks, bulleted lists, and numbered lists that aren't specified by a style, select the **Allow AutoFormat to override formatting restrictions** check box.

   • To permit only the current document theme, theme colors, and theme fonts, select the **Block Theme or Scheme switching** check box.

   • To permit only the current style set, select the **Block Quick Style Set switching** check box.

5. Click **OK** to implement the restricted set of styles. Word displays a message warning you that restricted styles will be removed.

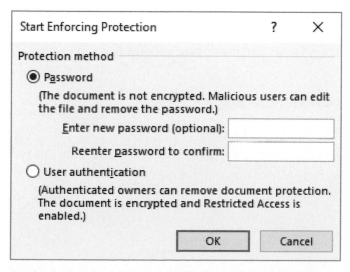

Word displays this warning regardless of whether the document contains restricted styles

6. In the message box, click **Yes** to remove any restricted formatting and revert restricted styles to Normal.

7. In the **Start enforcement** area of the **Restrict Editing** pane, click **Yes, Start Enforcing Protection** to open the **Start Enforcing Protection** dialog box.

11

People who don't know the password can't turn off the restrictions

8. If you want to require a password to turn off the restrictions, enter the password in the **Enter new password** and **Reenter password to confirm** boxes. Otherwise, leave the boxes blank.

9. In the **Start Enforcing Protection** dialog box, click **OK** to turn on the restrictions.

To restrict the editing permitted in a document

1. Display the **Restrict Editing** pane.

2. In the **Editing restrictions** area of the pane, select the **Allow only this type of editing in the document** check box.

3. In the **Allow only this type of editing in the document** list, click one of the following:

    • Tracked changes

    • Comments

    • Filling in forms

    • No changes (Read only)

4. In the **Start enforcement** area of the **Restrict Editing** pane, click the **Yes, Start Enforcing Protection** button to open the **Start Enforcing Protection** dialog box.

5. If you want to require a password to turn off the restrictions, enter the password in the **Enter new password** and **Reenter password to confirm** boxes. Otherwise, leave the boxes blank.

6. In the **Start Enforcing Protection** dialog box, click **OK** to turn on the restrictions.

To remove restrictions for specific people

1. Display the **Restrict Editing** pane.

2. In the **Editing restrictions** area of the pane, select the **Allow only this type of editing in the document** check box and then select the type of editing you want to permit for all users.

3. In the document, select the content that you want to permit a specific person or specific people to freely edit.

4. In the **Exceptions** area, if the **Groups** or **Individuals** box does NOT list the people or person you want to permit to edit the selection, do the following:

   a. Click the **More users** link to display the **Add Users** dialog box.

   b. Enter the user credentials of the person or people you want to allow to freely edit the selection.

Add Users	? ✕
Enter user names, separated by semicolons:	
joan@contoso.com;trinity@contoso.com	
Example: user1; DOMAIN\name; someone@example.com	
	OK Cancel

When granting restriction exceptions to multiple people, separate the entries by using semicolons

   c. In the **Add Users** dialog box, click **OK**.

5. In the **Exceptions** area, select the check box that precedes each group or person you want to permit to edit the selection.

6. If you want to permit the editing of additional sections of content, repeat steps 3 through 5.

7. In the **Start enforcement** area of the **Restrict Editing** pane, click the **Yes, Start Enforcing Protection** button to open the **Start Enforcing Protection** dialog box shown in the earlier procedure to restrict the styles permitted in a document.

8. In the **Start Enforcing Protection** dialog box, click **User authentication**, and then click **OK** to turn on the restrictions.

11

To remove editing and formatting restrictions

1. Display the **Restrict Editing** pane.

2. At the bottom of the pane, click the **Stop Protection** button.

3. The **Unprotect Document** dialog box opens regardless of whether a password is required.

When protecting a document, always use a password you can remember, because it can't be reset

4. In the **Unprotect Document** dialog box, enter a password in the **Password** box if one is required. Otherwise, leave the **Password** box blank. Then click **OK** to remove the restrictions.

Restrict access by using a password

Sometimes, you might want only certain people to be able to open and change a document. The simplest way to do this for an individual document is to assign a password to protect the file so that a person who wants to modify the document must enter a password when opening it to permit changes.

You can assign a password to a document while working in the document or when saving the document. Word offers two levels of password protection:

- **Encrypted** The document is saved in such a way that people who do not know the password cannot open it at all.

- **Unencrypted** The document is saved in such a way that only people who know the password can open it, make changes, and save the file. People who don't know the password can open a read-only version. If they make changes and want to save them, they have to save the document with a different name or in a different location, preserving the original.

Assigning a password to open a document encrypts the document; assigning a password to modify the document does not encrypt it

> ⚠ **IMPORTANT** Don't use common words or phrases as passwords, and don't use the same password for multiple documents. After assigning a password, make a note of it in a safe place. If you forget it, you won't be able to open the password-protected document.

To recommend against changes to a document

1. Display the **Save As** page of the Backstage view.

2. Using locations in the Places list, the current folder, or recent folders as a starting point, navigate to the folder you want to save the document in. If necessary, click **Browse** to display the **Save As** dialog box.

3. If you want to protect a copy of the document instead of the original, enter a name for the copy in the **File name** box.

4. Near the lower-right corner of the **Save As** dialog box, click the **Tools** button. Then in the **Tools** list, click **General Options**.

5. In the **General Options** dialog box, select the **Read-only recommended** check box, and then click **OK**.

To prevent unauthorized changes by setting a password

1. On the **Save As** page of the Backstage view, navigate to the folder you want to save the password-protected document in. If necessary, click **Browse** to display the **Save As** dialog box.

2. If you want to protect a copy of the document instead of the original, enter a name for the copy in the **File name** box.

11

3. Near the lower-right corner of the **Save As** dialog box, click the **Tools** button. Then in the **Tools** list, click **General Options**.

4. In the **General Options** dialog box, enter the password you want to assign to the document in the **Password to modify** box. Then click **OK** to display the **Confirm Password** dialog box.

> ✓ **TIP** As you enter the password, Word obscures it for security.

5. Enter the same password in the **Reenter password to modify** box, and then click **OK** to set the password.

6. In the **Save As** dialog box, click **Save**. If Word prompts you to overwrite the original document, click **Yes**.

To test the security of a password-protected document

1. Open the document and verify that Word displays the **Password** dialog box.

You can open a read-only version of an unencrypted document but must enter the password to open an encrypted document

2. Enter an incorrect password, click **OK**, and verify that Word denies you access to the document.

To open a password-protected document for reading

1. Open the document.

2. In the **Password** dialog box, click the **Read Only** button to open a read-only version of the document.

> ✓ **TIP** When using the default settings, Word opens the document in Read Mode.

To open a password-protected document for editing

1. Open the document.

2. In the **Password** dialog box, enter the password that you assigned to the document, and then click **OK** to open a read/write version of the document.

To remove password protection from an unencrypted document

1. On the **Save As** page of the Backstage view, in the **Current Folder** area, click the current folder.

2. At the bottom of the **Save As** dialog box, in the **Tools** list, click **General Options**.

3. In the **General Options** dialog box, select the contents of the **Password to modify** box, press **Delete**, and then click **OK**.

4. In the **Save As** dialog box, click **Save**.

To prevent document access by setting a password

1. Display the **Info** page of the Backstage view.

2. Click the **Protect Document** button, and then click **Encrypt with Password**.

11

After you assign the password, you will no longer be able to open the document without it

3. In the **Encrypt Document** dialog box, enter the password you want to assign in the **Password** box, and then click **OK**.

4. In the **Confirm Password** dialog box, enter the same password in the **Password** box, and then click **OK**.

The protected status of the document is displayed on the Info page of the Backstage view

5. Close the document and save your changes.

Or

1. On the **Save As** page of the Backstage view, navigate to the folder you want to save the password-protected document in. If necessary, click **Browse** to display the **Save As** dialog box.

2. If you want to make a password-protected copy of the document, enter a name for the copy in the **File name** box.

3. Near the lower-right corner of the **Save As** dialog box, click the **Tools** button. Then in the **Tools** list, click **General Options**.

4. In the **General Options** dialog box, enter the password you want to assign to the document in the **Password to open** box. Then click **OK** to display the **Confirm Password** dialog box.

5. Enter the same password in the **Reenter password to modify** box, and then click **OK** to set the password.

6. In the **Save As** dialog box, click **Save**. If Word prompts you to overwrite the original document, click **Yes**.

To remove password encryption from a document

1. Open the document and enter the correct password.

2. On the **Info** page of the Backstage view, in the **Protect Document** list, click **Encrypt with Password**.

3. In the **Encrypt Document** dialog box, delete the password from the **Password** box, and then click **OK**.

Restrict access by using rights management

If information rights management (IRM) is configured on your computer, you can control who can view and work with the documents you create. If you have this capability, a Restrict Permission By People option appears in the Protect Document list on the Info page of the Backstage view. Clicking Restrict Permission By People and then Restricted Access displays the Permission dialog box. In this dialog box, you can click Restrict Permission To This Document and then allow specific people to perform specific tasks, such as opening, printing, saving, or copying the document. When this protection is in place, other people cannot perform these tasks. The assigned permissions are stored with the document and apply no matter where the file is stored.

Before you can work on a document to which access has been restricted, you must verify your credentials with a licensing server. You can then download a use license that defines the tasks you are authorized to perform with the document. You need to repeat this process with each restricted document.

IMPORTANT To restrict permissions, your computer must be configured for IRM with a digital certificate that validates your identity. After you configure your computer for IRM, the Protect Document list on the Info page of the Backstage view includes a Restrict Permission By People option.

11

Coauthor documents

Whether you work for a large organization or a small business, you might need to collaborate with other people on the development of a document. No matter what the circumstances are, it can be difficult to keep track of different versions of a document produced by different people. If you store a document in a shared location such as a SharePoint document library or Microsoft OneDrive folder, multiple people can edit the document simultaneously.

After you save a document to a shared location, you can open and edit the document that is stored on the site just as you would if it were stored on your computer. Other people can also open and edit the document either by browsing to it or from an invitation that you send. This facilitates efficient collaboration between people regardless of location, schedule, or time zone.

When other people open a shared file for editing, Word alerts you by updating the Share button label on the ribbon and in the Share pane.

Dozens of people can work in a document at the same time

Word keeps track of the content that people are editing and locks paragraphs until the changes are shared to other editors. You can choose to automatically share your changes, or share them only when you save the document.

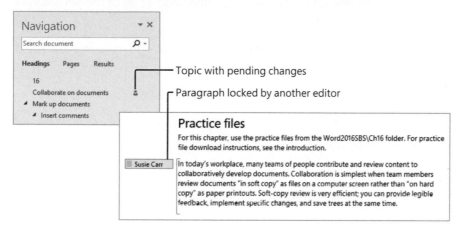

Word indicates the areas of the document that are being edited

If each person working in the document tracks his or her changes, the tracked changes remain available so that the document owner can accept or reject changes when the team has finished working on the document.

To make a document available for coauthoring

1. Save the document to a SharePoint document library or OneDrive folder.

To begin coauthoring a document

1. If the document is stored in a SharePoint document library, do NOT check it out.

2. Open the document directly from the document library or OneDrive folder.

3. Edit the document as you would normally.

To display the Share pane

1. Do either of the following:

   - Click the **Share** button located at the right end of the ribbon.

   - On the **Share** page of the Backstage view, click the **Share with People** button.

11

To invite other people to edit a shared document

1. Display the **Share** pane.

2. In the **Invite people** box, enter the names or email addresses of the people you want to send a document link to.

3. In the message box, enter any specific message you want to include in the sharing invitation.

4. Click the **Share** button to send an email message that contains a link to the document.

To identify areas locked by other reviewers

1. Display the **Navigation** pane.

2. Scan the **Navigation** pane for icons.

Or

1. Scan the left margin of the document for nametags and paragraph selection brackets.

To display changes made by coauthors

1. Do either of the following:

   • Save the document.

   • On the status bar, click the **Updates Available** button.

The Updates Available button appears on the status bar when other editors save changes

To configure Word to quickly make your changes available to coauthors

1. Display the **Share** pane.

2. In the **Automatically share changes** list, click **Always**.

Or

1. Display the **General** page of the **Word Options** dialog box.

2. In the **Real-time collaboration options** area, in the **When working with others...** list, click **Always**.

> **Real-time collaboration options**
>
> When working with others, I want to automatically share my changes: | Always ▾ |
> ☑ Show names on presence flags

If you want to see only that someone is working within a section but don't need to know who, you can clear the Show Names On Presence Flags check box

3. In the **Word Options** dialog box, click **OK**.

Skills review

In this chapter, you learned how to:

- Mark up documents
- Display and review document markup
- Compare and merge documents
- Control content changes
- Coauthor documents

11

Practice tasks

The practice files for these tasks are located in the Word2016SBS\Ch11 folder. You can save the results of the tasks in the same folder.

Mark up documents

Open the TrackChanges document in Word, display the document in Print Layout view, and then perform the following tasks:

1. Turn on change tracking.

2. In the last column of the table, select the words *some good*, and then attach the comment **They carry the new Ultra line.**

3. Configure the review settings to display the All Markup view of changes and to display only comments and formatting in balloons.

4. If necessary, scroll the document to display the table. Perform these tasks in the **Fabrikam** row of the table:

    -   In the **Prices** column, delete the word *much* from the phrase *Some much lower*.

    -   In the **Service** column, insert **but slow** after the word *Adequate*.

5. Perform these tasks in the **Northwind Traders** row of the table:

    -   In the **Quality** column, replace the word *Poor* with **Substandard**.

    -   Point to the deleted word and then to the inserted word to display information about the changes in ScreenTips.

6. Configure the review settings to display revisions in balloons instead of inline.

7. Restore the inline revision indicators and remove the balloons.

8. Move the last sentence in the paragraph to the beginning of the paragraph.

9. Turn off change tracking.

10. Configure the review settings to display the Simple Markup view.

11. Save and close the document.

Display and review document markup

Open the ReviewComments document in Word, display the document in Print Layout view, and then perform the following tasks:

1. Configure the review settings to display the **Simple Markup** view of changes.

2. Display only revisions made by Mike Nash.

3. Use the **Next Comment** button to move to the first comment shown in the document, which is attached to the word *competitors*. Delete the comment.

4. Move to the second comment, which is attached to the word *Adequate* in the **Service** column of the table. Point to the word in the table to display a Screen-Tip that contains the name of the person who inserted the comment and the date and time the comment was inserted. Notice that the ScreenTip displays more information than the comment bubble.

5. Click the **Reply to Comment** button in the second comment bubble. In the reply box, enter **If you had been a real customer, would you have left?**

6. Display the **Revisions** pane on the left side of the app window. Then drag the pane away from the side of the window so that it floats independently.

7. In the **Revisions** pane, expand the detailed summary of revisions and note the types of revisions in the document.

8. Configure the review settings to display revisions made by all reviewers.

9. Scroll through the revisions in the pane, and then close it.

10. Configure the review settings to display the **All Markup** view of changes.

11. Hide all comments in the document.

12. Move between the tracked changes in the document. Accept all the changes in the text paragraph. Process the changes in the table as follows:

    - Reject the table formatting change.

    - Accept the deletion of the word *much*.

    - Reject the changes associated with the addition of the words *but slow*.

    - Accept both of the changes associated with the replacement of *Poor* with *Substandard*.

13. Configure the review settings to display the **No Markup** view of changes. Then change the balloon setting to the one you like best.

14. Save and close the document.

Compare and merge documents

Open a new, blank document in Word, and then perform the following tasks:

1. Compare the MergeDocs1 and MergeDocs2 documents, by using the following settings:

   - Label unmarked changes from MergeDocs2 with your name.

   - Select all available comparison settings.

   - Mark the differences in a separate document.

2. When Word completes the comparison, ensure that the **Revisions** pane is open on the left, the merged document in the center, and the two original documents on the right.

> **TIP** If the Revisions pane is not open, click the Reviewing Pane button in the Tracking group on the Review tab. If the source documents are not displayed, click the Compare button, click Show Source Documents, and then click Show Both.

3. In the center pane, scroll through the document to review all the revisions, and then in the **Revisions** pane, scroll through the individual revisions.

   Before changes can be accepted in the document, conflicting changes must be resolved.

4. In the **Revisions** pane, locate the deleted instance of *March* and then accept the deletion.

5. Click each change that remains in the **Revisions** pane to display that location in the three document panes.

6. Click the merged document in the center pane to activate it. Then accept all the changes in the document at the same time.

7. Close the **Revisions** pane, and then close the two windows on the right side of the screen.

8. Save the merged document as **MyMergedDocument**, and then close it.

Control content changes

Open the ControlChanges document, and then complete the following tasks:

1. Save a copy of the document, naming the copy **MyControlChanges**, and require the password **P@ssw0rd1** to modify the document but no password to read the document.

2. Configure the document options to recommend that people open a read-only copy of the document.

3. Close the document, and then open a read-only version of it.

4. Attempt to make a change and verify that you can't save the changed document.

5. Close the document, and then use the password to open an editable version of it.

6. Remove the password protection from the document.

7. Encrypt the document and require the password **P@ssw0rd2** to open it.

8. Restrict the formatting in the document to only the recommended minimum styles.

9. Block users from switching schemes or style sets.

10. Turn on the restrictions and remove any formatting and styles that don't meet the requirements you selected. Notice the changes to the document.

11. Configure the editing restrictions so that you can edit only the first paragraph of the document but other people aren't permitted to make any changes.

12. Save and close the document.

Coauthor documents

There is no practice task for this topic because it requires that documents be stored in a shared location.

Finalize and distribute documents

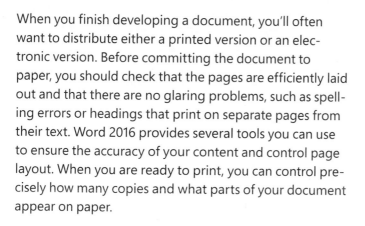

When you finish developing a document, you'll often want to distribute either a printed version or an electronic version. Before committing the document to paper, you should check that the pages are efficiently laid out and that there are no glaring problems, such as spelling errors or headings that print on separate pages from their text. Word 2016 provides several tools you can use to ensure the accuracy of your content and control page layout. When you are ready to print, you can control precisely how many copies and what parts of your document appear on paper.

If you intend to distribute your document electronically, Word provides tools for ensuring that the document doesn't contain unresolved revisions, hidden text, or identifying information that you might not want to send out. It also provides tools for indicating that a document is final and ready to distribute, and makes it easy to send the document by using email.

This chapter guides you through procedures related to locating and correcting text errors, previewing and adjusting page layout, controlling what appears on each page, preparing documents for electronic distribution, and printing and sending documents.

In this chapter

- Locate and correct text errors
- Preview and adjust page layout
- Control what appears on each page
- Prepare documents for electronic distribution
- Print and send documents

Practice files

For this chapter, use the practice files from the Word2016SBS\Ch12 folder. For practice file download instructions, see the introduction.

Locate and correct text errors

In the days of handwritten and typewritten documents, people might have tolerated a typographical or grammatical error or two because correcting such errors without creating a mess was difficult. Word-processing apps such as Word have built-in spelling and grammar checkers, so now documents that contain these types of errors are likely to reflect badly on their creators.

> ✓ **TIP** Although Word can help you eliminate misspellings and grammatical errors, its tools are not infallible. You should always read through your document to catch any problems that the Word tools can't detect—for example, homonyms such as *their*, *there*, and *they're*.

Word provides these three tools to help you with the chore of eliminating spelling and grammar errors:

- **AutoCorrect** This feature corrects common spelling and grammatical errors, replaces text codes with mathematical symbols, and automatically applies formatting based on text cues. AutoCorrect has a built-in list of frequently misspelled words and their correct spellings. If you frequently misspell a word that AutoCorrect doesn't change, you can add it to the list in the AutoCorrect dialog box. If you deliberately enter a word that is on the AutoCorrect list and don't want to accept the AutoCorrect change, you can reverse the correction by clicking the Undo button before you enter anything else, or by pointing to the bar that appears below the word and then clicking Undo.

> 🔍 **SEE ALSO** For information about modifying the AutoCorrect settings, see the "Manage proofing options" section of "Change default Word options" in Chapter 16, "Customize options and the user interface."

- **Error indicators** Word indicates possible spelling errors with red wavy underlines, possible grammatical errors with green wavy underlines, and possible formatting errors with blue wavy underlines. You can right-click an underlined word or phrase to display suggested corrections and links to proofing resources.

> ✓ **TIP** Word's grammar checker helps identify phrases and clauses that don't follow traditional grammatical rules, but it's not always accurate. It's easy to get in the habit of ignoring green wavy underlines. However, it's wise to scrutinize them all to be sure that your documents don't contain any embarrassing mistakes.

- **Spelling and grammar checker** To check the spelling or grammar of selected text or the entire document, click the Spelling & Grammar button in the Proofing group on the Review tab. Word then works its way through the selection or the document and displays the Spelling pane or Grammar pane if it encounters a potential error.

 TIP Press F7 to start checking the spelling and grammar from your current location in the document.

The pane that appears displays an explanation of the likely problem and suggests corrections. You can implement a suggestion by double-clicking it.

As you know, operating an import business in the global arena requ... economic and environmental conditions, as well as of political issue... maintain a viable business. When we select our product sorces, we ... local economy but to to ensure the preservation of fragile ecologie... we are commited to maximizing our positive impacts while causing ...

This is an exciting and challenging venture, and we wood like to invi... discuss your needs with our purchasing agent Cristina Potra. You m... number at (925) 555-0167, through email at cristina@wideworldim... our corporate address.

In the meantime, here is a packet of informational material that inc... a travel manual used by our purchasing agents in the field, and our ... our commitment to supporting grass-root businesses such as Conto...

Sincerely,

Florian Stiller

President

Spelling   ▾ ✕

sorces

[Ignore] [Ignore All] [Add]

sources
sores
scores
forces
source's

[Change] [Change All]

sources 🔊

1. a generative force : cause
2. the point of origin of a stream of water : fountainhead
3. a firsthand document or primary reference work

See more...

Powered by: Merriam-Webster

English (United States) ▾

The options in the Spelling pane are specific to the suspected error

Word saves your responses to suggested spelling and grammar changes with the document. If you choose to ignore a flagged error, the error will not be reflagged when you run the spelling and grammar checker again in the same document. To check the spelling and grammar of a document from scratch, click the Recheck Document button on the Proofing page of the Word Options dialog box.

12

> ✓ **TIP** You can specify the behavior of the spelling and grammar checker on the Proofing page of the Word Options dialog box. For information, see the "Manage proofing options" section of "Change default Word options" in Chapter 16, "Customize options and the user interface."

To review and correct the spelling and grammar in a document

1. If you want to begin checking from the beginning of the document, press **Ctrl+Home** to move there.

2. On the **Review** tab, in the **Proofing** group, click the **Spelling & Grammar** button to begin the review. The **Spelling** pane opens and displays the first possible error. The corresponding location in the document is highlighted.

As you know, operating an import business in the global arena requ
economic and environmental conditions, as well as of political issue
maintain a viable business. When we select our product sources, w
local economy but to to ensure the preservation of fragile ecologies
we are commited to maximizing our positive impacts while causing

This is an exciting and challenging venture, and we wood like to invi
discuss your needs with our purchasing agent Cristina Potra. You m
number at (925) 555-0167, through email at cristina@wideworldim
our corporate address.

In the meantime, here is a packet of informational material that inc
a travel manual used by our purchasing agents in the field, and our
our commitment to supporting grass-root businesses such as Conto

Sincerely,

Spelling ▾ ✕
to
[Ignore] [Delete]
(No Suggestions)

Repeated Word
English (United States) ▾

The spelling checker highlights misspelled or duplicated words and suggests corrections

3. In the **Spelling** pane, review the explanation and the suggested responses, and then do any of the following:

   - If the selection is identified as a possible spelling error, do any of the following:

     - Click **Ignore** to continue the review without changing the highlighted word or **Ignore All** to continue and to ignore other instances of the word in the current document.

- Click **Add** to add the word to the Spelling Checker dictionary on your computer.

- Select the correct spelling of the word in the suggestions list, and then click **Change** to change only this instance of the word or **Change All** to change all instances of this word in the document.

- If the selection is identified as a duplicated word, do either of the following:

  - Click **Ignore** to continue the review without making a change.

  - Click **Delete** to delete the highlighted instance of the duplicated word.

- If the selection is identified as a possible grammatical or formatting error, do either of the following:

  - Click **Ignore** to continue the review without making a change.

  - Select the correct usage in the suggestions list, and click **Change** to change the selection to the new usage.

The Grammar pane displays the definitions of the original word and the suggested replacement

When you click a button to fix or ignore the issue, the spelling and grammar checker moves to the next word that Word does not recognize.

4. After the last selection has been addressed, Word displays a message indicating that it has finished checking the spelling and grammar of the document. Click **OK** to close the message box.

To manage the custom dictionary

1. From the Backstage view, open the **Word Options** dialog box.

2. Display the **Proofing** page. In the **When correcting spelling in Microsoft Office programs** section of the Proofing page, click the **Custom Dictionaries** button.

3. The Custom Dictionaries dialog box displays the dictionaries that Office apps consult. Select the dictionary that has *(default)* after the name. Then click the **Edit Word List** button.

4. In the dialog box for the selected dictionary, do any of the following:

   - To review the content of the dictionary, scroll the **Dictionary** pane.

   - To remove a word from the dictionary, click it in the **Dictionary** pane, and then click **Delete**.

   - To clear the entire dictionary, click **Delete All**.

   - To add a word to the dictionary, enter it in the **Word(s)** box and then click **OK**.

The dictionary includes words that you've added from the Spelling pane or entered manually

To correct spelling errors from within the document

1. Right-click any word that has a wavy red underline. Word displays suggested spelling corrections at the top of the shortcut menu.

As·you·know,·operating·an·import·business·in·the·global·arena·requires·careful·consideration·of·current· economic·and·environmental·conditions,·as·well·as·of·political·issues·that·could·affect·our·ability·to· maintain·a·viable·business.·When·we·select·our·product·sorces, ~~nprove·the·~~
local·economy·but·to·<u>to</u>·ensure·the·preservation·of·fragile·ecolo ~~icing·act,·but·~~
we·are·<u>commited</u>·to·maximizing·our·positive·impacts·while·caus

| sources |
| sores |
| scores |
| forces |
| source's |
| <u>I</u>gnore All |
| <u>A</u>dd to Dictionary |
| <u>H</u>yperlink... |
| New Co<u>m</u>ment |

This·is·an·exciting·and·challenging·venture,·and·we·wood·like·to ~~porate·office·to·~~
discuss·your·needs·with·our·purchasing·agent·Cristina·Potra.·Yo ~~ough·our·main·~~
number·at·(925)·555-0167,·through·email·at·cristina@wideworl ~~gular·mail·at·~~
our·corporate·address.¶

In·the·meantime,·here·is·a·packet·of·informational·material·tha ~~s·and·suppliers,·~~
a·travel·manual·used·by·our·purchasing·agents·in·the·field,·and· ~~hich·outlines·~~
our·commitment·to·supporting·grass-root·businesses·such·as·C

The shortcut menu lists spelling options from the dictionary and related actions

SEE ALSO For information about the hyperlink option on the shortcut menu, see the sidebar "Hyperlink to additional resources" in Chapter 13, "Reference content and content sources."

2. Click any of the suggested corrections to replace the word.

Preview and adjust page layout

Working on your document in the default Print Layout view means that you always know how the document content will appear on the printed page. While you're work-ing in the document, you can use the commands in the Page Setup group on the Page Layout tab to adjust the page settings (such as the margins and page orientation) to best suit your content and delivery method. If you're planning to deliver the docu-ment at a page size other than the default, you can format the document to display and print correctly by changing the paper size.

Although the layout of each page is visible in Print Layout view, it's also a good idea to preview the whole document before you print it. This gives you more of a high-level overview of the document than when you're working directly in the content. Preview-ing is essential for multipage documents but is helpful even for one-page documents. You can preview a document as it will appear when printed, on the Print page of the

12

Backstage view. The preview area shows exactly how each page of the document will look when printed on the selected printer.

The Print page displays a preview of the document as it will appear when printed

> **TIP** Press Ctrl+P to display the Print page of the Backstage view. For more information about keyboard shortcuts, see "Keyboard shortcuts" at the end of this book.

If you don't like what appears in the preview pane of the Print page, you don't have to leave the Backstage view to make adjustments. The left pane of the Print page provides access to many of the commands that are available in the Page Setup group on the Page Layout tab, allowing you to change the following document settings while previewing their effect on the printed page:

- **Orientation** You can switch the direction in which a page is laid out on the paper. The default orientation is Portrait, in which the page is taller than it is wide. You can set the orientation to Landscape, in which the page is wider than it is tall.

- **Paper size** You can switch to one of the sizes available for the selected printer by making a selection from a list.

- **Margins** Changing the margins of a document changes where information can appear on each page. You can select one of Word's predefined sets of top, bottom, left, and right margins, or set custom margins.

All the pages of a document have the same orientation and margins unless you divide the document into sections. Then each section can have independent orientation and margin settings.

> **SEE ALSO** For more information about sections, see "Control what appears on each page" later in this chapter.

By default, hidden text does not print with the document. If your document contains hidden text that you want to print, you can configure that option in the Print settings.

If you want to configure multiple print layout settings in one place, or configure settings for only specific sections of the document, use the Page Setup dialog box. This dialog box provides the most comprehensive set of tools for page layout.

> **IMPORTANT** You must have a printer installed to perform the following procedures. On a default installation of Office 2016, the Microsoft XPS Document Writer and Send To OneNote 2016 options appear in your Printers list. You can perform the procedures by using one of those options or an actual local or network printer connection.

To adjust page layout settings from the Page Setup dialog box

1. Do either of the following:

   - On the **Print** page of the Backstage view, at the bottom of the left pane, click **Page Setup**.

   - On the **Layout** tab, click the **Page Setup** dialog box launcher.

2. In the **Page Setup** dialog box, do any of the following:

   - On the **Margins** tab, make the margin adjustments you want.

   > **SEE ALSO** For information about working with margins, see the "To modify document margins" procedure later in this topic.

12

- On the **Paper** tab, make any necessary changes to the paper settings.

- On the **Layout** tab, make the layout adjustments you want.

3. When you have the settings as you want them, click **OK**.

To preview a document as it will appear when printed

1. Display the **Print** page of the Backstage view. The page navigator below the preview pane indicates the number of pages the document will print on.

2. Do any of the following:

- To move between pages, click the **Next Page** or **Previous Page** button, or enter the number of the page you want to display in the page navigator box.

- To preview multiple pages, reduce the magnification until two or more pages fit in the preview pane.

You can move between pages, change the magnification, or fit a page to the available space

> **TIP** If you want to preview a multipage document as it will look when printed on both sides of the page and bound, add a blank page or a cover page to the beginning of the document before previewing it.

- To display a single page at the largest size that fits in the preview pane, click the **Zoom to Page** button in the lower-right corner.

To modify document margins

1. From the **Print** page of the Backstage view, do either of the following to display the margin settings:

   - In the **Settings** area, click the current margin setting to display the **Margins** menu.

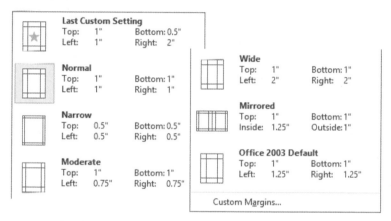

You can select from predefined margin settings, or you can set your own

> **TIP** While editing a document, you can display the same Margins menu by clicking the Margins button in the Page Setup group on the Layout tab.

   - At the bottom of the left pane, click the **Page Setup** link to display the **Margins** tab of the **Page Setup** dialog box.

12

The Mirror Margins setting is a good choice when you plan to print and bind a double-sided document

2. From the menu or in the dialog box, configure the margin settings as you want them. The preview area reflects the change.

To change the page orientation

1. On the **Print** page of the Backstage view, in the **Settings** area, click the current orientation to display the **Orientation** menu.

2. Click either **Landscape Orientation** or **Portrait Orientation**. The preview area reflects the change.

To include hidden text when printing documents

1. Open the **Word Options** dialog box, and then click the **Display** page tab.

2. In the **Printing options** area of the Display page, select the **Print Hidden Text** check box. Then click **OK**.

> **TIP** Changing the Print Hidden Text option in the Word Options dialog box changes this setting for all documents.

Control what appears on each page

When a document includes more content than will fit between its top and bottom margins, Word creates a new page by inserting a *soft page break* (a page break that moves if the preceding content changes). If you want to break a page in a place other than where Word would normally break it, you can insert a manual page break. As you edit the content of a document, Word changes the location of the soft page breaks, but not of any manual page breaks that you insert.

> **TIP** It's important to set manual page breaks and layout options from the beginning of a document to the end, because each change you make affects the content from that point forward.

If a paragraph breaks so that most of it appears on one page but its last line appears at the top of the next page, the line is called a *widow*. If a paragraph breaks so that its first line appears at the bottom of one page and the rest of the paragraph appears on the next page, the line is called an *orphan*. These single lines of text can make a document hard to read, so by default, Word specifies that a minimum of two lines should appear at the top and bottom of each page. As with so many other aspects of Word, however, you have control over this setting. You can also control the following options:

-   **Keep with next** This option controls whether Word will break a page between the paragraph and the following paragraph.

-   **Keep lines together** This option controls whether Word will break a page within the paragraph.

-   **Page break before** This option controls whether Word will break a page before the paragraph.

12

·Office·Procedures¶

General·Administration¶

Contact·Information¶
For·general·deliveries:¶

    1234·Main·Street↵
    New·York,·NY··90012¶

Deliveries·of·shipping·supplies·should·be·directed·to·the·door·at·the·back·of·the·building.·(The·loading·dock·staff·will·check·items·against·the·packing·slip·and·then·bring·the·slip·to·the·office.·The·office·employees·will·be·responsible·for·entering·the·packing·slip·information·into·the·inventory·database.)¶

Phone·numbers:¶

    Telephone:·(972)·555-0123↵
    Fax:·(972)·555-0124¶

A small black square in the left margin indicates that one of the Keep options is on for that paragraph

> **TIP** By selecting Keep With Next instead of inserting a page break, you allow the content to move from page to page as long as it stays with the following paragraph. You can apply these options to individual paragraphs, or you can incorporate them into the styles you define for document elements such as headings. For information about styles, see "Create and modify styles" in Chapter 15, "Create custom document elements."

When you want to format part of a document differently from the rest—for example, with page layout settings that are different from the surrounding text, you do so by inserting section breaks above and below it. A common example of this is when you need to print a wide table on a page with a Landscape orientation within a report that has a Portrait page orientation. There are four types of section breaks:

- **Next Page** Starts the following section on the next page

- **Continuous** Starts a new section without affecting page breaks

- **Even Page** Starts the following section on the next even-numbered page

- **Odd Page** Starts the following section on the next odd-numbered page

When hidden formatting marks are displayed, a section break appears in Print Layout view as a double-dotted line from the preceding paragraph mark to the margin, with the words *Section Break* and the type of section break in the middle of the line.

> **TIP** Formatting selected text in columns automatically inserts section breaks. For more information, see "Present information in columns" in Chapter 5, "Organize information in columns and tables."

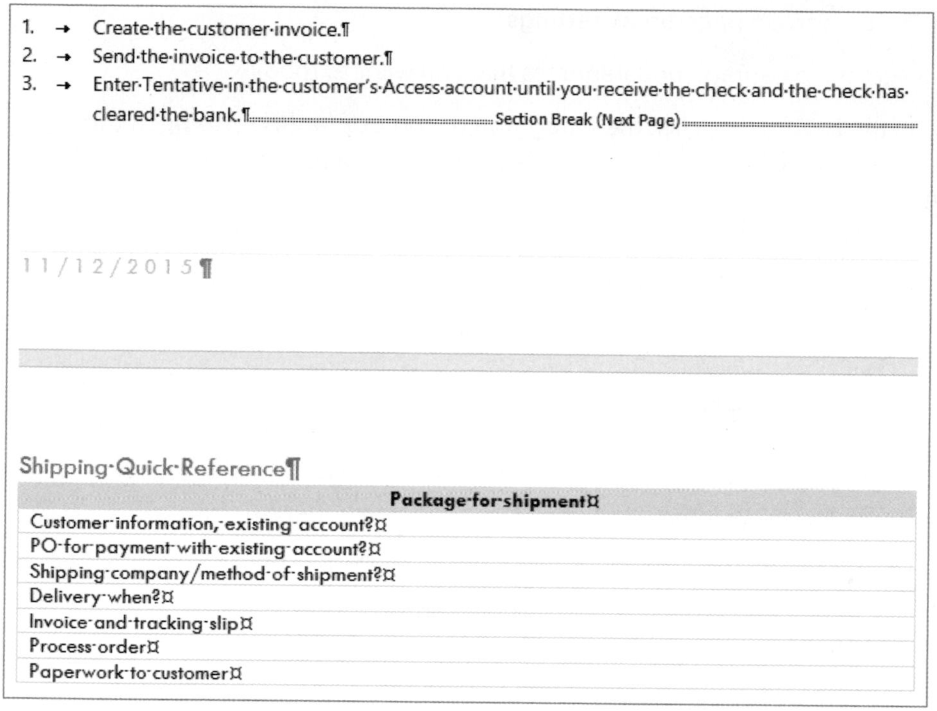

1. → Create·the·customer·invoice.¶
2. → Send·the·invoice·to·the·customer.¶
3. → Enter·Tentative·in·the·customer's·Access·account·until·you·receive·the·check·and·the·check·has·
   cleared·the·bank.¶·························· Section Break (Next Page) ··························

1 1 / 1 2 / 2 0 1 5 ¶

Shipping·Quick·Reference¶

Package·for·shipment¤
Customer·information,~existing~account?¤
PO·for·payment·with·existing·account?¤
Shipping·company/method·of·shipment?¤
Delivery·when?¤
Invoice·and·tracking·slip¤
Process·order¤
Paperwork·to·customer¤

The heading and table move to the next page, after the section break indicator

You can configure individual page layout, page setup, and headers and footers for each section.

> 🔍 **SEE ALSO** For information about headers and footers, see "Insert headers, footers, and page numbers" in Chapter 9, "Add visual elements."

To insert a manual page break

1. Position the cursor where you want to insert the page break in the document, and then do any of the following:

   - On the **Insert** tab, in the **Pages** group, click **Page Break**.

   - On the **Layout** tab, in the **Page Setup** group, click **Breaks**, and then click **Page**.

   - Press **Ctrl+Enter**.

To control paragraph page break settings

1. Select the paragraph or paragraphs that you want to modify.

2. On the **Layout** tab, click the **Paragraph** dialog box launcher to open the Paragraph dialog box. Then click the **Line and Page Breaks** tab.

Filled check boxes indicate that the setting is not the same for all selected content

3. On the **Line and Page Breaks** tab, do any of the following:

- Select the **Widow/Orphan control** check box to have Word control widows and orphans.

- Select the **Keep with next** check box to prevent Word from breaking a page between the paragraph and the following paragraph.

- Select the **Keep lines together** check box to prevent Word from breaking a page within the paragraph.

- Select the **Page break before** check box to have Word break a page before the paragraph.

To insert a section break

1. Position the cursor where you want to insert the section break in the document.

2. On the **Layout** tab, in the **Page Setup** group, click **Breaks**, and then do any of the following:

- Click **Next Page** to start the new section at the top of the next page.

- Click **Continuous** to start a new section without affecting page breaks.

- Click **Even Page** to start the following section on the next even-numbered page.

- Click **Odd Page** to start the following section on the next odd-numbered page.

To remove a page break or section break

12

1. Click at the left end of the break, or select the break, and then press the **Delete** key.

Prepare documents for electronic distribution

When a document is complete, you can distribute it in two ways: printed on paper or electronically. When you distribute a printed document, only the printed information is visible to the reader. When you distribute a document electronically, you should ensure that no confidential information is attached to the file and that it can be viewed by the people to whom you are sending it. Some of the information that is attached to the document is available with the document properties on the Info page of the Backstage view. You can change or remove some types of information from this page and more from either the Document Panel or the Properties dialog box.

> **SEE ALSO** For information about properties, see "Display and edit file properties" in Chapter 2, "Create and manage documents."

Many documents go through several revisions, and some are scrutinized by multiple reviewers. During this development process, documents can accumulate information that you might not want in the final version, such as the names of people who worked on the document, the time spent working on the document, and comments that reviewers have added to the file. There might also be hidden tracked changes. This information is not a concern if the final version is to be delivered as a printout. However, it has become very common to deliver documents electronically, making this information available to anyone who wants to read it.

Word includes these three tools that you can use to check for hidden and personal information, accessibility issues, and version compatibility issues:

- **Document Inspector** Automates the process of finding and removing all extraneous and potentially confidential information.

- **Accessibility Checker** Identifies document elements and formatting that might be difficult for people with certain kinds of disabilities to read or for assistive devices such as screen readers to access.

This tool checks for many common accessibility issues and provides explanations and recommendations for fixing them. You can leave the Accessibility Checker open while you work—its contents will automatically update to indicate the current issues. After you run the Accessibility Checker, information about document content issues is also shown in the Inspect Document area of the Info page of the Backstage view.

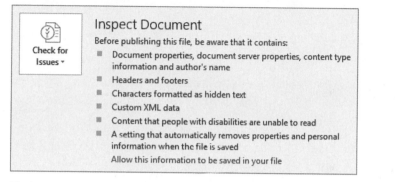

The Inspect Document area displays information about the document content

> **SEE ALSO** For more information about designing documents for accessibility, run the Accessibility Checker and then click the Read More link at the bottom of the Accessibility Checker pane.

- **Compatibility Checker** Identifies formatting and features not supported in earlier versions of Word.

After you determine that a document is ready to distribute, you can mark the document as final, so that other people know that they should not make changes to this released document.

> **IMPORTANT** By default, Word 2016 is configured to remove certain personal properties when saving a document. If you want to change this setting, display the Trust Center page of the Word Options dialog box, click Trust Center Settings, and then on the Privacy Options page of the Trust Center dialog box, clear the Remove Personal Information From File Properties On Save check box. Then click OK in each of the open dialog boxes to save the setting.

Accessibility issues

Whenever you create a document that will be distributed electronically, particularly if it will be displayed as a webpage, think about whether its content will be accessible to all the people you want to reach. For example, consider the following:

- Not all people will display the document in Word 2016 or in the same web browser in which you preview it.

- Some people might set their default web browser font sizes larger than usual, or display their web browser content at an increased zoom level.

- Some people can't differentiate changes in color. Others might have their computers configured to display a high-contrast color scheme that changes the default colors of text so they can read it better.

- People with visual impairments might use an assistive device such as a screen reader to "read" content to them from the document or webpage.

- Web browsers might be configured to not display certain page elements.

- A slow connection might prevent the display of large images.

If you intend to publish the document on a public webpage, consider also whether the terms that your prospective viewers might search for are accessible to search engines.

There are some things you can do to make a document display more uniformly on screen (or on paper) and be more accessible to assistive devices and Internet search engines:

- Use styles to format content, rather than applying manual formatting. This allows readers to move directly to specific headings from the document Navigation pane, and to apply style sets that use legible fonts and high-contrast colors to make content easier to read on the screen.

- Similarly, when specifying colors, use the theme colors so that they change appropriately when viewers choose high-contrast themes.

- If your content includes graphics, add a caption to each image and add a written description of the image to the image properties as alternative text (frequently referred to as *alt text*). The alt text is displayed in place of the image when the image can't be displayed on screen. It can also be read aloud by screen readers.

- Also to assist screen readers, wrap text around images by using the In Line With Text setting, so that images do not interrupt text.

- Do not use watermarks or background colors, patterns, or images that might interfere with the readability of the document content.

- Present information in the standard content of the document rather than in text boxes. Content in text boxes might not be accessible to screen readers.

- To ensure that screen readers can access content in the intended reading order, present it in text paragraphs rather than in tabbed lists or tables. If you must present information in a table, follow these guidelines:

    - Use the standard table formats—don't "draw" the table manually, merge or split cells, or nest tables. Variances in the table might cause assistive devices to incorrectly interpret the content.

    - If your table will span multiple pages, select the option to repeat the header row so that the headers are both visible and accessible to assistive devices.

    - Add alt text and captions to tables in the event that they are incorrectly displayed or interpreted.

- When formatting hyperlinks, provide ScreenTip text.

    SEE ALSO For information about creating ScreenTips for hyperlinks, see he sidebar "Hyperlink to additional resources" in Chapter 13, "Reference content and content sources."

12

To inspect a document for common issues

1. Display the **Info** page of the Backstage view.

2. In the **Inspect Document** area on the left side of the **Info** page, click the **Check for Issues** button, and then click **Inspect Document** to open the Document Inspector dialog box, which lists the items that will be checked.

3. If Word prompts you to save changes to the file, click **Yes**.

4. Clear the check boxes for any of the properties you don't want to check for, and then click **Inspect** to view the **Document Inspector** report on the presence of the properties you selected. In addition to the basic properties that are displayed in the Properties section of the Info page, the inspector might return information on headers and footers and custom XML data.

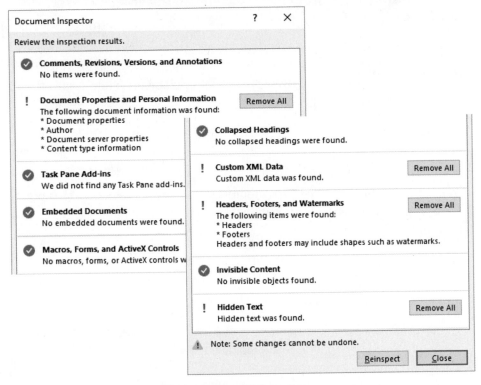

The Document Inspector evaluates 10 categories of information

5. Review the results, and then click the **Remove All** button for any category of information that you want to remove.

> **TIP** You can choose to retain content identified by the Document Inspector if you know that it is appropriate for distribution.

6. In the **Document Inspector** dialog box, click **Reinspect**, and then click **Inspect** to verify the removal of the properties and other data you selected.

7. When you're satisfied with the results, close the **Document Inspector** dialog box.

To inspect a document for accessibility issues

1. On the **Info** page of the Backstage view, click the **Check For Issues** button, and then click **Check Accessibility** to run the Accessibility Checker.

2. In the **Accessibility Checker** pane, review the inspection results and make any changes you want to the document.

3. When you are done, do either of the following:

   - Click the **X** in the upper-right corner of the **Accessibility Checker** pane to close the pane.

   - Leave the pane open to continue checking for accessibility issues as you work with the document.

To check a document for compatibility with earlier versions of Word

1. On the **Info** page of the Backstage view, click the **Check Compatibility** button to run the Compatibility Checker.

2. In the **Microsoft Word Compatibility Checker** dialog box, review the results, make any changes you want, and then click OK.

> **TIP** By default, Word always checks for compatibility whenever you save a document. If you don't want Word to do this, clear the Check Compatibility When Saving Documents check box in the Microsoft Word Compatibility Checker dialog box.

12

To mark a document as final

1. On the **Info** page of the Backstage view, in the **Protect Document** area, click the **Protect Document** button, and then click **Mark As Final**. A message tells you that the document will be marked as final and then saved.

2. In the message box, click **OK**. A message tells you that the document has been marked as final, the status property has been set to Final, and typing, editing commands, and proofing marks are turned off.

3. In the message box, click **OK**. The document title bar indicates that the document is read-only (no changes can be saved), and the Protect Document area indicates that the file has been marked as final.

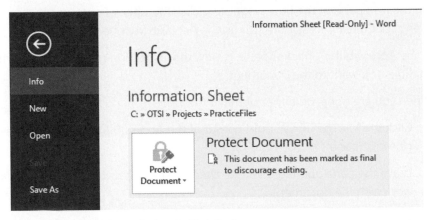

The Info page reminds people that the file is final

4. Click the **Return** button (the arrow) above the Backstage view page tabs to return to the document. Notice that only the ribbon tabs are visible; the commands are hidden.

5. Click the **Insert** tab to temporarily expand it, and notice that all the buttons are inactive (dimmed). Then click away from the tab to contract it. Word displays an information bar, notifying you that the document has been marked as final.

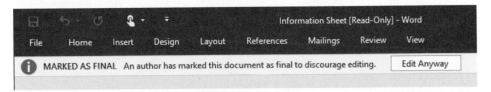

The information bar discourages people from making casual changes

To make changes to a document that has been marked as final

1. On the information bar, click the **Edit Anyway** button to remove the Final designation and read-only protection from the file.

Print and send documents

When you're ready to distribute your document to other people, you can do so either by printing it on paper or by sending or posting the file for people to access electronically.

The available printing options change, depending on the printer that is selected. This is either the default or the most recently used printer. You can display a list of installed printers on the Print page of the Backstage view.

Apps you can print to, such as Microsoft OneNote are available with local and network printers

> **TIP** You can display a ScreenTip that contains information about a printer, such as the printer status, manufacturer, model, and connection method, by selecting it in the Printer list and then pointing to it. You can manage the apps and printers shown on the Printer menu from the Devices And Printers Control Panel window.

From the Settings area of the Print page, you can specify what part of the document is printed and whether markup (tracked changes) is indicated in the printed document. In addition, you have the option of printing the following information instead of the document content:

- Document properties

- Tracked changes

- Styles

- AutoText entries

- Custom shortcut keys

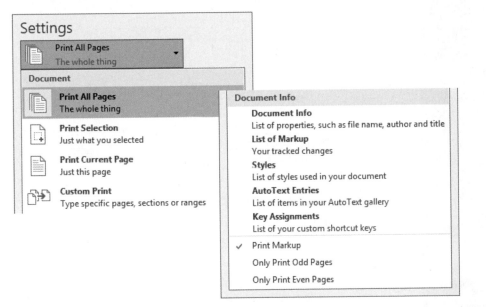

You can choose to print all or part of a document, or to print information that is stored with the document

You can choose to print a multipage document on one or both sides of the paper. If your printer supports double-sided printing, you have the option of flipping the double-sided page on the long edge or the short edge (depending on how you plan to bind and turn the document pages).

> ⚠️ **IMPORTANT** Some of the settings on the Print page of the Backstage view are dependent on the functionality supported by your printer. These settings might vary when you select a different device in the Printer list.

You can choose to print multiple copies of a document and whether to print collated pages (all pages of each copy together) or uncollated pages (all copies of each page together).

Finally, you have the option of specifying the number of pages to print per sheet of paper, up to 16. You can use this option to print a booklet with two pages per sheet that will be folded in the middle. You might also use this option to save paper when you're printing a long document, but bear in mind that as the number of pages per sheet increases, the size of the content printed on the page decreases.

> ✓ **TIP** If your printer has multiple paper trays or a manual paper feeder, you can select the paper source you want to use, on the Paper page of the Page Setup dialog box.

When Outlook is set as your default email app, you can send a document from Word while you're working in the file. You have the option of sending a copy of the file as a message attachment or, if the file is stored in a shared location, you can send a link to the file.

> ⚠️ **IMPORTANT** To use the Email sharing option, you must have Outlook installed and configured on your computer. If you're running another email app, the Email option will be available on the Share page of the Backstage view but might not generate an email message.

12

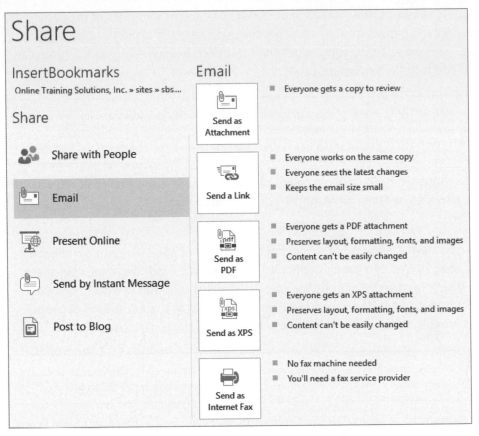

You can share an Office document as an attachment to an Outlook email message

When using the Share function, an interesting option that you have is to send a document as a PDF or XPS file. When you choose one of these options, Word creates the selected version of the document and attaches it to an email message for you to send. The PDF or XPS file is not saved to your computer.

> **TIP** If you have an account with a fax service provider that permits the transmission of fax messages by email, you can click the Send As Internet Fax option and provide the fax number to address the message in the format required by the fax service. For example, if your fax service provider is Contoso and the fax number is (425) 555-0199, the email might be addressed to 14255550199@contoso.com. The fax service relays the message electronically to the recipient's fax number.

To print one copy of a document with the default settings

1. Do either of the following:

   - Display the **Print** page of the Backstage view, and then click the **Print** button.

   - On the Quick Access Toolbar, click the **Quick Print** button.

   Word prints the document to the default printer with the default settings.

To print multiple copies of a document

1. Display the **Print** page of the Backstage view.

2. In the **Copies** box at the top of the page, enter the number of copies you want to print.

3. Click the **Print** button to print the specified number of copies of the document on the selected printer and return to the document.

To print only specific pages of a document

1. On the **Print** page of the Backstage view, click the first box in the **Settings** area to open a list of page options.

2. In the list, do any of the following:

   - Click **Print All Pages** to print the entire document. This is the default setting if there is currently no content selected in the document.

     > **TIP** If you first select text in the document and then display the Print page of the Backstage view, the Print Selection option will be active. Then when you click the Print button, Word will print only the selected text.

   - Click **Print Current Page** to print the page that is currently shown in the preview pane.

   - Click **Custom Print**, and then in the **Pages** box, enter the specific pages (in the format 1,3 or 1-3), sections (in the format s1 or s1-s3), or ranges (in the format p1s1-p3s2) you want to print.

3. Click the **Print** button to print the specified pages of the document on the selected printer and return to the document.

12

To display the list of installed printers

1. Display the **Print** page of the Backstage view.

2. In the **Printer** area, click the active printer.

To select a printer

1. On the **Print** page of the Backstage view, display the **Printer** list, and then click the printer you want to use.

To display printer status information

1. On the **Print** page of the Backstage view, point to the **Information** icon in the upper-right corner of the **Printer** area, or to the selected printer name, to display a ScreenTip that contains printer status information.

To send a document by email from within Word

1. In the document, click the **File** tab to display the Backstage view.

2. On the **Share** page of the Backstage view, click **Email** to display the email options.

3. In the **Email** pane, do one of the following:

   - Click **Send as Attachment** to attach a copy of the document to an email message.

   - Click **Send a Link** to insert a link to the shared file into an email message.

   > **TIP** The Send A Link button is available only if the document is saved in a shared location.

   - Click **Send as PDF** or **Send as XPS** to save a version of the document in that format and attach it to an email message.

4. If Outlook isn't already running, Word starts it before generating the email message. Enter your password if you are prompted to do so.

> **SEE ALSO** For information about the many fabulous features of Outlook 2016, refer to *Microsoft Outlook 2016 Step by Step* by Joan Lambert (Microsoft Press, 2016).

Skills review

In this chapter, you learned how to:

- Locate and correct text errors
- Preview and adjust page layout
- Control what appears on each page
- Prepare documents for electronic distribution
- Print and send documents

12

Practice tasks

The practice files for these tasks are located in the Word2016SBS\Ch12 folder. You can save the results of the tasks in the same folder.

> **IMPORTANT** You must have a printer installed to perform some of the following procedures. On a default installation of Office 2016, the Microsoft XPS Document Writer and Send To OneNote 2016 options appear in your Printers list. You can perform the procedures by using one of those options or an actual local or network printer connection.

Locate and correct text errors

Open the CorrectErrors document, and then complete the following tasks:

1. In the first paragraph, display a list of suggested spellings for the word *sorces*, (the first word with a red wavy underline). In the list, click **sources** to replace the misspelled word.

2. Position the cursor at the beginning of the document, and then do the following:

   - Check the spelling and grammar of the entire document.

   - Review each error that the spelling checker locates, and correct it as appropriate.

   - When the spelling checker flags the purchasing agent's last name, *Potra*, add the name to the custom dictionary so that Word doesn't flag it as an error in the future.

3. Save and close the document.

Preview and adjust page layout

Open the PreviewPages document, and then complete the following tasks:

1. Display the print preview of the document and zoom out to show both pages side by side in the preview pane.

2. Change the margins to **Wide**. Notice that the change is immediately reflected in the preview pane, and the page navigator indicates that the document now has three pages.

3. Scroll the preview pane to display the new third page.

4. From the preview pane, open the **Page Setup** dialog box. Turn on **Mirror margins** to set margins for facing pages. Then set the **Inside** margin to 2".

5. Review the other page settings and then return to the preview pane.

6. If you have a printer installed, print the document and compare it to what was shown on the screen. Then save and close the document.

Control what appears on each page

Open the ControlLayout document, display formatting marks, and then complete the following tasks:

1. Scroll through the document, noticing any awkward page breaks, such as a topic or list that starts close to the bottom of a page.

2. Near the bottom of page **1** and continuing onto page **2**, select the paragraph that begins with *The front office space*. Turn on the **Keep lines together** setting for the selection to move the entire paragraph to the beginning of the next page so that it is not split over two pages.

3. At the bottom of page **2** and top of page **3**, select the *Office Supplies* heading and the two lines that follow the heading. Turn on the **Keep with next** setting for the selected text.

4. Insert a **Next Page** section break immediately before the **Shipping Quick Reference** heading.

5. In the new section, set the **Margins** to **Wide** so the table better fits the page.

6. Return to the document and review your changes. Then save and close the document.

Prepare documents for electronic distribution

Open the PrepareDocument document, and then complete the following tasks:

1. On the **Info** page, notice the properties that are shown for the document.

2. Run the **Document Inspector** to check the document for all the default issues, and then do the following:

   - Examine the results of the report.

   - Remove all document properties and personal information from the document.

- If custom XML data was found, remove that.

- Reinspect the document and verify the removal of the properties and XML data.

3. Close the **Document Inspector** dialog box and notice the changes in the properties shown in the **Properties** area of the **Info** page.

4. Mark the document as **Final**. Notice the results on the **Info** page of the Backstage view. Then return to the document content and notice the results there.

5. Click the **Insert** tab to temporarily expand it, and notice that all the buttons are inactive (dimmed). Then click away from the tab to hide it. Word displays an information bar, notifying you that the document has been marked as final.

6. Save and close the document.

Print and send documents

Open the PrintDocument document, and then complete the following tasks:

> ⚠ **IMPORTANT** You must have an active printer connection to complete this exercise. You must also have configured Outlook to connect to your email account.

1. Display the **Print** page of the Backstage view. Notice that this is a two-page document. The colored document background is not displayed in the preview pane, because it will not be printed.

2. In the **Printer** area, display the list of installed printers, and then click the printer you want to use. Notice whether any of the available print options change.

3. Display the **Printer Status** ScreenTip for the selected printer.

4. Configure the print settings to print only page 2, and to print two copies of that page. Then print the document and confirm that it printed correctly as configured.

5. From the **Share** page of the Backstage view, send the document to yourself as an email message attachment. Then send the document to yourself as a PDF file attachment.

6. Review the received messages and their attachments to confirm the expected behavior.

7. Close the open documents.

Part 5

Use advanced Word functions

Reference content and content sources

Word has many types of reference tools that you can use to help readers locate information in or about a document. Many of these reference tools pull information directly from the document content based on its formatting. For example, you can format paragraphs as headings, and then insert a table of contents built from those headings. Similarly, you can insert index tags and then generate an index that references or links to them, or insert citations and then generate a bibliography from them.

In addition, you can insert named bookmarks as anchors that you can hyperlink to for cross-referencing purposes. You can also provide supporting information without interrupting the flow of the primary content by inserting information in footnotes or endnotes.

Another way to reference information that exists within a document or as a document property is by inserting a field that references the property. Changes to the property are automatically reflected in the fields that reference it. By using fields in this way, you can easily generate custom documents by updating the document properties.

This chapter guides you through procedures related to inserting bookmarks and cross-references, displaying document information in fields, inserting and modifying footnotes and endnotes, creating and modifying tables of contents, creating and modifying indexes, and citing sources and compiling bibliographies.

In this chapter

- Insert bookmarks and cross-references

- Display document information in fields

- Insert and modify footnotes and endnotes

- Create and modify tables of contents

- Create and modify indexes

- Cite sources and compile bibliographies

Practice files

For this chapter, use the practice files from the Word2016SBS\Ch13 folder. For practice file download instructions, see the introduction.

Insert bookmarks and cross-references

Word provides two tools that you can use to jump easily to designated places within the same document: bookmarks and cross-references.

Whether the document you're reading was created by you or by someone else, you can insert bookmarks to flag information to which you might want to return later. Like a physical bookmark, a Word bookmark marks a specific named place in a document. Each bookmark is identified by a unique name. (Bookmark names can contain only letters, numbers, and underscore characters.)

You can quickly go directly to any bookmark from the Bookmark dialog box, from the Go To tab of the Find And Replace dialog box, or from a hyperlink to the bookmark. Bookmarks are hidden by default, but you can configure Word options to display their markers, if you want to. The markers indicate only the bookmark locations. Bookmarks that mark individual locations are indicated by large, gray I-beams. Bookmarks that mark spans of text are indicated by gray square brackets at the beginning and end.

I-beams and brackets indicate bookmarks

You can create cross-references to bookmarks, headings, figures, tables, numbered items, footnotes, endnotes, and equations. Word automatically creates anchors for all of these items other than bookmarks. Cross-references can include hyperlinks, so that clicking a cross reference in the electronic document takes the reader directly to the specified location.

4. Storage

4.1 No bicycles, tricycles, scooters, roller skates, skateboards, wagons, toys, or other personal belongings shall be stored or left in any Common Area.

4.2 No trailers, boats, vans, campers, house trailers, buses, or trucks shall be stored in any parking space in any Common Area. (See 6. Parking for more information.)

4.3 No Owner shall use his or her garage to store personal belongings in such a way that there is not enough space for his or her vehicles.

Cross references are shaded when the cursor is in them

To insert a bookmark

1. Do either of the following:

   - Position the cursor in the location where you want to insert the bookmark. This is usually at the beginning of the content that you want to reference.

   - Select the text that you want to include in the bookmark.

2. On the **Insert** tab, in the **Links** group, click the **Bookmark** button to open the Bookmark dialog box.

If other bookmarks exist in the document, a bookmark is selected and its name displayed in the Bookmark Name box

3. In the **Bookmark name** box, enter a name for the bookmark you want to create (or replace the name that is currently in the Bookmark Name box.).

4. Click **Add** or press **Enter**.

> ✅ **TIP** Bookmark names cannot contain characters other than letters, numbers, and underscores. If you enter a prohibited character (such as a space or hyphen), the Add button becomes inactive. To name bookmarks with multiple words and maintain readability, either run the words together and capitalize each word (known as *camel caps*) or replace the spaces with underscores.

To display bookmarks in text

1. From the Backstage view, open the **Word Options** dialog box, and then click the **Advanced** page tab.

2. In the **Show Document Content** area of the **Advanced** page, select the **Show bookmarks** check box.

Word Options	? ✕
General	**Show document content**
Display	☑ Show background colors and images in Print Layout view
Proofing	☐ Show text wrapped within the document window
Save	☐ Show picture placeholders ⓘ
Language	☑ Show drawings and text boxes on screen
Advanced	☑ Show bookmarks
	☐ Show text boundaries

You can display bookmark indicators in a document

3. Click **OK**.

To go to any bookmark

1. Open the **Bookmark** dialog box, and then do either of the following:

   - In the **Bookmark name** list, double-click the bookmark you want to go to.

   - Click the bookmark you want to go to, and then click the **Go To** button.

Or

1. Do either of the following to display the Go To tab of the Find And Replace dialog box:

   - On the **Home** tab, in the **Editing** group, in the **Find** list, click **Go To**.

   - Press **Ctrl+G**.

2. In the **Go to what** list, click **Bookmark**.

3. Do either of the following in the **Enter bookmark name** list:

   - Click the bookmark you want.

   - Enter the name of the bookmark you want.

4. Click the **Go To** button.

To insert a cross-reference to a bookmark or document element

> ✓ **TIP** Word does not add text to introduce the cross-reference, so it's a good idea to enter text such as *See also* before the cross-reference.

1. On the **Insert** tab, in the **Links** group, click the **Cross-reference** button to open the Cross-reference dialog box.

You can cross-reference to many types of content

2. In the **Reference type** list, click the type of item you want to reference (for example, Heading).

3. In the **Insert reference to** list, click the text you want the cross-reference to display. (For example, when cross-referencing to a bookmark, you can display the bookmark text (when the bookmark includes a span of text), the page or paragraph number of the bookmark, or the word *above* or *below* depending on the location of the bookmark in relation to the location of the cross-reference.)

4. If you want the cross-reference to include a hyperlink, select the **Insert as hyperlink** check box. If you plan to distribute the document only on paper, it isn't necessary to hyperlink the cross-reference.

5. In the **For which** *item* pane, click the specific item you want to reference.

6. Click **Insert**, and then click **Close**.

7. Review the cross-reference, and add any words or punctuation that are necessary to assist the reader.

To go to a cross-referenced location

1. Hold down the **Ctrl** key, and then click the cross-reference.

> **TIP** Pointing to the inserted cross-reference displays a ScreenTip containing information about the cross-reference target.

> **IMPORTANT** If you delete the target of a cross-reference, you must manually delete the cross-reference by selecting the cross-reference text and deleting it as you would any other text. If you modify an item you have designated as the target of a cross-reference, delete the existing cross-reference and create a new one.

Hyperlink to additional resources

Many documents include URLs of websites that the reader can visit to obtain additional information related to the document topic. When a document will be viewed electronically, the URLs can be formatted as hyperlinks so that the websites can be accessed directly from the document. Hyperlinks can also provide direct access to bookmarks or headings in the document, or to a separate file; or you can use a hyperlink to create a new document or to open a pre-addressed email message window.

Hyperlinks are most frequently in text format, but you can attach a hyperlink to any object—for example, an image such as a shape, logo, or picture. Clicking the hyperlinked object then takes you directly to the linked location. Editing the object does not disrupt the hyperlink; however, deleting the object also deletes the hyperlink.

Word automatically adds hyperlink functionality and applies the Hyperlink format when you enter a standard website address and then press the Spacebar or Enter key.

To attach a hyperlink to text or an object, follow these steps:

1. Select the text or object that you want to hyperlink from.

2. On the **Insert** menu, in the **Links** group, click **Hyperlink** to open the Insert Hyperlink dialog box (or press **Ctrl+K**).

3. In the **Link to** list, click the type of target you're linking to. Often this is a webpage or another place in the file.

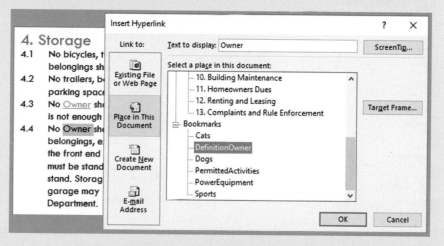

You can link to internal and external locations

4. If you're linking to a webpage, enter the URL in the **Address** box. If you're linking to a heading or bookmark in the current file, click it in the **Select a place in this document** pane. Then click **OK**.

Display document information in fields

A *field* is a placeholder that tells Word to supply specified information or to perform a specified action in a specified way. You can use fields to insert information that can be updated with the click of a button if the information changes. You don't simply enter a field in your document; instead, you tell Word to insert the field you want. One way to do this is to use the Field dialog box. This dialog box also allows access to various settings for the selected field type.

The Field dialog box provides a comprehensive list of all the available fields

More often, however, you will insert preconfigured fields, which you can do by clicking various options on the Insert tab. For example, clicking the Date & Time button on the Insert tab opens the Date And Time dialog box, which you can use to insert a date and time field. When you insert a date and time field, Word retrieves the date and time from your computer's internal calendar or clock. You can set a date and time field to be updated every time you open a document or whenever you save the document, or you can lock the field so that it does not update at all.

You can specify the date and time format you want

Another type of preconfigured field you might want to insert in a document—for example, in its header or footer—is one that contains a document property, such as the author, title, or last modification date. You can easily insert this type of information from the Document Property submenu of the Quick Parts menu. (If you edit the contents of the field in the document, the change is carried over to the list of properties displayed on the Info page in Backstage view.)

When you insert the Author document property field, the author's name appears in the document

> **SEE ALSO** For information about document properties, see "Prepare documents for electronic distribution" in Chapter 12, "Finalize and distribute documents."

13

To insert a date and time field

1. Position the cursor in the document where you want to insert the field.

2. On the **Insert** tab, in the **Text** group, click the **Date & Time** button to open the Date And Time dialog box.

> ✅ **TIP** If you want to insert a date and time field in a header or footer, you can also open the Date And Time dialog box from the Design tool tab. For more information about headers and footers, see "Insert headers, footers, and page numbers" in Chapter 9, "Add visual elements."

3. In the **Available formats** list, click the date and time format you want.

4. If you want the field to automatically update each time you open the document, select the **Update automatically** check box.

5. Click **OK**.

To edit a date and time field so that it is updated when the file is saved

1. Right-click the date and time field, and then click **Edit Field** to open the Field dialog box and display the properties and options for the current field.

2. In the **Categories** list, click **Date and Time** to filter the **Field names** list to display only the fields that relate to dates and times.

3. In the **Field names** list, click **SaveDate**.

4. In the **Date formats** list, click the format you want.

5. Select the **Preserve formatting during updates** check box.

6. Click **OK**.

To manually update a date and time field

1. Do either of the following:

   - Select the field, and then click the **Update** button that appears above it.

   - Right-click the field and click **Update Field**.

   The field will be updated to the current date and time, to the date and time it was last saved, or to the date and time it was last printed, depending on the setting of the field.

To lock a selected date and time field

1. Press **Ctrl+F11**.

> ✅ **TIP** To unlock the field, select it, and then press Ctrl+Shift+F11.

To insert a document property field

1. On the **Insert** tab, in the **Text** group, click the **Quick Parts** button, click **Document Property**, and then click the document property you want to insert.

📑 A̲utoText ▶		
📋 D̲ocument Property ▶	Abstract	
▣ F̲ield...	Author	
🗐 B̲uilding Blocks Organizer...	Category	
🖫 S̲ave Selection to Quick Part Gallery...	Comments	
	Company	
	Company Address	
	Company E-mail	
	Company Fax	
	Company Phone	
	Keywords	
	Manager	
	Publish Date	
	Status	
	Subject	
	Title	

You can insert document property fields into your document

13

Insert and modify footnotes and endnotes

When you want to make a comment about a statement in a document—for example, to explain an assumption or cite the source for a different opinion—you can enter the comment as a footnote or an endnote. Doing so inserts a number or symbol called a *reference mark* in the body of your document. The associated comment appears with the same number or symbol, either as a footnote at the bottom of the page or as an endnote at the end of the document or document section. In most views, footnotes or endnotes are divided from the main text by a note separator line.

MOVING TO A NEW HOME

Bamboos grow best in a moderately acidic loamy soil. A forest plant, it's best if mulch[1] is kept over the roots and rhizomes.

Bamboo can be planted any time of the year in areas with mild climates. A newly planted bamboo requires frequent and liberal watering, twice a week or more often during hot or windy weather.

To control spread of any of the running bamboo varieties, dig a trench[2] that is at least 30 inches wide and 30 inches deep around the area that you want the newly planted bamboo to occupy. Line the trench with a polyethylene bamboo barrier, and fill the lined trench with gravel. Tightly compact the soil next to the barrier to discourage deep rhizome growth.

---

[1] Grass makes a good mulch, because it's high in nitrogen and silica, as do chipped trees, bark, and straw.
[2] Examine the trench each fall to determine whether any rhizomes have tried to cross it. If so, cut them off.

Footnotes appear on the same page as their reference marks, and endnotes appear at the end of the document

 TIP You can quickly display the actual footnotes or endnotes (rather than their reference marks) by clicking the Show Notes button.

You can insert and manage footnotes and endnotes by using the commands in the Footnotes group on the References tab.

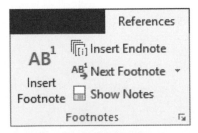

Footnote and endnote tools

You can use commands in the Footnote And Endnote dialog box to change various settings, such as where the footnote or endnote should appear, how it should be laid out, and what number format to use. By default, footnote reference marks use the *1, 2, 3* number format, and endnote reference marks use the *i, ii, iii* number format.

You can change the numbering format before or after you create footnotes or endnotes

To insert a footnote

1. Click in the document where you want the footnote reference to appear.
2. On the **References** tab, in the **Footnotes** group, click **Insert Footnote**.
3. Word creates a blank footnote at the bottom of the page and displays a blinking cursor. Enter the footnote text, and then click anywhere outside of the footnote area to return to the document.

To insert an endnote

1. Click in the document where you want the endnote reference to appear.
2. On the **References** tab, in the **Footnotes** group, click **Insert Endnote**.
3. Word creates a blank endnote at the end of the document and displays a blinking cursor. Enter the endnote text, and then click anywhere outside of the endnote area to return to the document.

To convert a footnote to an endnote

1. Right-click the footnote, and then click **Convert to Endnote**.

To convert an endnote to a footnote

1. Right-click the endnote, and then click **Convert to Footnote**.

To move among footnote or endnote references

1. Do either of the following:

   - On the **References** tab, in the **Footnotes** group, click the **Next Footnote** button.

   - In the **Footnotes** group, in the **Next Footnote** list, click **Next Footnote**, **Previous Footnote**, **Next Endnote**, or **Previous Endnote**.

To display footnotes or endnotes

1. Do either of the following:

   - Double-click a reference mark in the body of the document to display its corresponding footnote or endnote.

   - On the **References** tab, in the **Footnotes** group, click the **Show Notes** button to display the list of footnotes or endnotes.

To change the number format of footnotes or endnotes

1. On the **References** tab, click the **Footnotes** dialog box launcher to open the Footnote And Endnote dialog box.

2. In the **Location** area of the **Footnote and Endnote** dialog box, click **Footnotes** or **Endnotes** to indicate the element you want to modify.

3. In the **Format** area, in the **Number format** list, click the number format you want to use.

4. Click **Apply**.

To delete a footnote or endnote

1. In the document text, select the footnote or endnote marker, and then press **Delete**.

Create and modify tables of contents

When you create a long document that includes headings, such as an annual report or a catalog that has several sections, you might want to add a table of contents to the beginning of the document to give your readers an overview of the document content and help them navigate to specific sections. In a document that will be printed, you can indicate with a page number the page where each heading is located. If the document will be distributed electronically, you can link each entry in the table of contents to the corresponding heading in the document so that readers can jump directly to the heading with a click of the mouse.

The table of contents is a field that can be updated

13

By default, Word creates a table of contents based on paragraphs within the document that you have formatted with the standard heading styles: Heading 1, Heading 2, and so on. Word can also create a table of contents based on outline levels or on fields that you have inserted in the document. When you tell Word to create a table of contents, Word identifies the entries and inserts the table at the cursor as a single field.

> **SEE ALSO** For information about applying styles, see "Apply built-in styles to text" in Chapter 4, "Modify the structure and appearance of text."

The Table Of Contents controls are available from the References tab. In the Table Of Contents gallery, you can select from three standard options:

- **Automatic Table 1** This option inserts a table of contents that has the heading *Contents* and includes all text styled as Heading 1, Heading 2, or Heading 3.

- **Automatic Table 2** This option inserts a table of contents that has the heading *Table of Contents* and includes all text styled as Heading 1, Heading 2, or Heading 3.

- **Manual Table** This option inserts a table of contents that has the heading *Table of Contents* and includes placeholders that are not linked to the document content.

You can choose from three main options in the Table Of Contents gallery

Entries in a table of contents are formatted by using nine levels of built-in TOC styles (TOC 1, TOC 2, and so on). By default, Word uses the styles that are assigned in the template attached to the document. If you want to use a different style, you can create a custom table from the Table Of Contents dialog box. Here, you can choose from several formats, including Classic, Distinctive, Fancy, Modern, Formal, and Simple. (The Print Preview and Web Preview panes display a preview of the selected format.) You can also apply a different leader—that is, the set of characters used between the text and the corresponding page number in the table of contents. After you create a table of contents, you can format it manually by selecting text and then applying character or paragraph formatting or styles.

You can choose a different set of formatting styles for your table of contents

> **TIP** The TOC styles are based on the Body font of the document theme. Each style has specific indent and spacing settings. If you create a table of contents based on the document template, you can customize the TOC styles during the creation process. To do so, click From Template in the Formats list. Then click the Modify button. The Style dialog box opens, displaying the nine TOC styles. You can modify the font, paragraph, tabs, border, and other formatting of these styles the same way you would modify any other style. For information about creating styles, see "Create and modify styles" in Chapter 15, "Create custom document elements."

13

You can modify the elements on which Word bases the table at any time, and update the table with a single click to reflect your changes. If you change a heading in the document or if edits to the text change the page breaks, you can update the table of contents to reflect those changes. You have the option of updating only the page numbers or, if you have changed, added, or deleted headings, you can update (re-create) the entire table.

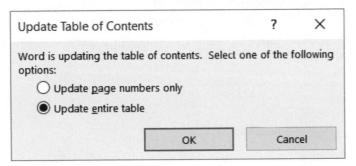

If headings or page breaks change, you can easily update the table of contents

You can use the table of contents to navigate within your document. For example, you can hold down the Ctrl key and click on a heading in a table of contents to access the corresponding section in the text.

Contents

Current Document
Ctrl+Click to follow link

General Administration ....

   Contact Information ....

   Facilities ....

     Office ....

     Warehouse ....

     Phone System...

   Ordering Stationery and Supplies ....

Hyperlink navigation functionality is built into the table of contents

Other reference tables

If a document includes figures, tables, or equations, you can easily create a table of figures so that readers can locate and quickly navigate to them. A table of figures is built from the tools in the Captions group on the References tab of the ribbon. You must insert a caption for each figure, table, or equation you want to include, and then generate the table.

If a legal document contains items such as regulations, cases, and statutes that are identified as legal citations, you can tell Word to create a table of authorities. In the table, citations are categorized as cases, statutes, rules, treatises, regulations, or other authorities.

Word uses the citations to create this type of table the same way it uses headings to create a table of contents and captions to create a table of figures. You must insert a citation for each legal reference you want to include, and then generate the table.

To insert a table of contents for a document with headings

1. Position the cursor in the document where you want to insert the table of contents.

2. On the **References** tab, in the **Table of Contents** group, click the **Table of Contents** button to display the **Table of Contents** menu.

3. In the **Table of Contents** gallery, select the table of contents style you want.

To create a custom table of contents

1. Position the cursor in the document where you want to add a custom table of contents.

2. Click the **Table of Contents** button, and click **Custom Table of Contents** to open the Table Of Contents dialog box.

3. In the **General** area of the **Table of Contents** tab, in the **Formats** list, click the format you want.

13

4. In the **Tab leader** list, click the leader option you want.

5. Click **OK**.

To update a table of contents

1. Do either of the following to display the Update Table Of Contents dialog box:

   - Click anywhere in the table of contents to select it, and then click the **Update** button that appears above the table.

     > **TIP** The table of contents is contained in one large field. When you click it, you select the entire field. For information about fields, see "Display document information in fields" earlier in this chapter.

   - On the **References** tab, in the **Table of Contents** group, click the **Update Table** button.

2. In the dialog box, do either of the following:

   - Click **Update page numbers only** to update the page numbers but not the headings.

   - Click **Update entire table** to update the headings and page numbers.

3. Click **OK**.

To jump to a location in the document from the table of contents

1. Point to any entry in the table of contents.

2. Press and hold the **Ctrl** key. The pointer changes to a hand.

3. Click the entry to move directly to that heading.

> **SEE ALSO** For more information about linking to other parts of a document, see "Insert bookmarks and cross-references" earlier in this chapter.

To delete a table of contents

1. On the **References** tab, in the **Table of Contents** group, click the **Table of Contents** button.

2. Click **Remove Table of Contents**.

Create and modify indexes

To help readers find specific concepts and terms that they might not be able to read-ily locate by looking at a table of contents, you can include an index at the end of a document. Word creates an index by compiling an alphabetical listing with page numbers based on index entry fields that you mark in the document. As with a table of contents, an index is inserted as a single field.

> **TIP** You don't need to create indexes for documents that will be distributed electroni-cally, because readers can use the Navigation pane to find the information they need. For more information, see "Find and replace text" in Chapter 3, "Enter and edit text."

animals	2	guest parking spaces	3
Association	1, 3, 4, 5, 6	Limited Common Area	1, 3, 4, 5, 6
Bellevue Fire Department	2	Maintenance Committee	4, 5, 6
bicycles	2	Maintenance Request Form	5, 6
Board	1, 2, 3, 4, 5, 6, 7, 8	Parking	3
boats	2	parking spaces	2, 3
Bylaws	1, 7	pet	2
common garage	2, 3	Plant containers	4
damage	1, 3, 5, 6	seeing-eye dogs	2
Declaration	1, 7	special assessment	6
dirt bikes	3	speed limit	3
Elevator	5	sprinkler	3
garage	*See* parking	trailers	2
Garage doors	4	vehicle	3
garbage	2		

You can generate an index for your document to help readers find important topics

In the index, an entry might apply to a word or phrase that appears on one page or one that is discussed on several pages. The entry might have related subentries. For example, in the index to this book, the main index entry *text effects* might have below it the subentries *applying* and *live preview of*. An index might also include cross-reference entries that direct readers to related entries. For example, the main index entry *text wrapping breaks* might be cross-referenced to *line breaks*. You can use cross references to direct readers to index terms they might not think of when looking for specific information.

> **TIP** When building an index, bear in mind the terms that readers are likely to look up. For example, one reader might expect to find information about cell phones by looking under *cell*, whereas another might look under *mobile*, another under *phones*, and another under *telephones*. A good index will include all four entries.

13

Before you can generate an index for your document, you must insert index entry fields throughout the document. Word then compiles the entries in these fields into the index. To insert an index entry field into the document, you use the Mark Index Entry dialog box. In this dialog box, you can do the following:

- Modify the selected text to alter how it appears in the index.

- Add a subentry.

- Designate the entry as a cross-reference, one-page entry, or, if the selected text spans multiple pages, a page-range entry. In the case of page-range entries, Word creates a bookmark for the selected text and prompts you to enter a name for it in the Mark Index Entry dialog box.

- Format the page number associated with the entry—for example, to make it appear bold or italic in the index.

You can edit, add a subentry to, and otherwise adjust the index entry in this dialog box

After you set the options in the dialog box, you can insert an index entry field adjacent to the selected text by clicking Mark, or adjacent to every occurrence of the selected text in the document by clicking Mark All.

> **TIP** The Mark Index Entry dialog box remains open to simplify the process of inserting multiple index entry fields, so you don't have to click the Mark Entry button for each new entry. You can move the dialog box off to the side so that it doesn't block the text you're working with.

Index entry fields are formatted as hidden. They are not visible unless you display formatting marks and hidden characters. When the index entry field is visible, the entry appears in the document enclosed in quotation marks within a set of braces, with the designator *XE* and a dotted underline.

To compile an index that is based on the index entries in a document, you work in the Index dialog box.

You use the Index dialog box to set up the index

In this dialog box, you can specify the following:

- Whether the index formatting should use styles from the current template or be based on one of four predefined formats, which you can preview in the Print Preview box

- Whether page numbers should be right-aligned, and if so, whether they should have dotted, dashed, or solid tab leaders

- Whether the index should be indented, with each subentry on a separate line below its main entry, or run-in, with subentries on the same line as the main entries

- The number of columns you want

When you click OK in the Index dialog box, Word calculates the page numbers of all the entries and subentries, consolidates them, and inserts the index as one field in the specified format at the specified location in the document.

You can edit the text of the index generated from the entries, but the changes you make are not permanent. If you regenerate the index, the original entries will be

13

restored. It is more efficient to edit the text within the quotation marks in the index entry fields. You can move and copy index entries by using the same techniques you would for regular text. If you make changes to a document that affect index entries or page numbering, you can update the index.

To mark a word or short phrase as an index entry

1. Select the word or phrase you want to mark.

2. Do any of the following to open or activate the Mark Index Entry dialog box:

    - On the **References** tab, in the **Index** group, click the **Mark Entry** button.

    - Press **Alt+Shift+X**.

    - If the **Mark Index Entry** dialog box is already open, click its title bar.

    Notice that the selected word or phrase has already been entered in the Main Entry box.

3. If you want, select the text and enter replacement text—for example, making a word plural or lowercase.

> **TIP** Index entries will appear in the index exactly as they appear in the Mark Index Entry dialog box. For consistency, make all nouns except proper nouns lowercase, and make all nouns plural unless only one of the items exists.

4. Do either of the following:

    - Click **Mark** to insert an index entry field next to just this occurrence of the selected word or phrase.

    - Click **Mark All** to insert index entry fields adjacent to every occurrence of the selected word or phrase in the document.

> **TIP** Index entries are case sensitive. If you mark an entry that is lowercase, any instances of the word or phrase that are uppercase will not be marked with index entries, because their capitalization does not match the selected word.

> **TIP** The Mark Index Entry dialog box remains open even after you insert the index entry, so that you can quickly add more index entries. When you're finished marking index entries, simply close the dialog box.

To mark text that is longer than one page as an index entry

1. Select the text segment that you want to mark.

2. Open the **Mark Index Entry** dialog box or, if it is already open, click its title bar to activate it.

3. The selected text appears in the Main Entry box. Replace the text segment with an appropriate index entry.

4. Click **Page Range**.

5. In the **Bookmark** field, enter a bookmark name for the selected text.

> ✓ **TIP** Bookmark names can contain only numbers, letters, and underscore characters. To name bookmarks with multiple words, either run the words together and capitalize each word or replace the spaces with underscores for readability.

6. Click the **Mark** button.

To add a cross-reference to an index entry

1. After marking a word, phrase, or longer text as an index entry, without leaving the **Mark Index Entry** dialog box, in the **Options** area, select the **Cross-reference** option. Notice that the cursor moves to the space after the word *See* in the adjacent box.

2. Without moving the cursor, enter the text you want to use for a cross-reference. This text should exactly match another index entry in the document.

3. Click **Mark** to insert a cross-reference to the new index entry adjacent to the current index entry.

To enter a subentry for an index entry

1. Select the word or phrase you want to mark.

2. Open the **Mark Index Entry** dialog box or, if it is already open, click its title bar to activate it.

3. In the **Subentry** box, enter the subentry.

4. Click **Mark** to insert an index entry with the entry and subentry separated by a colon.

13

To edit an index entry

1. Click within the index entry in the document (not in the Mark Index Entry dialog box), and make the changes you want.

To insert an index in a document

1. In a document with previously marked index entries, position the cursor where you want to insert the index—usually at the end of the document.

2. On the **Home** tab, in the **Paragraph** group, click the **Show/Hide ¶** button to hide formatting marks, fields, and content that is formatted as hidden.

> ⚠️ **IMPORTANT** When hidden content is visible, the document might not be paginated correctly. Always turn off the display of formatting marks and hidden characters before creating an index.

3. On the **References** tab, in the **Index** group, click the **Insert Index** button to open the Index dialog box.

4. Optionally, change the number of columns and the format.

5. Click **OK** to compile an index based on the index entries you previously marked.

To delete an index entry

1. On the **Home** tab, in the **Paragraph** group, click the **Show/Hide ¶** button to show formatting marks, fields, and content that is formatted as hidden.

2. Scroll to the index entry you want to delete.

3. Select the entire entry and press the **Delete** key.

> ✅ **TIP** Dragging through any part of an index entry field that includes one of the enclosing braces selects the entire field. If you find it hard to select only this entry, try pointing to the right of the closing brace (}) and dragging slightly to the left.

To update an index

1. Do either of the following:

   - Click anywhere in the index, and then, on the **References** tab, in the **Index** group, click the **Update Index** button.

   - Right-click the index and then click **Update Field**.

Cite sources and compile bibliographies

Many types of documents that you create might require a bibliography that lists the sources of the information that appears or is referenced in the document. Whether your sources are books, periodicals, websites, or interviews, you can record details about them. You can also select a common style guide, such as the *Chicago Manual of Style*, to have Word automatically list your sources in that style guide's standard format.

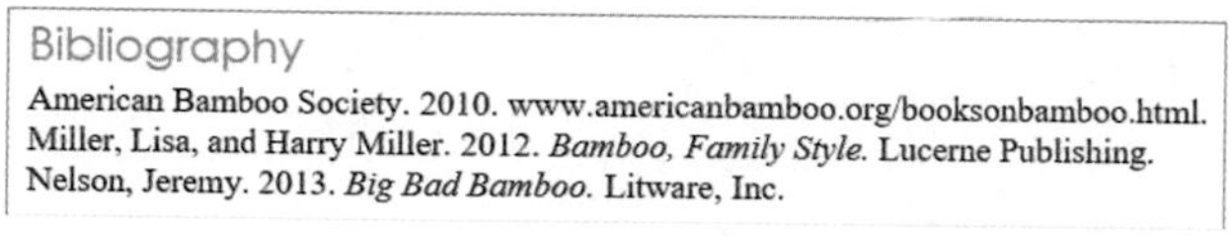

Bibliography

American Bamboo Society. 2010. www.americanbamboo.org/booksonbamboo.html.
Miller, Lisa, and Harry Miller. 2012. *Bamboo, Family Style*. Lucerne Publishing.
Nelson, Jeremy. 2013. *Big Bad Bamboo*. Litware, Inc.

A bibliography formatted to meet the specifications of the Chicago Manual of Style Sixteenth Edition

Word offers a tool, called the Source Manager, to help you keep track of sources and to ensure that you reference them in the proper format. When you enter source information, Word stores the information in a separate file on your computer's hard disk so that you can cite the sources in any document you create. The Source Manager offers easy access to this master list of sources, in addition to access to the list of sources cited in your current document.

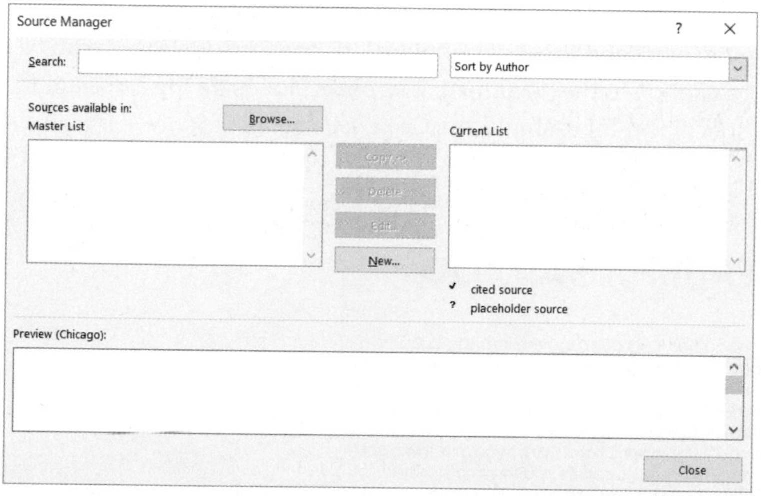

The Source Manager accumulates sources from all documents, so if other documents already contain citations, their source information might appear here

> **TIP** To add a source in the master list to the current document, click it in the Master List box in the Source Manager dialog box and then click the Copy button to copy it to the Current List box.

13

To create sources, you use the Create Source dialog box. In this dialog box, you can select the type of source—for example, whether it's a book, a journal article, or other type of source. You can then enter the author of the source, the title of the source, and other key information. If the source has multiple authors, you can open the Edit Name dialog box to enter them all.

Create Source dialog box

You use the Create Source dialog box to create a source

Within your document, you can cite the sources you create by using the Source Manager dialog box or by using the Insert Citation menu available from the Citations & Bibliography group of the References tab. You can also use the Insert Citation menu to create new citations as you work and to set placeholders for citations, which you can fill in later. When you add a citation to the document, it appears alongside the associated text in the format you specified—for example, the *Chicago Manual of Style*.

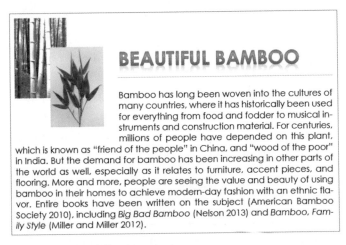

This document includes three citations

If you know you need to insert a citation, but you don't have all the information about your source handy, you can insert a placeholder. Then, when you gather the information you need, you can update the placeholder.

After you enter citations in a document, you can compile their sources into a list with one of three headings: *Bibliography*, *References*, or *Works Cited*. (The heading you choose is usually specified by the organization or person for whom you are preparing the document, such as your company, your instructor, or the publication in which you intend to publish the document.) You can also insert a source list with no heading at all.

You can choose from three built-in styles or insert a bibliography with no heading

When you compile a bibliography, Word inserts it at the cursor as one field. You can edit the text of a bibliography, but if the source information changes, it is more efficient to edit the source in the Source Manager and then update the bibliography the same way you would update a table of contents or index.

To set the style rules for citations

1. On the **References** tab, in the **Citations & Bibliography** group, display the **Style** list.

The available styles change from time to time

2. In the style list, click the style guide you want Word to use when creating the bibliography.

To create a bibliography source

1. In the **Citations & Bibliography** group, click the **Manage Sources** button to open the Source Manager dialog box.

2. In the **Source Manager** dialog box, click **New** to open the Create Source dialog box.

3. In the **Type of Source** list, click the type of source (book or magazine, for example) that you want to add.

> **⚠ IMPORTANT** The fields in the Bibliography Fields For section vary depending on what type of source you select. Also, the data required is specific to the style guide that is selected.

4. In the **Bibliography Fields for** *Style* area, enter the required bibliographic data.

5. Click **OK** to add the source to both the **Master List** and the **Current List**.

To create a source with multiple authors

1. In the **Create Source** dialog box, click **Edit** to open the Edit Name dialog box.

If a source has more than one author, create a multiple-name entity

2. In the **Add name** area, enter an author's name in the **Last**, **First**, and/or **Middle** boxes, and then click **Add** to add the name to the Names box.

3. Repeat step 2 to add other authors, clicking **Add** after each author.

4. Reorder the names as needed by selecting a name in the **Names** box and then clicking the **Up** or **Down** button to change its place in the order.

5. When you are finished adding authors, click **OK**.

6. In the **Create Source** dialog box, enter the bibliographic data, and then click **OK**.

7. In the **Source Manager** dialog box, click **Close**.

13

To insert a citation to an existing source in a document

1. Position the cursor in the document at the location where you want to insert a citation.

2. On the **References** tab, in the **Citations & Bibliography** group, click the **Insert Citation** button to display the list of available sources.

> **American Bamboo Society**
> 2010
>
> **Miller, Lisa, Miller, Harry**
> Bamboo, Family Style,
> (2012)
> **Nelson, Jeremy**
> Big Bad Bamboo, (2013)
>
> ---
> 📇 Add New Source...
>
> 🔖 Add New Placeholder...

You can cite sources from the Insert Citation menu

3. On the **Insert Citation** menu, click a source to insert it in the document.

To create a source while inserting a citation

1. On the **Insert Citation** menu, click **Add New Source** to open the Create Source dialog box.

2. Enter source information as described in the procedure "To create a bibliography source" earlier in this topic.

3. Click **OK** to add the citation to the document and add the source information to both the Master List and the Current List in the Source Manager.

To insert a citation placeholder

1. On the **References** tab, in the **Citations & Bibliography** group, click **Insert Citation**, and then click **Add New Placeholder**.

2. In the **Placeholder Name** dialog box, enter a descriptive name for the placeholder (without spaces), and then click **OK**.

To update a placeholder

1. Do either of the following:

   - Click the placeholder in the document, click the arrow that appears, and then click **Edit Source**.

   - In the **Source Manager** dialog box, in the **Current List** box, click the placeholder, and then click the **Edit** button.

2. In the **Edit Source** dialog box, enter the necessary source information, and then click **OK**.

To generate and insert a bibliography

1. In the **Citations & Bibliography** group, click **Bibliography** to display the Bibliography gallery.

2. Select a bibliography format from the gallery to insert a bibliography containing all the citations in the document in alphabetical order.

To update a bibliography

1. Do either of the following:

   - Click anywhere in the bibliography to activate it. Then above the bibliography, click the **Update Citations and Bibliography** button.

   - Right-click the bibliography, and then click **Update Field**.

Skills review

In this chapter, you learned how to:

- Insert bookmarks and cross-references

- Display document information in fields

- Insert and modify footnotes and endnotes

- Create and modify tables of contents

- Create and modify indexes

- Cite sources and compile bibliographies

13

Practice tasks

The practice files for these tasks are located in the Word2016SBS\Ch13 folder. You can save the results of the tasks in the same folder.

Insert bookmarks and cross-references

Open the InsertBookmarks document in Print Layout view, and then perform the following tasks:

1. Position the cursor at the beginning of the *10. Building Maintenance* heading (don't select any text).

2. Insert a bookmark named **BuildingMaintenance.**

3. In section 10.3, select the bulleted list, and then add a bookmark named **LimitedCommonAreas**.

4. Use the commands on the **Advanced** page of the **Word Options** dialog box to display bookmarks in the document.

5. Use any of the methods described in this chapter to go to each bookmark in turn.

6. At the end of section 4.2, enter **See also** followed by a space and a period.

7. Position the cursor before the period, and then insert a hyperlinked cross-reference to the section 6 heading.

8. Use the cross-reference to go directly to section 6.

9. Save and close the document.

Display document information in fields

Open the DisplayFields document in Print Layout view, and then perform the following tasks:

1. Display the document's headers and footers.

2. Activate the document footer, and then position the cursor at the left end of the footer.

3. Use the commands in the **Date & Time** dialog box to insert a field that displays both the date and time and that updates automatically.

4. Edit the field to change it to a **SaveDate** field that displays both the date and time and that preserves formatting during updates.

5. Save the document.

6. Update the footer to display the time that you saved the document.

7. Lock the **SaveDate** field, and then save the document again.

8. Right-click the field. Notice that the **Update Field** command is not available.

9. Unlock the **SaveDate** field.

10. In the middle of the footer, insert the **Author** document property field.

11. If your name doesn't appear in the field, display the **Info** page of the Backstage view, expand the **Properties** list to include the **Author** property, and enter yourself as the author. Then return to the document to verify that the field displays your name.

12. Save and close the document.

Insert and modify footnotes and endnotes

Open the InsertFootnotes document in Print Layout view, and then perform the following tasks:

1. In the first paragraph after the heading *Moving to a New Home*, locate the word *mulch*. Insert a footnote immediately after the word.

2. In the footnote area that appears at the bottom of the page, enter Grass makes a good mulch, because it's high in nitrogen and silica.

3. In the second paragraph under the heading *Moving to a New Home*, insert an endnote immediately after the word *trench*.

4. In the endnote area that appears at the end of the document, enter Examine the trench each fall to determine whether any rhizomes have tried to cross it. If so, cut them off.

5. Convert the endnote to a footnote.

6. Move the cursor to the beginning of the document, and then go to the first footnote reference.

7. Double-click the footnote reference mark to display the corresponding footnote.

8. Display the list of footnotes in the document.

9. Change the format of the footnote markers from numbers to symbols. Notice the effect of the change.

10. Save and close the document.

Create and modify tables of contents

Open the CreateTOC document in Print Layout view, and then perform the following tasks:

1. With the cursor positioned at the beginning of the document, insert an **Automatic Style 2** table of contents. Review the table of contents, and then delete it.

2. Position the cursor at the beginning of the document, and then open the **Table of Contents** dialog box.

3. Use the commands in the dialog box to insert a **Formal** table of contents with no tab leader.

4. From the table of contents, go directly to the *Phone System* heading in the document.

5. In the heading, replace the word *Phone* with **Telecommunications**.

6. Update the entire table of contents, and verify that it reflects the change in the heading.

7. Save and close the document.

Create and modify indexes

Open the CreateIndexes document in Print Layout view, display formatting marks, and then perform the following tasks:

1. At the beginning of the document, in the first bulleted list item, select the word *Declaration*. Then mark all instances of that word in the document as index entries.

2. In section 2.3, select the word *sports*. Mark only this instance of the word as an index entry.

3. In section 3.2, select the word *animal*. Mark all instances of the word as index entries, but change the main entry to **animals**.

4. In section 3.3, in the first bulleted list item, select the word *dog*. Mark all instances of the word as index entries. Then add a *See* cross-reference from *dog* to *animals*.

5. In section 5.1, mark the first instance of the word *garbage* as an index entry. Then add the subentry **recycling**.

6. In section 11.4, select the entire bulleted list.

7. In the **Mark Index Entry** dialog box, replace the text in the **Main entry** box with **delinquency**.

8. In the **Options** area of the dialog box, click **Page Range**.

9. In the **Bookmark** field, enter **delinquency**. Then click the **Mark** button.

10. If you want to create a more extensive index, add other index entries.

11. Position the cursor at the end of the document, after the **Index** heading.

12. Hide formatting marks so that they don't affect the page numbers of the index entries.

13. Insert an index in the **Simple** format, with page numbers right-aligned and with dots as tab leaders. Review the index. Notice that the delinquency entry points to an invalid bookmark.

14. Show formatting marks, fields, and content that is formatted as hidden.

15. In section 11.4, delete the *delinquency* index entry.

16. Hide formatting marks, and then update the index.

17. Save and close the document.

Cite sources and compile bibliographies

Open the CompileBibliography document in Print Layout view, and then perform the following tasks:

1. Set the bibliography style to **Chicago Sixteenth Edition**.

2. Create a new source in the **Source Manager** by using the following information:

   Type of Source: Book
   Author: Jeremy Nelson
   Title: Big Bad Bamboo
   Year: 2015

Publisher: Litware, Inc.

3. Create a second source in the **Source Manager**, this time using the commands in the **Edit Name** dialog box to accommodate multiple authors. Use the following information:

    Type of Source: Book
    Authors: Lisa Miller and Harry Miller
    Title: Bamboo, Family Style
    Year: 2014
    Publisher: Lucerne Publishing

4. Close the **Source Manager** dialog box.

5. In the first paragraph of the document, position the cursor immediately after *Big Bad Bamboo*, and then insert the Nelson citation.

6. Position the cursor immediately after *Bamboo, Family Style*, and then insert the Miller citation.

7. Move the cursor to the end of the document, and then insert the bibliography. Use the **Bibliography** option.

8. In the first paragraph of the document, position the cursor after *Entire books have been written on the subject*, and insert a new citation with the following information:

    Type of Source: Web site
    Corporate Author: American Bamboo Society
    Name of Web Page: Bamboo, Family Style
    Year: 2010
    URL: www.americanbamboo.org/booksonbamboo.html

9. Update the bibliography and verify that it includes the new citation.

10. Save and close the document.

Merge data with documents and labels

Many organizations communicate with customers or members by means of letters, newsletters, and promotional pieces that are sent to everyone on a mailing list. You can use a reasonably simple process called *mail merge* to easily insert specific information from a data source into a Word document to create personalized individual items such as form letters, labels, envelopes, or email messages. You can also use this process to create a directory, catalog, or other listing that incorporates information from the data source.

The primary requirement for a mail merge operation is a well-structured data source. You can pull information from a variety of data sources—even your Outlook address book—and merge it with a starting document or a content template to create the output you want. Word has a wizard that can guide you through the processes, but this chapter provides information about each of the individual processes so you can quickly get started with your merging projects.

This chapter guides you through procedures related to choosing and refining data sources, choosing the output type and starting documents, previewing the results and completing the merge, and creating individual envelopes and labels.

In this chapter

- Understand the mail merge process
- Start the mail merge process
- Choose and refine the data source
- Insert merge fields
- Preview and complete the merge
- Create individual envelopes and labels

Practice files

For this chapter, use the practice files from the Word2016SBS\Ch14 folder. For practice file download instructions, see the introduction.

Understand the mail merge process

The process for creating a mail merge document is quite straightforward and logical. All the tools for performing mail merge operations are available from the Mailings tab. From this tab, you can run the wizard or perform individual steps of the mail merge process on your own.

Mail merge tools are located on the Mailings tab

Three important terms that are used when discussing mail merge processes are:

- **Data source** The file or storage entity that contains the variable information you want to pull into the merge output.

- **Field** A specific category of information, such as a first name, last name, birthdate, customer number, item number, or price.

- **Record** A set of the information that goes in the fields; for example, information about a specific person or transaction. A record doesn't have to contain information for every field, but it must have a placeholder for any missing information.

The mail merge process varies slightly depending on whether you're creating one document per record or one document containing all the records. However, the basic process is this:

1. Identify a data source that contains the records you want to use.

2. Create a document into which you want to merge the records.

3. In the document, identify the fields from the data source that you want to merge into the document.

4. Preview the results and make any necessary adjustments.

5. Merge the data into the document to either create one or more new documents or to print the merge results directly to the printer.

You can perform the mail merge process by using the commands on the Mailings tab of the ribbon, or you can get step-by-step guidance from the Mail Merge wizard. The wizard displays options in a series of panes, and you choose the options you want. If you're new to mail merge, the wizard can provide a helpful framework. If you are comfortable with the mail merge process and know what you want to create, it can be faster to perform the steps manually.

To use the Mail Merge wizard

1. Start Word and display the **Mailings** tab.

2. In the **Start Mail Merge** group, click the **Start Mail Merge** button, and then click **Step-by-Step Mail Merge Wizard**.

3. In each of the six panes of the wizard, select an option or provide the requested information.

4. In the last pane, specify whether to send the merge output directly to the printer or to create one or more documents that you can review and save.

This chapter provides in-depth information about how to get the results that you want from the mail merge process, whether you use the wizard or the commands on the Mailings tab.

Start the mail merge process

For most mail merge projects, you need a starting document that provides structure and common content, and that identifies the locations where you want to insert data. You specify the data to merge into each location by inserting *merge fields*. The merge fields pull data from the data source fields into the starting document. To identify the data fields that are available for the mail merge operation, you must select the data source and import its records into the Mail Merge Recipients list.

The best starting point varies based on the type of output that you want to create. The output categories include letters, email messages, envelopes, labels, and directories.

In this topic, we discuss ways of getting started with a mail merge process based on the output type.

14

> **TIP** If you find that you need help, you can start the wizard from any point in the process and move back to make changes or forward to keep the work you've done.

Get started with letters

If you're creating a form letter or similar document, you can write the document, connect to the data source, and then insert the merge fields, or you can start with a blank
document, connect to the data source, and then insert the merge fields as you write
the document. Either way, you can't insert merge fields in a document until you connect to the data source.

If you're creating a document that needs to go through a review process, it's easier
to do that before you connect to the data source; otherwise, the document tries to
connect to the data source each time a reviewer opens it. When that's the case, you
can insert placeholders in the document where you plan to insert merge fields later.
You can set off the placeholders from the real text by using brackets or highlighting
to indicate to reviewers that the placeholders aren't final content, and to make them
easy to locate later.

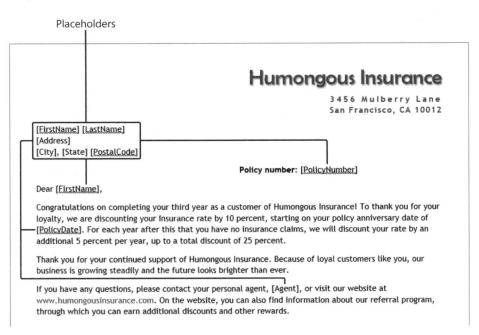

It's easiest to write and edit your document before starting the mail merge process

If you need a bit of help creating a document for your intended purpose, you can use
any of the Word content templates. A wide variety of templates are available from the
New page of the Backstage view.

To start a letter mail merge

1. Open a blank document or a document that contains the static content you want to pull data into.

2. On the **Mailings** tab, in the **Start Mail Merge** group, click the **Start Mail Merge** button.

3. On the **Start Mail Merge** menu, click **Letters**. There is no visible change to the document.

4. To continue and complete the process:

   a. Use the procedures described in "Choose and refine the data source" later in this chapter to identify the data source and available fields.

   b. Create or edit the document content, and use the procedures described in "Insert merge fields" later in this chapter to insert the merge fields.

   c. Use the procedures described in "Preview and complete the merge" later in this chapter to finish creating the letter.

Get started with labels

The mail merge processes for labels are designed not only for stickers but also for name tags, badge inserts, business cards, tab inserts for page dividers, CD labels, postcards, notecards, printable magnets, and anything else that you print onto paper or other sheet-fed media that is divided into fixed areas. Many of these products are available from office supply and craft supply retailers. Common manufacturers of label materials include Avery and 3M, but there are many others.

> **SEE ALSO** For more information about creating mailing labels, see "Create individual envelopes and labels" later in this chapter.

14

When generating labels from a data source, you're usually printing data from multiple records onto each sheet, but you can also print a full sheet of each record.

When creating labels, you select the manufacturer and product number of the specific printing media, and then Word creates a table that defines the printable area of the label sheet. You insert merge fields into the first cell as a template for all the other cells, format the content as you want it, and then copy the cell content to the other fields. If you're making sheets of labels that pull data from multiple records, each additional field starts with a «Next Record» tag that signals Word to move to the next record.

The starting document and first page of results for a label mail merge

It's important that you select the correct manufacturer and product, because the document page setup is very precisely controlled to match the media.

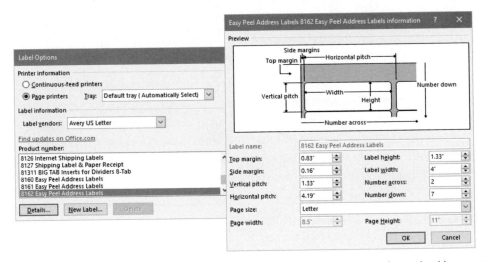

The definition for each label product includes the dimensions of the printable and nonprintable areas of the sheet

To start a label mail merge

1. Open a blank document and display paragraph marks and formatting symbols.

2. On the **Mailings** tab, in the **Start Mail Merge** group, click the **Start Mail Merge** button.

3. On the **Start Mail Merge** menu, click **Labels**. The Label Options dialog box opens.

Thousands of label products are available from this dialog box

4. In the **Printer information** area, choose the correct printer type for the label forms and, for standard printers, choose the input tray (or manual feed) for the label sheets.

5. On the label package, identify the manufacturer and product number of the labels you will be using. In the **Label information** area, do the following:

   • In the **Label vendors** list, click the label manufacturer.

   • In the **Product number** list, click the product number.

> **TIP** To save time, click in the Product Number box and then press the keyboard key corresponding to the first character of the product number to jump to that section of the list. Then scroll to locate the specific product number. If the label product you're using doesn't already appear in the list, click the Find Updates On Office.Com link to refresh the list.

14

6. In the **Label Options** dialog box, click **OK** to return to the document. Word creates the label form in which you will enter the merge fields and any static content.

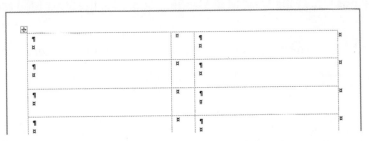

Ensure that paragraph symbols and formatting marks are shown before continuing

7. To continue and complete the process:

   a. Use the procedures described in "Choose and refine the data source" later in this chapter to identify the data source and available fields.

   b. Create or edit the static label content, and use the procedures described in "Insert merge fields" later in this chapter to insert the merge fields.

   c. Use the procedures described in "Preview and complete the merge" later in this chapter to finish creating the labels.

Get started with email messages

When you want to send the same information to all the people on a list—for example, all your customers, or all the members of a club or your family—you don't have to print letters and physically mail them. Instead, you can use mail merge to create a personalized email message for each person in a data source. As with a form letter that will be printed, you can either use the Mail Merge wizard or use the buttons on the Mailings tab to insert merge fields into a document. These merge fields will be replaced with information from the specified data source and the starting document will be converted to individual email messages.

Many email messages need no merge fields other than a greeting line.

«GreetingLine»

Thank you for your recent visit to our store. It was a pleasure to be able to answer your decorating questions and offer suggestions. As you requested, we have added your name to our online mailing list. You will be receiving our monthly newsletter, as well as advance notice of upcoming shipments and in-store events.

You can also visit our website at www.wideworldimporters.com for a schedule of events, links to online decorating resources, articles on furniture care, and more.

Contact us at customerservice@wideworldimporters.com, or call (925) 555-0167, for answers to all your decorating questions.

If you want to edit the custom greeting, right-click the merge field and then click Edit Greeting Line

Because email messages tend to be less formal than printed letters, you might want to start the messages with a custom greeting rather than one of the predefined greeting options (Dear and To).

If you send the messages, you can locate them in your Sent Items folder

To start an email mail merge

1. Open a blank document or a document that contains the static content you want to pull data into.

2. On the **Mailings** tab, in the **Start Mail Merge** group, click the **Start Mail Merge** button.

14

3. On the **Start Mail Merge** menu, click **E-mail Messages**. Word displays the current content in Web view.

> **SEE ALSO** For information about the available views, see "Display different views of documents" in Chapter 2, "Create and manage documents."

4. To continue and complete the process:

   a. Use the procedures described in "Choose and refine the data source" later in this chapter to identify the data source and available fields.

   b. Create or edit the document content, and use the procedures described in "Insert merge fields" later in this chapter to insert the merge fields.

   c. Use the procedures described in "Preview and complete the merge" later in this chapter to finish creating the messages.

Choose and refine the data source

The mail merge process combines variable information from a data source with static information in a starting document. The basic data source requirement is the same regardless of the output format: it must be a container that stores information in a consistent structure.

```
Brian,LaMee,816 Sycamore St,Roanoke,GA,37684
Andrew,Lan,133 Sycamore St,Reading,KS,96696
Ingelise,Lang,944 Mahogany Cove,Indianapolis,CT,92016
Rebecca,Laszlo,679 Oak Ct,El Paso,NV,15523
Kenneth,Ledyard Jr.,30 Gum
Aaron,Lee,637 Willow Drive
Mark,Lee,46 Redbud Way,Mob
Anna,Lidman,534 Crabwood C
Paulo,Lisboa,855 Beech Bay
Kevin,Liu,513 Palo Verde R
Andre,Ludick,459 Buckeye C
Richard,Lum,443 Madrone Rd
Vidur,Luthra,408 Palm Terr
Jenny,Lysaker,702 Mesquite
```

	A	B	C	D	E	F
1	FirstName	LastName	Address	City	State	PostalCode
2	Humberto	Acevedo	421 Hawthorn Ct	Tucson	MA	11491
3	David	Ahs	699 Fir Cove	Sacramento	TN	58292
4	Michelle	Alexander	716 Mangrove Rd	Albuquerque	MN	52101
5	Sean	Alexander	214 Pine Dr	Memphis	WA	31039
6	Tony	Allen	736 Acacia Terrace	Nassau	FL	18689
7	Thomas	Andersen	18 Fir Blvd	Scranton	MA	43666
8	Jose Luis	Auricchio	82 Ash Boulevard	Boston	VT	83896
9	Mary	Baker	671 Conifer Cove	Charlotte	TN	76644
10	Dave	Barnett	888 Hazel Court	Cedar Rapids	MO	67393
11	Shai	Bassli	877 Aspen Boulevard	Burlington	WY	44360
12	Mark	Bebbington	122 Aspen Lane	Mansfield	MI	69555
13	Bradley	Beck	750 Maple Cove	Springfield	TN	54087

Customers

Data sources store information in a consistent structure

Most data source structures store data in a tabular format, with fields identified at the top and records following. The most straightforward example of this, and the one we work with throughout this chapter, is a Microsoft Excel workbook.

Each field in a data source must be identified by a unique name so you can pull data from the field into the starting document. In Excel, the field names are the table headers or column headers.

The Mail Merge Recipients dialog box displays all the records from the data source

Select an existing data source

The full list of acceptable data source file types is lengthy. Typical data sources include Excel worksheets and delimited text files, but you can also pull data from tables in Microsoft Word, Access, or SQL Server; from a Microsoft Outlook contact list; or from a variety of other, less common sources.

14

```
All Data Sources (*.odc;*.mdb;*.mde;*.accdb;*.accde;*.ols;*.udl;*.dsn;*.xlsx;*.xlsm;*.xlsb;*.xls;*.htm;*.html;*.
Office Database Connections (*.odc)
Access Databases (*.mdb;*.mde)
Access 2007 Database (*.accdb;*.accde)
Microsoft Office Address Lists (*.mdb)
Microsoft Office List Shortcuts (*.ols)
Microsoft Data links (*.udl)
ODBC File DSNs (*.dsn)
Excel Files (*.xlsx;*.xlsm;*.xlsb;*.xls)
Web Pages (*.htm;*.html;*.asp;*.mht;*.mhtml)
Rich Text Format (*.rtf)
Word Documents (*.docx;*.doc;*.docm)
All Word Documents (*.docx;*.doc;*.docm;*.dotx;*.dot;*.dotm;*.rtf;*.htm;*.html)
Text Files (*.txt;*.prn;*.csv;*.tab;*.asc)
Database Queries (*.dqy;*.rqy)
OpenDocument Text Files (*.odt)
```

All the file types that are accepted as data sources

> **TIP** If your company or organization uses another contact-management system, you can probably export information to one of these formats. Delimited text files are the most basic format of structured information storage and should be an export option from any other information storage system.

The data source doesn't have to be stored on your computer; the wizard can link to remotely stored data. If the data source is stored on a server that requires you to log on, you can provide your credentials and, optionally, store your password.

> **TIP** It isn't necessary for the data source file to be closed during the import operation; you can import records from an open file, edit and save the file, and refresh the list with the changes.

If you use Outlook to manage your email, contacts, and calendar information that is stored in Microsoft Exchange or Exchange Online, you can import data from an Exchange account contact folder to use as a mail merge data source. The Mail Merge wizard polls your Outlook data folders and provides a list of contact folders that you can use. When you choose a contact folder, the wizard imports the contact list.

It's likely that your contact list contains a variety of contacts—clients, employees, friends, relatives, and other people you have corresponded with. Many of these contacts might not be current, and many of them might not be people to whom you want to direct the specific form letter or email message that you're creating. But that's okay—you can import the entire contact list and then use the filtering function in the

Mail Merge Recipients dialog box to identify only those people you want to include in your current mail merge project.

A selected check box indicates that a record will be included in the mail merge

> **SEE ALSO** For information about filtering records for a mail merge, see "Refine the data source records" later in this topic.

To select an existing data source

1. On the **Mailings** tab, in the **Start Mail Merge** group, click the **Select Recipients** button to display the data source options.

You must choose or create a data source file

2. On the **Select Recipients** menu, do either of the following:

    - Click **Use an Existing List**. In the **Select Data Source** dialog box, browse to and select the data source file, and then click **Open**.

    - Click **Choose from Outlook Contacts**. If the **Select Contacts** dialog box opens, select the contact folder that you want to import and click **OK**.

Create a new data source

If the information that you want to include in your data source isn't already stored in a file or address list, you can create a "Microsoft Office Address List" while working in the Mail Merge wizard; the wizard saves your list as a table in an Access database (.mdb) file in the My Data Sources subfolder of your Documents folder.

The process of entering information through the Address List interface is somewhat tedious, because you must manually populate each field—so if you have a lot of records, it's easier to enter your data into an Excel worksheet. However, it's fine for an impromptu mail merge process, such as creating a set of name tags for a meeting.

Creating a simple list through the wizard

You're not limited to collecting contact information; you can add, remove, and reorder the fields to store the type of data that is pertinent to your mail merge process.

To create a data source from the Mailings tab

1. On the **Mailings** tab, in the **Start Mail Merge** group, click the **Select Recipients** button, and then click **Type a New List**.

2. In the **New Address List** dialog box, do the following:

   a. Click **Customize Columns**. Add any fields to the column list that you plan to include in the mail merge operation. To keep things tidy, you can remove fields that you don't plan to use.

   b. Enter the information for each record, clicking **New Entry** to create another.

3. When you finish, click **OK**.

4. In the **Save Address List** dialog box, provide a name for the database file, and then click **Save**.

Refine the data source records

The data source you choose doesn't have to be specific to the item you're creating. For example, you could create postcards announcing an in-store sale only for customers who live in that area, or create gift certificates only for people who have birthdays in the next month.

If you don't want to include all the data source records in your mail merge operation, you can now whittle down the list to those you want. You can use the following processes to remove a record from the recipient list:

- **Filter the list on one or more fields** You can filter the list to display only the records that you want to include, or to locate (and then remove) the records that you want to exclude.

- **Remove duplicates** The wizard can help to identify entries that might be duplicates. You can either clear the check boxes for the duplicate versions that you don't want to use, or you can remove the entries from the data source file, save the file, and refresh the recipients list.

- **Manually exclude records** Each record has a check box. Clearing the check box removes the record from the mail merge operation.

14

Excluding records from the mail merge operation does not remove them from the Mail Merge Recipients list or from the original data source file. They will still be available for you to use in this or another mail merge operation.

In addition to limiting the set of information used in a mail merge, you can also sort the records to specify the order in which they appear in the mail merge document— for example, in postal code order for a bulk mailing.

> **IMPORTANT** The Refine Recipient List in the Mail Merge Recipients dialog box includes a Validate Addresses link. At the time of this writing, clicking the link displays a message that an address validation add-in is required. Clicking the link to locate the add-in returns an error. This feature might be fixed by the time you read this book; when it is, you can validate mailing addresses against standards to filter out recipients whose mailing addresses don't appear to be valid per postal regulations.

To display the Mail Merge Recipients list

1. On the **Mailings** tab, in the **Start Mail Merge** group, click **Edit Recipient List**.

To filter the recipients list to display only records you want to include

1. Display the **Mail Merge Recipients** list.

2. In the **Refine recipient list** area, click **Filter** to display the **Filter Records** tab of the **Filter and Sort** dialog box.

3. In the **Field** list, click the field you want to filter by.

4. In the **Comparison** list, click one of the following:

   - Equal to
   - Not equal to
   - Less than
   - Greater than
   - Less than or equal

   - Greater than or equal
   - Is blank
   - Is not blank
   - Contains
   - Does not contain

5. In the **Compare to** list, enter the criterion for the field filter.

6. To apply multiple criteria, click **And** or **Or** in the leftmost list and then enter the additional criteria.

A multi-filter operation that returns only specific insurance policy subscribers

7. In the **Filter and Sort** dialog box, click **OK**. Records that are not displayed in the filtered list are not included in the mail merge operation.

To filter records out of the recipients list

1. Following the instructions in the previous procedure, filter the **Mail Merge Recipients** list to display the records you want to exclude.

2. Click the check box in the column heading area (twice if necessary) to clear the check boxes of all the records returned by the filter operation.

Clearing a check box removes a record from the recipient list but not from the data source

3. In the **Refine recipient list** area, click **Filter** to redisplay the Filter Records tab of the Filter And Sort dialog box.

4. On the **Filter Records** tab, click the **Clear All** button, and then click **OK** to remove the filter. The records that you excluded while the filter was applied are still excluded.

To remove duplicate records from the recipients list

1. Display the **Mail Merge Recipients** list.

2. In the **Refine recipient list** area, click **Find duplicates** to display records that have similar field entries.

Data Source		LastName	FirstName	Address	City	State
CustomerList.xlsx	☑	Alexander	Michelle	716 Mangrove Rd	Albuquerque	MN
CustomerList.xlsx	☑	Alexander	Sean	716 Mangrove Rd	Albuquerque	MN
CustomerList.xlsx	☐	Cox	Oliver		Lincoln	ID
CustomerList.xlsx	☑	Cox	Oliver	448 Gum Loop	Lincoln	ID
CustomerList.xlsx	☐	Fort	Garth		Reno	ID
CustomerList.xlsx	☑	Fort	Garth	499 Sumac Bay	Reno	ID
CustomerList.xlsx	☐	Gode	Scott	780 Palmetto T...	Augusta	ID
CustomerList.xlsx	☑	Gode	Scott		Augusta	ID

Review possible duplicates

3. In the **Find Duplicates** dialog box, clear the check boxes of any records that you want to exclude from the mail merge operation. Then click **OK**.

To sort records in a data source

1. Display the **Mail Merge Recipients** list.

2. To sort the records by one field, click the field name (the column header) of the field you want to sort by. (Click the field name again to sort in the opposite order.)

   Or

   To sort the records by multiple fields, do the following:

   a. In the **Refine recipient list** area, click **Sort** to display the Sort Records tab of the Filter And Sort dialog box.

   You can sort by up to three fields

   b. In the **Sort by** list, click the first field you want to sort by. Then click the adjacent **Ascending** or **Descending** option to specify the sort order.

   c. In the first **Then by** list, click the second field you want to sort by, and the adjacent **Ascending** or **Descending** option.

   d. In the second **Then by** list, specify the third sort field and order, or click (None).

   e. In the **Filter and Sort** dialog box, click **OK**.

To manually exclude records from the recipients list

1. Display the **Mail Merge Recipients** list.

2. If necessary, sort or filter the list to locate records.

3. Clear the check boxes of any records that you want to exclude from the mail merge operation.

14

Refresh data

You can save and close the document at any point in the mail merge process. When you reopen the document, if you've already connected to the data source and inserted merge fields, Word prompts you to refresh the data connection.

Microsoft Word ✕

⚠ Opening this document will run the following SQL command:

SELECT * FROM `AnniversaryList$`

Data from your database will be placed in the document. Do you want to continue?

Show Help >>

Yes   No

The recipient list reflects changes to the source data when you reopen the document

You can also refresh the data manually at any time from within the document by clicking the Refresh button in the Data Source area of the Mail Merge Recipients dialog box.

Insert merge fields

In the document, merge fields are enclosed in chevrons (« and »). However, you can't simply type the chevrons and the field name; you must insert the merge field by using the commands on the Mailings tab. This creates a link from the merge field to the data source field.

The commands that you use to insert merge fields in a starting document are in the Write & Insert Fields group on the Mailings tab.

References   Mailings   Review   View

Highlight Merge Fields   Address Block   Greeting Line   Insert Merge Field ▾   🗋 Rules ▾   Match Fields   Update Labels

Write & Insert Fields

The tools for inserting fields in mail merge documents

Every field in the data source is available to insert as an individual merge field. Additionally, two merge fields are available that can save you a bit of time:

- **Address Block** This merge field inserts elements of a standard address block (the recipient's name, company name, and postal address) that you select so you can insert all the information with one merge field.

You can customize the Address Block merge field

- **Greeting Line** This merge field inserts a personalized salutation or substitutes a generic salutation for records that are missing the necessary information.

You can select from multiple greetings and name forms

14

After you insert the first merge field in a document, the Highlight Merge Fields button in the Write & Insert Fields group on the Mailings tab becomes active. Click this button to highlight (in gray) all the merge fields in the document so they're easier to locate.

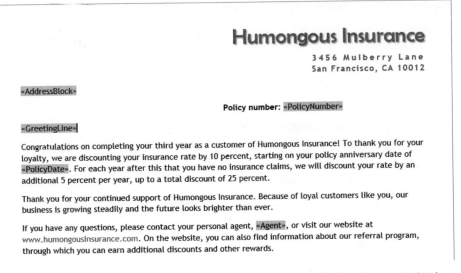

Congratulations on completing your third year as a customer of Humongous Insurance! To thank you for your loyalty, we are discounting your insurance rate by 10 percent, starting on your policy anniversary date of «PolicyDate». For each year after this that you have no insurance claims, we will discount your rate by an additional 5 percent per year, up to a total discount of 25 percent.

Highlighting the merge fields makes them easier to locate and also verifies that they aren't simply placeholders

> ⚠️ **IMPORTANT** Before you can perform the procedures in this topic, you must select a data source. For more information, see "Choose and refine the data source" earlier in this chapter.

To insert a single merge field

1. Position the cursor in the location where you want to insert the merge field.

2. On the **Mailings** tab, in the **Write & Insert Fields** group, click **Insert Merge Field**, and then click the field you want to insert.

To insert an Address Block merge field

1. Position the cursor in the location where you want to insert the Address Block merge field.

2. On the **Mailings** tab, in the **Write & Insert Fields** group, click **Address Block**.

3. In the **Insert Address Block** dialog box, select the address block elements you want to include and select the format for the recipient's name.

4. In the **Preview** box displaying your first data record, check that the address block looks correct. You can move through additional records to check further.

5. When you finish, click **OK**.

To insert a Greeting Line merge field

1. Position the cursor in the location where you want to insert the Greeting Line merge field.

2. On the **Mailings** tab, in the **Write & Insert Fields** group, click **Greeting Line**.

3. In the **Insert Greeting Line** dialog box, select the greeting line elements you want to include and the generic format for records that don't have the elements you specify.

4. In the **Preview** box displaying your first data record, check that the greeting looks correct. You can move through additional records to check further.

5. When you finish, click **OK**.

Preview and complete the merge

After you specify the data source you want to use and enter merge fields in the main document, you can preview the effect of merging the records into the documents, and then perform the actual merge. You can further filter the source data during the preview process. When you're ready, you can either send the merged documents directly to the printer or you can merge them into a new document. If you merge to a new document, you have another chance to review and, if necessary, edit the merged documents before sending them to the printer.

14

> ⚠ **IMPORTANT** Before you can perform the procedures in this topic, you must select a data source and insert merge fields. For more information, see "Choose and refine the data source" and "Insert merge fields" earlier in this chapter.

To preview merged documents

1. Display the starting document with merge fields in place and the data source attached.

2. On the **Mailings** tab, in the **Preview Results** group, click the **Preview Results** button to display the data source information in place of the merge fields.

3. In the **Preview Results** group, do any of the following:

   - Click the **Next Record** or **Previous Record** button to move through the data source one record at a time.

   - Click the **First Record** or **Last Record** button to move to the first or last record in the data source.

   - Click the **Preview Results** button again to redisplay the merge fields.

To merge the data to a new document

1. On the **Mailings** tab, in the **Finish** group, click the **Finish & Merge** button, and then click **Edit Individual Documents**. The Merge To New Document dialog box opens.

You can limit the merge to one record or a range of records

2. In the **Merge to New Document** dialog box, indicate the record or records that you want to merge, and then click **OK**.

To merge the data and print the resulting file

1. On the **Mailings** tab, in the **Finish** group, click the **Finish & Merge** button, and then click **Print Documents**.

2. In the **Merge to Printer** dialog box, indicate the record or records that you want to merge, and then click **OK**.

3. In the **Print** dialog box, select your printer, configure any additional printer settings that are necessary, and then click **OK**.

To merge the data and email the resulting messages

1. On the **Mailings** tab, in the **Finish** group, click the **Finish & Merge** button, and then click **Send Email Messages**. The Merge To E-mail dialog box opens.

You specify the address field and subject line before sending the messages

2. In the **Message options** area, do the following:

   - In the **To** list, click the field that contains the recipients' email addresses.

   - In the **Subject line** box, enter the message subject you want the email message to display.

   - In the **Mail format** list, click **Attachment**, **Plain text**, or **HTML**.

3. In the **Send records** area, indicate the record or records that you want to merge. Then click **OK**.

14

Create individual envelopes and labels

If you want to print a lot of envelopes or mailing labels based on data source fields, you can use the mail merge function to create documents, and then print the documents onto envelopes or sheet-fed labels rather than regular paper.

However, you can also use the prominently placed Envelope and Labels functions to create one or more individually addressed envelopes or address labels. Because these functions are related to "mailing" envelopes or packages, they have been (somewhat confusingly) placed on the Mailing tab of the ribbon, which is otherwise home to only the mail merge functionality.

Generate individual envelopes

The Envelope function prints a delivery address and can also print a return address and electronic postage, if you have the necessary software installed. You can manually enter the delivery address or you can pick it up from a document (usually a letter) that contains an address.

You can edit the address information before creating or printing the envelope

> ✓ **TIP** You can save time by storing the return address with your user information. The address then appears by default as the return address in the Envelopes And Labels dialog box.

When creating envelopes, you can specify the envelope size, the address locations, and the fonts for the addresses. You can also specify the paper source, the envelope feed method (horizontally or vertically and face up or face down), and the alignment of the envelope. Then Word configures the page layout options and print options as required for your selections.

You can position the addresses on the envelope exactly where you want them

When you create an envelope based on an address in a letter, you can print the envelope immediately or add the envelope page to the document, and then print the envelope and letter at a later time.

14

Samantha Smith
99 Magnolia Court
Flower Hill, CA 98052

Max Stevens
Principal
Elm Street Elementary
321 Elm Street
Flower Hill, CA 98052

Samantha Smith
99 Magnolia Court
Flower Hill, CA 98052

October 15, 2015

Max Stevens
Principal
Elm Street Elementary
321 Elm Street
Flower Hill, CA 98052

Dear Principal Stevens,

Adding the envelope to the document inserts it as a separate document section with unique page layout settings

> ⚠ **IMPORTANT** The electronic postage options on the Envelopes tab of the Envelopes And Labels dialog box require the installation of an electronic postage add-in. Clicking the link to locate the add-in returns an error. This feature might be fixed by the time you read this book; when it is, you can print electronic postage directly onto envelopes.

To save your mailing address for use in Word documents

1. Open the **Word Options** dialog box, and then click the **Advanced** tab.

2. On the **Advanced** page, in the **General** section, enter your name and address in the **Mailing Address** box. Then click **OK**.

To set up an envelope with a manually entered address

1. Open any document.

2. On the **Mailings** tab, in the **Create** group, click the **Envelopes** button to open the Envelopes And Labels dialog box.

The Return Address box contains your user name or your mailing address, if you saved that in the Word Options dialog box. (If you saved and then deleted your mailing address, the Return Address box might be blank.)

3. In the **Return address** area, do either of the following:

    *   Review the return address information and modify it as necessary.

    *   If you plan to print to envelopes that have a preprinted return address, select the **Omit** check box.

4. In the **Delivery address** box, enter the name and address that you want Word to print on the envelope.

To set up an envelope from an address in a document

1. Open the document and select the address.

2. On the **Mailings** tab, in the **Create** group, click the **Envelopes** button to open the Envelopes And Labels dialog box with the selected address in the Delivery Address box. The Return Address box contains your user name, and also contains your return address if you've saved that in Word.

3. Review the addresses and make any changes you want. If you plan to print on an envelope that has a preprinted return address, select the **Omit** check box in the **Return address** area.

To configure or confirm the envelope printing options

1. At the bottom of the **Envelopes** tab of the **Envelopes and Labels** dialog box, click the **Options** button to open the Envelope Options dialog box.

2. On the **Envelope Options** tab, set the envelope size, delivery address font and position, and return address font and position.

3. On the **Printing Options** tab, set the feed method, rotation, and paper source.

14

> ⚠ **IMPORTANT** If the printer shown at the top of the Printing Options tab is not the correct printer, click OK in each of the open dialog boxes to save your settings and return to the source document. Then select the correct printer in the source document and return to the Envelopes And Labels dialog box to finish creating the envelope.

4. Click **OK** to return to the Envelopes And Labels dialog box.

To print or save the envelope

1. After you set up the envelope and configure the envelope printing options, do either of the following:

   - Load an envelope into the printer in the manner configured in the Envelope Options dialog box. Then at the bottom of the **Envelopes and Labels** dialog box, click **Print** to print the envelope.

   - At the bottom of the **Envelopes and Labels** dialog box, click **Add to Document** to insert the envelope content as a separately formatted section at the beginning of the current document.

Generate individual mailing labels

The Labels function is designed to print one address (a delivery address or a return address) onto a sheet of labels, either to create a single label or a full sheet of the same label. Instead of selecting an envelope size, you select a label form by first selecting the label manufacturer and then selecting the specific product number. Word sets up a document to precisely match the content layout areas of the selected form.

Samantha Smith 99 Magnolia Court Flower Hill, CA 98052	Samantha Smith 99 Magnolia Court Flower Hill, CA 98052
Samantha Smith 99 Magnolia Court Flower Hill, CA 98052	Samantha Smith 99 Magnolia Court Flower Hill, CA 98052
Samantha Smith 99 Magnolia Court Flower Hill, CA 98052	Samantha Smith 99 Magnolia Court Flower Hill, CA 98052
Samantha Smith	Samantha Smith

The content cells defined by the table match the printing areas of the label sheets

As discussed in "Get started with labels" earlier in this chapter, the term "labels" refers not only to rectangular stickers, but also to many other things that you print onto sheet-fed media that is divided into fixed areas. You can use the Labels function to print on any of these. It's important that you select the correct form because the print areas are very specifically defined.

To set up individual mailing labels

1. Open any document.

2. On the **Mailings** tab, in the **Create** group, click the **Labels** button to open the Envelopes And Labels dialog box.

3. In the **Address** area, do either of the following:

   - If you've saved your return address information in Word and want to create a return address label, select the **Use return address** check box to insert the saved address into the Address box. Then review the return address information and modify it as necessary.

   - Enter the name and address that you want Word to print on the label.

Although the field specifies an address, you can print any text on the labels

4. In the **Print** area, do either of the following to correctly configure the label output:

   - If you want to print one full sheet of labels, click **Full page of the same label**.

   - If you want to print only one label, click **Single label** and then enter the row and column of the position on the sheet of the label you want to print on.

   > **TIP** This feature permits you to easily reuse a partial sheet of blank labels.

5. In the **Label** area, confirm that the label type is the correct one for the printed label forms you are using. If it is not, configure the label settings in the **Label Options** dialog box.

   > 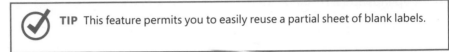 **SEE ALSO** For information about configuring label settings, see "Get started with labels" earlier in this chapter.

To print or save the mailing label

1. After you set up the label and configure the label printing options, do either of the following:

   - Load a label form into the printer in the manner configured in the Label Options dialog box. Then at the bottom of the **Envelopes and Labels** dialog box, click **Print** to print the label.

   - At the bottom of the **Envelopes and Labels** dialog box, click **New Document** to generate a new document that contains the merged labels.

Skills review

In this chapter, you learned how to:

- Understand the mail merge process
- Start the mail merge process
- Choose and refine the data source
- Insert merge fields
- Preview and complete the merge
- Create individual envelopes and labels

Practice tasks

The practice files for these tasks are located in the Word2016SBS\Ch14 folder. You can save the results of the tasks in the same folder.

Understand the mail merge process

Start Word, open a new blank document, and then perform the following tasks:

1. Start the Mail Merge wizard and investigate the options provided therein.

2. Using the wizard, create any mail merge item you want to. Use the **CustomerList** workbook from the practice file folder as your data source.

3. If you create a mail merge document, save it as **MyMerge**, and then close it.

Start the mail merge process

Open the StartMerge document from the practice file folder, and then perform the following tasks:

1. Start a letter mail merge. Notice that the document does not change.

2. Next start an email mail merge. Notice that the document view changes to Web Layout.

3. Start a label mail merge, and investigate the options in the Label Options dialog box. Choose a label vendor and product number, and display the label details.

4. Create the label sheet, and allow Word to replace the contents of the StartMerge document when prompted to do so.

5. Close the **StartMerge** document without saving it.

Choose and refine the data source

Open the RefineData document, and then perform the following tasks:

1. Start a letter mail merge. Select the **CustomerList** workbook from the practice file folder as the data source, and select the **Customers$** table of the workbook when prompted to do so.

2. Sort the recipient list alphabetically, in ascending order, by the customers' last names.

3. Remove duplicate records from the recipient list.

4. Filter the list to display only those records for customers who live either in the state of Texas (TX) or the state of Louisiana (LA).

5. Manually exclude all of the Louisiana (LA) records from the recipient list, and then return to the letter.

6. From the **Select Recipients** menu, create a new data source. Add your name and the names of two other people. Add any other information you want, and then save the new list as **PracticeList.mdb**.

7. Save and close the **RefineData** document.

Insert merge fields

Open the InsertFields document, and then perform the following tasks:

1. Start a letter mail merge. Select the **PolicyholdersList** workbook from the practice file folder as the data source, and select the **PolicyHolders$** table of the workbook when prompted to do so.

2. Replace each placeholder in the document with its corresponding merge field.

3. Save the **InsertFields** document, but don't close it.

4. Create a new blank document and start a new letter mail merge. Use the same data source as in step 1.

5. Open the **Insert Address Block** dialog box. Review the settings and make any changes you want, and then insert the merge field.

6. In the document, two lines below the address block, insert a **Greeting Line** merge field.

7. Save the document as **MyFields**, and then close it. Leave the **InsertFields** document open for the next set of practice tasks.

Preview and complete the merge

Complete the previous set of practice tasks to modify the InsertFields document. Then perform the following tasks:

1. Use the tools in the **Preview Results** group on the **Mailings** tab to preview the results of completing the mail merge. Then redisplay the merge fields.

2. Merge the data source into the document to create a new document. Save the document as **MyLetter**, and then close it.

3. Redisplay the **InsertFields** document, and follow the procedure to merge the output directly to the printer. (If you don't want to print the file, click **Cancel** in the final dialog box.)

4. Follow the procedure to merge the output to email messages. Explore the settings, and then click **Cancel**.

5. Save and close the **InsertFields** document.

Create individual envelopes and labels

Open the CreateEnvelopes document, and then perform the following tasks:

1. Open the **Word Options** dialog box, and display the **Advanced** page. In the **General** section, check whether you have saved your mailing address. If you have not, do so now.

2. Open the **Envelopes and Labels** dialog box. Verify that the **Return Address** box contains your saved mailing address.

3. In the **Delivery address** box, enter the name and address of another person. Then add the envelope to the document.

4. In the document, select the letter recipient's name and address, and then open the **Envelopes and Labels** dialog box. Verify that the **Return Address** box contains your mailing address, and the **Delivery Address** box contains the letter recipient's name and address.

5. In the **Envelope Options** dialog box, configure the envelope printing options and then, if you want, load an envelope into your printer, and print the addresses onto the envelope.

6. Save and close the **CreateEnvelopes** document.

7. Create a new blank document.

8. Display the **Labels** tab of the **Envelopes and Labels** dialog box. If your saved mailing address is not already shown in the Address box, select the **Use return address** check box to add your saved information to the **Address** box.

9. Configure the merge output to print one full sheet of labels.

10. If you have a sheet of labels to print to, configure the label settings. Then load a sheet of labels into the printer and print the addresses onto the labels.

11. If you don't have a sheet of labels, generate a new document that contains the merged labels. Then save the document as MyLabels, and close it.

Create custom document elements

When it comes to maximizing your efficiency while creating documents in Word, styles and templates are among the most powerful tools available to you.

You can greatly enhance your efficiency when developing a series of related custom documents by creating themes that specify the colors and fonts to use, styles that specify the formatting appropriate to the document, and templates that store and apply those styles. You can also create building blocks that save preformatted content segments so you can insert them anywhere in any document.

This chapter guides you through procedures related to creating and modifying styles, creating and managing custom themes, creating and attaching templates, and creating custom building blocks.

In this chapter

- Create and modify styles
- Create and manage custom themes
- Create and attach templates
- Create custom building blocks

Practice files

For this chapter, use the practice files from the Word2016SBS\Ch15 folder. For practice file download instructions, see the introduction.

Create and modify styles

Even if you don't want to create your own templates, it's very useful to know how to create and modify styles. When you apply direct character formatting or paragraph formatting, you affect only the selected characters or paragraphs. If you change your mind about how you want to format a particular document element, you have to change the formatting manually everywhere it is applied. When you format characters or paragraphs by applying a style, you can change the way all of those characters or paragraphs look simply by changing the style definition. With one change in one place, you can completely change the look of the document.

You can modify existing styles, or create new styles. When you modify a style, document content that has that style applied immediately reflects your changes. When you create or modify styles, you can choose to make them active in the current document only, or in all documents based on the template you're working in.

You can modify the content of the Style gallery for the current template by adding and removing styles, so the styles you want are available from the gallery and the styles you rarely use don't distract you.

A customized Style gallery

Adding and removing styles in the gallery doesn't affect the styles in the Styles pane. If you create or modify styles and don't want to save them as part of a template, you can save the style definitions as a custom style set.

To open the Modify Style dialog box

1. Do any of the following:

   - In the **Style** gallery, right-click the style you want to modify, and then click **Modify**.

   - In the **Styles** pane, point to the style you want to modify, click the arrow that appears to the right of the style name, and then click **Modify**.

   - In the **Apply Styles** dialog box, click the style you want to modify, and then click **Modify**.

To modify an existing style

1. Apply the style you want to modify to a paragraph or selected text.

2. Adjust the formatting so that the paragraph or selection looks the way you want it.

3. Do either of the following to update the style definition with the new formatting:

   - In the **Style** gallery, right-click the style, and then click **Update** *<style>* **to Match Selection**.

   - In the **Styles** pane, point to the style, click the arrow that appears to the right of the style name, and then click **Update** *<style>* **to Match Selection**.

Or

1. Open the **Modify Style** dialog box for the style.

2. In the **Formatting** area or from the **Format** menu, change the settings to achieve the look you want.

15

You can modify as many aspects of a style as you can of the document text

3. To save the style modification in the template, click **New documents based on this template** (otherwise, the style will be modified in this document only).

4. Click **OK**.

> ⊘ **SEE ALSO** For information about configuring a custom personal templates location, see "Change default Word options" in Chapter 16, "Customize options and the user interface."

To create a simple style

1. Apply the formatting that you want to include in the style to a paragraph or selection of text.

2. On the **Home** tab, in the **Styles** group, click the **More** button (in the lower-right corner of the Style gallery) and then on the menu, click **Create a Style**.

   A minimal version of the Create New Style From Formatting dialog box opens.

   The Paragraph Style Preview box displays the style formatting

3. In the **Create New Style from Formatting** dialog box, enter a name for the style in the **Name** box, and then click **OK**.

To create a style that is linked to other styles

> **TIP** To save steps later, you can insert the cursor in the style you want to base the new style on, and then apply the formatting that you want to that style.

1. Do either of the following to open the full version of the Create New Style From Formatting dialog box:

   • In the lower-left corner of the **Styles** pane, click the **New Style** button.

   • Open the minimal version of the dialog box, and then click the **Modify** button.

15

Basing a style on another simplifies global updates

2. Do the following:

   a. In the **Name** box, insert a name for the style.

   b. In the **Style based on** list, verify or click the style that you want to build the new style on. Updating the base style updates all styles based on it.

3. Do either of the following:

   - In the **Formatting** section, select the font, font size, font effects, font color, alignment, line spacing, space before and after, and indent.

   - Click the **Format** button, and then from the Format list, format the font, paragraph, tabs, border, language, frame, numbering, shortcut key, or text effects.

4. If you're creating a paragraph style, in the **Style for following paragraph** list, click the style that you want to create when the user presses **Enter** in a paragraph of this style.

5. If you want to include this style in the Style gallery, select the **Add to the Styles gallery** check box.

6. If you want to automatically update the style definition whenever formatting is applied to this style in a document, select the **Automatically update** check box. (You probably do not want to select this because it can modify the style when you don't want it to.)

7. If you want to save the style as part of the currently attached document template, click **New documents based on this template**.

8. Click **OK**.

To add a style to the Style gallery

1. In the **Styles** pane, do either of the following:

   • Right-click the style, and then click **Add to Style Gallery**.

   • Point to the style, click the arrow that appears, and then click **Add to Style Gallery**.

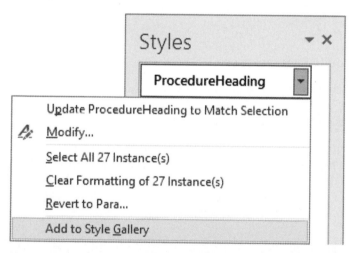

You can manage a style and the content it's applied to from the Styles pane

Or

1. Open the **Modify Style** dialog box for the style.

2. Select the **Add to the Styles gallery** check box, and then click **OK**.

15

To remove a style from the Style gallery

1. Do either of the following:

   - In the **Styles** pane, point to the style, click the arrow that appears, and then click **Remove from Style Gallery**.

   - In the **Styles** pane or **Style** gallery, right-click the style, and then click **Remove from Style Gallery**.

AaBbCcD	Update List1GraphicCaption to Match Selection
List1Gra.	Modify...
	Select All 12 Instance(s)
AaBbCcD	Rename...
SbarList.	Remove from Style Gallery
	Add Gallery to Quick Access Toolbar

You can manage a style from the Style gallery

Or

1. Open the **Modify Style** dialog box for the style.

2. Clear the **Add to the Styles gallery** check box, and then click **OK**.

To save the current style definitions as a style set

1. On the **Design** tab, in the **Document Formatting** group, click the **More** button (in the lower-right corner of the gallery pane) to expand the Style Set gallery and menu.

2. On the menu, click **Save as a new Style Set**.

3. In the **Save as a New Style Set** dialog box, enter a name for the style set in the **File name** box.

4. Click **Save** to save the style set in the QuickStyles folder and add it to the Style Set gallery.

> **SEE ALSO** For information about switching style sets, see "Apply built-in styles to text" in Chapter 4, "Modify the structure and appearance of text."

To delete a custom style

1. In the **Styles** pane, click the arrow to the right of the style, click **Delete** or **Revert To** <*style*>, and then click **Yes** to confirm the deletion.

> ✓ **TIP** The Delete command appears on the menu for styles that aren't based on other styles. The Revert To command appears for styles that are based on other styles. You cannot delete a built-in style, but if you have modified it, you can revert it back to its original formatting.

Create and manage custom themes

Chapter 4, "Modify the structure and appearance of text," contains information about applying themes, changing the default theme, and changing the colors, fonts, or effect styles of a theme within an individual document.

If you create a combination of theme elements that you would like to be able to use with other documents, you can save the combination as a new theme. By saving the theme in the default Document Themes folder, you make the theme available in the Themes gallery. However, you don't have to store custom themes in the Document Themes folder; you can store them anywhere on your hard disk, on removable media, or on a network location.

> ✓ **TIP** The default Document Themes folder is stored within your user profile. On a default freestanding installation, the folder is located at C:\Users\<*user name*>\AppData\Roaming\Microsoft\Templates\Document Themes. In a corporate environment with managed computer configurations, the user profile folder might be located elsewhere.

If multiple people create corporate documents for your company, you can ensure that everyone's documents have a common look and feel by assembling a custom theme and making it available to everyone. Use theme elements that reflect your corporate colors, fonts, and visual style, and then save the theme to a central location or send the theme file by email and instruct your colleagues to save it to the default Document Themes folder.

15

To save a custom theme

1. Apply a base theme, and then modify the theme colors, fonts, and effects the way you want them.

2. On the **Design** tab, in the **Document Formatting** group, click the **Themes** button.

3. At the bottom of the **Themes** menu, click **Save Current Theme** to display the contents of the Document Themes folder in the Save Current Theme dialog box.

4. In the **File name** box, replace the suggested name, and then click **Save**.

To apply a custom theme

1. Display the **Themes** menu. If custom themes are saved in the Document Themes folder, the Themes menu includes a Custom section that contains those themes.

2. In the **Custom** section of the **Themes** menu, click the theme.

To apply a theme from a nonstandard location

1. On the **Design** tab, in the **Document Formatting** group, click the **Themes** button.

2. At the bottom of the **Themes** menu, click **Browse for Themes**.

3. In the **Choose Theme or Themed Document** dialog box, browse to the theme you want to apply, and then click **Open**.

To find the location of your Document Themes folder

1. On the **Design** tab, in the **Document Formatting** group, click the **Themes** button.

2. At the bottom of the **Themes** menu, click **Save Current Theme**.

3. In the **Save Current Theme** dialog box, click the icon at the left end of the address bar to display the full path to the Document Themes folder.

To delete a custom theme

1. Do either of the following:

   - Open File Explorer, browse to the **Document Themes** folder, and delete the theme file.

   - In Word, display the **Themes** menu, right-click the custom theme, and then click **Delete**.

   Note that the second method removes the theme choice from the gallery but does not remove the theme file from your Themes folder.

Create and attach templates

Although most Word users rarely need to concern themselves with this fact, all Word documents are based on templates. New blank documents are based on the built-in Normal template, which defines paragraph styles for regular text paragraphs, a title, and different levels of headings. It also defines a few character styles that you can use to change the look of selected text. These styles appear in the Styles pane and are also available in the Style gallery on the Home tab. You can apply these template styles to format the content in the document.

> **SEE ALSO** For information about applying styles, see "Apply built-in styles to text" in Chapter 4, "Modify the structure and appearance of text."

Depending on the types of documents you create and the organization for which you create them, it might be quite realistic for you to work in the Normal template for the entire length of your word-processing career. If none of the templates that come with Word or that you download from Office.com meets your needs, you can create your own template. You can also distribute the custom template to other people. By doing so, you can ensure that documents you and your co-workers create adhere to a specific set of styles or are based on the same content.

Chapter 4, "Modify the structure and appearance of text," discusses how to assign formats and outline levels to content by applying styles, and how to change the appearance of styled content by using style sets. You can apply local character formatting to modify the appearance of text, and change the paragraph spacing for an entire document. All of these actions, however, are effective only in the document you're working on. If you want to consistently create coordinated documents, your most efficient option is to create a template that contains styles and colors specific to your purpose.

If you work for a company that has specific corporate fonts and colors, you can save a significant amount of time (and create very professional documents) by creating a corporate template.

Creating a custom template is easy—you simply create a document containing the content, styles, and settings that you want, and then save it as a document template (a .dotx file) rather than as a document (a .docx file). You can save a custom template with text in it, which is handy if you create many documents with only slight variations. Or you can delete the text so that a new document based on the template

15

will open as a blank document with the set of predefined styles available to apply to whatever content you enter.

You can save a custom template anywhere and then browse to and double-click the file name to open a new document based on the template. However, if you save the template in your default Personal Templates folder, it will be available when you click Personal at the top of the New page of the Backstage view. If you want to make changes to the content or formatting that is part of an existing template, you must open the template file instead of creating a document based on the template.

> **TIP** In earlier versions of Office, the default Templates location was a hidden folder stored at C:\Users\<*user name*>\AppData\Roaming\Microsoft\Templates. Word 2016 allows you to choose your own Personal Templates folder from the Save page of the Word Options dialog box. If you create a lot of your own templates, you can organize them by storing them in subfolders of your personal templates folder. You can create subfolders either by browsing to your personal templates folder in File Explorer and clicking the New Folder button, or by clicking the New Folder button in the Save As dialog box.

If you're working with an existing document and want to convert it to your custom template, you can either attach the custom template to the existing document or create a new document based on the custom template and import or paste in the content of the existing document. You attach a template by using the Document Template command, which is located in the Templates group on the hidden Developer tab.

> **TIP** You can load additional templates as *global templates* to make their contents available in all documents that you work on. Two global templates are automatically loaded by Word—the Normal template and the Building Blocks template—but you can load others. For example, your organization might have a Custom Building Blocks template containing corporate-themed document parts that it wants you to use in all documents.

If you modify the Normal template, you can easily revert to the original by closing all open Word documents, deleting the Normal.dotx template file from the default template location, and then restarting Word. If Word doesn't find the Normal template, it automatically creates a new one for you with the default settings.

To save a document as a personal template

1. In the Backstage view, click the **Save As** page tab.

2. In the left pane of the **Save As** page, click the **Browse** button to open the Save As dialog box.

3. In the **Save as type** list, click **Word template**. The folder path in the Address bar changes to display your default personal templates folder.

4. In the **File name** box, enter a name for the template, such as Company Fax Template. Then click **Save**.

5. Close the template. It is now available from the Personal view of the New page of the Backstage view.

To create a document based on a personal template

1. On the **New** page of the **Backstage** view, below the search box, Featured and Personal appear above the thumbnails if custom templates are saved in the default personal templates location. Click **Personal** to display the contents of your personal templates folder.

2. In the **Personal** templates view, click a thumbnail. Word creates a new document based on your custom template.

To edit a personal template

1. Display your personal templates folder.

2. Right-click the template that you want to edit, and then click **Open**.

Or

1. On the **Open** page of the Backstage view, browse to your personal templates folder.

2. Set the file type to **Word Templates**, and then double-click the template you want to edit.

To access the Document Template command

1. Do the following to display the Templates group on the Quick Access Toolbar:

   a. Display the **Quick Access Toolbar** page of the **Word Options** dialog box.

   b. In the **Choose commands from** list, click **Developer Tab**.

   c. In the **Choose commands from** pane, click **Templates**.

   d. Click **Add,** and then click **OK**.

Or

15

1. Do the following to display the Developer tab on the ribbon:

    a. Display the **Customize Ribbon** page of the **Word Options** dialog box.

    b. In the **Customize the Ribbon** pane displaying the main tabs, select the check box to the left of **Developer**, and then click **OK**.

> ⊘ **SEE ALSO** For information about customizing the Quick Access Toolbar and ribbon, see Chapter 16, "Customize options and the user interface."

To attach a different template to an open document

1. Display the **Templates** group on the Quick Access Toolbar, or display the **Developer** tab on the ribbon.

2. On the **Quick Access Toolbar** or **Developer** tab, in the **Templates** group, click **Document Template** to display the Templates page of the Templates And Add-ins dialog box.

Templates and Add-ins   ?   ✕

| Templates | XML Schema | XML Expansion Packs | Linked CSS |

Document template

C:\OTSI\Templates\OTSI-Corp.dotx   [Attach...]

☑ Automatically update document styles

☐ Attach to all new e-mail messages

Global templates and add-ins

Checked items are currently loaded.

[⌃]   [Add...]
                                                    [Remove]
[⌄]

Full path:

[Organizer...]   [OK]   [Cancel]

You can attach a template from any location you can browse to

3. In the **Document template** section, click **Attach** to open the Attach Template dialog box.

4. Navigate to the template you want to attach, and then double-click it to enter the path to the template in the Document Template box.

5. In the **Templates and Add-ins** dialog box, select the **Automatically update document styles** check box, and then click **OK** to attach the new template and update the document styles.

   If the styles in the new template have the same names as the styles in the original template, the formatting associated with the styles will change when you attach the new template. If the styles have different names, you can quickly restyle the document content by using commands available from the Styles pane.

To replace the styles attached to content

1. In the **Styles** pane, point to the old style name, click the arrow that appears, and click **Select All.** Then click the new style name.

To load a global template and make it available for use

1. Display the **Templates and Add-ins** dialog box. In the **Global templates and add-ins** section, click **Add** to open the Add Template dialog box.

2. In the **Add Template** dialog box, navigate to the template you want to load, and then double-click it to enter the template name in the Global Templates And Add-Ins pane. A check mark indicates that the template is active.

3. In the **Templates and Add-ins** dialog box, click **OK**.

> ✅ **TIP** You can deactivate a global template (but keep it available for future use) by clearing its check box, and you can unload it by selecting it in the list and clicking Remove.

Create custom building blocks

A building block is a document element that is saved in the Building Blocks global template. A building block can be as straightforward as a single word, or as complicated as a page full of formatted elements. Many building blocks are provided with Word 2016, including professionally designed page elements such as cover pages, headers and footers, and sidebars; and content elements such as bibliographies, common equations, Quick Tables, and watermarks. You can use these building blocks to assemble or enhance a document.

15

> **SEE ALSO** For information about working with building blocks to insert document elements such as cover pages, headers, footers, and page numbers, see Chapter 9, "Add visual elements."

You can save information and document elements that you use frequently as custom building blocks so that you can easily insert them into documents. A custom building block can be a simple phrase or sentence that you use often, or it can include multiple paragraphs, formatting, graphics, and more.

Wide World Importers
Furniture and accessories for your world
(925) 555-0167
www.wideworldimporters.com

Beautiful Bamboo

Bamboo has long been woven into the cultures of many countries, where it has historically been used for everything from food and fodder to musical instruments and construction material. For centuries, millions of people have depended on this plant, which is known as "friend of the people" in China,

ORDERING
INFORMATION

To order the Room Planner for just $39.99 plus shipping and handling, visit our website, at www.wideworldimporters.com or call us at 925-555-0167. We accept all major credit cards.

Custom building blocks, such as a company name and address block, make it easy to insert specific text and objects in any document

You need to create the element exactly as you want it only one time; then you can save it as a building block and use it confidently wherever you need it. You insert a custom building block into a document from the Quick Parts gallery on the Quick Parts menu.

Company Information

Contact Block

Wide World Importers
Furniture and accessories for your world
(925) 555-0167
www.wideworldimporters.com

Ordering Sidebar

ORDERING
INFORMATION

To order the Room Planner for just $39.99 plus shipping and handling, visit our website, at www.wideworldimporters.com

 AutoText ▶
Document Property ▶
Field...
Building Blocks Organizer...
Save Selection to Quick Part Gallery...

The building blocks in the Quick Parts gallery reflect the color scheme of the current document

> **TIP** The Quick Parts gallery displays only the building blocks you create. The built-in building blocks are available from other galleries, such as the Cover Page gallery.

> **IMPORTANT** When you exit Word after saving a custom building block, Word prompts you to save changes to the Building Blocks template, which is a separate template from the document template. If you want the building block to be available for future documents, save the changes.

To save content as a building block

1. Select the content that you want to save as a building block.

2. On the **Insert** tab, in the **Text** group, click the **Quick Parts** button to open the Quick Parts gallery.

3. Click **Save Selection to Quick Part Gallery** to open the Create New Building Block dialog box.

Word suggests text from the selection as the name of the building block

4. In the **Name** box, enter a name for your new building block.

5. In the **Category** list, do either of the following:

   - Click the category you want to save the building block in. General is the default.

   - If you want to create a custom category, click **Create New Category**, and in the **Create New Category** dialog box, enter a new category name in the name box, and then click **OK**.

15

6. In the **Create New Building Block** dialog box, add a description and make a selection in the **Options** box if you want, and then click **OK** to add the selected content to the **Quick Parts** gallery and the **Building Blocks** template.

> ✓ **TIP** To save changes to a custom building block, modify the building block in the document and then save it to the Quick Parts gallery with the same name as the original, and then click Yes when Word prompts you to indicate whether you want to redefine the building block.

To insert a custom building block in a document

1. Position the cursor in the document where you want to insert a building block.

2. Do any of the following:

   - In the **Quick Parts** gallery, select a building block.

   - In the **Quick Parts** gallery, click **Building Blocks Organizer**, and then, in the **Building Blocks Organizer** dialog box, select the building block and click the **Insert** button.

   - In the document, enter the name of the building block, and then press **F3** to replace the building block name with the building block.

   The building block picks up the formatting information from the document into which you insert it.

Or

1. Position the cursor anywhere in the document.

2. In the **Quick Parts** gallery, right-click a building block, and then click one of the specified locations.

General

Payment Schedule

Payment Schedule	
Interest Rate	
Years	
Loan Amount	$155,0
Monthly Payment	$4,5
Cost of Loan	$163,7
3-Year Lease Cost	$180,0
Savings	$16,

Insert at <u>C</u>urrent Document Position

Insert at Page <u>H</u>eader

Insert at Page <u>F</u>ooter

Insert at Be<u>g</u>inning of Section

Insert at E<u>n</u>d of Section ▶

Insert at <u>B</u>eginning of Document ▶

Insert at End of Document

Edit <u>P</u>roperties...

<u>O</u>rganize and Delete...

<u>A</u>dd Gallery to Quick Access Toolbar

- <u>A</u>utoText
- <u>D</u>ocument Pro
- <u>F</u>ield...
- <u>B</u>uilding Block
- <u>S</u>ave Selection

You can insert a custom building block by selecting a location from a list

To delete a custom building block

1. In the **Building Blocks Organizer** dialog box, select a building block, click the **Delete** button, and then click **Yes** when Word prompts you to indicate whether you want to delete the selected building block.

Skills review

In this chapter, you learned how to:

- Create and modify styles
- Create and manage custom themes
- Create and attach templates
- Create custom building blocks

15

Practice tasks

The practice files for these tasks are located in the Word2016SBS\Ch15 folder. You can save the results of the tasks in the same folder.

Create and modify styles

Open the CreateStyles document in Word, and then perform the following tasks:

1. Open the **Styles** pane, and review the styles that are part of the document template. Notice that they use fonts and colors that are different from the Normal template.

2. In the **Styles** pane, point to the **Heading 1** style to display its properties. Notice that it is based on the Normal style. Point to **Heading 2** and **Heading 3**, and notice that each is based on the previous heading level.

3. Change the font of the **Normal** style from Candara to **Franklin Gothic Book**, and notice the effect on the document content.

4. Select the heading *America's Finest Publishing Team*, and change the font color to **Green**.

5. With the heading still selected, update the **Heading 1** style to match the selection. Notice the effect on the Heading 2 and Heading 3 styles.

6. In the *Description of Services* section, under *Management*, select *Project Management*.

7. Change the font color to **Orange**. Remove the bold formatting and apply italic formatting.

8. Create a new character style based on the formatting, and name it **ServiceName**.

9. Apply the **ServiceName** style to the words *Document Management* at the beginning of the next paragraph. Then apply it to the other services in the *Description of Services* section of the document.

10. Save and close the document.

Create and manage custom themes

Open the CreateThemes document in Word, and then perform the following tasks:

1. Change the theme font set from Candara/Candara to a font set of your choice.

2. Change the theme colors to a color set of your choice.

3. Save the customized theme in the default theme location as **MyTheme**.

4. From the practice file folder, open the **ChangeTheme** document. Review the document content and note the fonts and colors.

5. Apply the **MyTheme** theme to the document. Then review the document and notice the changes.

6. Save and close the open documents.

Create and attach templates

Open the CreateTemplates document in Word, and then perform the following tasks:

1. Delete the content from the body of the document (but not the header or footer).

2. Open the **Styles** pane and display a preview of the styles that are in the document.

3. Save the blank document in the default template location, as a template named **MyTemplate**. Then close the file.

4. Start Word or switch to an open document, and display the **New** page of the Backstage view.

5. Click the **Personal** link that is now available at the top of the page, to display your personal templates.

6. Create a new document based on the **MyTemplate** template. Notice that the new document includes the header and footer.

7. In the **Styles** gallery, notice that the styles in the new document are the same as those in the **CreateTemplates** document.

8. Close the open documents without saving changes.

9. If you want to delete your custom template, browse to the default template location and delete the **MyTemplate.dotx** file.

Create custom building blocks

Open the CreateBuildingBlocks document in Word, and then perform the following tasks:

1. Activate the footer and select all the footer content.

2. Save the selected content as a building block with the following properties:

   Name: MyFooter
   Gallery: **Footers**
   Category: Create a new category named MyBlocks
   Description: My custom footer
   Save in: **Building Blocks**
   Options: **Insert content only**

3. Create a new, blank document. On the **Insert** tab, display the **Footer** gallery, locate the **MyFooter** building block, and insert it in the document.

4. Open the **Building Blocks Organizer**. Locate the **MyFooter** building block, and delete it.

5. Close the open documents without saving changes.

Customize options and the user interface

After you become accustomed to using Word 2016, you might notice certain default behaviors that don't fit the way you work. For example, you might always select a non-default paste option. The default Word functionality is based on the way that most people work with documents, or in some cases, because one option had to be selected as the default. You can modify the default behavior of many functions so that you can work more efficiently. You can also change aspects of the program to make it more suitable for the kinds of documents you create.

When working in Word, you interact with commands (in the form of buttons, lists, and galleries) on the various tabs of the ribbon. Most people use a few commands from each tab often, and others not at all. You can centralize and streamline your interactions with the ribbon by adding the commands (from ribbon tabs other than Home) that you use most often to the Quick Access Toolbar, and positioning the Quick Access Toolbar below the ribbon so it's closer to the document content. You can also hide or display specific ribbon tabs and modify the content that appears on the ribbon.

This chapter guides you through procedures related to changing default Word options, customizing the Quick Access Toolbar and ribbon, and managing add-ins and security options.

In this chapter

- Change default Word options
- Customize the Quick Access Toolbar
- Customize the ribbon
- Manage add-ins and security options

Practice files

No practice files are necessary to complete the practice tasks in this chapter.

Change default Word options

Many of the options available in the Word Options dialog box are discussed in context in other chapters in this book. This topic includes information about all the available options, including a few that power users of Word might particularly find useful to modify.

All the options I discuss in this topic are available in the Word Options dialog box, which you open from the Backstage view. Each Office app has its own Options dialog box. Because so many options are available for each app and for Office, they are divided among pages (and in some cases, additional dialog boxes that you open from the pages). The pages are represented by page tabs in the left pane of the Word Options dialog box.

Shading indicates the active page tab

The left pane of the Word Options dialog box is divided into three sections:

- The first section contains the General, Display, Proofing, Save, Language, and Advanced page tabs. These are the pages of options that standard Word users will most commonly make changes to when customizing the app functionality.

- The second section contains the Customize Ribbon and Quick Access Toolbar page tabs. These are the pages on which you customize the presentation of commands in the user interface.

- The third section contains the Add-ins and Trust Center page tabs. These pages are access points for higher-level customizations that can affect the security of your computer, and are not often necessary to modify.

> **TIP** This topic discusses the options on the General, Display, Proofing, Save, Language, and Advanced pages. For information about customizing the ribbon, Quick Access Toolbar, add-ins, and security options, see the related topics later in this chapter.

A brief description of the page content appears at the top of each page. Each page is further divided into sections of related options. The General page contains information that is shared among the Office apps. Other pages contain options that are specific to the app or to the file you're working in.

The images in this topic depict the default selections for each option. Many options have only on/off settings as indicated by a selected or cleared check box. Options that have settings other than on or off are described in the content that follows the image.

Manage general Office and Word options

Options that affect the user interface and startup behavior of Word are available from the General page of the Word Options dialog box.

16

General options for working with Word.

User Interface options

☑ Show Mini Toolbar on selection ⓘ
☑ Enable Live Preview ⓘ
☑ Update document content while dragging ⓘ
ScreenTip style: [Show feature descriptions in ScreenTips ▾]

Personalize your copy of Microsoft Office

User name: [Samantha Smith]
Initials: [SS]
☐ Always use these values regardless of sign in to Office.
Office Background: [No Background ▾]
Office Theme: [Colorful ▾]

Options for all Office apps

The options in the User Interface Options and Personalize Your Copy Of Microsoft Office sections of the General page are shared among the Office apps installed on the computer you're working on, and include the following:

- You can turn off the Mini Toolbar, which hosts common formatting commands and appears by default when you select content.

- You can turn off the Live Preview feature if you find it distracting to have content formatting change when the pointer passes over a formatting command.

- You can minimize or turn off the display of ScreenTips when you point to buttons.

- You can specify the user name and initials you want to accompany your comments and tracked changes, and override the display of information from the account associated with your installation of Office.

- You can choose the background graphics (Office background) and color scheme (Office theme) for the Office app windows.

> **TIP** You can also set the Office background and theme on the Account page of the Backstage view. For information about Office backgrounds and themes, see "Manage Office and app settings" in Chapter 1, "Word 2016 basics."

The Start Up Options section contains options related to setting Word as the default document editor, and a couple of options that you might want to configure: to open documents in Reading view if you can't edit them, and to turn off the Start screen that appears when you start Word without opening a specific file. When the Start screen is turned off, starting the app without opening a specific file automatically creates a new, blank file.

Start up options

Choose the extensions you want Word to open by default: Default Programs...

☑ Tell me if Microsoft Word isn't the default program for viewing and editing documents.

☐ Open e-mail attachments and other uneditable files in reading view ⓘ

☑ Show the Start screen when this application starts

Real-time collaboration options

When working with others, I want to automatically share my changes: Always ▾

☐ Show names on presence flags

General options for Word

To open the Word Options dialog box

1. Click the **File** tab to display the Backstage view.

2. In the left pane, click **Options**.

To display a specific page of the Word Options dialog box

1. Open the **Word Options** dialog box.

2. In the left pane, click the tab of the page that you want to display.

To close the Word Options dialog box

1. Do either of the following:

   • To commit to any changes, click **OK**.

   • To cancel any changes, click **Cancel** or click the **Close** button (**X**) in the upper-right corner of the dialog box.

To enable or disable the Mini Toolbar

1. Open the **Word Options** dialog box, and display the **General** page.

2. In the **User Interface options** section, select or clear the **Show Mini Toolbar on selection** check box.

16

To enable or disable the Live Preview feature

1. Display the **General** page of the **Word Options** dialog box.

2. In the **User Interface options** section, select or clear the **Enable Live Preview** check box.

To control the display of ScreenTips

1. Display the **General** page of the **Word Options** dialog box.

2. In the **User Interface options** section, display the **ScreenTip style** list, and then click any of the following:

   - Show feature descriptions in ScreenTips

   - Don't show feature descriptions in ScreenTips

   - Don't show ScreenTips

To change the user identification that appears in comments and tracked changes

> ⚠ **IMPORTANT** The User Name and Initials settings are shared by all the Office apps, so changing them in any one app immediately changes them in all the apps.

1. Display the **General** page of the **Word Options** dialog box.

2. In the **Personalize your copy of Microsoft Office** section, do the following:

   - In the **User name** and **Initials** boxes, enter the information you want to use.

   - Select the **Always use these values regardless of sign in to Office** check box.

To enable or disable the Word Start screen

1. Display the **General** page of the **Word Options** dialog box.

2. In the **Start up options** section, select or clear the **Show the Start screen when this application starts** check box.

Manage display options

Options on the Display page control what is shown in the content pane and how documents are printed. The default settings on this page are appropriate for most types of documents. You can turn on and off the display of formatting marks from within the app window, and set many of the printing options when you print a document.

Change how document content is displayed on the screen and when printed.

Page display options

☑ Show white space between pages in Print Layout view ⓘ
☑ Show highlighter marks ⓘ
☑ Show document tooltips on hover

Always show these formatting marks on the screen

☐ Tab characters   →
☐ Spaces   •••
☐ Paragraph marks   ¶
☐ Hidden text   abc
☐ Optional hyphens   ¬
☑ Object anchors   ⚓
☐ Show all formatting marks

Printing options

☑ Print drawings created in Word ⓘ
☐ Print background colors and images
☐ Print document properties
☐ Print hidden text
☐ Update fields before printing
☐ Update linked data before printing

Options for displaying document content

16

Manage proofing options

Options that affect the spelling and grammar-checking and automatic text replacement functions of Word are available from the Proofing page of the Word Options dialog box.

Editorial options for working with document content

You might find that you want to modify the spelling and grammar correction options in the When Correcting Spelling And Grammar In Word section of the page. These options control whether Word automatically checks for spelling errors, grammar errors, and writing style issues. When automatic checking is turned on, Word displays squiggly red lines under words it thinks are spelled wrong, and squiggly blue lines under words that don't meet its grammar and style guidelines. If you find those lines to be distracting, you can turn off the automatic checking, modify the grammar and style issues Word is checking for, or turn off the display of the lines for the current document or for all documents.

When reviewing spelling in a document, you have options to ignore one or all instances of suspected spelling errors. You choose to ignore all instances of a flagged spelling error in a document either from the shortcut menu or from the Spelling pane. Word remembers your selection and removes the squiggly underlines from all instances of that word. If you want Word to forget those settings and conduct a fresh spelling check, you can do that from this page.

The AutoCorrect settings do affect the way Word processes specific text and character combinations that you enter, so it's good to be familiar with them.

Reasons to modify the AutoCorrect settings include:

- If you find that Word is consistently changing text that you enter, in a way that you don't want it to.

- If you consistently make a spelling mistake that you would like Word to correct for you.

- If you want to create a shortcut for entering longer text segments. (For example, if you want Word to enter *Wide World Importers* whenever you type *WW*.)

To turn off the automatic spelling checking function

1. Display the **Proofing** page of the **Word Options** dialog box.

2. In the **When correcting spelling and grammar in Word** section, clear the **Check spelling as you type** check box.

To specify the grammar and style issues Word checks for

1. Display the **Proofing** page of the **Word Options** dialog box.

2. In the **When correcting spelling and grammar in Word** section, click the **Settings** button to open the Grammar Settings dialog box. By default, all grammar and style options are selected.

16

Grammar Settings	?	X

Writing style:

Grammar ▾

Grammar and style options:

☑ Capitalization
☑ Capitalization in Sentences
☑ Hyphenation
☑ Misused Words
☑ Noun Phrases
☑ Punctuation
☑ Spacing
☑ Subject Verb Agreement
☑ Verb Phrases

Reset All   OK   Cancel

You can specify the types of grammar and style issues Word checks for

3.   In the **Grammar Settings** dialog box, clear the check boxes of any grammar or style issues you don't want Word to check for. Then click OK.

> **TIP** Typically, the issues you might want to ignore are those that you consistently click Ignore for when running a spelling and grammar check from the Review tab.

To hide squiggly underlines that indicate spelling or grammar errors

1.   Display the **Proofing** page of the **Word Options** dialog box.

2.   In the **Exceptions for** list, do either of the following:

- Click **All New Documents** to hide error indicators until you change this selection.

- Click a specific document file name to hide error indicators in that document.

3.   In the **Exceptions for** section, select one or both of the following check boxes:

- **Hide spelling errors in this document only**

- **Hide grammar errors in this document only**

To clear hidden errors and check spelling and grammar against the current criteria

1. Display the **Proofing** page of the **Word Options** dialog box.

2. In the **When correcting spelling and grammar in Word** section, click the **Recheck Document** button.

To stop Word from automatically correcting a specific type of text entry

1. Display the **Proofing** page of the **Word Options** dialog box.

2. In the **AutoCorrect options** section, click the **AutoCorrect Options** button.

3. In the **AutoCorrect** dialog box, display the **AutoCorrect** or **Math AutoCorrect** tab.

Automatic text correction options

4. Locate the correction that you want to turn off, and clear the check box. Then click **OK**.

16

To stop Word from automatically applying formatting

1. Display the **Proofing** page of the **Word Options** dialog box.

2. In the **AutoCorrect options** section, click the **AutoCorrect Options** button.

3. In the **AutoCorrect** dialog box, display the **AutoFormat** or **AutoFormat As You Type** tab.

Automatic formatting options

4. Locate the formatting that you want to turn off, and clear the check box. Then click **OK**.

To automatically change a specific text entry to another

1. Display the **Proofing** page of the **Word Options** dialog box.

2. In the **AutoCorrect options** section, click the **AutoCorrect Options** button.

3. In the **AutoCorrect** dialog box, on the **AutoCorrect** tab, do the following, and then click **OK**:

    - In the **Replace** box, enter the misspelling or abbreviated text. The list scrolls to display the closest entries.

    - In the **With** box, enter the corrected spelling or full-length text you want Word to replace the original entry with.

Manage file saving options

The Save page of the Word Options dialog box contains two sections of options that control the behavior of the app, and one section that is specific to the document you're working in.

Options that affect where and when Word saves and looks for documents and templates are available in the Save Documents and Offline Editing Options sections. These options can be rather important—not necessarily to change them, but to know where Word stores files so that you can browse to them if necessary.

Customize your save options

Two options that you might find useful are these:

- **Save AutoRecover Information** If you're making a lot of changes that you don't want to lose, or feel that your system might run into trouble (for example, if you're in a location that is experiencing frequent power outages and you don't have battery backup), you can automatically save drafts more frequently than the default of every 10 minutes.

- **Default Local File Location** You can specify the folder that Word displays in the Save As dialog box when you select This PC in the Places list. The default is your Documents folder, but if you routinely save in another location, you can save yourself a few clicks by choosing that instead. (Or you can pin the location to the top of the location list.)

The location specified in the Offline Editing section is where Word stores local copies of online files it's working with. It's best to not change anything in this section.

Options for saving fonts with the current document are available in the Preserve Fidelity section. When you distribute a Word document electronically (as a .docx file), the fonts in the document render correctly on-screen only if they are installed on the computer that's displaying the document. If you use fonts in your document other than those that come with Office, or if you have reason to believe that the fonts you use won't be available on a computer or device that displays the document, you can embed the fonts in the document.

Preserve fidelity when sharing this document:	Document1	⌄
☐ Embed fonts in the file ⓘ		
☐ Embed only the characters used in the document (best for reducing file size)		
☑ Do not embed common system fonts		

Embed nonstandard fonts in documents so they display correctly on other computers

Embedding fonts in a document increases the size of the file. You can minimize the increase by embedding only the characters that are used in the document. Letters, numbers, and symbols that aren't in the document when you embed the fonts will not be available. Embedding all the characters of a font requires more storage space, especially if you use multiple fonts in the document, but makes the characters available on other systems so the document content can be gracefully edited.

To change the automatic draft saving frequency

1. Display the **Save** page of the **Word Options** dialog box.

2. In the **Save documents** section, set the saving frequency in the **Save AutoRecover information every** box.

To change the default local folder

1. Start File Explorer and browse to the folder you want to set as the default.

2. Do either of the following to copy the folder path to the Clipboard:

   - Click the folder icon at the left end of the **Address** box to display the folder path. Then press **Ctrl+C**.

   - Right-click the **Address** box, and then click **Copy address as text**.

3. Display the **Save** page of the **Word Options** dialog box.

4. In the **Save documents** section, select the content of the **Default local file location** box.

5. Do either of the following to paste the folder path into the box:

   - Press **Ctrl+V**.

   - Right-click the selection, and then click **Paste**.

To embed fonts in a document

1. Display the **Save** page of the **Word Options** dialog box.

2. In the **Preserve fidelity when sharing this document** section, select the **Embed fonts in the file** check box.

3. If you want to embed the entire character set of all fonts used in the document, click **Embed all characters**.

> **TIP** Additional fidelity-related options are located in the Preserve Fidelity When Sharing This Document section of the Advanced page of the Word Options dialog box. For information about those settings, see the "Manage advanced options" section of this topic.

16

Manage language options

Most people use only one editing and display language when working in documents, but people who work in a multilingual environment might be able to use additional languages. The Language page of the Word Options dialog box contains options for adding, removing, and prioritizing language options in all the Office apps that are installed on the computer.

You can install additional language packs

You can configure two types of language options on the Language page:

- Editing languages, which control the keyboard and proofing settings

- Display languages, which control the language of user interface labels (such as ribbon tab names and button names) and built-in user assistance features (such as ScreenTips)

The keyboard languages are installed through Windows, but you can start the process from this page. If you've already installed a language on your computer through

Windows, that language is automatically available to you in Office as a keyboard language. The Office proofing tools and display languages are specific to Office and aren't provided by Windows.

To add an editing language to Office

1. Display the **Language** page of the **Word Options** dialog box.

2. In the **Choose Editing Languages** section, in the **Add additional editing languages** list, click the language you want to add. Then click the **Add** button adjacent to the list.

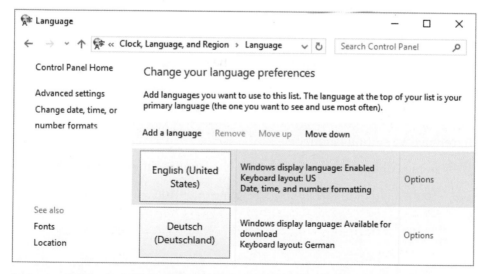

You must specifically install the proofing tools through Office

To enable the keyboard layout for a language

1. In the **Editing Language** pane, click the **Not enabled** link to display the Language window of the Windows Control Panel.

Languages that you install through Windows are available to you as keyboard languages

16

2. In the **Language** window, click **Add a language**.

3. On the **Add a language** page, locate the language that you want to enable the keyboard for. Click the language, and then click **Add**.

To install the proofing tools for a language or to install a display language

1. In the **Editing Language** pane, click the **Not installed** link to display the Language Accessory Pack For Office 2016 page of the Office website.

2. On the **Language Accessory Pack** page, locate the language that you want to install the proofing tools for.

German	de-de	Deutsch	Full	The pack includes:	Download
				▪ Display in selected language	
				▪ Help in selected language	
				▪ Proofing tools for selected language	

The language accessory pack includes the proofing tools and display language, if available

3. Click the **Download** link for the language.

4. In the prompt that appears, click **Run** to begin the installation of the selected language accessory pack. An Office message box informs you that you must close all Office apps and Internet Explorer to install the language pack.

To set a default editing language

1. In the **Editing Language** pane, click the language that you want to set as the default.

2. To the right of the pane, click the **Set as Default** button.

To remove an editing language

1. In the **Editing Language** pane, click the language that you want to remove.

2. To the right of the pane, click the **Remove** button.

To prioritize a display language or Help language

1. In the **Display Language** or **Help Language** pane, click the language you want to prioritize.

2. Click the **Move Up** button adjacent to the pane.

Manage advanced options

The most interesting and useful options are, of course, gathered on the Advanced page of the Word Options dialog box. There are many options here; some affect the app behavior, and others are specific to the document you're working in.

The Advanced page is divided into 12 sections.

Manage the ways you can edit content

The options in the Editing Options and Cut, Copy, And Paste sections are self-explanatory, other than the Use Smart Cut And Paste option. This option is very useful when working with text in a Word document because it controls whether the app tries to

16

merge content into adjacent lists when you cut it from one location and paste it in another.

Manage the ways Word pastes content

Most of the options in the Image Size And Quality and Chart sections are specific to the current document. These options can frequently be useful:

- **Discard editing data** When you insert images in a document and then edit them by using the tools on the Format tool tab for pictures, Word saves the editing data so you can undo your changes. You can decrease the file size of a document by discarding the editing data.

- **Do not compress images in file** When you're finalizing a document for distribution, you have the option to compress the media within the file. This results in a smaller file size, but also a lower quality. You also have the option to exclude images from the media compression.

Manage the impact of images on file size

The options in the Chart section control whether custom data labels and formatting stay with data points in charts. It seems likely that this would always be the better option, but if you find that it presents a problem, you can turn it off here.

Display

Show this number of Recent Documents: 25   (i)

☐ Quickly access this number of Recent Documents: 4

Show this number of unpinned Recent Folders: 20

Show measurements in units of: Inches

Style area pane width in Draft and Outline views: 0"

☐ Show pixels for HTML features

☑ Show shortcut keys in ScreenTips

☑ Show horizontal scroll bar

☑ Show vertical scroll bar

☑ Show vertical ruler in Print Layout view

☐ Optimize character positioning for layout rather than readability

☐ Disable hardware graphics acceleration

☑ Update document content while dragging (i)

☑ Use subpixel positioning to smooth fonts on screen

Configure the display of information in the Backstage view and in the app window

Options in the Display section are among those that you might want to configure for the way you work. You can change the number of documents that appear in the Recent file list in the right pane of the Open page of the Backstage view. You can also display your most recently edited documents directly in the left pane of the Backstage view, below the Options button, for easy access. This can be very convenient, but the option is not turned on by default.

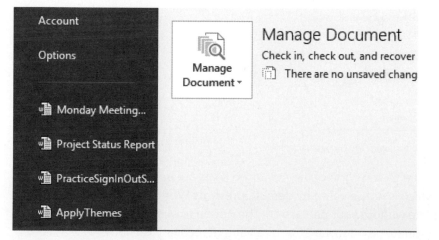

Quickly access recent documents from the left pane of the Backstage view

You configure the display of ScreenTips and whether they include feature descriptions on the General page of the Word Options dialog box. However, the option to display keyboard shortcuts within ScreenTips is here in the Display section of the Advanced page. If you're a person who likes to work from the keyboard and you don't have the full list of keyboard shortcuts memorized, you can learn them by including them in ScreenTips.

> **SEE ALSO** For an extensive list of keyboard shortcuts that you can use in Word 2016 and globally throughout Office 2016, see "Keyboard shortcuts" at the end of this book.

There are two sections of printing options; the first are general printing options and the second are specific to the document you're working in. You can configure the same options for printing the current document on the Print page of the Backstage view. The advantage to configuring the document-specific options here is that they travel with the document.

Save specific print options with the current document

The options in the Save section of the Advanced page are important to consider. The first option, which is not selected by default, prevents Word from overwriting the Normal template without your permission. The option to allow background saves, which is on by default, is important for the saving of recovery versions.

Save

- ☐ Prompt before saving Normal template ⓘ
- ☐ Always create backup copy
- ☐ Copy remotely stored files onto your computer, and update the remote file when saving
- ☑ Allow background saves

Preserve fidelity when sharing this document: 📄 Project Status Report ▽

- ☐ Save form data as delimited text file
- ☑ Embed linguistic data

Advanced options related to saving documents

> **TIP** Additional fidelity-related options are located in the Preserve Fidelity When Sharing This Document section of the Save page of the Word Options dialog box. For information about those settings, see the "Manage file saving options" section of this topic.

The General section of the Advanced page is a bit of a catch-all for options that don't fit elsewhere. One item of note here is the Mailing Address box. If you enter your name and address in this box, Word automatically fills it in for you when you create envelopes and mailing labels.

General

- ☐ Provide feedback with sound
- ☑ Provide feedback with animation
- ☐ Confirm file format conversion on open
- ☑ Update automatic links at open
- ☐ Allow opening a document in Draft view
- ☑ Enable background repagination
- ☐ Show add-in user interface errors

Mailing address:

[File Locations...] [Web Options...]

Provide your address to Word for use in mail merge documents

16

The options in the Layout Options section of the Advanced page are document-specific and reasonably specialized. Few Word users will need to modify these settings.

Layout options for:	▥ Project Status Report	⌄

☐ Add space for underlines

☐ Adjust line height to grid height in the table

☐ Balance SBCS characters and DBCS characters

☐ Convert backslash characters into yen signs

☐ Don't center "exact line height" lines

☐ Don't expand character spaces on a line that ends with SHIFT+RETURN

☐ Draw underline on trailing spaces

☐ Suppress extra line spacing at bottom of page

☐ Suppress extra line spacing at top of page

☐ Use line-breaking rules

Layout options modify the positioning of content

Customize the Quick Access Toolbar

By default, buttons representing the Save, Undo, and Redo commands appear on the Quick Access Toolbar. If you regularly use a few commands that are scattered on various tabs of the ribbon and you don't want to switch between tabs to access the commands, you might want to add them to the Quick Access Toolbar so that they're always available to you.

You can add commands to the Quick Access Toolbar directly from the ribbon, or from the Quick Access Toolbar page of the Word Options dialog box.

> **✓ TIP** You can display a list of commands that do not appear on the ribbon by clicking Commands Not In The Ribbon in the Choose Commands From list on the Quick Access Toolbar or Customize Ribbon page of the app-specific Options dialog box.

The Quick Access Toolbar is a convenient command organization option

You can customize the Quick Access Toolbar in the following ways:

- You can define a custom Quick Access Toolbar for all documents (referred to in the Word Options dialog box as documents), or you can define a custom Quick Access Toolbar for a specific document.

- You can add any command from any group of any tab, including tool tabs, to the toolbar.

- You can display a separator between different types of buttons.

- You can move commands around on the toolbar until they are in the order you want.

- You can reset everything back to the default Quick Access Toolbar configuration.

16

After you add commands to the Quick Access Toolbar, you can reorganize them and divide them into groups to simplify the process of locating the command you want.

As you add commands to the Quick Access Toolbar, it expands to accommodate them. If you add a lot of commands, it might become difficult to view the text in the title bar, or all the commands on the Quick Access Toolbar might not be visible, defeating the purpose of adding them. To resolve this problem and also position the Quick Access Toolbar closer to the file content, you can move the Quick Access Toolbar below the ribbon.

To add a command to the Quick Access Toolbar from the ribbon

1. Do either of the following:

   - Right-click a command on the ribbon, and then click **Add to Quick Access Toolbar**. You can add any type of command this way; you can even add a drop-down list of options or gallery of thumbnails.

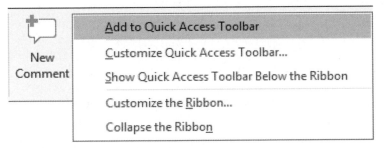

Add any button to the Quick Access Toolbar directly from the ribbon

   - At the right end of the Quick Access Toolbar, click the **Customize Quick Access Toolbar** button. On the menu of commonly used commands, click a command you want to add.

Commonly used commands are available from the menu

To display the Quick Access Toolbar page of the Word Options dialog box

1. Do any of the following:

   - At the right end of the Quick Access Toolbar, click the **Customize Quick Access Toolbar** button, and then click **More Commands**.

   - Click the **File** tab and then, in the left pane of the Backstage view, click **Options**. In the left pane of the **Word Options** dialog box, click **Quick Access Toolbar**.

   - Right-click any ribbon tab or empty area of the ribbon, and then click **Customize Quick Access Toolbar**.

16

To add a command to the Quick Access Toolbar from the Word Options dialog box

1. Display the **Quick Access Toolbar** page of the **Word Options** dialog box.

2. In the **Choose commands from** list, click the tab the command appears on, or click **Popular Commands**, **Commands Not in the Ribbon**, **All Commands**, or **Macros**.

3. In the left list, locate and click the command you want to add to the Quick Access Toolbar. Then click the **Add** button.

To move the Quick Access Toolbar

1. Do either of the following:

   - At the right end of the Quick Access Toolbar, click the **Customize Quick Access Toolbar** button, and then click **Show Below the Ribbon** or **Show Above the Ribbon**.

   - Display the **Quick Access Toolbar** page of the **Word Options** dialog box. In the area below the **Choose commands from** list, select or clear the **Show Quick Access Toolbar below the Ribbon** check box.

To define a custom Quick Access Toolbar for a specific document

1. Display the **Quick Access Toolbar** page of the **Word Options** dialog box.

2. In the **Customize Quick Access Toolbar** list (above the right pane) click **For** *file name*.

3. Add the commands to the toolbar that you want to make available to anyone who edits the file, and then click **OK**. The app displays the file-specific Quick Access Toolbar to the right of the user's own Quick Access Toolbar.

 TIP If a command is on a user's Quick Access Toolbar and also on a file-specific Quick Access Toolbar, it will be shown in both toolbars.

To display a separator on the Quick Access Toolbar

1. Display the **Quick Access Toolbar** page of the **Word Options** dialog box.

2. In the right pane, click the command after which you want to insert the separator.

3. Do either of the following:

   - In the left pane, double-click **<Separator>**.

   - Click **<Separator>** in the left pane, and then click the **Add** button.

To move buttons on the Quick Access Toolbar

1. Display the **Quick Access Toolbar** page of the **Word Options** dialog box.

2. In the right pane, click the button you want to move. Then click the **Move Up** or **Move Down** arrow until it reaches the position you want.

To reset the Quick Access Toolbar to its default configuration

1. Display the **Quick Access Toolbar** page of the **Word Options** dialog box.

2. In the lower-right corner, click **Reset**, and then click either of the following:

   - **Reset only Quick Access Toolbar**

   - **Reset all customizations**

3. In the **Microsoft Office** message box verifying the change, click **Yes**.

> ⚠️ **IMPORTANT** Resetting the Quick Access Toolbar does not change its location. You must manually move the Quick Access Toolbar by using either of the procedures described earlier.

Customize the ribbon

The ribbon was designed to make all the commonly used commands visible so that people can more easily discover the full potential of each Office app. But many people perform the same set of tasks all the time, and for them, buttons that they never use might be considered just another form of clutter.

If you don't want to entirely hide the ribbon, you can modify its content. From the Customize Ribbon page of the Word Options dialog box, you can control the tabs that appear on the ribbon, and the groups that appear on the tabs.

16

You can hide and display individual ribbon tabs

On this page, you can customize the ribbon in the following ways:

- You can hide an entire tab.

- You can remove a group of commands from a tab. (The group is not removed from the app, only from the tab.)

- You can move or copy a group of commands to another tab.

- You can create a custom group on any tab and then add commands to it. (You cannot add commands to a predefined group.)

- You can create a custom tab. For example, you might want to do this if you use only a few commands from each tab and you find it inefficient to flip between them.

Don't be afraid to experiment with the ribbon to come up with the configuration that best suits the way you work. If at any point you find that your new ribbon is harder to work with rather than easier, you can easily reset everything back to the default configuration.

> ⚠️ **IMPORTANT** Although customizing the default ribbon content might seem like a great way of making the app yours, I don't recommend doing so. A great deal of research has been done about the way that people use the commands in each app, and the ribbon has been organized to reflect the results of that research. If you modify the default ribbon settings, you might end up inadvertently hiding or moving commands that you need. Instead, consider the Quick Access Toolbar to be the command area that you customize and make your own. If you add all the commands you use frequently to the Quick Access Toolbar, you can hide the ribbon and have extra vertical space for document display. (This is very convenient when working on a smaller device.) Or, if you really want to customize the ribbon, do so by gathering your most frequently used commands on a custom tab, and leave the others alone.

To display the Customize Ribbon page of the Word Options dialog box

1. Do either of the following:

   - Display the **Word Options** dialog box. In the left pane, click **Customize Ribbon**.

   - Right-click any ribbon tab or empty area of the ribbon, and then click **Customize the Ribbon**.

To show or hide a tab

1. Display the **Customize Ribbon** page of the **Word Options** dialog box.

2. In the **Customize the Ribbon** list, click the tab set you want to manage:

   - All Tabs

   - Tool Tabs

   - Main Tabs

3. In the right pane, select or clear the check box of any tab other than the File tab. (You can't hide the File tab.)

16

To remove a group of commands from a tab

1. Display the **Customize Ribbon** page of the **Word Options** dialog box.

2. In the **Customize the Ribbon** list, click the tab set you want to manage.

3. In the **Customize the Ribbon** pane, click the **Expand** button (+) to the left of the tab you want to modify.

4. Click the group you want to remove, and then in the center pane, click the **Remove** button.

To create a custom tab

1. Display the **Customize Ribbon** page of the **Word Options** dialog box.

2. On the **Customize Ribbon** page, click the **New Tab** button to insert a new custom tab below the active tab in the Customize The Ribbon pane. The new tab includes an empty custom group.

Creating a new tab and group

To rename a custom tab

1. Display the **Customize Ribbon** page of the **Word Options** dialog box.

2. In the **Customize the Ribbon** pane, click the custom tab. Then click the **Rename** button.

3. In the **Rename** dialog box, replace the existing tab name with the tab name you want, and then click **OK**.

To rename a custom group

1. Click the custom group, and then click the **Rename** button to open the **Rename** dialog box in which you can specify an icon and display name for the group.

Assign an icon to appear when the group is narrow

2. In the **Rename** dialog box, do the following, and then click **OK**:

    •   In the **Display name** box, replace the current name with the group name that you want to display.

    •   In the **Symbol** pane, click an icon that you want to display when the ribbon is too narrow to display the group's commands.

To create a custom group

1. Display the **Customize Ribbon** page of the **Word Options** dialog box.

2. On the **Customize Ribbon** page, in the right pane, click the tab you want to add the group to. Then click the **New Group** button to add an empty custom group.

To add commands to a custom group

1. Display the **Customize Ribbon** page of the **Word Options** dialog box.

2. In the **Customize the Ribbon** list, expand the tab set you want to manage, and then click the group you want to add the commands to.

16

3. In the **Choose commands from** list, click the tab the command appears on, or click **Popular Commands**, **Commands Not in the Ribbon**, **All Commands**, or **Macros**.

4. In the left list, locate and click the command you want to add to the group. Then click the **Add** button.

To reset the ribbon to its default configuration

1. Display the **Customize Ribbon** page of the **Word Options** dialog box.

2. In the lower-right corner, click **Reset**, and then click either of the following:

- **Reset only selected Ribbon Tab**

- **Reset all customizations**

Manage add-ins and security options

The final section of pages in the Word Options dialog box contains the settings that you should definitely think carefully about before changing, because they can affect the security of your system.

Manage add-ins

Add-ins are utilities that add specialized functionality to a program but aren't full-fledged programs themselves. Word includes two primary types of add-ins: COM add-ins (which use the Component Object Model) and Word add-ins.

There are several sources of add-ins:

- You can purchase add-ins from third-party vendors; for example, you can purchase an add-in that allows you to assign keyboard shortcuts to Word commands that don't already have them.

- You can download free add-ins from the Microsoft website or other websites.

- When installing a third-party program, you might install an add-in to allow it to interact with Microsoft Office 2016 programs.

> **TIP** Be careful when downloading add-ins from websites other than those you know and trust. Add-ins are executable files that can easily be used to spread viruses and otherwise wreak havoc on your computer. For this reason, default settings in the Trust Center intervene when you attempt to download or run add-ins.

Information about the add-ins that are installed on your computer, and access to manage them, is available from the Add-ins page of the Word Options dialog box.

The Add-ins page displays installed add-ins of all types

16

Each type of add-in has its own management interface. You can add and remove add-ins, turn off installed add-ins, and enable add-ins that have been disabled.

Display and manage active and disabled add-ins

Many add-ins install themselves, but to use some add-ins, you must first install them on your computer and then load them into your computer's memory.

To display management options for a type of add-in

1. Display the **Add-Ins** page of the **Word Options** dialog box.

2. In the **Manage** list at the bottom of the page, click the type of add-in you want to manage. Then click the adjacent **Go** button.

To install an add-in

1. Display the dialog box for the type of add-in you want to manage.

2. In the dialog box, click **Add** or **Add New**.

3. In the **Add Add-In** dialog box, navigate to the folder where the add-in you want to install is stored, and double-click its name.

4. In the list of available add-ins in the **Add-In** dialog box, select the check box of the new add-in, and then click **OK** or **Load** to make the add-in available for use in Word.

Configure Trust Center options

The Trust Center is a separate multipage dialog box in which you can configure security and privacy settings. You open the Trust Center from the Trust Center page of the Word Options dialog box. The Trust Center settings aren't exposed directly on the page; you must click a button next to a warning recommending that you not change any of the settings.

> Help keep your documents safe and your computer secure and healthy.
>
> **Security & more**
>
> Visit Office.com to learn more about protecting your privacy and security.
>
> Microsoft Trustworthy Computing
>
> **Microsoft Word Trust Center**
>
> The Trust Center contains security and privacy settings. These settings help keep your computer secure. We recommend that you do not change these settings.
>
> [Trust Center Settings...]

Continue at your own risk

It's certainly true that if you don't take care when modifying the Trust Center settings, you could expose Word, your computer, and your network to malicious software. Depending on the type of files you work with and the breadth of your work network, you might find it appropriate to modify some of these settings in Word. Review the available settings so you can evaluate whether any of them would be appropriate to change in your specific situation.

The Trust Center has 11 pages of options that you can configure. When you first open the Trust Center from the Backstage view, the Macro Settings page is active. As in the Word Options dialog box, you click a page tab name in the left pane to display that page in the right pane.

16

It is safest to run macros only from trusted sources

Most pages display options that are very specific to the page name. When you're working in Word, some circumstances will send you directly to this dialog box—for example, if you open a document that contains macros, and then click the info bar to enable them, Word takes you to this page.

Many of the Trust Center options are beyond the scope of any needs that you'd usually have when creating documents. Some of those that might be of interest are those that make it easier to work in documents that you trust, but that Word might not know are safe.

When you open a document from an online location (such as a cloud storage location or email message) or from a location that has been deemed unsafe, Word opens the file in Protected view, with most editing functions disabled. The purpose of this is to prevent any malicious code that is embedded in the file from gaining access to your computer. If you're uncertain about the origin of a file that you're opening, you can choose to open the file in Protected view.

In Protected view, the title bar displays *Read-Only* in brackets to the right of the file name, and a yellow banner at the top of the content pane provides information about why the file has been opened in Protected view. If you know that the document is from a safe location or sender, and you want to edit the file content, you can choose to enable editing.

If you find that you frequently need to edit documents that open in Protected view, you can modify options on three pages of the Trust Center to affect this:

- If you want to open any document that is stored in a specific location without going into Protected view, you can add that folder (and its subfolders, if you want) to your Trusted Locations list.

Trust the contents of specific storage folders

If you want to trust folders on other computers on your network, you must first specifically choose that option. Otherwise, when you try to add a network folder as a trusted location, the Trust Center displays a message that it is not permitted by your current security settings. Before selecting the option to allow network locations, consider what people or computers have access to the network locations you intend to allow, and whether the locations are secure or could host malicious content.

16

- If you want to be able to edit all files of a specific type (based on the file extension) you can modify the File Block settings.

File Block Settings

For each file type, you can select the Open and Save check boxes. By selecting Open, Word blocks this file type, or opens it in Protected View. By selecting Save, Word prevents saving in this file type.

File Type	Open	Save
Word 2007 and later Documents and Templates	☐	☐
OpenDocument Text Files	☐	☐
Word 2007 and later Binary Documents and Templates	☐	☐
Web Pages	☐	☐
RTF Files	☐	☐
Plain Text Files	☐	☐
Legacy Converters for Word	☐	☐
Office Open XML Converters for Word	☐	☐
PDF Files	☐	

Open behavior for selected file types:
- ◯ Do not open selected file types
- ◉ Open selected file types in Protected View
- ◯ Open selected file types in Protected View and allow editing

Restore Defaults

Block specific file types or permit editing in Protected view

- You can exclude an entire class of files (files originating from the Internet, stored in unsafe locations, or received as email attachments) from Protected view.

Protected View

Protected View opens potentially dangerous files, without any security prompts, in a restricted mode to help minimize harm to your computer. By disabling Protected View you could be exposing your computer to possible security threats.

- ☑ Enable Protected View for files originating from the Internet
- ☑ Enable Protected View for files located in potentially unsafe locations ⓘ
- ☑ Enable Protected View for Outlook attachments ⓘ

Turn off Protected view for a class of files

Before doing any of these things, you should carefully consider whether the "rule" you're making will always yield the results you want.

If you frequently work with a specific Word document that contains active content, and you feel that the security prompts are unnecessarily slowing you down, you can choose to trust the document. When you do so, it is added to the Trusted Documents list. You can manage the Trusted Documents list from the Trusted Documents page of the Trust Center. You can stipulate whether to trust documents that aren't stored locally, turn off the Trusted Documents function completely (to stop trusting all documents), or clear the Trusted Documents list to start over.

Trusted Documents

Warning: Trusted Documents open without any security prompts for macros, ActiveX controls and other types of active content in the document. For a Trusted Document, you will not be prompted the next time you open the document, even if new active content was added to the document or changes were made to existing active content. Therefore, you should only trust documents if you trust the source.

☑ Allow documents on a network to be trusted

☐ Disable Trusted Documents

Clear all Trusted Documents so that they are no longer trusted | Clear |

If you experience trouble with a trusted document, you can reset the list here

If you track changes and insert comments in documents, you might run into this surprising behavior—Word changing your user information to "Author" when you save the document. To correct that problem, clear the Remove Personal Information From File Properties On Save check box in the Document-specific Settings section of the Privacy Options page.

Document-specific settings

☐ Warn before printing, saving or sending a file that contains tracked changes or comments

☑ Store random numbers to improve Combine accuracy ⓘ

☑ Make hidden markup visible when opening or saving

☐ Remove personal information from file properties on save ⓘ

| Document Inspector... |

Research & Reference

| Translation Options... |

| Research Options... |

Important option to manage if you use the collaboration features

16

From the Research & Reference section of this page, you can configure translation options and manage the reference books and research sites that are available in Word.

Add reference services to your available resources

Some, but not all, of the Trust Center pages include buttons that you can click to reset that set of options to the defaults, so take care when making changes; if you're uncertain whether you should invoke a change, click Cancel to close the Trust Center without committing to the changes.

As with options in the Word Options dialog box, you should take the time to familiarize yourself with the Trust Center settings so you know what changes it is possible to make, in the event that it is appropriate to do so in your computing environment.

To open the Trust Center

1. In the left pane of the Backstage view, click the **Trust Center** page tab.

2. On the **Trust Center** page, click the **Trust Center Settings** button.

Skills review

In this chapter, you learned how to:

- Change default Word options
- Customize the Quick Access Toolbar
- Customize the ribbon
- Manage add-ins and security options

16

Practice tasks

No practice files are necessary to complete the practice tasks in this chapter.

Change default Word options

Start Word, display any document, and then perform the following tasks:

1. Open the **Word Options** dialog box.

2. Explore each page of the dialog box.

3. On the **General**, **Display**, **Proofing**, **Save**, **Language**, and **Advanced** pages, do the following:

   - Notice the sections and the options in each section.

   - Note the options that apply only to the current file.

   - Modify the options on each page as necessary to fit the way you work.

4. Close the **Word Options** dialog box.

Customize the Quick Access Toolbar

Start Word, display any document, and then perform the following tasks:

1. Move the Quick Access Toolbar below the ribbon. Consider the merits of this location versus the original location.

2. From the **Customize Quick Access Toolbar** menu, add the **Print Preview & Print** command to the Quick Access Toolbar.

3. From the **Design** tab of the ribbon, add the following commands to the Quick Access Toolbar:

   - From the **Document Formatting** group, add the **Paragraph Spacing** command.

   - From the **Page Background** group, add the **Watermark** command.

   Notice that each of the commands is represented on the Quick Access Toolbar exactly as it is on the ribbon. Clicking the Paragraph Spacing arrow displays a list, and clicking Watermark displays a gallery.

4. From the **Show** group on the **View** tab, add the **Ruler** command and the **Grid-lines** command to the Quick Access Toolbar. Notice that the commands are represented on the Quick Access Toolbar as check boxes.

5. Point to the commands you added to the Quick Access Toolbar and then to the same commands on the View tab. Notice that ScreenTips for commands on the Quick Access Toolbar are identical to those for commands on the ribbon.

6. Display the **Quick Access Toolbar** page of the **Word Options** dialog box, and then do the following:

   • In the left pane, display the commands that appear on the **Layout** tab.

   • Add the **Grid Settings** button from the Layout tab to the Quick Access Toolbar.

   • In the right pane, move the **Paragraph Spacing** button to the bottom of the list so that it will be the rightmost button on the Quick Access Toolbar (immediately to the left of the Customize Quick Access Toolbar button).

   • Insert a separator between the original commands and the commands you added in this task set.

   • Insert two separators between the **Watermark** and **Ruler** commands.

7. Close the **Word Options** dialog box and observe your customized Quick Access Toolbar. Note the way that a single separator sets off commands, and the way that a double separator sets off commands.

8. Redisplay the **Quick Access Toolbar** page of the **Word Options** dialog box.

9. Reset the Quick Access Toolbar to its default configuration, and then close the dialog box. Notice that resetting the Quick Access Toolbar does not change its location.

10. Close the document without saving it.

Customize the ribbon

Start Word, display any document, and then perform the following tasks:

1. Display the **Customize Ribbon** page of the **Word Options** dialog box.

2. Remove the **Mailings** tab from the ribbon, and add the **Developer** tab (if it isn't already shown).

3. Create a custom tab and name it MyShapes.

4. Move the **MyShapes** tab to the top of the right pane so that it will be the left-most optional ribbon tab (immediately to the right of the File tab).

5. Change the name of the custom group on the **MyShapes** tab to Curved Shapes, and select a curved or circular icon to represent the group.

6. Create three more custom groups on the **MyShapes** tab; name them **Angular Shapes**, **Connectors**, and **Quick Erase**; and add appropriate icons to represent the groups.

7. In the **Choose commands from** list, click **Commands Not in the Ribbon**. From the list, add the **Arc** and **Oval** commands to the **Curved Shapes** group, the **Isosceles Triangle** and **Rectangle** commands to the **Angular Shapes** group, the **Elbow Arrow Connector** and **Elbow Connecto**r commands to the **Connectors** group, and the **Clear** and **Clear Formats** commands to the **Quick Erase** group.

8. Close the **Word Options** dialog box and display your custom tab. Click the **Arc** command, and then drag on the page to draw an arc.

9. Change the width of the app window to collapse at least one custom group, and verify that the group button displays the icon you selected.

10. Restore the app window to its original width and redisplay the **Customize Ribbon** page of the **Word Options** dialog box.

11. Reset the ribbon to its default configuration, and then close the dialog box.

12. Close the document without saving it.

Manage add-ins and security options

Start Word, display any document, and then perform the following tasks:

1. Open the **Word Options** dialog box.

2. Display the **Add-ins** page, and then do the following:
   - Review the add-ins that are installed on your computer.
   - Notice the types of add-ins that are active, and display the dialog box for that type of add-in.
   - Notice add-ins that are turned on or off, and modify the setting if you want to.
   - Close the dialog box.

3. Display the **Trust Center** page, and then do the following:
   - Open the Trust Center.
   - Review the settings therein, but don't make any changes.
   - Close the Trust Center.

4. Close the **Word Options** dialog box.

Keyboard shortcuts

Throughout this book, we provide information about how to perform tasks quickly and efficiently by using keyboard shortcuts. The following shortcuts were excerpted from Word Help and Office.com and formatted in tables for convenient lookup.

> ✓ **TIP** In the following lists, keys you press at the same time are separated by a plus sign (+), and keys you press sequentially are separated by a comma (,).

Word 2016 keyboard shortcuts

This section provides a comprehensive list of keyboard shortcuts built into Word 2016.

Perform common tasks

Action	Keyboard shortcut
Create a nonbreaking space	Ctrl+Shift+Spacebar
Create a nonbreaking hyphen	Ctrl+Shift+Hyphen
Make letters bold	Ctrl+B
Make letters italic	Ctrl+I
Make letters underlined	Ctrl+U
Decrease font size one value	Ctrl+Shift+<
Increase font size one value	Ctrl+Shift+>
Decrease font size 1 point	Ctrl+[
Increase font size 1 point	Ctrl+]
Remove paragraph or character formatting	Ctrl+Spacebar
Copy the selected text or object	Ctrl+C
Cut the selected text or object	Ctrl+X

Action	Keyboard shortcut
Paste text or an object	Ctrl+V
Refine paste action (Paste Special)	Ctrl+Alt+V
Paste formatting only	Ctrl+Shift+V
Undo the last action	Ctrl+Z
Redo the last action	Ctrl+Y
Open the Word Count dialog box	Ctrl+Shift+G

Work with documents and webpages

Create, view, and save documents

Action	Keyboard shortcut
Create a new document	Ctrl+N
Open a document	Ctrl+O
Close a document	Ctrl+W
Split the document window	Alt+Ctrl+S
Remove the document window split	Alt+Shift+C or Alt+Ctrl+S
Save a document	Ctrl+S

Find, replace, and browse through text

Action	Keyboard shortcut
Open the Navigation pane (to search the document)	Ctrl+F
Repeat a Find action (after closing the Find And Replace dialog box)	Alt+Ctrl+Y
Replace text, specific formatting, and special items	Ctrl+H
Go to a page, bookmark, footnote, table, comment, graphic, or other location	Ctrl+G
Switch between the last four places that you have edited	Alt+Ctrl+Z

Action	Keyboard shortcut
Open a list of browse options	Alt+Ctrl+Home
Move to the previous browse object (set in browse options)	Ctrl+Page Up
Move to the next browse object (set in browse options)	Ctrl+Page Down

Switch to another view

Action	Keyboard shortcut
Switch to Print Layout view	Alt+Ctrl+P
Switch to Outline view	Alt+Ctrl+O
Switch to Draft view	Alt+Ctrl+N

Work in Outline view

Action	Keyboard shortcut
Promote a paragraph	Alt+Shift+Left Arrow
Demote a paragraph	Alt+Shift+Right Arrow
Demote to body text	Ctrl+Shift+N
Move selected paragraphs up	Alt+Shift+Up Arrow
Move selected paragraphs down	Alt+Shift+Down Arrow
Expand text under a heading	Alt+Shift+Plus sign
Collapse text under a heading	Alt+Shift+Minus sign
Expand or collapse all text or headings	Alt+Shift+A
Hide or display character formatting	The slash (/) key on the numeric keypad
Show the first line of body text or all body text	Alt+Shift+L
Show all headings with the Heading 1 style	Alt+Shift+1
Show all headings up to the Heading n style	Alt+Shift+9
Insert a tab character	Ctrl+Tab

Work in Read Mode

Action	Keyboard shortcut
Go to the beginning of the document	Home
Go to the end of the document	End
Go to page *n*	*n*, Enter
Exit Read Mode	Esc

Print and preview documents

Action	Keyboard shortcut
Print a document	Ctrl+P
Display the Print page of the Backstage view	Alt+Ctrl+I
Move around the preview page when zoomed in	Arrow keys
Move by one preview page when zoomed out	Page Up or Page Down
Move to the first preview page when zoomed out	Ctrl+Home
Move to the last preview page when zoomed out	Ctrl+End

Review documents

Action	Keyboard shortcut
Insert a comment	Alt+Ctrl+M
Turn change tracking on or off	Ctrl+Shift+E
Close the Reviewing pane if it is open	Alt+Shift+C

Work with references, footnotes, and endnotes

Action	Keyboard shortcut
Mark a table of contents entry	Alt+Shift+O
Mark a table of authorities entry (citation)	Alt+Shift+I
Mark an index entry	Alt+Shift+X

Insert a footnote	Alt+Ctrl+F
Insert an endnote	Alt+Ctrl+D

Work with webpages

Action	Keyboard shortcut
Insert a hyperlink	Ctrl+K
Go back one page	Alt+Left Arrow
Go forward one page	Alt+Right Arrow
Refresh	F9

Edit and move text and graphics

Delete text and graphics

Action	Keyboard shortcut
Delete one character to the left	Backspace
Delete one word to the left	Ctrl+Backspace
Delete one character to the right	Delete
Delete one word to the right	Ctrl+Delete
Cut selected content to the Clipboard	Ctrl+X
Undo the last action	Ctrl+Z
Cut selected content to the Spike	Ctrl+F3

Copy and move text and graphics

Action	Keyboard shortcut
Open the Clipboard	Press Alt+H to move to the Home tab, and then press F,O
Copy selected text or graphics to the Clipboard	Ctrl+C
Cut selected text or graphics to the Clipboard	Ctrl+X
Paste the most recent addition or pasted item from the Clipboard	Ctrl+V
Move text or graphics once	F2 (then move the cursor and press Enter)
Copy text or graphics once	Shift+F2 (then move the cursor and press Enter)
When text or an object is selected, open the Create New Building Block dialog box	Alt+F3
When a building block—for example, a SmartArt graphic—is selected, display the shortcut menu that is associated with it	Shift+F10
Copy the header or footer used in the previous section of the document	Alt+Shift+R

Insert special characters

Action	Keyboard shortcut
A field	Ctrl+F9
A line break	Shift+Enter
A page break	Ctrl+Enter
A column break	Ctrl+Shift+Enter
An em dash	Alt+Ctrl+Minus sign
An en dash	Ctrl+Minus sign

Action	Keyboard shortcut
An optional hyphen	Ctrl+Hyphen
A nonbreaking hyphen	Ctrl+Shift+Hyphen
A nonbreaking space	Ctrl+Shift+Spacebar
The copyright symbol	Alt+Ctrl+C
The registered trademark symbol	Alt+Ctrl+R
The trademark symbol	Alt+Ctrl+T
An ellipsis	Alt+Ctrl+Period
An AutoText entry	Enter (after the ScreenTip appears)

Insert characters by using character codes

Action	Keyboard shortcut
Insert the Unicode character for the specified Unicode (hexadecimal) character code. For example, to insert the euro currency symbol (€), enter 20AC, and then hold down Alt and press X	The character code, Alt+X
Find out the Unicode character code for the selected character	Alt+X
Insert the ANSI character for the specified ANSI (decimal) character code. For example, to insert the euro currency symbol, hold down Alt and press 0128 on the numeric keypad	Alt+ the character code (on the numeric keypad)

Select text and graphics

Action	Keyboard shortcut
Select text and graphics	Hold down Shift and use the arrow keys to move the cursor

Extend a selection

Action	Keyboard shortcut
Turn extend mode on	F8
Select the nearest character	F8+Left Arrow or Right Arrow
Increase the size of a selection	F8 (press once to select a word, twice to select a sentence, and so on)
Reduce the size of a selection	Shift+F8
Turn extend mode off	Esc
Extend a selection one character to the right	Shift+Right Arrow
Extend a selection one character to the left	Shift+Left Arrow
Extend a selection to the end of a word	Ctrl+Shift+Right Arrow
Extend a selection to the beginning of a word	Ctrl+Shift+Left Arrow
Extend a selection to the end of a line	Shift+End
Extend a selection to the beginning of a line	Shift+Home
Extend a selection one line down	Shift+Down Arrow
Extend a selection one line up	Shift+Up Arrow
Extend a selection to the end of a paragraph	Ctrl+Shift+Down Arrow
Extend a selection to the beginning of a paragraph	Ctrl+Shift+Up Arrow
Extend a selection one screen down	Shift+Page Down
Extend a selection one screen up	Shift+Page Up
Extend a selection to the beginning of a document	Ctrl+Shift+Home
Extend a selection to the end of a document	Ctrl+Shift+End
Extend a selection to the end of a window	Alt+Ctrl+Shift+Page Down
Extend a selection to include the entire document	Ctrl+A

Action	Keyboard shortcut
Select a vertical block of text	Ctrl+Shift+F8, and then use the arrow keys; press Esc to cancel
Extend a selection to a specific location in a document	F8+arrow keys; press Esc to cancel

Select text and graphics in a table

Action	Keyboard shortcut
Select the next cell's contents	Tab
Select the preceding cell's contents	Shift+Tab
Extend a selection to adjacent cells	Hold down Shift and press an arrow key repeatedly
Select a column	Use the arrow keys to move to the column's top or bottom cell, and then do either of the following: ■ Press Shift+Alt+Page Down to select the column from top to bottom ■ Press Shift+Alt+Page Up to select the column from bottom to top
Extend a selection (or block)	Ctrl+Shift+F8, and then use the arrow keys; press Esc to cancel selection mode
Select an entire table	Alt+5 on the numeric keypad (with Num Lock off)

Move through documents

Action	Keyboard shortcut
One character to the left	Left Arrow
One character to the right	Right Arrow
One word to the left	Ctrl+Left Arrow
One word to the right	Ctrl+Right Arrow
One paragraph up	Ctrl+Up Arrow

Action	Keyboard shortcut
One paragraph down	Ctrl+Down Arrow
One cell to the left (in a table)	Shift+Tab
One cell to the right (in a table)	Tab
Up one line	Up Arrow
Down one line	Down Arrow
To the end of a line	End
To the beginning of a line	Home
To the top of the window	Alt+Ctrl+Page Up
To the end of the window	Alt+Ctrl+Page Down
Up one screen (scrolling)	Page Up
Down one screen (scrolling)	Page Down
To the top of the next page	Ctrl+Page Down
To the top of the previous page	Ctrl+Page Up
To the end of a document	Ctrl+End
To the beginning of a document	Ctrl+Home
To a previous revision	Shift+F5
Immediately after opening a document, go to the location you were working in when the document was last closed	Shift+F5

Move around in a table

Action	Keyboard shortcut
To the next cell in a row	Tab
To the previous cell in a row	Shift+Tab
To the first cell in a row	Alt+Home
To the last cell in a row	Alt+End
To the first cell in a column	Alt+Page Up
To the last cell in a column	Alt+Page Down

Action	Keyboard shortcut
To the previous row	Up Arrow
To the next row	Down Arrow

Insert characters and move content in tables

Action	Keyboard shortcut
New paragraphs in a cell	Enter
Tab characters in a cell	Ctrl+Tab
Move content up one row	Alt+Shift+Up Arrow
Move content down one row	Alt+Shift+Down Arrow

Apply character and paragraph formatting

Copy formatting

Action	Keyboard shortcut
Copy formatting from text	Ctrl+Shift+C
Apply copied formatting to text	Ctrl+Shift+V

Change or resize the font

> **TIP** The following keyboard shortcuts do not work in Read Mode.

Action	Keyboard shortcut
Open the Font dialog box to change the font	Ctrl+Shift+F
Increase the font size	Ctrl+Shift+>
Decrease the font size	Ctrl+Shift+<
Increase the font size by 1 point	Ctrl+]
Decrease the font size by 1 point	Ctrl+[

Apply character formats

Action	Keyboard shortcut
Open the Font dialog box to change the formatting of characters	Ctrl+D
Change the case of letters	Shift+F3
Format all letters as capitals	Ctrl+Shift+A
Apply bold formatting	Ctrl+B
Apply an underline	Ctrl+U
Underline words but not spaces	Ctrl+Shift+W
Double-underline text	Ctrl+Shift+D
Apply hidden text formatting	Ctrl+Shift+H
Apply italic formatting	Ctrl+I
Format letters as small capitals	Ctrl+Shift+K
Apply subscript formatting (automatic spacing)	Ctrl+Equal sign
Apply superscript formatting (automatic spacing)	Ctrl+Shift+Plus sign
Remove manual character formatting	Ctrl+Spacebar
Change the selection to the Symbol font	Ctrl+Shift+Q

View and copy text formats

Action	Keyboard shortcut
Display nonprinting characters	Ctrl+Shift+8
Review text formatting	Shift+F1 (then click the text with the formatting you want to review)
Copy formats	Ctrl+Shift+C
Paste formats	Ctrl+Shift+V

Set the line spacing

Action	Keyboard shortcut
Single-space lines	Ctrl+1
Double-space lines	Ctrl+2
Set 1.5-line spacing	Ctrl+5
Add or remove one line space preceding a paragraph	Ctrl+0 (zero)

Align paragraphs

Action	Keyboard shortcut
Switch a paragraph between centered and left-aligned	Ctrl+E
Switch a paragraph between justified and left-aligned	Ctrl+J
Switch a paragraph between right-aligned and left-aligned	Ctrl+R
Left align a paragraph	Ctrl+L
Indent a paragraph from the left	Ctrl+M
Remove a paragraph indent from the left	Ctrl+Shift+M
Create a hanging indent	Ctrl+T
Reduce a hanging indent	Ctrl+Shift+T
Remove paragraph formatting	Ctrl+Q

Apply paragraph styles

Action	Keyboard shortcut
Open the Apply Styles pane	Ctrl+Shift+S
Open the Styles pane	Alt+Ctrl+Shift+S
Start AutoFormat	Alt+Ctrl+K
Apply the Normal style	Ctrl+Shift+N
Apply the Heading 1 style	Alt+Ctrl+1
Apply the Heading 2 style	Alt+Ctrl+2
Apply the Heading 3 style	Alt+Ctrl+3
Close the active Styles pane	Ctrl+Spacebar, C

Work with mail merge and fields

Perform mail merges

Action	Keyboard shortcut
Preview a mail merge	Alt+Shift+K
Merge a document	Alt+Shift+N
Print the merged document	Alt+Shift+M
Edit a mail-merge data document	Alt+Shift+E
Insert a merge field	Alt+Shift+F

Work with fields

Action	Keyboard shortcut
Insert a Date field	Alt+Shift+D
Insert a LIstNum field	Alt+Ctrl+L
Insert a Page field	Alt+Shift+P
Insert a Time field	Alt+Shift+T
Insert an empty field	Ctrl+F9
Update linked information in a Word source document	Ctrl+Shift+F7
Update selected fields	F9
Unlink a field	Ctrl+Shift+F9
Switch between a selected field code and its result	Shift+F9
Switch between all field codes and their results	Alt+F9
Run GoToButton or MacroButton from the field that displays the field results	Alt+Shift+F9
Go to the next field	F11
Go to the previous field	Shift+F11
Lock a field	Ctrl+F11
Unlock a field	Ctrl+Shift+F11

Use the Language bar

Action	Keyboard shortcut
Switch between languages or keyboard layouts	Left Alt+Shift
Display a list of correction alternatives	Windows logo key+C
Turn handwriting on or off	Windows logo key +H
Turn Japanese Input Method Editor (IME) on 101 keyboard on or off	Alt+~
Turn Korean IME on 101 keyboard on or off	Right Alt
Turn Chinese IME on 101 keyboard on or off	Ctrl+Spacebar

> ✓ **TIP** The Windows logo key is available on the bottom row of keys on most keyboards.

Perform function key tasks

Function keys

Action	Keyboard shortcut
Get Help or visit Office.com	F1
Move text or graphics	F2
Repeat the last action	F4
Choose the Go To command (Home tab)	F5
Go to the next pane or frame	F6
Choose the Spelling command (Review tab)	F7
Extend a selection	F8
Update the selected fields	F9
Show KeyTips	F10
Go to the next field	F11
Choose the Save As command	F12

Shift+function key

Action	Keyboard shortcut
Start context-sensitive Help or reveal formatting	Shift+F1
Copy text	Shift+F2
Change the case of letters	Shift+F3
Repeat a Find or Go To action	Shift+F4
Move to the last change	Shift+F5
Go to the previous pane or frame (after pressing F6)	Shift+F6
Choose the Thesaurus command (Review tab, Proofing group)	Shift+F7
Reduce the size of a selection	Shift+F8
Switch between a field code and its result	Shift+F9
Display a shortcut menu	Shift+F10
Go to the previous field	Shift+F11
Choose the Save command	Shift+F12

Ctrl+function key

Action	Keyboard shortcut
Expand or collapse the ribbon	Ctrl+F1
Choose the Print Preview command	Ctrl+F2
Close the window	Ctrl+F4
Go to the next window	Ctrl+F6
Insert an empty field	Ctrl+F9
Maximize the document window	Ctrl+F10
Lock a field	Ctrl+F11
Choose the Open command	Ctrl+F12

Ctrl+Shift+function key

Action	Keyboard shortcut
Insert the contents of the Spike	Ctrl+Shift+F3
Edit a bookmark	Ctrl+Shift+F5
Go to the previous window	Ctrl+Shift+F6
Update linked information in a Word source document	Ctrl+Shift+F7
Extend a selection or block	Ctrl+Shift+F8, and then press an arrow key
Unlink a field	Ctrl+Shift+F9
Unlock a field	Ctrl+Shift+F11
Choose the Print command	Ctrl+Shift+F12

Alt+function key

Action	Keyboard shortcut
Go to the next field	Alt+F1
Create a new building block	Alt+F3
Exit Word	Alt+F4
Restore the app window size	Alt+F5
Move from an open dialog box back to the document, for dialog boxes that support this behavior	Alt+F6
Find the next misspelling or grammatical error	Alt+F7
Run a macro	Alt+F8
Switch between all field codes and their results	Alt+F9
Display the Selection And Visibility pane	Alt+F10
Display Microsoft Visual Basic code	Alt+F11

Alt+Shift+function key

Action	Keyboard shortcut
Go to the previous field	Alt+Shift+F1
Choose the Save command	Alt+Shift+F2
Display the Research pane	Alt+Shift+F7
Run GoToButton or MacroButton from the field that displays the field results	Alt+Shift+F9
Display a menu or message for an available action	Alt+Shift+F10
Select the Table Of Contents button when the Table Of Contents is active	Alt+Shift+F12

Ctrl+Alt+function key

Action	Keyboard shortcut
Display Microsoft System Information	Ctrl+Alt+F1
Choose the Open command	Ctrl+Alt+F2

Office 2016 keyboard shortcuts

This section provides a list of keyboard shortcuts available in all Office 2016 apps, including Word.

Display and use windows

Action	Keyboard shortcut
Switch to the next window	Alt+Tab
Switch to the previous window	Alt+Shift+Tab
Close the active window	Ctrl+W or Ctrl+F4
Restore the size of the active window after you maximize it	Alt+F5

Action	Keyboard shortcut
Move to a pane from another pane in the app window (clockwise direction)	F6 or Shift+F6
If pressing F6 does not display the pane that you want, press Alt to put the focus on the ribbon, and then press Ctrl+Tab to move to the pane	
Switch to the next open window	Ctrl+F6
Switch to the previous window	Ctrl+Shift+F6
Maximize or restore a selected window	Ctrl+F10
Copy a picture of the screen to the Clipboard	Print Screen
Copy a picture of the selected window to the Clipboard	Alt+Print Screen

Use dialog boxes

Action	Keyboard shortcut
Move to the next option or option group	Tab
Move to the previous option or option group	Shift+Tab
Switch to the next tab in a dialog box	Ctrl+Tab
Switch to the previous tab in a dialog box	Ctrl+Shift+Tab
Move between options in an open drop-down list, or between options in a group of options	Arrow keys
Perform the action assigned to the selected button; select or clear the selected check box	Spacebar
Select an option; select or clear a check box	Alt+ *the underlined letter*
Open a selected drop-down list	Alt+Down Arrow
Select an option from a drop-down list	*First letter of the list option*
Close a selected drop-down list; cancel a command and close a dialog box	Esc
Run the selected command	Enter

Use edit boxes within dialog boxes

An edit box is a blank box in which you enter or paste an entry.

Action	Keyboard shortcut
Move to the beginning of the entry	Home
Move to the end of the entry	End
Move one character to the left or right	Left Arrow or Right Arrow
Move one word to the left	Ctrl+Left Arrow
Move one word to the right	Ctrl+Right Arrow
Select or unselect one character to the left	Shift+Left Arrow
Select or unselect one character to the right	Shift+Right Arrow
Select or unselect one word to the left	Ctrl+Shift+Left Arrow
Select or unselect one word to the right	Ctrl+Shift+Right Arrow
Select from the insertion point to the beginning of the entry	Shift+Home
Select from the insertion point to the end of the entry	Shift+End

Use the Open and Save As dialog boxes

Action	Keyboard shortcut
Open the Open dialog box	Ctrl+F12 or Ctrl+O
Open the Save As dialog box	F12
Open the selected folder or file	Enter
Open the folder one level above the selected folder	Backspace
Delete the selected folder or file	Delete
Display a shortcut menu for a selected item such as a folder or file	Shift+F10

Action	Keyboard shortcut
Move forward through options	Tab
Move back through options	Shift+Tab
Open the Look In list	F4 or Alt+I
Refresh the file list	F5

Use the Backstage view

Action	Keyboard shortcut
Display the Open page of the Backstage view	Ctrl+O
Display the Save As page of the Backstage view (when saving a file for the first time)	Ctrl+S
Continue saving an Office file (after giving the file a name and location)	Ctrl+S
Display the Save As page of the Backstage view (after initially saving a file)	Alt+F+S
Close the Backstage view	Esc

> **TIP** You can use dialog boxes instead of Backstage view pages by selecting the Don't Show The Backstage When Opening Or Saving Files check box on the Save page of the Word Options dialog box. Set this option in any Office app to enable it in all Office apps.

Navigate the ribbon

Follow these steps:

1. Press **Alt** to display the KeyTips over each feature in the current view.

2. Press the letter shown in the KeyTip over the feature that you want to use.

> ✓ **TIP** To cancel the action and hide the KeyTips, press Alt.

Change the keyboard focus without using the mouse

Action	Keyboard shortcut
Select the active tab of the ribbon and activate the access keys	Alt or F10. Press either of these keys again to move back to the document and cancel the access keys
Move to another tab of the ribbon	F10 to select the active tab, and then Left Arrow or Right Arrow
Expand or collapse the ribbon	Ctrl+F1
Display the shortcut menu for the selected item	Shift+F10
Move the focus to select each of the following areas of the window: ■ Active tab of the ribbon ■ Any open panes ■ Status bar at the bottom of the window ■ Your document	F6
Move the focus to each command on the ribbon, forward or backward, respectively	Tab or Shift+Tab
Move among the items on the ribbon	Arrow keys
Activate the selected command or control on the ribbon	Spacebar or Enter
Display the selected menu or gallery on the ribbon	Spacebar or Enter

Action	Keyboard shortcut
Activate a command or control on the ribbon so that you can modify a value	Enter
Finish modifying a value in a control on the ribbon, and move focus back to the document	Enter
Get help on the selected command or control on the ribbon	F1

Move around in and work in tables

Action	Keyboard shortcut
Move to the next cell	Tab
Move to the preceding cell	Shift+Tab
Move to the next row	Down Arrow
Move to the preceding row	Up Arrow
Insert a tab in a cell	Ctrl+Tab
Start a new paragraph	Enter
Add a new row at the bottom of the table	Tab at the end of the last row

Access and use panes and galleries

Action	Keyboard shortcut
Move to a pane from another pane in the app window	F6
When a menu is active, move to a pane	Ctrl+Tab
When a pane is active, select the next or previous option in the pane	Tab or Shift+Tab
Display the full set of commands on the pane menu	Ctrl+Spacebar
Perform the action assigned to the selected button	Spacebar or Enter
Open a drop-down menu for the selected gallery item	Shift+F10
Select the first or last item in a gallery	Home or End

Action	Keyboard shortcut
Scroll up or down in the selected gallery list	Page Up or Page Down
Close a pane	Ctrl+Spacebar, C
Open the Clipboard	Alt+H, F, O

Access and use available actions

Action	Keyboard shortcut
Display the shortcut menu for the selected item	Shift+F10
Display the menu or message for an available action or for the AutoCorrect Options button or the Paste options button	Alt+Shift+F10
Move between options in a menu of available actions	Arrow keys
Perform the action for the selected item on a menu of available actions	Enter
Close the available actions menu or message	Esc

Find and replace content

Action	Keyboard shortcut
Open the Find dialog box	Ctrl+F
Open the Replace dialog box	Ctrl+H
Repeat the last Find action	Shift+F4

Use the Help window

Action	Keyboard shortcut
Open the Help window	F1
Close the Help window	Alt+F4
Switch between the Help window and the active app	Alt+Tab

Action	Keyboard shortcut
Return to the Help table of contents	Alt+Home
Select the next item in the Help window	Tab
Select the previous item in the Help window	Shift+Tab
Perform the action for the selected item	Enter
Select the next hidden text or hyperlink, including Show All or Hide All at the top of a Help topic	Tab
Select the previous hidden text or hyperlink	Shift+Tab
Perform the action for the selected Show All, Hide All, hidden text, or hyperlink	Enter
Move back to the previous Help topic (Back button)	Alt+Left Arrow or Backspace
Move forward to the next Help topic (Forward button)	Alt+Right Arrow
Scroll small amounts up or down, respectively, within the currently displayed Help topic	Up Arrow, Down Arrow
Scroll larger amounts up or down, respectively, within the currently displayed Help topic	Page Up, Page Down
Display a menu of commands for the Help window. This requires that the Help window have the active focus (click in the Help window)	Shift+F10
Stop the last action (Stop button)	Esc
Print the current Help topic If the cursor is not in the current Help topic, press F6 and then press Ctrl+P	Ctrl+P
In a Table of Contents in tree view, select the next or previous item, respectively	Up Arrow, Down Arrow
In a Table of Contents in tree view, expand or collapse the selected item, respectively	Left Arrow, Right Arrow

Create custom keyboard shortcuts

If a command you use frequently doesn't have a built-in keyboard shortcut, or if you don't like the keyboard shortcut that is assigned to the command, you can create one either in a specific document or in a template. You can also modify the built-in keyboard shortcuts.

To manage keyboard shortcuts

1. Display the **Customize Ribbon** page of the **Word Options** dialog box.

2. Below the **Choose commands from** pane, to the right of **Keyboard shortcuts**, click the **Customize** button.

3. In the **Customize Keyboard** dialog box, select the category containing the command for which you want to create a keyboard shortcut, and then select the command.

   The Current Keys box displays any keyboard shortcut already assigned to the command.

4. Position the cursor in the **Press new shortcut key** box, and then press the key combination you want to use as a keyboard shortcut for the selected command.

   In the area below the Current Keys box, Word tells you whether the keyboard shortcut is currently assigned to a command or unassigned.

5. To delete an existing keyboard shortcut to make it available for reassignment, select it in the **Current keys** box, and then click the **Remove** button.

6. To assign an available keyboard shortcut to the selected command, do either of the following:

   - To save the keyboard shortcut in all documents based on the current template, verify that the template name is selected in the **Save changes in** list, and then click **Assign**.

   - To save the keyboard shortcut only in the current document, click the document name in the **Save changes in** list, and then click **Assign**.

7. To delete all custom keyboard shortcuts, click **Reset All**.

8. Close the **Customize Keyboard** dialog box and the **Word Options** dialog box.

Glossary

accessible content Content that is packaged and delivered in a way that supports access by all means of input methods and output devices.

add-in A utility that adds specialized functionality to an app but does not operate as an independent app.

All Markup view A view that displays all tracked changes, including formatting, text edits, and comments.

aspect ratio The ratio of the width of an image to its height.

attribute An individual item of character formatting, such as size or color, that determines how text looks.

AutoCorrect A feature that automatically detects and corrects misspelled words and incorrect capitalization. You can add your own AutoCorrect entries.

AutoShape One of an array of ready-made shapes provided by Word to assist you with creating more complex pictures.

background The colors, shading, texture, and graphics that appear behind the text and objects in a document.

balloon In Print Layout view or Web Layout view, a box that shows comments and tracked changes in the margins of a document, making it easy to review and respond to them.

bar chart A chart with bars that compares the quantities of two or more items.

blog A frequently updated online journal or column. Blogs are often used to publish personal or company information in an informal way. Short for *web log*.

bookmark A location or section of text that is electronically marked so that it can be returned to at a later time. Like a physical bookmark, a Word bookmark marks a specific location in a document. You can quickly display a specific bookmark from the Go To page of the Find And Replace dialog box or from the Insert Bookmark dialog box.

building block Frequently used text saved in a gallery, from which it can be inserted quickly into a document.

caption Descriptive text associated with a figure, photo, illustration, or screenshot.

category axis The horizontal reference line on a grid, chart, or graph that has horizontal and vertical dimensions. Also called the *x-axis*.

cell A box formed by the intersection of a row and column in a worksheet or a table, in which you enter information.

cell address The location of a cell, expressed as its column letter and row number, as in *A1*.

character formatting Formatting you can apply to selected characters.

character spacing The distance between characters in a line of text. Can be adjusted by pushing characters apart (expanding) or squeezing them together (condensing).

character style A combination of character formatting options identified by a style name. See also *paragraph style*; *Quick Style*; *style, table style*.

chart area A region in a chart that is used to position chart elements, render axes, and plot data.

chevron A small control or button that you can click to display or hide items, such as the chevron at the right end of the ribbon that you click to hide the ribbon. Also the « and » characters that surround each merge field in a main document; also known as *guillemet characters*.

Click and Type A feature that allows you to double-click a blank area of a document to position the cursor in that location, with the appropriate paragraph alignment already in place. You can turn this feature on or off in Advanced Options.

clip art A piece of free, ready-made art that is distributed without copyright. Usually cartoons, sketches, illustrations, or photographs.

Clipboard A storage area shared by all Microsoft Office apps, where cut or copied items are temporarily stored so they can be pasted elsewhere.

coauthor To collaborate with other people on the development of a document.

collaborate To work with other people to update or interact with content.

column Either the vertical arrangement of text into one or more side-by-side sections or the vertical arrangement of cells in a table.

column break A break inserted in the text of a column to force the text below it to move to the next column.

column chart A chart that displays data in vertical bars to facilitate data comparison.

comment A note or annotation that an author or reviewer adds to a document. Word displays the comment in a balloon in the margin of the document or in the Reviewing pane.

contextual tab See *tool tab*.

cross-reference entry An entry in an index that refers readers to a related entry.

cursor A representation on the screen of the input device pointer location.

cycle diagram A diagram that shows a continuous process.

data marker A customizable symbol or shape that identifies a data point on a chart. Data markers can be bars, columns, pie or doughnut slices, dots, and various other shapes and can be various sizes and colors.

data point An individual value plotted in a chart.

data series Related data points that are plotted in a chart. One or more data series can be plotted in a chart. A pie chart has just one data series.

data source A file containing variable information, such as names and addresses, that is merged with a main document containing static information.

demoting In an outline, changing a heading to a lower heading level or body text; for example, changing from Heading 5 to Heading 6. See also *promoting*.

desktop publishing A process that creates pages by combining text and objects, such as tables and graphics, in a visually appealing way.

destination file The file into which a linked or embedded object or mail merge data is inserted. When you change information in a destination file, the information is not updated in the source file. See also *source file*.

diagram A graphic in which shapes, text, and pictures are used to illustrate a process, cycle, or relationship.

dialog box launcher On the ribbon, a button at the bottom of some groups that opens a dialog box with features related to the group.

digital signature Data that binds a sender's identity to the information being sent. A digital signature might be bundled with any message, file, or other digitally encoded information, or transmitted separately. Digital signatures are used in public key environments and provide authentication and integrity services.

Display For Review options The four options for displaying comments in a Word document. The options are All Markup, Simple Markup, No Markup, and Original.

Document Inspector A tool that automates the process of detecting and removing all extraneous and confidential information from a document.

Draft view A document view that displays the content of a document with a simplified layout.

drag-and-drop editing A way of moving or copying selected text by dragging it from one location to another.

dragging A way of moving objects by selecting them and then, while the selection device is active (for example, while you are holding down the mouse button), moving the selection to the new location.

drawing canvas A work area for creating pictures in Word. The drawing canvas keeps the parts of the picture together, helps you position the picture, and provides a frame-like boundary between your picture and the text on the page.

drawing object Any graphic you draw or insert that can be changed and enhanced. Drawing objects include AutoShapes, curves, lines, and WordArt.

drop cap An enlarged, decorative capital letter that appears at the beginning of a paragraph.

embedded object An object that is wholly inserted into a file. Embedding the object, rather than simply inserting or pasting its contents, ensures that the object retains its original format. If you open the embedded object, you can edit it with the toolbars and menus from the app used to create it.

endnote A note that appears at the end of a section or document and that is referenced by text in the main body of the document. An endnote consists of two linked parts, a reference mark within the main body of text, and the corresponding text of the note. See also *footnote*.

Extensible Markup Language (XML) A format for delivering rich, structured data in a standard, consistent way. XML tags describe the content of a document, whereas HTML tags describe how the document looks. XML is extensible because it allows designers to create their own customized tags.

field A placeholder that tells Word to supply the specified information in the specified way. Also, the set of information of a specific type in a data source, such as all the last names in a contacts list.

field name A first-row cell in a data source that identifies data in the column below.

file format The structure or organization of data in a file. The file format of a document is usually indicated by the file name extension.

filtering Displaying files or records in a data source that meet certain criteria; for example, filtering a data source so that you display only the records for people who live in a particular state. Filtering does not delete files; it simply changes the view so that you display only the files that meet your criteria.

font A graphic design applied to a collection of numbers, symbols, and characters. A font describes a certain typeface, which can have qualities such as size, spacing, and pitch.

font effect An attribute, such as superscript, small capital letters, or shadow, that can be applied to a font.

font size The height (in points) of a collection of characters, where one point is equal to approximately 1/72 of an inch.

font style The emphasis placed on a font by using formatting such as bold, italic, underline, or color.

footer One or more lines of text in the bottom margin area of a page in a document, typically containing elements such as the page number and the name of the file. See also *header*.

footnote A note that appears at the end of a page that explains, comments on, or provides references for text in the main body of a document. A footnote consists of two linked parts, a reference mark within the main body of the document, and the corresponding text of the note. See also *endnote*.

formatting See *character formatting; paragraph formatting*.

formula A sequence of values, cell references, names, functions, or operators in a cell of a table or worksheet that together produce a new value. A formula always begins with an equal sign (=).

gallery A grouping of thumbnails that display options visually.

graphic Any piece of art used to illustrate or convey information or to add visual interest to a document.

grayscale The range of shades of black in an image.

gridlines In a table, thin lines that indicate the cell boundaries. Table gridlines do not print when you print a document. In a chart, lines that visually carry the y-axis values across the plot area.

group On a ribbon tab, an area containing buttons related to a specific document element or function.

grouping Assembling several objects, such as shapes, into a single unit so that they act as one object. Grouped objects can easily be moved, sized, and formatted.

hard copy Printed output on paper, film, or other permanent medium.

header A line, or lines, of content in the top margin area of a page in a document, typically containing elements such as the title, page number, or name of the author. See also *footer*.

hierarchy diagram A diagram that illustrates the structure of an organization or entity.

hyperlink A connection from a hyperlink anchor such as text or a graphic that you can follow to display a link target such as a file, a location in a file, or a website. Text hyperlinks are usually formatted as colored or underlined text, but sometimes the only indication is that when you point to them, the pointer changes to a hand.

Hypertext Markup Language (HTML) A markup language that uses tags to mark elements in a document to indicate how web browsers should display these elements to the user and how they should respond to user actions.

hyphenating Splitting a word that would otherwise extend beyond the right margin of the page.

icon A small picture or symbol representing a command, file type, function, app, or tool.

indent marker A marker on the horizontal ruler that controls the indentation of text from the left or right margin of a document.

index A list of the words and phrases that are discussed in a printed document, along with the page numbers they appear on.

index entry A field code that marks specific text for inclusion in an index. When you mark text as an index entry, Word inserts an XE (Index Entry) field formatted as hidden text.

index entry field The XE field, including the braces ({ }), that defines an index entry.

justifying Making all lines of text in a paragraph or column fit the width of the document or column, with even margins on each side.

keyboard shortcut Any combination of keystrokes that can be used to perform a task that would otherwise require a mouse or other pointing device.

landscape The orientation of a picture or page where the width is greater than the height.

legend A key in a chart that identifies the colors and names of the data series or categories that are used in the chart.

line break A manual break that forces the text that follows it to the next line. Also called a *text wrapping break*.

line graph or line chart A type of chart in which data points in a series are connected by a line.

link See *hyperlink*; *linked object*.

linked object An object that is inserted into a document but that still exists in the source file. When information is linked, the document can be updated automatically if the information in the original document changes.

list diagram A diagram in which lists of related or independent information are visually represented.

Live Preview A feature that temporarily displays the effect of applying a specific format to the selected document element.

mail merge The process of merging information into a main document from a data source, such as an email address book or database, to create customized documents, such as form letters or mailing labels.

main document In a mail merge operation in Word, the document that contains the text and graphics that are the same for each version of the merged document.

manual page break A page break inserted to force subsequent information to appear on the next page.

margin The blank space outside the printing area on a page.

markup Comments and tracked changes such as insertions, deletions, and formatting changes.

markup views Views that display tracked changes such as insertions, deletions, and formatting changes.

matrix diagram A diagram that shows the relationship of components to a whole.

merge field A placeholder in a document that is replaced with variable information from a data source during the merge process.

Microsoft Office Clipboard See *Clipboard*.

Navigation pane A pane that displays an outline of a document's headings, or thumbnails of a document's pages, and allows you to jump to a heading or page in the document by clicking it. Also provides content search capabilities.

nested table A table inserted into a cell of a table that is being used to arrange information on a page.

No Markup view A view that hides all tracked changes and comments.

object An item, such as a graphic, video clip, sound file, or worksheet, that can be inserted into a document and then selected and modified.

orientation The direction (horizontal or vertical) in which a page is laid out.

Original view A view that displays all content as it was originally entered in the document, with any tracked changes and comments hidden.

orphan The first line of a paragraph printed by itself at the bottom of a page.

Outline view A view that shows the headings of a document indented to represent their level in the document's structure.

palette A collection of color swatches that you can click to apply a color to selected text or an object.

paragraph In word processing, a block of text that ends when you press the Enter key.

paragraph formatting Formatting that controls the appearance of a paragraph. Examples include indentation, alignment, line spacing, and pagination.

paragraph style A combination of character formatting and paragraph formatting that is named and stored as a set. Applying the style to a paragraph applies all the formatting characteristics at one time.

path A sequence of folders that leads to a specific file or folder. A backslash is used to separate each folder in a Windows path, and a forward slash is used to separate each directory in an Internet path.

PDF (Portable Document Format) A fixed-layout file format in which the formatting of the document appears the same regardless of the computer on which it is displayed.

picture A photograph, clip art image, illustration, or another type of image created with an app other than Word.

picture diagram A diagram that uses pictures to convey information, rather than or in addition to text.

pie chart A round chart that shows the size of items in a single data series, proportional to the sum of the items.

plot area In a two-dimensional chart, the area bounded by the axes, including all data series. In a three-dimensional chart, the area bounded by the axes, including the data series, category names, tick-mark labels, and axis titles.

point The unit of measure for expressing the size of characters in a font, where 72 points equals approximately 1 inch.

pointing to Pausing the mouse pointer or other pointing device over an on-screen element.

Portable Document Format See *PDF*.

portrait The orientation of a picture or page where the page is taller than it is wide.

post A message published on a blog, discussion board, or message board.

Print Layout view A view of a document as it will appear when printed; for example, items such as headers, footnotes, columns, and text boxes appear in their actual positions.

process diagram A diagram that visually represents the ordered set of steps required to complete a task.

promoting In an outline, changing body text to a heading, or changing a heading to a higher-level heading. See also *demoting*.

pull quote Text taken from the body of a document and showcased in a text box to create visual interest.

pyramid diagram A diagram that shows foundation-based relationships.

query Selection criteria for extracting information from a data source.

Quick Access Toolbar A small, customizable toolbar that displays frequently used commands.

Quick Table A table with sample data that you can customize.

Read Mode A document view that displays a document in a simplified window with minimal controls, at a size that is optimized for reading documents on a computer screen. Previously referred to as Full Screen Reading view or Reading Layout view.

read-only A setting that allows a file to be read or copied, but not changed or saved. If you change a read-only file, you can save your changes only if you give the document a new name.

record A collection of data about a person, a place, an event, or some other item. Records are the logical equivalents of rows in a table.

reference mark The number or symbol displayed in the body of a document when you insert a footnote or endnote.

relationship diagram A diagram that shows convergent, divergent, overlapping, merging, or containment elements.

revision A change in a document.

ribbon A user interface design that organizes commands into logical groups that appear on separate tabs.

saturation In color management, the purity of a color's hue, moving from gray to the pure color.

screen clipping An image of all or part of the content displayed on a computer screen. Screen clippings can be captured by using a graphics capture tool such as the Screen Clipping tool included with Office 2016 apps.

ScreenTip A note that appears on the screen to provide information about the app interface or certain types of document content, such as proofing marks and hyperlinks within a document.

section break A mark you insert to show the end of a section. A section break stores the section formatting elements, such as the margins, page orientation, headers and footers, and sequence of page numbers.

selecting Highlighting text or activating an object so that you can manipulate or edit it in some way.

selection area An area in a document's left margin in which you can click and drag to select blocks of text.

series axis The third axis in a three-dimensional coordinate system, used in computer graphics to represent depth. Also called the *z-axis*.

SharePoint library A collection of files on SharePoint Server that is shared with other site users.

Simple Markup view A view for tracked changes that clearly identifies where changes and comments are in a document, and gives you easy access to them, without detracting from the readability.

sizing handle A small circle, square, or set of dots that appears at the corner or on the side of a selected object. You drag these handles to change the size of the object horizontally, vertically, or proportionally.

SmartArt graphic A predefined set of shapes and text used as a basis for creating a diagram.

soft page break A page break that Word inserts when the text reaches the bottom margin of a page.

source file A file that contains information that is linked, embedded, or merged into a destination file. Updates to source file content are reflected in the destination file when the data connection is refreshed. See also *destination file*.

stack A set of graphics that overlap each other.

status bar An app window element, located at the bottom of the app window, that displays indicators and controls.

status bar indicator A notification on the status bar that displays information related to the current app.

style Any kind of formatting that is named and stored as a set. See also *character style*; *paragraph style*; *Quick Style*; *table style*.

style area pane A pane that can be displayed along the left side of a document on the screen in Draft or Outline view and that displays the assigned paragraph style of the adjacent paragraph.

subentry An index entry that falls under a more general heading; for example, *Mars* and *Venus* might be subentries of the index entry *planets*.

tab A tabbed page on the ribbon that contains buttons organized in groups.

tab leader A repeating character (usually a dot or dash) that separates text before the tab from text or a number after it.

tab stop A location on the horizontal ruler that indicates how far to indent text or where to begin a column of text.

tabbed list A list that arranges text in simple columns separated by left, right, centered, or decimal tab stops.

table One or more rows of cells commonly used to display numbers and other items for quick reference and analysis. Items in a table are organized in rows and columns.

table of authorities A list of the references in a legal document, such as references to cases, statutes, and rules, along with the numbers of the pages on which the references appear.

table of contents A list of the headings in a document, along with the numbers of the pages on which the headings appear.

table of figures A list of the captions for pictures, charts, graphs, slides, or other illustrations in a document, along with the numbers of the pages on which the captions appear.

table style A set of formatting options, such as font, border style, and row banding, that are applied to a table. The regions of a table, such as the header row, header column, and data area, can be variously formatted.

target A file, location, object, or webpage that is displayed from a link or hyperlink.

template A file that can contain predefined formatting, layout, text, or graphics, and that serves as the basis for new documents with a similar design or purpose.

text box A container that contains text separately from other document content.

text wrapping The way text wraps around an object on the page.

text wrapping break A manual break that forces the text that follows it to the next line. Also known as a *line break*.

theme A set of unified design elements that combine color, fonts, and effects to provide a professional look for a document.

thumbnail A small representation of an item, such as an image, a page of content, or a set of formatting, usually obtained by scaling a snapshot of it. Thumbnails are typically used to provide visual identifiers for related items.

tick-mark A small line of measurement, similar to a division line on a ruler, that intersects an axis in a chart.

tool tab A tab containing groups of commands on the ribbon, that are pertinent only to a specific type of document element such as a picture, table, or text box. Tool tabs appear only when relevant content is selected.

value axis The vertical reference line on a grid, chart, or graph that has horizontal and vertical dimension. Also called the *y-axis*.

View Shortcuts toolbar A toolbar located at the right end of the status bar that contains tools for switching between views of document content and changing the display magnification.

view A common menu item that enables the user to select how the contents of the current app are displayed.

watermark A text or graphic image on the page behind the main content of a document.

web app See *Word Online*.

web browser Software that interprets HTML files, formats them into webpages, and displays them. A web browser, such as Edge or Internet Explorer, can follow hyperlinks, respond to requests to download files, and play sound or video files that are embedded in webpages.

Web Layout view A view of a document as it will appear in a web browser. In this view, a document appears as one page (without page breaks); text and tables wrap to fit the window.

webpage A World Wide Web document. A webpage typically consists of an HTML file, with associated files for graphics and scripts, in a particular folder on a particular computer. It is identified by a Uniform Resource Locator (URL).

widow The last line of a paragraph printed by itself at the top of a page.

wildcard character A keyboard character that can be used to represent one or many characters when conducting a search. The question mark (?) represents a single character, and the asterisk (*) represents one or more characters.

Word Online A Microsoft Office Online app that enables users to upload, view (in full fidelity), share, and edit Word files in a web browser. Users can create and edit a new Word file directly from the web app, and this file can be saved, viewed, edited, and opened in the Word desktop app.

word processing The writing, editing, and formatting of documents in an app designed for working primarily with text.

word wrap The process of breaking lines of text automatically to stay within the page margins of a document or within window boundaries.

WordArt A group of text effects that incorporate qualities such as shadows, reflections, edge glow, beveled edges, 3-D rotation, and transforms.

x-axis The horizontal reference line on a grid, chart, or graph that has horizontal and vertical dimensions. Also called the *category axis*.

y-axis The vertical reference line on a grid, chart, or graph that has horizontal and vertical dimensions. Also called the *value axis*.

z-axis The third axis in a three-dimensional coordinate system, used in computer graphics to represent depth. Also called the *series axis*.

Index

About the author

Joan Lambert has worked closely with Microsoft technologies since 1986, and in the training and certification industry since 1997. As President and CEO of Online Training Solutions, Inc. (OTSI), Joan guides the translation of technical information and requirements into useful, relevant, and measurable resources for people who are seeking certification of their computer skills or who simply want to get things done efficiently.

Joan is the author or coauthor of more than three dozen books about Windows and Office (for Windows, Mac, and iPad), video-based training courses for SharePoint and OneNote, and three generations of Microsoft Office Specialist certification study guides.

Joan is a Microsoft Certified Professional, Microsoft Certified Trainer, Microsoft Office Specialist Master (for all Office versions since Office 2007), Microsoft Certified Technology Specialist (for Windows and Windows Server), Microsoft Certified Technology Associate (for Windows), and Microsoft Dynamics Specialist.

Joan currently lives in a small town in Texas with her simply divine daughter, Trinity; an ever-growing menagerie of dogs, cats, and fish; and the DeLonghi Gran Dama super-automatic espresso machine that runs the house.

Acknowledgments

I appreciate the time and efforts of Carol Dillingham, Rosemary Caperton, and the team at Microsoft Press—past and present—who made this and so many other books possible.

I would like to thank the editorial and production team members at Online Training Solutions, Inc. (OTSI) and other contributors for their efforts. Angela Martin, Ginny Munroe, Jaime Odell, Jean Trenary, Jeanne Craver, Kate Shoup, Kathy Krause, Meredith Thomas, Steve Lambert, Susie Carr, and Val Serdy all contributed to the creation of this book.

OTSI specializes in the design and creation of Microsoft Office, SharePoint, and Windows training solutions and the production of online and printed training resources. For more information about OTSI, visit *www.otsi.com* or follow us on Facebook at *www.facebook.com/Online.Training.Solutions.Inc.*

I hope you enjoy this book and find it useful. The content of this book was guided in part by feedback from readers of previously published *Step by Step* books. If you find errors or omissions in this book, want to say something nice about it, or would like to provide input for future versions, you can use the feedback process outlined in the introduction.

Now that you've read the book...

Tell us what you think!

Was it useful?
Did it teach you what you wanted to learn?
Was there room for improvement?

Let us know at http://aka.ms/tellpress

Your feedback goes directly to the staff at Microsoft Press,
and we read every one of your responses. Thanks in advance!

 Microsoft